Lynda Weinman's | Hands-On Training

Adobe®
Dreamweaver® CS3

Includes Exercise Files and Demo Movies

lynda.com™

By Garrick Chow

Adobe® Dreamweaver® CS3 Hands-On Training

By Garrick Chow

lynda.com/books | Peachpit Press
1249 Eighth Street • Berkeley, CA • 94710
800.283.9444 • 510.524.2178 •
510.524.2221(fax)
http://www.lynda.com/books
http://www.peachpit.com

lynda.com/books is published
in association with Peachpit Press,
a division of Pearson Education
Copyright ©2008 by lynda.com

ISBN-13: 978-0-321-50985-7
ISBN-10:   0-321-50985-4

0 9 8 7 6 5 4

Printed and bound in the
United States of America

H•O•T Credits

Director of Product Development and Video Production: Tanya Staples

Senior Editor: Karyn Johnson

Production Coordinator: Tracey Croom

Compositor: David Van Ness

Technical Writer: Lauren Harmon

Copyeditor: Kim Wimpsett

Proofreader: Liz Welch

Interior Design: Hot Studio, San Francisco

Cover Design: Don Barnett

Cover Illustration: Bruce Heavin (bruce@stink.com)

Indexer: Jack Lewis

H•O•T Colophon

The text in *Adobe Dreamweaver CS3 H·O·T* was set in Avenir from Adobe Systems Incorporated. The cover illustration was painted in Adobe Photoshop and Adobe Illustrator.

This book was created using QuarkXPress and Microsoft Office on an Apple Macintosh using Mac OS X. It was printed on 60 lb. Influence Matte at Courier.

Table of Contents

Table of Contents

Table of Contents

Introduction

A Note from Lynda Weinman

Most people buy computer books to learn, yet it's amazing how few books are written by teachers. Garrick and I take pride that this book was written by experienced teachers who are familiar with training students in this subject matter. In this book, you'll find carefully developed lessons and exercises to help you learn Adobe Dreamweaver CS3—one of the most capable Web development tools available today.

This book is targeted at beginning- to intermediate-level Web designers and Web developers who are looking for a way to learn the basics of Dreamweaver quickly and easily. The premise of the hands-on approach is to get you up to speed quickly with Dreamweaver while actively working through the lessons in this book. It's one thing to read about a program, and it's another experience entirely to try the product and achieve measurable results. Our motto is, "Read the book, follow the exercises, and you'll learn the program." I have received countless testimonials, and it is our goal to make sure it remains true for all our hands-on training books.

This book doesn't set out to cover every single aspect of Dreamweaver, and it doesn't try to teach you how to hand-code a Web site from scratch. What we saw missing from the bookshelves was a process-oriented tutorial that teaches readers core principles, techniques, and tips in a hands-on training format.

I welcome your comments at **dwcs3hot@lynda.com**. If you run into any trouble while you're working through this book, check out the technical support link at **www.lynda.com/info/books/dwcs3**.

We hope this book will improve your skills in Dreamweaver CS3 and Web design in general. If it does, we have accomplished the job we set out to do!

—Lynda Weinman

About lynda.com

lynda.com was founded in 1995 by Lynda Weinman and Bruce Heavin in conjunction with the first publication of Lynda's revolutionary book, *Designing Web Graphics*. Since then, lynda.com has become a leader in software training for graphics and Web professionals and is recognized worldwide as a trusted educational resource.

lynda.com offers a wide range of HOT (**H**ands-**O**n **T**raining) books, which guide users through a progressive learning process using real-world projects. lynda.com also offers a wide range of video-based tutorials, which are available on CD-ROM and DVD-ROM and through the **lynda.com Online Training Library**. lynda.com also owns the **Flashforward** conference.

For more information about lynda.com, check out **www.lynda.com**. For more information about Flashforward, check out **www. flashforwardconference.com**.

Product Registration

Register your copy of *Adobe Dreamweaver CS3 Hands-On Training* today, and receive the following benefits:

- A free 24-hour pass to the lynda.com Online Training Library with more than 10,000 professionally produced video tutorials covering more than 150 topics by leading industry experts and teachers

- News, events, and special offers from lynda.com

- The lynda.com monthly newsletter

To register, visit **www.lynda.com/register/HOT/dwcs3**.

Additional Training Resources from lynda.com

To help you master and further develop your skills with Dreamweaver CS3, register to use the free, 24-hour pass to the lynda.com Online Training Library, and check out the following video-based training resources:

Dreamweaver CS3 Essential Training with Garrick Chow

Migrating from GoLive to Dreamweaver CS3 with Garrick Chow

Photoshop CS3 for the Web Essential Training with Jan Kabili

Fireworks CS3 Essential Training with Tom Green

CSS for Designers with Andy Clarke and Molly E. Holzschlag

CSS Web Site Design with Eric Meyer

XML Essential Training with Joe Marini

XHTML Essential Training with William E. Weinman

HTML Essential Training with William E. Weinman

JavaScript Essential Training with Charles G. Hollins

About Garrick Chow

Garrick Chow is a full-time training developer and evangelist for lynda.com. He is the author of four other books in the HOT series, covering Adobe Acrobat and Mac OS X, and he has created and recorded more than 20 video-based training titles for the lynda.com Online Training Library. In addition to his work with lynda.com, Garrick has led classes at numerous conferences, universities, government agencies, and private corporations.

His articles have appeared in *MacAddict* and *Mac|Life* magazines. In the evenings, he sheds his mild-mannered computer trainer appearance and rocks out as the bass player for the indie-rock band the Jellybricks (**www.thejellybricks.com**). He can often be found playing music when he should be working and working when he should be playing music.

How to Use This Book

The following sections outline important information to help you make the most of this book.

The Formatting in This Book

This book has several components, including step-by-step exercises, commentary, notes, tips, warnings, and video tutorials. Step-by-step exercises are numbered. File names, folder names, commands, keyboard shortcuts, and Web addresses are in bold so they pop out easily: **filename.htm**, the **images** folder, **File > New**, **Shift+click**, **www.lynda.com**.

Commentary is in dark gray text, as shown here:

This is commentary text.

Interface Screen Captures

Most of the screen shots in the book were taken on a Mac using Mac OS X, but the Dreamweaver interface is similar enough on Macs and Windows machines that there should be no confusion for Windows users. For screens and interface elements that are unique to Windows, Windows screen shots have been provided.

HTM versus HTML

All the exercise files on the CD-ROM end with the **.html** extension. As you design Web sites, you may see HTML files use the **.htm** extension. You can name your files either way, and any browser will recognize the file, but it's a good idea to use only one or the other.

What's on the Dreamweaver HOT CD-ROM?

You'll find a number of useful resources on the **Dreamweaver HOT CD-ROM**, including the following: exercise files, video tutorials, and information about product registration. Before you begin the hands-on exercises, read through the following sections so you know how to set up the exercise files and video tutorials.

Exercise Files

The files required to complete the exercises are on the **Dreamweaver HOT CD-ROM** in a folder called **exercise files**. These files are divided into chapter folders, and you should copy each chapter folder onto your desktop before you begin the exercise for that chapter. For example, if you're about to start Chapter 5, copy the **chap_05** folder from the **exercise files** folder on the **Dreamweaver HOT CD-ROM** onto your desktop.

On Windows, when files originate from a CD-ROM, they automatically become write-protected, which means you cannot alter them. Fortunately, you

can easily change this attribute. For complete instructions, read the "Making Exercise Files Editable on Windows Computers" section.

Video Tutorials

Throughout the book, you'll find references to video tutorials. In some cases, these video tutorials reinforce concepts explained in the book. In other cases, they show bonus material you'll find interesting and useful. To view the video tutorials, you must have the Apple QuickTime Player installed on your computer. If you do not have QuickTime Player, you can download it for free from Apple's Web site at **www.apple.com/quicktime**.

To view the video tutorials, copy the videos from the **Dreamweaver HOT CD-ROM** onto your hard drive. Double-click the video you want to watch, and it will automatically open in QuickTime Player. Make sure the volume on your computer is turned up so you can hear the audio content.

Making Exercise Files Editable on Windows Computers

By default, when you copy files from a CD-ROM to a Windows computer, the files are set to read-only (write-protected). This will cause a problem with the exercise files because you will need to edit and save many of them. You can remove the read-only property by following these steps:

1 Open the **exercise files** folder on the **Dreamweaver HOT CD-ROM**, and copy one of the subfolders, such as **chap_02**, to your **Desktop**.

2 Open the **chap_02** folder you copied to your **Desktop**, and choose **Edit > Select All**.

3 Right-click one of the selected files, and choose **Properties** in the contextual menu.

4 In the **Properties** dialog box, click the **General** tab. Deselect the **Read-Only** option to turn off the read-only properties for the selected files in the **chap_02** folder.

Making File Extensions Visible on Windows Computers

By default, you cannot see file extensions, such as **.htm**, **.fla**, **.swf**, **.jpg**, **.gif**, or **.psd**, on Windows computers. Fortunately, you can change this setting easily. Here's how.

Windows XP

1 On your **Desktop**, double-click the **My Computer** icon.

Note: If you (or someone else) has changed the name, it will not say My Computer.

2 Choose **Tools > Folder Options** to open the **Folder Options** dialog box. Click the **View** tab.

3 Deselect the **Hide extensions for known file types** option to make all file extensions visible.

Windows Vista

1 Click the **Start** button, and open **Control Panel**.

2 Double-click **Folder Options**.

3 On the **View** tab, deselect the **Hide extensions for known file types** option to make all file extensions visible.

Right-clicking and Ctrl-clicking

Throughout this book, you will be instructed to right-click certain elements on your screen. This means press the secondary button on your mouse, which oftentimes opens a contextual menu of items from which you can select commands. If you are using a Mac with a single-button mouse, you can reproduce the effect of right-clicking by holding down the Ctrl button on your keyboard while clicking your mouse.

Dreamweaver CS3 System Requirements

Windows

- Intel Pentium 4, Intel Centrino, Intel Xeon, or Intel Core Duo (or compatible) processor and newer

- Microsoft Windows XP with Service Pack 2 or Windows Vista Home Premium, Business, Ultimate, or Enterprise (certified for 32-bit editions)

- 512 MB RAM (1 GB recommended to run more than one CS3 product simultaneously)

- 1024 x 768, 16-bit display (32-bit recommended)

- 1 GB available disk space

- Internet connection (broadband recommended)

Mac

- PowerPC G4 or G5 or multicore Intel processor

- Mac OS X 10.4.8 or later

- 512 MB RAM (1 GB recommended to run more than one CS3 product simultaneously)

- 1024 x 768, thousands of colors display (millions of colors recommended)

- 1.4 GB available disk space

- Internet connection (broadband recommended)

Getting Demo Versions of the Software

If you'd like to try demo versions of the software used in this book, you can download demo versions as follows:

Firefox: www.getfirefox.com

Dreamweaver CS3: www.adobe.com/go/dreamweaver

Fireworks CS3: www.adobe.com/go/fireworks

Photoshop CS3: www.adobe.com/go/photoshop

1

Getting Started

I could start this book with lots of exercises, throwing you right into working with Adobe Dreamweaver CS3 without any preparation, but then you would be flying blind, without understanding basic Web design fundamentals such as XHTML (e**X**tensible **H**yper**T**ext **M**arkup **L**anguage), CSS (**C**ascading **S**tyle **S**heets), DHTML (**D**ynamic **HTML**), XML (e**X**tensible **M**arkup **L**anguage), and JavaScript. Instead, I'll start you off with some definitions, concepts, and guidelines to help with your hands-on Dreamweaver CS3 training. Feel free to scan this chapter for information if you already know some of what is here or jump right to the exercises in the next chapter.

What Is Dreamweaver CS3?

Dreamweaver CS3 is the ninth version of Dreamweaver, and it's also the first version of the application to be released as an Adobe product. In 2005, Adobe acquired Macromedia and their entire product line, including Dreamweaver. Dreamweaver is now part of the Adobe CS3 suite of applications, boasting new features and tight integration with the rest of the CS3 suite.

At its roots, Dreamweaver CS3 is a WYSIWYG (**W**hat **Y**ou **S**ee **I**s **W**hat **Y**ou **G**et) XHTML generator. This means if you change something on the screen in Dreamweaver CS3, it will show you the results instantly and write the proper code for you. In contrast, if you were to code the XHTML by hand in a non-WYSIWIG editor, you would have to write the code and then view the results in a browser, write more code, and check the browser again. The instant feedback of a live design environment such as Dreamweaver CS3 speeds up your workflow tremendously, because you can see whether you like the results while you are working.

HTML vs. XHTML

We are at a rather interesting crossover point in the evolution of the World Wide Web. For many years, HTML (**H**yper**T**ext **M**arkup **L**anguage) was the only code you could use to create a Web page. Sure, you could use other technologies such as JavaScript and CSS and server-side languages such as ASP (**A**ctive **S**erver **P**ages), JSP (**J**ava**S**erver **P**ages), Adobe ColdFusion, and such, but at the heart of every Web page was simple HTML. As of October 4, 2001, the W3C (**W**orld **W**ide **W**eb **C**onsortium), which is the Web standards committee, decided to discontinue HTML. Taking its place is XHTML, a language almost identical to HTML with the exception that it has a stricter format and follows XML syntax rules. Does this mean that if you learned HTML you wasted your time? Heck, no. You can still use HTML, as well as XHTML, to create Web pages. In fact, knowing HTML will help you make the transition to XHTML, so don't worry.

Over the past several years most Web designers have begun to embrace XHTML and have started using it to develop their Web pages. In an effort to ensure you learn the most up-to-date methods, you will see only XHTML code examples throughout this book. Even though you can still use HTML to create Web pages, not using XHTML would be a disservice to you, because it's the most current standard for creating Web pages. This chapter will give you more information about XHTML so you better understand the role it plays in Web design.

Roundtrip XHTML

Dreamweaver has gained and maintained a lot of great reviews and customer loyalty because of its use of Roundtrip XHTML, which lets you easily move between Dreamweaver and another text editor, such as BBEdit from Bare Bones Software or Macromedia HomeSite from Adobe, with very little or no change to your code. Unless you are a programmer (and chances are you aren't if you are reading this book), this probably won't mean a whole lot to you right now. However, moving between different development tools can be important when you are working with a programmer or in a team environment where everyone might not be using Dreamweaver. It's nice to know you can do this and not worry about Dreamweaver breaking your code by inserting unwanted or proprietary changes. Don't you wish all programs were so respectful?

Many programmers have looked at WYSIWYG editors with skepticism because of their reputation for inflexibility and inclusion of nonstandard code. Dreamweaver CS3 is one of the few WYSIWYG XHTML editors to win the approval of programmers and designers alike. Programmers like the product because they don't have to worry about their code being changed by Dreamweaver. Designers like it because it writes clean code with-

out inserting a lot of proprietary and self-serving tags, and it lets them visually lay out pages without touching a line of code. It's hard to believe a tool could please both of these divergent groups, but Dreamweaver CS3 does it.

Now, truth be told, Dreamweaver can make some minor changes to a page once it's opened. Since the few changes it makes are usually cleaning up bad code, no one really frowns on these changes. In fact, Dreamweaver lets you control how code is rewritten (if at all) within the **Preferences** area of the program, so you still have full control over this feature. We won't get into those issues now; I cover these changes and how to turn them off (if you want to do so) in Chapter 12, *"Using XHTML."*

Do You Need to Learn XHTML to Use Dreamweaver?

Yes and no. If you use a WYSIWYG XHTML editor, then technically you can create an entire Web page without writing a single line of code. However, at some point you will have to edit the code manually to troubleshoot a problem, such as when you encounter an incompatibility between browsers.

For some, XHTML can be quite intimidating at first glance—your first reaction may be to avoid it at all costs. After all, when you design pages using Adobe Photoshop, QuarkXPress, or Adobe InDesign, you don't need to look at raw Adobe PostScript code anymore, even though the early pioneers of desktop publishing had to know how to program in PostScript just to create a page layout. Designing for print also doesn't include the inherent problem of having to design for multiple browsers and devices displaying the page; a printed page is a printed page, no matter who's viewing it.

In the past, if you didn't know some XHTML, you were at the mercy of a programmer, who might have more control over your design than you liked.

With Dreamweaver CS3, you can get by without understanding or writing a single line of code. However, it won't be long before you need to look at the code and make some changes manually, especially if you intend to be a true professional Web designer or developer. So, I strongly recommend you take the time to learn XHTML. Most people who don't learn XHTML are at a disadvantage in the workplace, especially when they need to troubleshoot problems on their Web pages.

How do you learn XHTML? You can learn it in lots of ways—you can take a class at school, take an online class, buy a training CD-ROM, or buy a book. An easy way to learn XHTML (and the way many designers first begin to learn XHTML) is to view the source code of pages you like. In XHTML, the code is visible to anyone who uses a browser. To view the source code of a page—whether it is in HTML or XHTML—in your browser, choose **View > Page Source** (Firefox), **View > Source** (Internet Explorer), or **View > View Source** (Safari). Once you get comfortable with some of the elements, you will likely be able to deconstruct how these pages were made.

What Does XHTML Do?

XHTML is a derivative of SGML (**S**tandard **G**eneralized **M**arkup **L**anguage), an international standard for representing text in an electronic form that can be used for exchanging documents in an independent manner. XHTML is also the replacement for HTML.

At its heart, XHTML allows for the markup of text and the inclusion of images, as well as the capability to link documents. **Hyperlinks**, which are at the core of any Web page's success, are what let you jump between pages in a site or to view pages on other Web sites. These hyperlinks, or **links**, are references contained within the markup. If the source of the link moves, or the reference to the link is misspelled, it won't work. One of the great attributes of Dreamweaver CS3 is its many site management capabilities, which help you manage your internal links so they are automatically updated if the links are changed.

The last published version of HTML was 4.01. It was replaced by the newer standard, XHTML 1.0, which already exists as a formal recommendation sanctioned by the W3C. The next version of XHTML, version 1.1, is a formal recommendation but is more suitable for internal applications and isn't quite ready for mass public consumption.

So then, how is XHTML different from its close companion HTML? The most visible difference between the two markup languages is in their syntax, with all opening tags requiring a closing tag. Here are some of the key differences:

- All element and attribute names are in lower-case. For example, `<p>` is a valid XHTML element, but `<P>` is not valid.

- All attribute values must be contained within quotation marks (single or double). For example, in HTML you can write `<td nowrap>`, but in XHTML you have to write `<td nowrap="nowrap">`. Be consistent in the type of quotation marks

you use; don't mix single quotation marks with double quotation marks, or vice versa.

- All nonempty elements must have a closing tag. For example, `<p>This is good text.</p>` is a valid XHTML element, but `<p>This is bad text.` is not valid.

- All empty tags should be written with a space and a slash at the end of the tag. For example, `<br />` is a valid XHTML tag, but `<br>` is not. This method of closing empty tags ensures your pages are compatible with older browsers while honoring the XHTML specifications.

Before you panic, I'll point out that Dreamweaver CS3 will write all the XHTML code for you. This gives you the freedom to create your Web pages in a visual way while letting Dreamweaver CS3 create the code behind the scenes. So if you don't have the patience or desire to learn XHTML, you really don't have to do so. Of course, I strongly suggest you take the time to learn XHTML because it will help you build and troubleshoot more complex pages.

XHTML follows the XML rules and syntax guidelines. Because XML has very rigid requirements for writing code, XHTML is a more structured markup language than HTML. This more structured approach to markup languages allows one document to be viewed on multiple devices (browsers, cell phones, personal digital assistants, and so on) by simply creating different style sheets for each device. (You will learn about style sheets later in the book.) In a nutshell, XHTML is basically HTML 4.01 reformatted using the syntax of XML, which is described later in this chapter. You will be glad to know Dreamweaver CS3 has full support for XHTML. In fact, Dreamweaver CS3 can even convert your existing HTML documents to XHTML. You will learn more about this in Chapter 12, *"Using XHTML."*

What Does XHTML Look Like?

If you have ever seen HTML code, you will find instant comfort in looking at XHTML code. Because XHTML is a reformatting of HTML, many things look the same or have minor differences. Although XHTML and HTML have some distinct and critical differences, they are both markup languages and share many common traits, which lessens the learning curve if you're already familiar with HTML.

Here are some of the basic elements of an XHTML document written in correct syntax:

1. `<!DOCTYPE html PUBLIC "-//W3C//DTD XHTML 1.0 Transitional//EN" "http://www.w3.org/TR/xhtml1/DTD/xhtml1-transitional.dtd">`

2. `<html xmlns="http://www.w3.org/1999/xhtml">`

3. `<head>`

4. `<title>Untitled Document</title>`

5. `</head>`

6. `<body>` This is where the content of your page will be placed.

7. `</body>`

8. `</html>`

Here is a breakdown of these XHTML code elements:

1. **DTD (Document Type Definition) or DOCTYPE:** This URL (**U**niform **R**esource **L**ocator) points to a file outlining the available elements, their attributes, and their appropriate usage. Three XHTML DTDs are available:

   - XHTML Transitional lets you maintain backward compatibility with older browsers while still providing access to HTML 4.01 elements. (This is the DOCTYPE I'll be using throughout this book.)

   - XHTML Strict removes many of the HTML elements that were designed to control the appearance of a page and how the user interacts with those elements. This is the truest form of XHTML elements.

   - XHTML Frameset gives you access to the HTML elements needed to create framesets.

2. **XML namespace:** This URL points to a file that gives detailed information about the particular XML vocabulary used on the page, which is XHTML in this case.

3. **Opening head tag:** The `<head>` tag contains all the header information.

4. **Opening title tag:** The `<title>` tag defines the page title, which appears at the top of the browser window and in a user's bookmark list.

5. **Closing head tag:** All XHTML tags must be closed, so this is the closing `</head>` tag.

6. **Opening body tag:** All your visible content will be placed inside the `<body>` tag.

7. **Closing body tag:** You guessed it! This is the closing `</body>` tag.

8. **Closing html tag:** Last, but not least, is the closing `</html>` tag.

This example represents only a smidgen of the available XHTML tags, attributes, and values. But it covers the basics and is a great place to start your XHTML education. I give more examples of XHTML in Chapter 4, *"Learning the Basics,"* and Chapter 12, *"Using XHTML."*

File-Naming Conventions

Working with XHTML is much more restrictive than working with other types of computer media. One of the strictest parts about XHTML is its file-naming conventions:

- **Don't use spaces:** Save your files using no spaces between the file name elements. For example, the file name **about lynda.html** is illegal because of the space between the words *about* and *lynda*. Instead, write this file name as **about_lynda.html** or **aboutlynda.html**.

- **Avoid capital letters:** Avoid capitalization in your file names. **AboutLynda.html** will work as a file name, but any time you link to the file you will have to remember the correct capitalization. If you're using a Unix or Linux server, file names are case-sensitive; users typing the link directly into their browsers will most likely type everything lowercase. It is far easier to simply use all lowercase letters.

- **Avoid illegal characters:** The following chart lists the characters to avoid when naming files:

File-Naming Conventions	
Character	**Usage**
. (dot)	Periods are reserved for file name extensions or suffixes, for example .gif and .jpg.
"	Quotation marks are reserved for HTML to indicate the value of tags and attributes.
**/ or **	Slashes (/) indicate files are nested in folders. If you include a slash in your file name, HTML may lose your references, thinking you are specifying a folder. A backslash (\) isn't allowed on Windows servers.
:	Colons are used to separate certain script commands on Windows and Mac computers. Avoid them in your file names so as to not confuse a file name with a script command.
!	Exclamation marks are used in comment tags.

File Name Extensions

You may be curious about the many extensions used after the dot at the end of a file name. The following chart lists the meaning of some extensions you'll run across during your development adventures:

File Name Extensions	
Extension	**Usage**
.htm, .html	These two extensions are commonly used to denote an HTML file. The three-letter extension works just as well as the four-letter version. Older DOS systems didn't allow for four-letter extensions, which is why you sometimes see .html abbreviated as .htm.

continues on next page

File Name Extensions *continued*	
Extension	**Usage**
.gif	GIF images.
.jpg	JPEG images.
.png	PNG images (also used for Adobe Fireworks CS3 source files).
.swf	Adobe Flash files.
.mov	Apple QuickTime movie files.
.avi	AVI movie files.
.aif	AIFF sound files.
.flv	Flash Video files.

What Is CSS?

CSS is used for many purposes, but its primary function is to separate the presentation of a page from its structure. **Presentation** has to do with the way a page "looks," whereas **structure** has to do with the "meaning" of the page's content. For example, an **<h1>** tag defines that the text within is a header and that the text carries some special meaning (the text may be a headline or title, for instance). Whether that header is blue, purple, big, small, italic, or whatever, has to do with its presentation. It's important to separate the two so the structure of a page isn't compromised in order to make it look good. Using CSS has several other advantages, which are discussed in Chapter 6, *"Working with Cascading Style Sheets."*

You can use CSS to specify the font used for the text on the page, to lay out an entire Web page, and to do much more. CSS today plays a much

more important role in the Web development process than it did just a few years ago. With better support for CSS between browsers, many developers use it on all their pages. In fact, Dreamweaver CS3 uses CSS by default for setting page properties, such as background color and image, default text colors, page margins, and such. Formatting and presentation that used to be done with HTML (which is considered improper usage of HTML these days) is now being done with CSS. Using CSS will help every Web designer create efficient and modern Web pages.

Dreamweaver CS3 has incredible support for CSS, including creating complex and modern CSS layouts, that far exceeds previous versions of the product. You will learn a lot of basic CSS in this book in Chapter 6, *"Working with Cascading Style Sheets,"* and Chapter 9, *"Using Layout Tools."*

What Does CSS Look Like?

Unless you've already begun exploring CSS, you probably don't have any idea what CSS looks like. CSS is a deceptively simple language with few pieces to the puzzle.

Here is a basic CSS rule written in correct syntax:

```
1. body {
2.     font-family: Verdana, Arial, Helvetica,
       sans-serif;
3.     color: #000000;
4.     background-color: #FFFFFF;
5. }
```

Here's a breakdown of these CSS elements:

1. **Selector and start of declaration block:** The selector tells the browser which element to style in the document. This can be an HTML element, an element with a specific class applied, or even an element with a specific ID. The text **body** is the selector, and the left curly braces ({) is the start of the declaration block.

2. **Declaration:** A declaration consists of a property (in this case **font-family**) followed by a value (**Verdana, Arial, Helvetica, sans-serif**) followed by a semicolon to end the declaration. This declaration specifies the font for the entire document. You can specify as many declarations as you want inside the declaration block.

3. **Declaration:** This declaration specifies the color for the body text on the page to **#000000**, which is the hex value for black. Color declarations can use either hex colors or certain named colors, but it's always best to stick with hex.

4. **Declaration:** This declaration sets the background color of the page to white.

5. **End of declaration block:** The right curly brace ends the CSS rule. Once you've ended a declaration, you're ready to start the next one.

What Is XML?

XML is a set of guidelines for delimiting text through a system of tags so it can be read and processed by any device capable of reading a text file. You can think of it as a system for customizing Web content that must follow a set of specific syntax rules. Since XML is a text format following rigid guidelines, you can imagine why so many developers like to work with XML data; you can do just about anything with a text file, regardless of what computer and operating system you are using. For this reason, XML is used to move data between different computers and different operating systems, which makes it perfect for e-commerce solutions and for sending and retrieving data from a database.

Dreamweaver supports templates, covered in Chapter 16, *"Using Templates and Library Items."* One of the advanced features of Dreamweaver CS3 is the ability to export and import XML files through a template. Because XML is so complex and deep and because the use of databases is outside the scope of this book, I don't include any XML exercises in any of the chapters. Here are some places you can go to learn more about XML:

- **World Wide Web Consortium:** www.w3.org/xml/

- **W3 Schools—XML:** www.w3schools.com/xml/

- **A List Apart:** www.alistapart.com/stories/usingxml/

What Is DHTML?

DHTML is a collection of different technologies. This can include any combination of XHTML, JavaScript, CSS, and the DOM (**D**ocument **O**bject **M**odel). By combining these technologies, you can author more dynamic content than what basic HTML affords.

Some of the effects possible with DHTML include animation, drag and drop, and complicated roll-overs (buttons that change when a cursor moves over them). With Dreamweaver CS3, you can create some fancy DHTML just by clicking a few buttons.

Just like with XHTML, Dreamweaver CS3 codes DHTML effects behind the scenes. However, DHTML has some serious cross-platform issues, because the behind-the-scenes code is supported quite differently between browsers. Fortunately, Dreamweaver CS3 lets you target specific browsers, as well as test the compatibility of your DHTML effects.

DHTML uses a combination of XHTML, JavaScript, CSS, and the DOM. The following chart gives a short description of each:

DHTML Technologies	
Technology	**Explanation**
XHTML	eXtensible HyperText Markup Language—the default markup for basic Web pages and the root of DHTML.
JavaScript	A scripting language used to manipulate Web pages.
CSS	Cascading Style Sheets—a presentation language supported by version 4.0 and newer browsers, which allows for better control over the appearance and positioning of elements on a Web page.
DOM	Document Object Model—the specification for how objects in a Web page are represented. The DOM defines what attributes are associated with each object and how the objects and attributes can be manipulated.

What Is JavaScript?

JavaScript was developed by in 1995 and has become almost as popular as HTML. It actually has nothing to do with the Java programming language, but Netscape licensed the name from Sun Microsystems in hopes of increasing acceptance of the new scripting protocol. It's not certain whether it was the name that did the trick, but JavaScript has become almost as widely adopted as HTML itself. The most common uses of JavaScript are creating rollovers, resizing browser windows, and checking for browser compatibility.

You can access most of the JavaScript routines through the **Behaviors** panel in Dreamweaver CS3, which you will learn about in Chapter 11, "*Adding Rollover Images*," and Chapter 14, "*Applying Behaviors*." This book covers many JavaScript techniques, including rollovers, browser sniffing, and external browser windows. You will not have to learn to write JavaScript by hand in order to use it within Dreamweaver CS3, which is fortunate for non-programmers, because JavaScript programming is far more complicated than XHTML.

What Is a Web Application?

In broad terms, a **Web application** is a Web site that delivers dynamic data instead of static data that has to be updated manually. (Amazon.com and eBay.com are great examples of a Web application.) Web applications have also been referred to as *data-driven*, *database-driven*, and *dynamic* sites. In almost all cases, a Web application involves a database and server-side scripting, such as ASP, Adobe ColdFusion, PHP, and so on. Web applications aren't just one thing; they can take on many forms and serve many purposes. They can be used to handle e-commerce, inventory tracking, online auctions, and just about anything using a large amount of information. So, what do Web applications have to do with learning Dreamweaver CS3? Well, Dreamweaver CS3 can create complete Web applications, in addition to static Web sites. Although creating Web applications is outside the scope of this book, you should know that you can use Dreamweaver CS3 to create them. As you advance your skills, you will find that you will not outgrow Dreamweaver—the sky is the limit as far as its capabilities are concerned.

Extending Dreamweaver

One of the greatest features of the Dreamweaver community is the way people share objects, commands, behaviors, and server behaviors, which are like plug-ins for Dreamweaver that let you add programming functionality without typing a single line of code. These prebuilt elements can be shared and distributed, much the way Photoshop plug-ins work. If you visit the Adobe Dreamweaver Exchange (**www.adobe.com/cfusion/exchange/index.cfm?view=sn120**), you'll find numerous ways to get more out of Dreamweaver CS3 (and other versions of Dreamweaver) without having to learn a complex programming language. In addition, you'll find a collection of third-party sites to help you extend the capabilities of Dreamweaver CS3. Tons of extension developers are out there, so I can't list them all. You can find a pretty comprehensive list at **www.dwfaq.com/Resources/Extensions/**.

Now that you have a basic foundation in these key areas, you are ready to learn more about Dreamweaver CS3. The next chapter will introduce you to the Dreamweaver CS3 interface and prepare you for the many step-by-step exercises throughout the rest of the book.

2

Exploring the Interface

One of the most daunting aspects of working with any HTML (**H**yper**T**ext **M**arkup **L**anguage) editor is learning its interface. With HTML editors becoming more and more powerful and capable of so many functions, it's not surprising their interfaces have gotten more complex over the years. But compared to other editors, the Adobe Dreamweaver CS3 interface is a model of efficiency. No other HTML editor offers a robust editing environment with such an efficient, intuitive interface. Other HTML editors require you to open many different-sized windows and panels to reach all the features, which means you're constantly hunting for the right tool at the right time. Dreamweaver CS3, however, uses a system of adjustable panels and panel groups to suit your needs depending on the context. This saves screen real estate and makes learning the interface a lot easier. Although the Dreamweaver CS3 interface can seem overwhelming at first, learning how to use it is probably one of the easier challenges ahead of you.

This chapter will introduce the basic concepts of the program's interface. In addition, I'll also share how to set up my favorite Dreamweaver CS3 preferences and configurations.

You might be antsy to start on the step-by-step exercises in later chapters, but you should review this chapter first to identify the toolbars, panels, and windows you'll be using throughout this book.

Touring the Interface

In Windows, the Dreamweaver CS3 interface is contained within an integrated workspace, which means the **Document** window and all the panels are positioned within a larger window. This layout can make working with multiple documents and panels easier because the panels don't float all over the screen as separate objects.

The integrated workspace is available in Windows only, though. Because the Windows and Mac versions of Dreamweaver CS3 are significantly different, I cover both interfaces in this chapter. Regardless of your operating system, the interface has six main parts.

Windows Interface

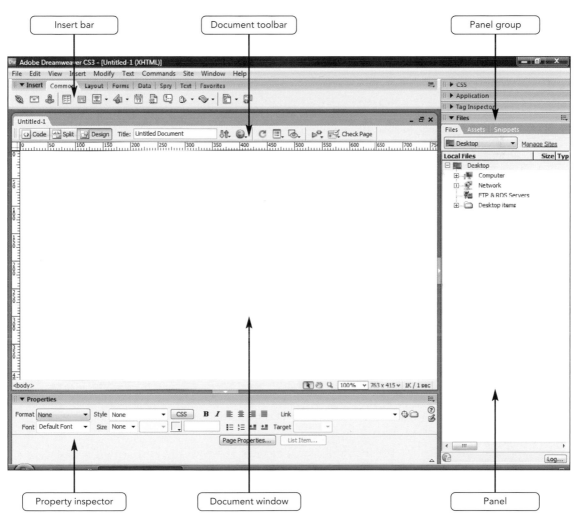

Insert bar

Document toolbar

Panel group

Property inspector

Document window

Panel

The six main elements of the Windows interface are as follows: the **Insert** bar, **Document** toolbar, **Document** window, **Property inspector**, panels, and panel groups. By default, each time you open Dreamweaver CS3, it opens with the **Welcome Screen** (which you'll see in just a bit).

Mac Interface

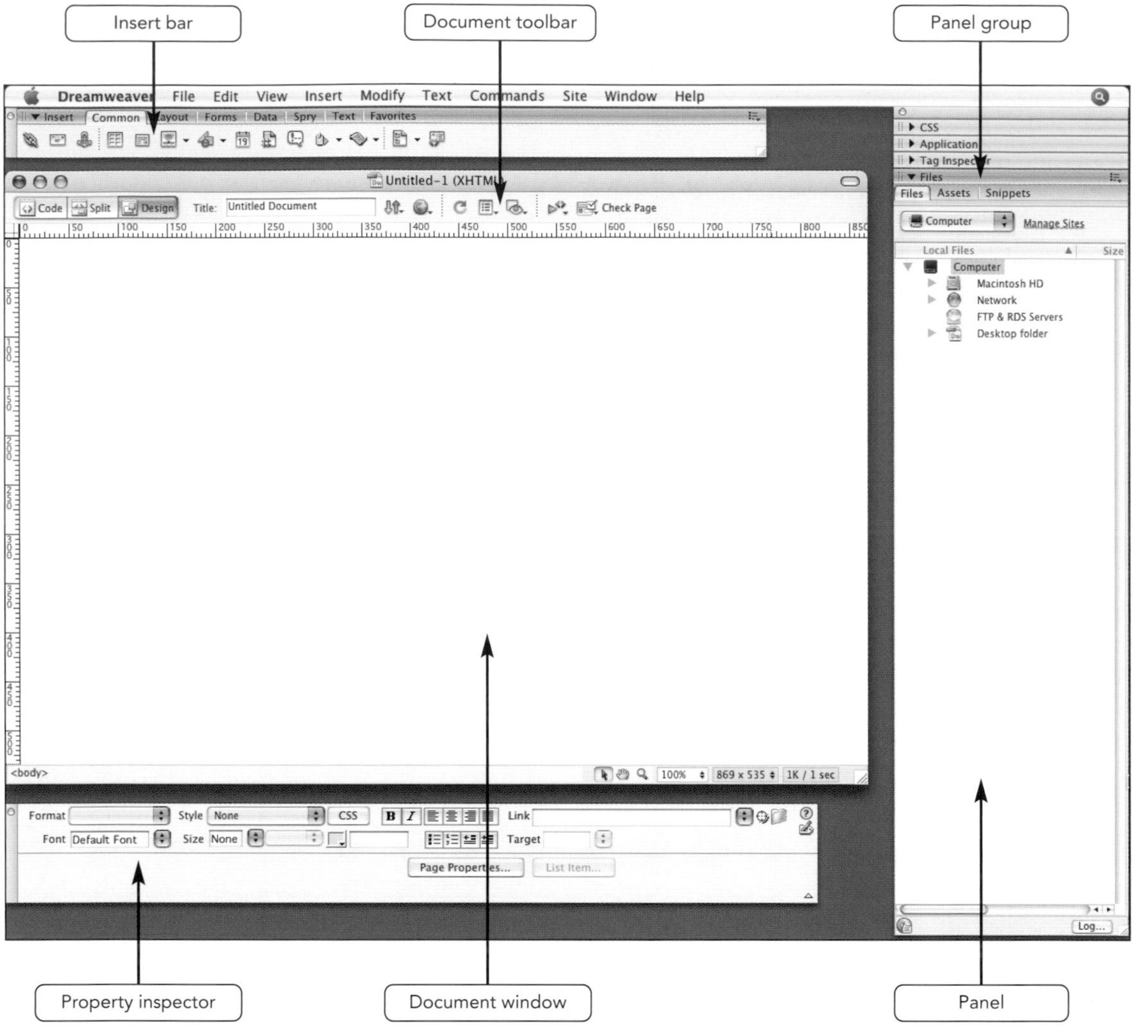

The six main elements of the Mac interface are also as follows: the **Insert** bar, **Document** toolbar, **Document** window, **Property inspector**, panels, and panel groups. By default, each time you open Dreamweaver CS3, it opens with the **Welcome Screen** (which you'll learn about shortly).

The Welcome Screen

The **Welcome Screen** offers a quick way to perform common tasks, such as opening recently viewed files, creating new documents, accessing templates, and more. You can even access some online tutorials and the Adobe Dreamweaver Exchange by clicking its respective link. (You'll learn more about the Dreamweaver Exchange in Chapter 21, "*Getting Your Site Online.*") The **Welcome Screen** is a nice way to introduce you to Dreamweaver CS3 because it visually represents these common tasks.

The **Welcome Screen** behaves and looks the same in Windows and on a Mac, except the **Welcome Screen** on a Mac is a floating window, and the **Welcome Screen** in Windows is part of the integrated workspace.

If, for whatever reason, you don't want to use the **Welcome Screen**, you can disable it by selecting the **Don't show again** check box in the lower-left corner of the **Welcome Screen** or by choosing **Edit > Preferences > General** (Windows) or **Dreamweaver > Preferences > General** (Mac) and deselecting the **Show Welcome Screen** check box, as shown in the illustration here. Both options cause Dreamweaver CS3 to open without the **Welcome Screen** showing.

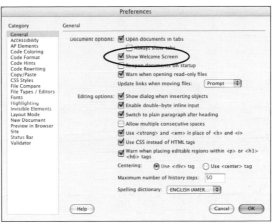

VIDEO: **welcome_screen.mov**

For a more in-depth look at the Welcome Screen, check out **welcome_screen.mov** in the **videos** folder on the **Dreamweaver HOT CD-ROM**.

The Insert Bar

The **Insert** bar contains rows of object icons and is used as a one-click stop for many operations. If you move your cursor over the icons in the **Insert** bar and pause for a moment, you will see a **tool tip** appear, which explains what each of the icons does.

By default, the **Insert** bar is divided into tabbed categories, with each tab containing a different set of related icons. So, for example, if you were creating a form, you would click the **Forms** tab to access all of Dreamweaver's available form objects.

If you don't like the tabs, you also have the option of displaying the **Insert** bar with a pop-up menu of categories. Just click the **Panel Options** button, and choose **Show as Menu**. You can then select among the different categories in the pop-up menu at the left of the **Insert** bar. To return to the tabbed interface, choose **Show as Tabs** in the menu.

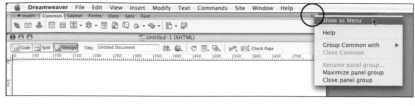

Select to return to the tabbed layout.

Many items in the **Insert** bar also appear on the **Insert** menu in the top menu bar. The **Insert** bar provides one-click alternatives to using that menu bar. You may be comfortable clicking the icons, or you may prefer the menu access. There is no right or wrong way to do this; it's just a matter of personal preference.

Types of Insert Bar Categories

The **Insert** bar is grouped into six categories, plus one additional area for Favorites. Each category contains a related set of objects. Here is a brief description of each of the **Insert** bar categories.

The **Common** group contains the most frequently used objects in Dreamweaver CS3, including images, tables, **<div>** tags, simple rollovers, Flash objects, and so on. You will use this panel a lot.

The **Layout** group is really useful, and you will find yourself using it a lot as you build your pages. This panel lets you switch between editing modes, work with absolutely positioned **<div>** tags, and do so much more. You'll learn about these items in Chapter 9, *"Using Layout Tools."*

The **Forms** group contains all the objects essential for creating forms for your Web pages. These objects include text boxes, buttons, menus, and, new to Dreamweaver CS3, Spry validation widgets. You'll learn about these items in Chapter 13, *"Working with Forms."*

The **Data** group is new to Dreamweaver CS3. It lets you insert Spry data objects as well as other dynamic elements such as record sets, repeated regions, and record insertion and update forms.

The **Spry** group is also new to Dreamweaver CS3. It contains buttons for building Spry pages, including Spry data objects and widgets. The Spry framework is used to create rich Internet applications and is a more advanced technique for experienced Web developers. However, I'll still take the time to cover the basics of using the **Spry** group in Chapter 20, *"Using Spry Tools."*

The **Text** group provides an easy way to add formatting to text on your page, though truth be told, you'll probably do most of your formatting using the **Property inspector** because you'll find it inconvenient to open the **Text** group in the **Insert** bar every time you want to format some text.

Throughout the book, you'll learn how and when to use many of the objects in the **Insert** bar. For now, this is just a sneak peek to let you know they're there.

Adding Favorites to the Insert Bar

As you build your Web pages, you may find yourself constantly switching back and forth among the different categories in the **Insert** bar, which can become tedious, especially if you're always using the same set of items. As you become more experienced with Dreamweaver, you'll get a better idea of which **Insert** bar objects you find yourself using most of the time, and you might find it convenient to have them all located in one place rather than spread across several categories. To make life a little easier for you, Dreamweaver CS3 offers the ability to create a **Favorites** group in the **Insert** bar to contain your most commonly used items.

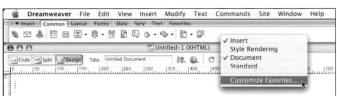

With any document open, simply right-click the **Insert** bar anywhere, and choose **Customize Favorites** to open the **Customize Favorite Objects** dialog box.

Here you can select your most commonly used objects from the list on the left and add them to the **Favorite objects** column on the right. Use the **up arrow** and **down arrow** buttons to move items up and down the list, and click the **Add separator** button to add a separator line between objects. Click **OK** when you're done.

You'll find all your favorites in the **Favorites** category, and you can just keep this group open to access the items you need. Of course, if you need to select an object that isn't listed here, you can just click its tab to find it or even add it to your favorites if you're going to use it often.

The Property Inspector

The **Property inspector** is context-sensitive, meaning it changes depending on what type of element is selected on your Web page. If you have text selected, you'll see text properties in the **Property inspector** (as shown in the illustration here); if you have an image selected, you'll see image properties.

Collapse/Expand

Without the **Property inspector**, you wouldn't be able to change the properties of many elements on your page, so it's a good idea to keep it open at all times. You'll also want to make sure it's fully expanded at all times by clicking the **arrow** icon in its lower-right corner. When the **Property inspector** is collapsed, you won't be able to see all the available properties.

The Document Toolbar

You can access many of the options you need directly in the **Document** toolbar, which is attached to the top of each **Document** window. The **Document** toolbar contains a series of buttons and pop-up menus that let you change the document view, set the page title, preview the page in a browser, and interact with a server hosting your site.

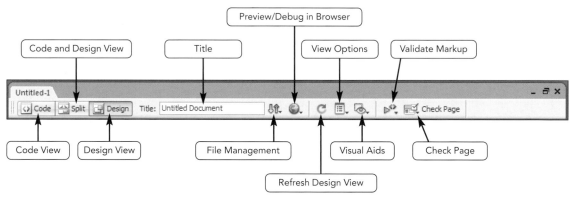

This is what the **Document** toolbar looks like in Windows.

This is what the **Document** toolbar looks like on a Mac.

Redundancy in the Interface

As you learn Dreamweaver CS3, you'll notice that there is some redundancy in the interface. For example, you can insert an image by clicking the **Image** button in the **Insert** bar or by choosing **Insert > Insert Image**. You can align objects by using the **Property inspector** or by using a command on a menu. Different options are convenient at times, but it can also be confusing to learn a program that has two or three ways to accomplish the same task. Just remember that there is no right or wrong method. As you continue to work with Dreamweaver, you'll figure out which methods work best for you.

As you can see, the **Document** toolbar on a Mac is essentially the same as in Windows. The following chart describes what all these buttons do:

Document Toolbar Features	
Feature	**Description**
Code View	**Code** view displays the code that creates your page. You can use this to edit the code directly and make changes without having to use a separate text editor, such as BBEdit from Bare Bones Software or Macromedia HomeSite from Adobe. **Code** view is helpful if you are comfortable coding your pages or need to create or modify custom code, such as JavaScript, ASP (**A**ctive **S**erver **P**ages), and so on. You'll have numerous opportunities throughout the book to learn to work with **Code** view.
Code and Design View	Also called **Split** view, the **Code and Design** view splits your document in half, displaying the code and the page layout. This view is helpful if you want to make some minor changes to the code and see the visual effect they have on your page immediately.
Design View	**Design** view is the default view for your **Document** window. This view displays your page in WYSIWYG (**W**hat **Y**ou **S**ee **I**s **W**hat **Y**ou **G**et) mode, which means you will see images, text, and other media as you add them to your page. This view is helpful if you aren't familiar with HTML or just don't want to take the time to type all the code yourself; in addition, it gives you a pretty accurate preview of what your page will look like in a browser as it's being designed.
Title	This text field lets you specify the title for your page. The title you type here appears at the top of your visitors' browser windows and is used by some search engines to describe your site listing. It is also the name identifying the page when it's saved as a bookmark or favorite in a browser. You can also set the title in the **Page Properties** dialog box.

continues on next page

Document Toolbar Features *(continued)*

Feature	Description
File Management	This pop-up menu lets you manage the files of your site by uploading and downloading files, unlocking them, and checking them in or out. It's great to have access to all these options directly in the **Document** window. You'll learn how to upload and download files in Chapter 21, *"Getting Your Site Online."*
Preview/Debug in Browser	This pop-up menu lets you choose a browser to preview your page or debug the JavaScript. You can also access the **Define Browsers** dialog box, which lets you define new browsers or change references to existing browsers you have already defined.
Refresh Design View	This button refreshes the contents of the **Design** view. This can be helpful if you make edits to your page in **Code** view and don't immediately see the changes in **Design** view.
View Options	This menu performs different functions based on whether you're in **Code** view or **Design** view. In **Code** view, you can set the view to wrap words, display line numbers, display syntax coloring, and so on. In **Design** view, you can determine whether you want to see items such as the rulers or guides. And in **Split** view, you can also set the view options for both **Code** view and **Design** view as well as swap their positions by placing **Design** view in the top pane.
Visual Aids	This pop-up menu lets you turn many of the visual aids on and off in **Design** view. You can turn off invisible elements, table borders, CSS (**C**ascading **S**tyle **S**heets) layout backgrounds, and other cool CSS rendering features, which you'll learn more about in Chapter 6, *"Working with Cascading Style Sheets."*
Validate Markup	This pop-up menu lets you validate your code against various HTML and XHTML (e**X**tensible **H**yper**T**ext **M**arkup **L**anguage) standards. You can validate the current document, a group of selected documents, or the entire site. You can also access various options to determine which items the validator will check against.
Check Page	This menu gives you a quick way to check your code against various browsers and their different versions. Using this pop-up menu, you can check your code and define which browsers and what versions your code is being checked against. You can also set an option so your pages are automatically validated each time you open them. You will learn more about this feature in Chapter 21, *"Getting Your Site Online."*

The Document Window

The **Document** window is where all the action happens when you're creating a Web site. This is where you assemble your page elements and design your pages. The **Document** window is similar in appearance to a browser window.

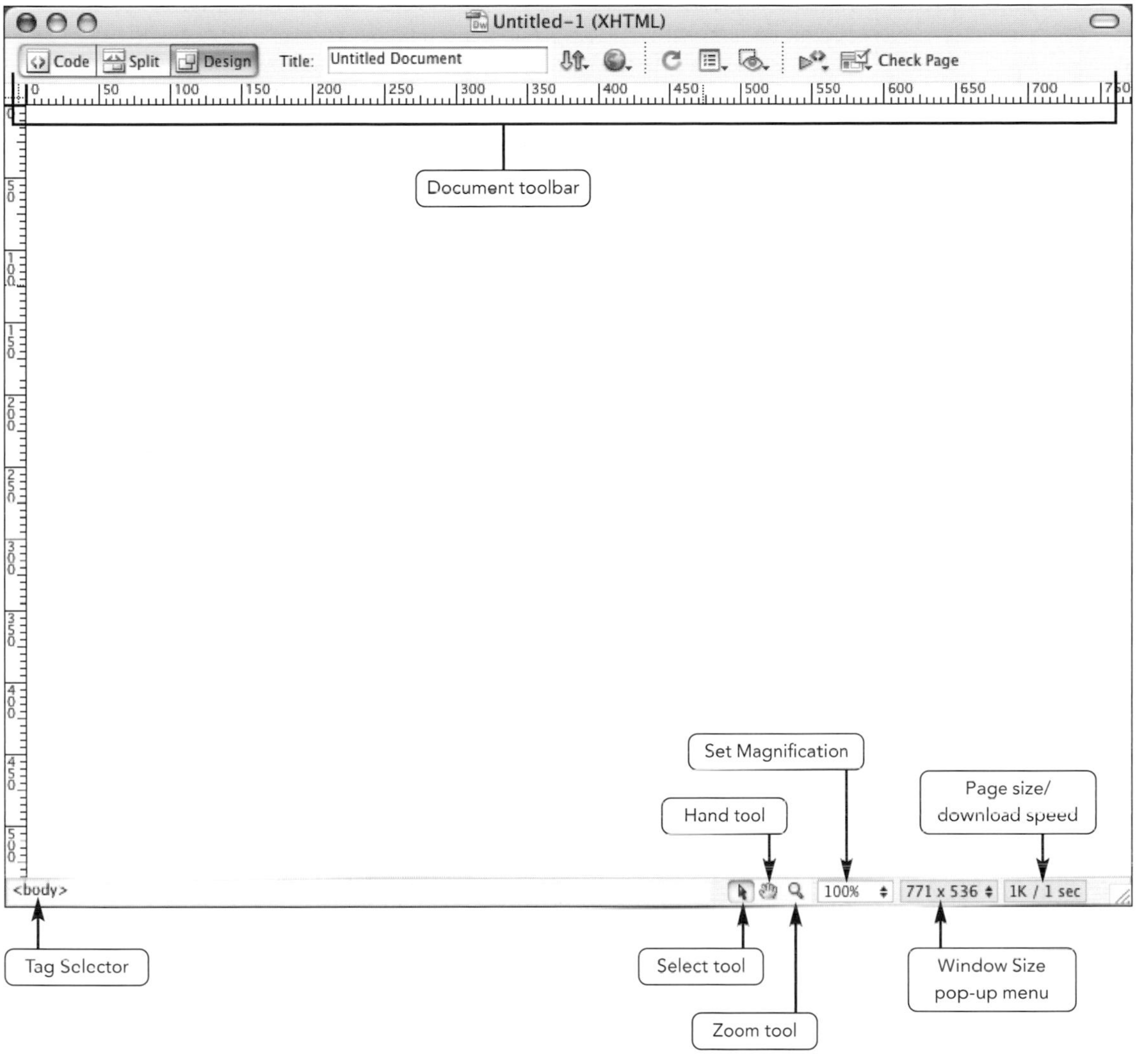

Untitled-1 (XHTML)
Code
Split
Design
Title:
Untitled Document
Check Page
Document toolbar
Set Magnification
Hand tool
Page size/
download speed
<body>
100%
771 x 536
1K / 1 sec
Tag Selector
Select tool
Zoom tool
Window Size
pop-up menu

The following chart explains the **Document** window features:

Document Window Features

Feature	Description
Document toolbar	Each **Document** window has its own **Document** toolbar, which contains a series of buttons to perform actions such as change the view of the **Document** window, change layout modes, add a page title, preview in a browser, and so much more. Earlier in this chapter, you'll find a detailed explanation of each function of the **Document** toolbar.
Tag Selector	As you select visual elements on your screen, the **Tag Selector** highlights the corresponding HTML tag. It's a fast and easy way to select different items on your page. You'll learn how to use the **Tag Selector** in many chapters throughout the book.
Window Size	This pop-up menu lets you resize your window to various preset or custom pixel dimensions. It has no effect on the final layout of your page—it's simply a way to see what your page might look like in different window sizes.
Page size/ download speed	This area gives you the approximate size (kilobytes) and download time for the current page. By choosing **Preferences > Status Bar**, you can change this display to match the download speed of your typical user's computer.
Select tool	The **Select** tool is the default choice when editing a document. This lets you place your cursor on the page to type, select images and tables, and interact with all the elements on your page.
Hand tool	Use the **Hand** tool to grab and move the **Document** view when you're at a magnification greater than 100 percent. If you're zoomed into **Design** view at 200 percent, you can use the **Hand** tool to move the document in the **Document** window to view different areas of the page.
Zoom tool	Select this tool to quickly zoom into a specific area of the page. When you select the **Zoom** tool, your cursor will change to a magnifying glass, and you can click and drag an area to zoom in.
Set Magnification	This pop-up menu lets you to choose a predefined zoom level. The **Document** window will zoom in to whatever element is currently selected. You can also select the current percentage value and type a specific value.

Document Window Views

Dreamweaver gives you the added control and flexibility of viewing your pages in one of three different views: **Code** view, **Split** view, and **Design** view. By default, all new documents will open in the view of the current document. If you don't have a document open, new documents will open in the view of the last document you had opened. So if the last document you worked on was in **Code** view when you closed it, the next new document will open in **Code** view. The three buttons on the left of the **Document** toolbar let you change between the three different views.

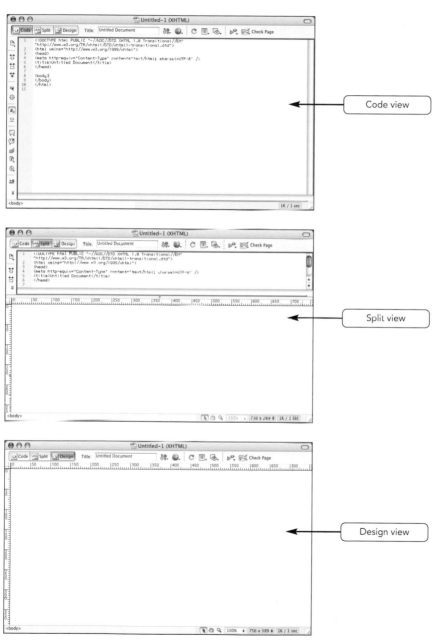

Code view

Split view

Design view

Multiple Document Windows

When you're working on a site with multiple pages, you'll need to work with several documents open at the same time, which can be a pain to manage, even with a large monitor. Dreamweaver CS3 makes it easy to work with multiple **Document** windows by placing a small tab for each open page at the top of the **Document** window. You can jump from one page to another by clicking a tab. **Note:** In Windows, your page must be maximized in order to see the tabs; otherwise, the page will float around as a separate object.

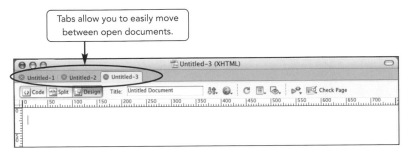

Panels and Panel Groups

Dreamweaver makes it easy to manage an otherwise complex interface through a system of panels and panel groups. These two interface elements work together to help you customize your workspace so you can quickly access just the panels you need. Each panel group can contain several panels, each identified by a tab. You can click each tab to move between panels.

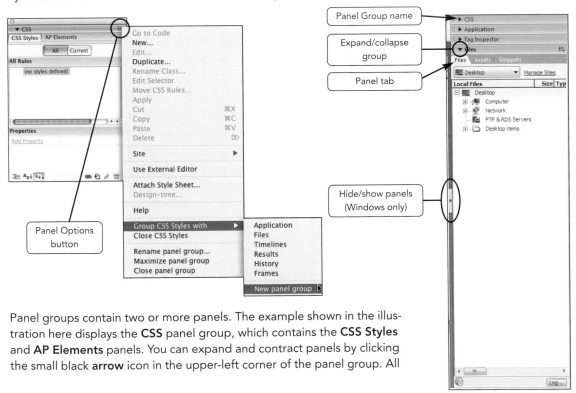

Panel groups contain two or more panels. The example shown in the illustration here displays the **CSS** panel group, which contains the **CSS Styles** and **AP Elements** panels. You can expand and contract panels by clicking the small black **arrow** icon in the upper-left corner of the panel group. All the panels are accessible from the **Window** menu or by using a keyboard shortcut. You can customize panel groups or create your own by adding and removing panels by choosing the **Group <panel> with** and **Close <panel>** commands in the **Panel Options** menu.

You can rename panel groups by choosing **Rename panel group**, or you can make new panel groups by choosing **Group <panel> with > New panel group** in the **Panel Options** menu. This is a great way to customize the interface. You can also click and drag the panels to add or remove them from other panel groups.

By default, all the panel groups are docked along the right side of the screen. You can undock a panel group by clicking the small dots in the upper-left corner of a panel group (referred to as the **gripper**) and dragging the group to a new position.

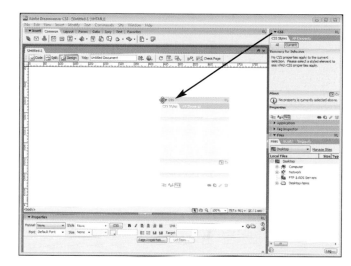

You can easily redock by clicking the gripper (in the upper-left area) and dragging over any of the other panels. When a blue line appears between the panel groups, you'll know where the panel group will end up when you release the mouse.

In Windows, you can also dock panels along the left and right sides of the **Document** window by clicking the upper-left "gripper" area and dragging over any part of the right or left side of the **Document** window. A thick black line will preview where the panel will appear when you release the mouse. If you are on a Mac, you can drag your panels and groups to the left side of the screen; they just won't dock and resize as nicely as they do in Windows.

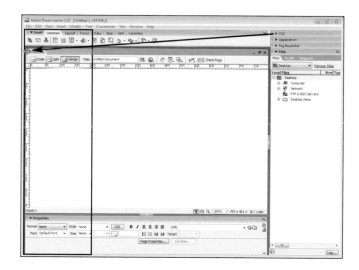

A lot of Dreamweaver developers like to arrange their panels along the left and right sides of the **Document** window. Of course, you really do need a large monitor to work effectively with your panels arranged this way. Remember, there is no wrong or right way to do this; it's simply a matter of personal preference.

Setting a Default Workspace

As you experiment with different panel layouts and groupings, you may find that you've really changed Dreamweaver's workspace from its nice default layout into something a little…less nice. If you're on a Mac, you can set everything back to the way it was by choosing **Window > Workspace Layout > Default**. If you're on Windows, you can also choose **Window > Workspace Layout**, but

instead of **Default**, you have the choice of **Designer** or **Coder**. The **Designer** option in Windows is the equivalent to the **Default** option on a Mac; it sets all your panel groups to the right side of the interface. The **Coder** option is for developers who prefer to work primarily in **Code** view; therefore, unless you like to type code, choose **Designer**.

NOTE:

Dual Screen Mode

Also in the **Window > Workspace Layout** menu is **Dual Screen**. This option is for people fortunate enough to have two monitors hooked to their computers. If you're one of these lucky people, you can choose **Dual Screen** to spread your panel groups onto your second monitor, giving you much more room on your primary monitor to work with your Web pages.

Saving Workspace Layouts

If you've spent the time to customize your workspace layout, chances are good that you'll be interested in saving your layout so you can call it up again in case you or someone one else accidentally messes up your workspace. Also, many developers work on several different types of sites. You might work on a dynamic site one day and need the **Application** panel and **Tag Inspector**, and you might work on a static XHTML site the next day and need only the **CSS** panel. Saving workspace layouts lets you set up a layout for each workflow so you can easily switch between the two (or three or four).

After you configure your panels and panel groups, choose **Window > Workspace Layout > Save Current** to open the **Save Workspace Layout** dialog box. Type a name for your saved workspace, and click **OK**.

To access a custom workspace you created, choose **Window > Workspace Layout**, and choose the custom workspace you want to use. Your panels will magically rearrange themselves.

Defining a Default Browser

One of the most important steps of designing a Web site is to test your pages in various browsers, because when it comes down to it, a Web page is nothing more than a bunch of code, be it XHTML, JavaScript, CSS, or whatever. What you see when you view a page in a browser is that browser's interpretation of the code, and each browser might interpret a page differently. Now, as time has gone by, browser standards have gotten a little more reliable, but it's still a good idea to check your pages in as many browsers as possible before launching it on the Web.

Of course, you may be one of those browser snobs who says, "I designed my page for Firefox users, and that's that!" This is fine—as long as you don't mind that people coming to your site in other browsers might not be able to see the content the way you intended it. But if you're trying to reach as broad an audience as possible, you'll want to download and install all sorts of browsers such as Firefox, Netscape, Opera… the list goes on. At the least you should have the most current version of Internet Explorer, Netscape, and Firefox on your machine if you're working in Windows. If you're on a Mac, you should already have Safari, but you should probably download and install Firefox and Netscape too. If you're really serious about making sure your pages work, you'll want to check them cross-platform as well; if you're designing in Windows, check your pages out on a Mac, and vice versa.

As you saw earlier, Dreamweaver does have some built-in tools for validating your pages code against different browser types, but if you want to know what your page looks like in a certain browser, check it out in that browser.

And checking your pages in a browser isn't just something you should do right before you're ready to upload them to the Web. You should be checking them at each step along the way so you can catch potential problems as you go.

To set up your browser preference, follow these steps:

1 Choose **Edit > Preferences** (Windows) or **Dreamweaver > Preferences** (Mac).

2 In the **Category** list, click **Preview in Browser**.

3 Click the **+**, **–**, or **Edit** button to add, remove, or change a browser from the list of choices.

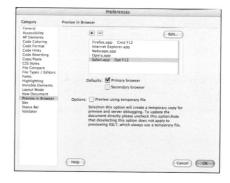

Note: The primary browser is the browser that launches when you press F12 (Windows) or Opt+F12 (Mac). The secondary browser is the browser that launches when you press Ctrl+F12 (Windows) or Cmd+F12 (Mac). Many designers like to preview their pages in multiple browsers so they can ensure their work looks the same on all browsers. Using a primary and secondary browser will allow you to do so easily.

The Preview in Browser preference sets the primary browser to open with the F12 (Windows) or Opt+F12 (Mac) shortcut key. You can add more than two browsers here, but you can access only the primary and secondary browsers using the shortcut keys. You can access the other browsers using the Preview in Browser button on the Document toolbar.

Using Shortcut Keys

Dreamweaver CS3 has lots of shortcut keys. The following chart lists some of my favorites:

Shortcuts in Dreamweaver		
Action	Mac	Windows
Create new document	Cmd+N	Ctrl+N
Insert line break	Shift+Return	Shift+Enter
Open Page properties	Cmd+J	Ctrl+J
Select a word	Double-click	Double-click
Select a paragraph	Triple-click	Triple-click
Check spelling	Shift+F7	Shift+F7
Find and replace	Cmd+F	Ctrl+F
Insert bar	Cmd+F2	Ctrl+F2
Property inspector	Cmd+F3	Ctrl+F3
Behaviors	Shift+F4	Shift+F4
Files	F8	F8
Results	F7	F7
History	n/a	Shift+F10
CSS styles	n/a	Shift+F11
Save	Cmd+S	Ctrl+S
Put	Cmd+Shift+U	Ctrl+Shift+U
Preview in primary browser	Opt+F12	F12
Preview in secondary browser	Cmd+F12	Ctrl+F12
Hide/show all panels	F4	F4

Customizing Keyboard Shortcuts

If you want to set up your own keyboard shortcuts, choose **Edit > Keyboard Shortcuts** (Windows) or **Dreamweaver > Keyboard Shortcuts** (Mac). You can change or add keyboard shortcuts to your heart's desire.

Dreamweaver CS3 lets you define your own custom keyboard shortcuts and choose from several predefined sets of shortcuts; you can even save your own custom settings and export an HTML file for a handy reference. This can be really useful if, for example, you want to create a keyboard shortcut to open the **History** and **CSS styles** panels on a Mac, which by default have no keyboard shortcuts associated with them.

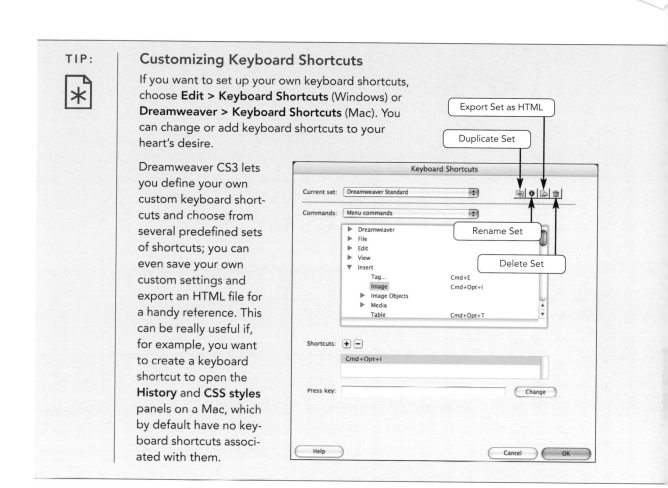

In this chapter, you got a quick tour of the Dreamweaver CS3 interface and learned how to configure your Dreamweaver CS3 preferences to your liking. Now that you know your way around Dreamweaver CS3, it's time to start building some Web pages. In the next chapter, you'll learn how to define a site in Dreamweaver CS3.

3

Managing Your Sites

If you've built one or two Web sites in the past, you'll likely agree that file management is one of the greatest challenges of this medium. But if you have yet to put up your first creation, you're probably wondering, "What is file management?" **File management** encompasses the organization, folder structure, and naming conventions of all the pages and graphics in your Web site. Few other disciplines require the creation of so many documents at once, because every individual Web page is usually comprised of numerous CSS (**C**ascading **S**tyle **S**heets), media, and image files, not to mention all the files linking back and forth to each other.

To compound the difficulty of managing numerous files, most people build Web sites from their hard drives, and when they've finished, they upload these files to a Web server so that the files can be viewed online. Let's say you created a folder on your hard drive called **HTML** and created another folder called **graphics**. If you put your HTML (**H**yper**T**ext **M**arkup **L**anguage) and graphics files inside those two folders, you would have to replicate this exact folder hierarchy when you uploaded those files to your Web server, or your links to those files would break. In this chapter, you will learn how to avoid such misfortune by building your Adobe Dreamweaver CS3 site management skills.

What Is a Local Root Folder?

Dreamweaver CS3 has a site management scheme that requires you to keep all your files within one main local root folder so you can easily duplicate the folder hierarchy on your hard drive when you publish to a Web server. A **local root folder** is no different from any other kind of folder on your hard drive, except you have told Dreamweaver CS3 that this is where all HTML and media files for your site reside.

If you think of the local root folder as the folder from which all other files stem, just like the roots of a tree, you will understand its function. A local root folder can contain many subfolders, but Dreamweaver CS3 cannot keep track of elements unless they are stored in the main local root folder.

Taking the concept further, let's say you decide midstream to change the folder hierarchy of your site by adding a folder or changing a folder name. If you were hand-coding the pages, making these changes would be a hassle because you would need to change all references to that folder in every page of your site. Dreamweaver CS3 makes this process painless, as long as you work within its site management structure.

By the time you are through with these exercises, you will have learned to define a site and a local root folder, create a site map, and reorganize files and folders.

WARNING:

⚠️

Don't Ignore Site Management

You might think site management in Dreamweaver CS3 is a neat (but optional) feature, and you would rather skip it now and return to it later when you're in the mood. Don't do it! Site management is integral to Dreamweaver CS3, and the program kicks up quite a fuss if you try to force it to work outside these boundaries. This book asks you to define a site with each new chapter, because if you have files outside your defined area, you will be constantly plagued by warnings that Dreamweaver is unable to find or link to files outside that defined site. So, stick with it, and make sure you grasp the concepts in this chapter before continuing.

---

1 | Defining a Site

This exercise shows you how to define a site in Dreamweaver CS3. You'll be working with a folder of HTML and image files from the **Dreamweaver HOT CD-ROM** you transfer to your hard drive. Once you've finished this exercise, the Dreamweaver CS3 site management feature will catalog all the files in this folder by building a **site cache file**—a small file that holds information such as the locations and names of all the files and folders in your site.

This exercise teaches you how to define a site from an existing Web site. You would use this process if you wanted to work with Dreamweaver CS3 on a site you or someone else had already created outside Dreamweaver CS3. Later in the chapter, an exercise shows you how to define a site from an empty folder, which will more likely simulate your approach when you are starting a site from scratch.

1 If you haven't already done so, copy the **chap_03** folder from the **Dreamweaver HOT CD-ROM** to your desktop. For clarity, leave this folder named **chap_03**.

The folder contains the required images and HTML files to complete the exercises in this chapter. You will be asked to add and change files, which requires you to have all the files on your hard drive.

2 Open Dreamweaver CS3. Close the **Welcome Screen**, and choose **Site > New Site** to open the **Site Definition** dialog box.

3 In the **Site Definition** dialog box, click the **Basic** tab to display the basic mode of the **Site Definition** dialog box.

The basic mode guides you through the process of defining a site by asking a series of questions about your site. As you use Dreamweaver CS3 more and more, you will find yourself using the Advanced tab—which you'll learn how to use later in this chapter—to define your sites.

4 Type **Chapter 3** in the **What would you like to name your site?** field. You can leave the **What is the HTTP Address (URL) of your site?** field blank for now. Click **Next**.

The site name is an internal naming convention, so you can use any kind of name you want without worrying about spaces or capitalization. Think of it as your own pet name for your project, just like you give a folder or hard drive a custom name. Dreamweaver CS3 will use the HTTP (**H**yper**T**ext **T**ransfer **P**rotocol) address you type to manage root relative links in your site. You'll find out more about root relative links later in this chapter.

---

5 The next screen asks whether you want to use a server technology for your site. Select the **No, I do not want to use a server technology** radio button, and click **Next**.

If you were creating a Web application or a site connected to a database, you would select Yes… to set up the proper options. However, a simple static Web site, like the one you'll create in this book, does not require any special server technology setup.

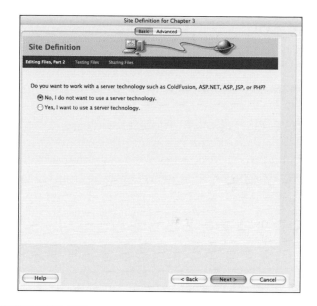

---

6 The next screen asks how you want to develop your pages. Select the **Edit local copies on my machine, then upload to server when ready (recommended)** radio button.

This option lets Dreamweaver CS3 know you will create and edit the Web pages on your computer and then upload them to the Web when you are ready. The other radio button lets you edit your pages over a network or directly on a remote Web server.

Browse button

7 Click the **Browse** button (the small folder icon), and browse to the **chap_03** folder on your desktop. Select the **chap_03** folder, and click **Select** (Windows) or **Choose** (Mac).

8 Click **Next**.

9 The next screen defines how you will connect to the remote Web server so you can upload your files. Select **None**, and then click **Next**.

Don't worry about this section for now—you'll learn more about connecting to a remote Web server in Chapter 21, *"Getting Your Site Online."*

Note: Changing the site definition settings is easy, even long after you've created them. Choose Site > Manage Sites, select the site you want modify, and click Edit.

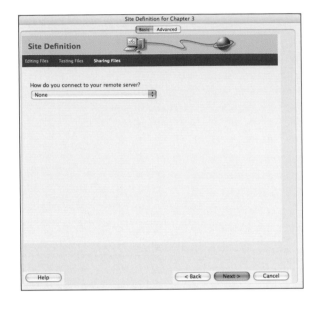

10 The next screen summarizes the settings you specified for your site. Take a moment to look over this screen to make sure you have everything set up properly. When you are ready, click **Done**.

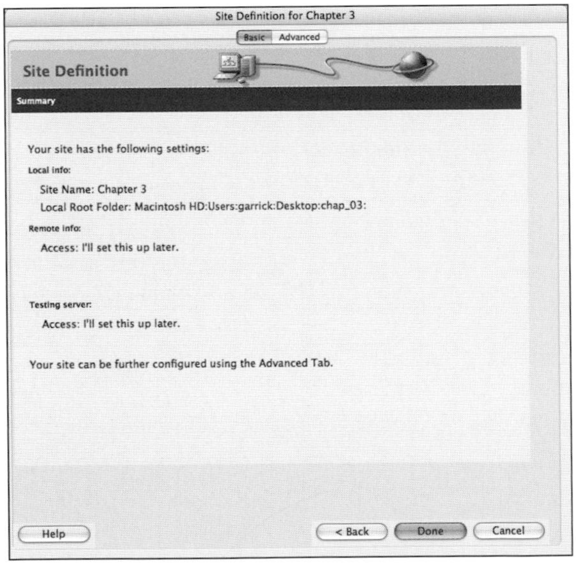

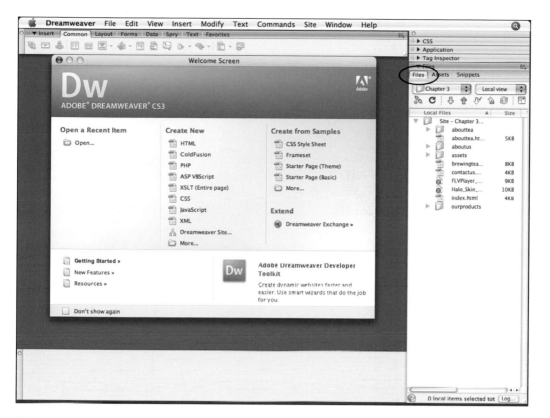

The site is now defined as Chapter 3. The Files panel displays the contents of the chap_03 folder on your desktop. Note that you didn't make a copy of this folder in Dreamweaver; you are looking at the actual contents of the folder on your desktop via Dreamweaver's Files panel. This is the folder containing all your HTML files and images, also referred to as your local root folder. Although you might think very little has happened, you'll see the advantages of defining a site in upcoming exercises where you'll move files around and put this feature to the test!

Note: In Windows, if you see lock icons next to the file or folder icons, refer to the introduction to learn how to remove the locks before proceeding.

NOTE:

Local Root Folder, Root Folder, Root

As you work through Dreamweaver CS3, you will notice references to a **local root folder**, a **root folder**, and a **root**. All these terms are interchangeable. Each refers to a folder on your hard drive that contains all the HTML, images, and so on, for your Web site. This can be any folder on your computer. It can be empty, or it can contain an entirely completed Web site. Don't be confused by this slight difference in terminology.

Importing and Exporting Site Definitions

If you ever work with other developers on a project, you may all need the same settings in your site definitions, especially if you're working on a dynamic site. Going back and forth in e-mail or on the phone trying to get things to match can be a hassle. ("What was the last octet of that IP address for the FTP server?") To take the pain out of configuring multiple copies of Dreamweaver with the same site setup, Dreamweaver CS3 lets you import and export your site definitions.

To export a site definition to share with someone else, choose **Site > Manage Sites** to open the **Manage Sites** dialog box. Select a defined site, and click **Export**.

If you have any FTP (**F**ile **T**ransfer **P**rotocol) settings defined for the site you selected in the **Manage Sites** dialog box, an **Exporting site** warning dialog box will open asking whether you want to back up your settings or share your settings with other users.

Select **Back up my settings** if you want to export all your login information, including your user name and password. Remember, choosing this option shares your user name and password, so make sure you're sharing it with someone you trust. If you'd rather not share your user name and password, choose **Share settings with other users** to omit the sensitive information. Click **OK** to close the **Exporting site** dialog box.

Type a file name, and click **Save** to create an **.ste** file containing your site definition. You can send this file as an e-mail attachment to share it with any other Dreamweaver CS3 user.

To import a site definition from another Dreamweaver CS3 user, save the **.ste** file on your computer. Choose **Site > Manage Sites** to open the **Manage Sites** dialog box, and click **Import**. Browse to the location where you saved the .ste file, and click **Open**. The site will then be added to the list in the **Manage Sites** dialog box in Dreamweaver CS3.

Understanding Relative and Absolute URLs

The term **URL** stands for **U**niform **R**esource **L**ocator. In plain English, they are the addresses you use when you go to a Web site. Some are simple, such as **http://www.lynda.com/**, and others are more complicated and hard to remember, such as **http://www.lynda.com/info/books/dw8/**. Regardless of whether a URL is short or long, they come in two forms: absolute and relative.

An absolute URL looks like this: **http://www.lynda.com/aboutus/**. A relative URL looks like this: **aboutus.html**, **pageone.html**, or **somefolder/pagetwo.html**.

An **absolute** URL is a complete URL specifying the exact location of a file on the Web, including the protocol (in this case, **http**), the host name (in this case, **www.lynda.com**), and the exact path to the

file location (in this case, **/aboutus.html**). Use absolute URLs when you want to link to a site outside your own.

A **relative** URL points to a page inside your Web site. For example, if you want to link from the Products page to the Home page, you don't need to include the **http://www.lynda.com/** information. Instead, you include just the file to which you want to link. For example, you can link to just **aboutus.html** instead of **http://www.lynda.com/aboutus.html**.

You can use absolute URLs within your own site, but it's not necessary, and most Web publishers opt to use relative URLs instead. If you use relative URLs for internal documents, it's easier to move them if you change your domain name.

NOTE:

Never Trust Your Own Browser

If for some reason (and you'd be hard-pressed to come up with one) you decide to work outside the Dreamweaver site setup, never trust your own browser to let you know whether a link is correct, especially if you're working locally. If you're working outside a defined site, Dreamweaver may write a link to an image, such as `src="file:///C/MySite/someimage.gif`. If you check this page on your local machine, the image will appear in all its magnificent glory because it's located in that folder on your machine. But as soon as Great Aunt Ruth looks at it on her machine across town, the image won't display correctly. That's just one more reason to always work within Dreamweaver.

EXERCISE 2 | Observing Links to Relative and Absolute URLs

Now that you understand the differences between relative and absolute URLs, it's time to learn how to identify them when you're working in Dreamweaver CS3. Here's an exercise to show you how.

1 In the **Files** panel, double-click **index.html** to open it.

Although you can also open files by choosing File > Open and opening the file from your hard drive, train yourself to open HTML files using the Files panel instead. Opening files in the Files panel uses the site definition you specified and ensures you use the site management features in Dreamweaver CS3.

2 Click the **teacloud** logo (**logo.png**) to select it.

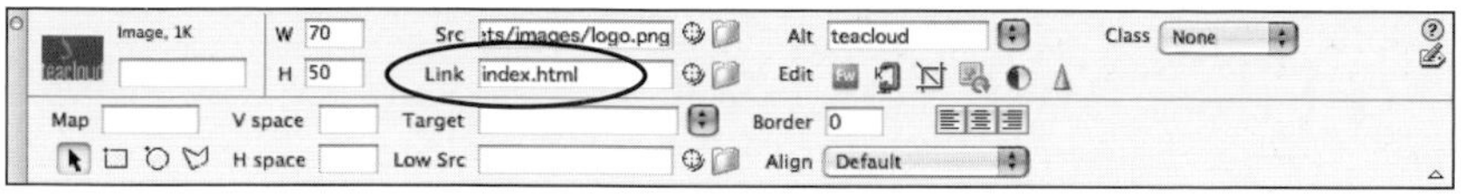

3 In the **Property inspector**, take a look at the **Link** field. Notice it links to **index.html**.

The link index.html is a relative link. It does not have additional information in front of it, as in http://www.teacloud.com/index.html. The file does not need that information because the file name is relative to other internal files in the site.

Tip: If the Property inspector doesn't show as many features as the one shown here, click the arrow icon in the lower-right corner to expand it.

---

4 Scroll to the bottom of the **index.html** file, and click anywhere in the **lynda.com** text link at the bottom of the **Document** window. (Click outside the table to get rid of the table width outlines if you can't see the link.)

In the Property inspector, notice this text links to http://www.lynda.com, which is an external link to another site on the Web. This type of link is an absolute link. It needs the additional information to specify its location because it is not relative to any internal documents, and it exists on its own server, separate from the site used in this book.

---

5 Close **index.html**. You don't need to save your changes.

---

3 | Managing Files and Folders

In the **Files** panel, you can create and move new folders and files from one directory to another. When you do this, you're actually adding folders and files to your hard drive, as you'll learn in this exercise. Accessing the files and folders directly in the **Files** panel in Dreamweaver CS3 is essential to site management practices because Dreamweaver CS3 can then keep track of where the files and folders have been moved, renamed, added, or deleted. This exercise shows you how to add folders and files to the Chapter 3 site you defined in Exercise 1.

1 In the **Files** panel, **right-click** the folder at the top of the local folder view. Choose **New Folder** in the contextual menu to add a new folder to the **chap_03** folder on your hard drive.

2 When the bounding box appears, type **html** for the folder name, and press **Enter** (Windows) or **Return** (Mac).

Note: Before you continue, make sure you close all open files in Dreamweaver CS3. If you have files open and you move their locations, Dreamweaver CS3 may not be able to maintain the links and image paths in the file. So, as a rule of thumb, always make sure you close all your files before you move them in the Files panel.

Next, you'll learn to select files to move them into the folder you just created. Additionally, you'll learn how to select **noncontiguous** files—files that are not listed adjacent to one another.

3 In the **Files** panel, click **abouttea.html** to select it. Hold down **Ctrl** (Windows) or **Cmd** (Mac) and click **brewingtea.html** and **contactus.html** to multiple-select the files.

---

4 With all three files selected, drag them to the **html** folder you created in Steps 1 and 2. The **Update Files** dialog box will open automatically.

Note: Don't worry if your html folder is in a slightly different location in the Files panel.

---

5 In the **Update Files** dialog box, click **Update**.

When you move items in the Files panel, Dreamweaver CS3 automatically prompts you to update their links by listing the files whose links were affected by the items you just moved. Once you click Update, Dreamweaver CS3 rewrites these files automatically to reflect the change in file structure. If you had moved the files directly on your hard drive instead of using the Files panel as you did in this exercise, you would not have been prompted to update the affected links, and the links would have been broken. Can you imagine how long it would take you to update the links manually?

TIP:

Always Use the Files Panel

If you want to add, modify, move, or delete files or folders in your Web site, always use the **Files** panel, as shown in this exercise. If you make these file or folder changes directly on your hard drive without using the **Files** panel in Dreamweaver CS3, you'll have to manually repair the links by editing the links on each page. If you make your changes in the **Files** panel, Dreamweaver CS3 will keep track of them and automatically update your pages, as shown in this exercise.

4 | Understanding Path Structure

This exercise shows how Dreamweaver CS3 creates and alters path structures when you move files in the local root folder. A **path structure** is how HTML represents the path to different files in your site, depending on where they are located. Relative and absolute URL paths can result in a variety of path structures. In this exercise, you will move files around the local root folder in three distinct ways, each demonstrating a different type of path structure you might encounter.

---

1 In the **Files** panel, double-click **index.html** to open it.

2 Click the **teacloud** logo in the upper-right corner to select it.

---

3 With the logo selected, look at the **Src** field in the **Property inspector**. Notice the **Src** (source) field is set to **assets/images/logo.png**, which means the image file, called **logo.png**, is nested inside the **assets** and **images** folders.

---

4 In the **Files** panel, click the **plus sign** (Windows) or **triangle** (Mac) to expand the contents of the **assets** folder and then the **images** folder. Notice **logo.png** resides in the **images** folder. This is the actual image file you're seeing on the Web page.

Next, you'll insert the logo image into another Web page and observe how Dreamweaver writes the correct path to the image.

5 Open **abouttea.html** in the **html** folder (which you moved here in Exercise 3). Notice that the logo is missing from this page.

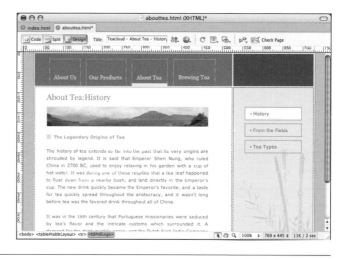

6 Drag **logo.png** from the **Files** panel to the table cell in the upper-right corner of the page to add it to the page, as shown in the illustration here. When you release the mouse, Dreamweaver inserts the image on the page, and the **Image Tag Accessibility Attributes** dialog box opens.

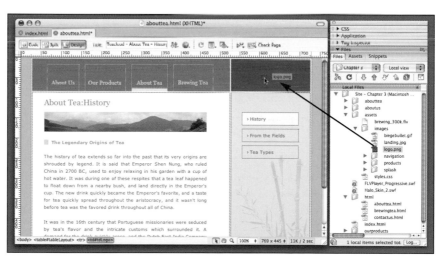

7 In the **Image Tag Accessibility Attributes** dialog box, type **teacloud logo** in the **Alternate text** field, and click **OK**.

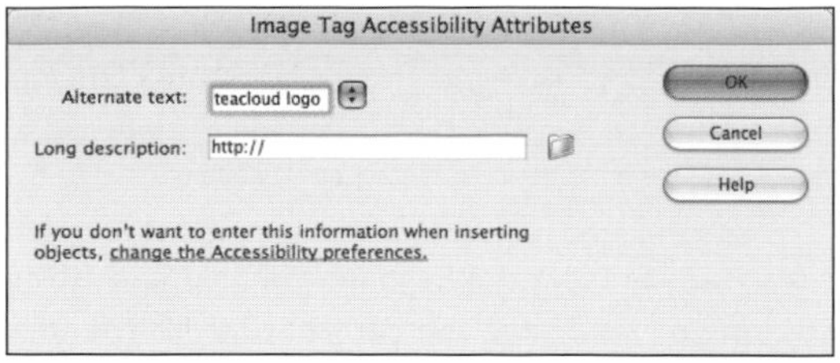

Specifying alternate text adds the necessary alt attribute to your <image> tag to ensure your images are accessible to those using screen readers or to those with images disabled in their browsers. As the dialog box states, you can get rid of this dialog box in your Preferences by clicking the link and deselecting the Images check box in the Accessibility category of the Preferences dialog box. We highly recommend leaving this feature turned on so you don't forget to add an alt attribute to all your images.

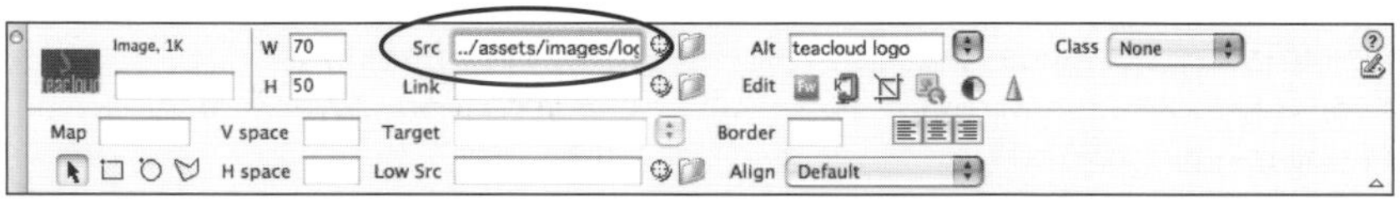

8 With the logo you just added selected, look at the **Src** field in the **Property inspector**.

Notice on this page, the Src field is set to ../assets/images/logo.png. The ../ means the image file is up one folder level and then nested inside the assets and images folders. It's the same image being used on the index.html page, but the abouttea.html file is at a different folder level than index.html, so Dreamweaver CS3 writes a different path to make sure the image displays correctly.

The purpose of this exercise was simply to show you how Dreamweaver CS3 generates different path structures depending on the locations of your files and folders in the Files panel. Path structures are something you'll encounter as you build HTML pages in Dreamweaver CS3, so you'll start to understand them more as you continue to build your site.

9 Close all open files. You don't need to save your changes.

Understanding Site Root and Document Relative Links

To complicate this lesson even more, there are two types of relative links—site root and document. In the previous exercise, you created document relative links to the **teacloud** logo image file. **Document relative links** are relative to a specific document. **Site root relative links** are relative to the *root* of a site.

So far, you've looked only at document relative links (which you'll continue to use throughout the book). A typical link to your site's homepage as a document relative link would be `href="index.html"`. A site root relative link to the same page would be `href="/index.html"`. The slash at the beginning of the link tells the browser to go back to the root of your site and then start looking for the page requested.

The following chart shows what different types of links resolve to, assuming the page you're on is at **http://www.mysite.com/somefolder/somepage.html**:

Site Root vs. Document Relative Links

Relative Link	Description
index.html	This document relative link tells the browser to find a page named **index.html** in the same folder as the current page, so this link points to **http://mysite.com/somefolder/index.html**.
/index.html	This site root relative link tells the browser to go to the root of the site and then find a page named **index.html**, so this link points to **http://mysite.com/index.html**.
foldername/page.html	This document relative link tells the browser to find a folder named **foldername** at the same level as the current page and then find a page named **page.html**, so this link points to **http://mysite.com/somefolder/foldername/page.html**.
../foldername/page.html	This document relative link tells the browser to go up one folder level (../) and then find **foldername/page.html**, so this link points to **http://mysite.com/foldername/page.html**.
/foldername/page.html	This site root relative link tells the browser to go to the root of the site and then find **foldername/page.html**, so this link points to **http://mysite.com/foldername/page.html**.

This chart should clarify how these links work. Document relative links always start at the current page, and site root relative links always start at the root of the site. Why is this important? When you're testing locally, you should *always* use document relative links. If you try using root relative links, the browser would start looking at the root of your hard drive for all your site files. (I'm sure that's not where you store all your files, right?) Using site root relative links makes far more sense once you start dealing with dynamic sites that use file includes and other dynamic tricks of the trade to generate pages on the fly. For now, just know that anytime you're creating links in Dreamweaver CS3, they should be document relative links to keep your gorgeous head of hair from going gray.

5 | Creating a Site Map

Creating a site map is a great way to examine the structure of your Web site because it lets you see the different levels of your Web site and the files and folders contained within those levels. Many designers use site maps to show their clients how their sites look from a structural viewpoint. You can easily create site maps in Dreamweaver CS3, and you can even render the site map as a BMP or PNG file. Anytime you change the structure of the site, the site map updates automatically. This exercise shows you how easy it is to create and save a site map.

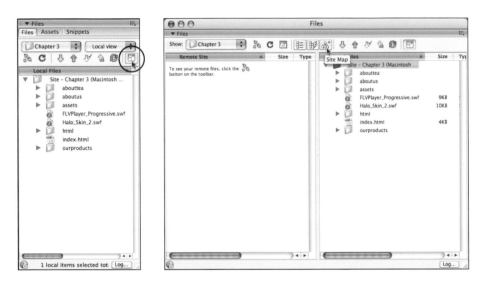

1 In the **Files** panel, click the **Expand/Collapse** button in the upper-right corner to expand the **Files** panel so it fills the entire screen.

By expanding the Files panel, you'll have access to the Site Map feature, which you'll use to create a site map.

Note: If you have not set up a connection to a remote site, you may see a different message in the Remote Site section of the Files panel.

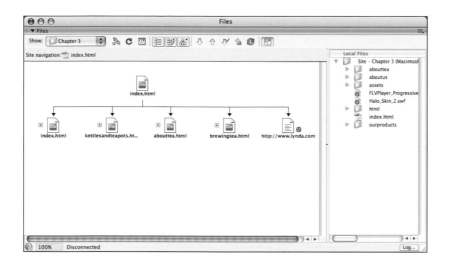

2 Click and hold the **Site Map** button in the **Files** panel, and choose **Map and Files** in the pop-up menu to display a site map of the Chapter 3 site.

Dreamweaver CS3 offers two ways to view a site map—the Map and Files view and the Map Only view. The illustration here shows the Map and Files view. The Map and Files view is great if you want to be able to see the files in your site (in the right pane) as well as the overall structure of your Web site and how the different pages link to each other (in the left pane). If you click any of the plus signs, you'll see the pages linked to that page. Next, you'll take a look at the Chapter 3 site using the Map Only view.

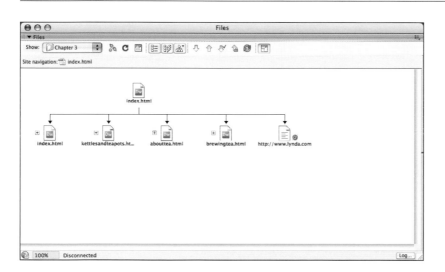

3 In the **Files** panel, click the **Site Map** button, and choose **Map Only**.

In the Map Only view, you can see the overall architecture of your Web site. Like with the Site Map view, if you click any of the plus signs, you will see the pages linked to that page.

Next, you'll learn how to save and print a site map.

4 The process of saving the site map as an image, so you can view or print it later, is a bit different between the Windows and Mac systems:

- **Windows:** While viewing the site map, click the **Panel Options** button, and choose **File > Save Site Map**. In the **Save Site Map** dialog box, type the name for the site map in the **File name** field, choose a location for the file, choose the format in the **Save as type** pop-up menu, and click **Save**.

- **Mac:** While viewing the site map, click the **Panel Options** button in the upper-right corner of the **Files** panel, and choose **File > Save Site Map** in the **Panel Options** menu. In the **Save** dialog box, name the map by typing the file name in the **Save As** field, choose a location for the file, and click **Save**. The map is saved as a .pict file.

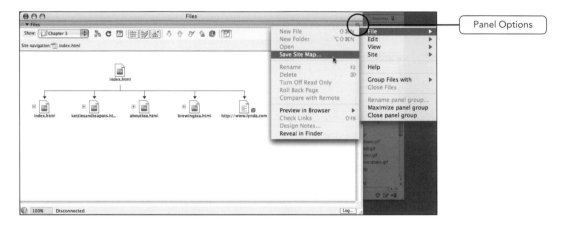

Panel Options

5 At the top of the window, click the **Expand/Collapse** button to return to the default Dreamweaver CS3 interface.

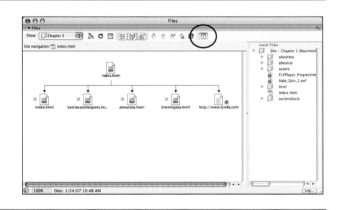

6 Close all open files. You don't need to save your changes.

VIDEO: | **site_maps.mov**

To learn more about creating site maps, check out **site_maps.mov** in the **videos** folder on the **Dreamweaver HOT CD-ROM**.

6 | Creating a Site from Scratch

So far, you've had a chance to work with the Dreamweaver CS3 site management window by defining a site based on folders and files from the **Dreamweaver HOT CD-ROM**. But what happens when you finish this book and go on to create your own Web sites? You might know how to define a Web site that already exists, but you may not know how to go about creating a site from scratch. Fortunately, the process is pretty much the same, but just in case you need a little more of a review, this exercise shows you how to define a site based on an empty folder and introduces you to the **Advanced** tab in the **Site Definition** dialog box.

---

1 Navigate to the desktop of your computer. Create a new empty folder on your desktop, and name it **mywebsite**.

---

2 Return to Dreamweaver CS3, and choose **Site > Manage Sites** to open the **Manage Sites** dialog box, where you can define a new site or edit/remove an existing site. Click **New**, and choose **Site** in the pop-up menu to open the **Site Definition** dialog box.

---

3 Click the **Advanced** tab. Type the **Site Name**. (I chose **My Website**, but you can name it anything you want.) Click the folder icon to the right of the **Local root folder** field, and browse to the empty folder you created on your desktop called **mywebsite**. Click **Select** (Windows) or **Choose** (Mac), and then click **OK**. In the **Manage Sites** dialog box, click **Done**.

Because you created a new site based on an empty folder, your Files panel will also be empty.

Next, you'll learn how to add files to your site. When you want to add, delete, or move files in your new site, make sure you use the Files panel, just as when you added, deleted, or moved files with an existing site earlier in this chapter. Using the Files panel ensures your files and links will be managed properly in Dreamweaver CS3 and will save you many headaches down the road.

4 **Right-click** the local root folder at the top of the **Files** panel, and choose **New File** in the contextual menu.

When you create a new file, Dreamweaver CS3 automatically names the file untitled.html, as shown in the illustration here.

5 Navigate to the **mywebsite** folder you created on your desktop in Step 1.

Notice the mywebsite folder contains an HTML document called untitled.html—this is the same HTML file you just created and viewed in the Files panel in Step 4.

6 Close all open files. You don't need to save your changes.

EXERCISE

7 | Deleting a Site Definition

As you continue building Web sites, sometimes you no longer are working on a particular site or just don't need to manage it with Dreamweaver anymore. This brief exercise shows you how to delete a site definition from Dreamweaver CS3, using the site you created in the previous exercise as an example.

1 You should still have the **mywebsite** site you created in Exercise 6 open. If not, complete Exercise 6, and then return to this exercise.

2 Choose **Site > Manage Sites** to view all your currently defined sites.

3 Select **My Website**, and click **Remove**. Dreamweaver warns you that this action cannot be undone. Click **Yes**. **My Website** disappears from the **Manage Sites** dialog box. Click **Done**.

It's important to note here that you deleted only the definition of the site in Dreamweaver. The actual mywebsite folder, and the single untitled.html file it contains, is still sitting safely on your desktop, so you could easily redefine the folder as a site again if you accidentally deleted the definition or just change your mind later. If you wanted to get rid of the files themselves, you would drag them from the desktop to your system Recycle Bin (Windows) or Trash (Mac).

4 Close all open files. You don't need to save any changes.

As you can see from the exercises in this chapter, the site management capabilities in Dreamweaver CS3 set it apart from every other Web development application available. Dreamweaver CS3 remembers everything about your site for you, including rewriting links and taking care of image paths, which is a huge boon to your productivity. The ability to define sites for existing work, create sites from scratch, and import and export your site definitions with your colleagues makes it easy to work with other developers on a site. Many users think this type of information is easily disregarded, but you've seen just how powerful these tools really are. Next, you'll learn some basics to help you perform common tasks in Dreamweaver CS3.

4

Learning the Basics

If you're the impatient type, this is the chapter you've been waiting to read. The following exercises teach you how to get started with Adobe Dreamweaver CS3, including creating and saving pages, inserting and aligning images and text, linking images and text, defining page properties with CSS (Cascading Style Sheets), and inserting metainformation such as keywords and descriptions for search engines. The purpose of this chapter is to get you comfortable with Dreamweaver by building a simple page and performing other common Web development tasks. The rest of this book will focus on many of these areas in greater detail. Digesting this much material may seem overwhelming, but fortunately Dreamweaver CS3 makes most of these operations as simple as accessing a menu or clicking a button.

By the time you're done with this chapter, you'll be well on your way to understanding the program's interface for creating pages and sites. The exercises here will be your foundation for building more complex pages in future chapters.

Creating and Saving a New Document

This exercise teaches you how to create and save a document in Dreamweaver CS3. You will be saving this document as **index.html**, which has special significance on the Web—it's almost always the beginning page of a site. Additionally, you will learn to set the title of the document—what visitors to your site see at the top of their browsers while viewing the page.

---

1 If you haven't already done so, copy the **chap_04** folder from the **Dreamweaver HOT CD-ROM** to your desktop. Define your site as **Chapter 4** using the **chap_04** folder as the local root folder. If you need a refresher on this process, visit Exercise 1 in Chapter 3, *"Managing Your Sites."*

---

2 If you already have documents open, save and close them as necessary. Each time you open Dreamweaver CS3, by default it will open to the **Welcome Screen**, which lets you create a wide variety of documents by simply clicking a link.

You can turn off the Welcome Screen in the preferences, which is explained in Chapter 2, *"Exploring the Interface."*

---

3 On the **Welcome Screen**, either click **More** or choose **File > New**. Either action opens the **New Document** dialog box, which lets you choose a template for your new document.

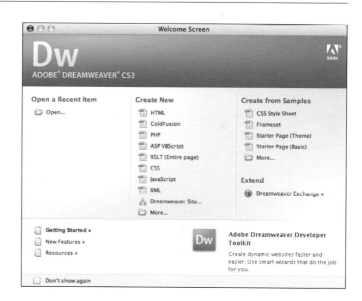

Using the Dreamweaver prebuilt pages lets you get started quickly with new XHTML documents. When you use Dreamweaver CS3 to create new files, it adds all the basic structure for a new page so you don't have to do the repetitive work of adding **<head>**, **<body>**, **<title>**, and other tags to a new document.

The Welcome Screen is a quick and easy way to create new documents. However, it does not give you access to all the new page templates in Dreamweaver CS3 or let you control some other options, such as creating a new page using XHTML (e**X**tensible **H**yper**T**ext **M**arkup **L**anguage) instead of HTML (**H**yper**T**ext **M**arkup **L**anguage). To access all the new page templates, follow the next few steps.

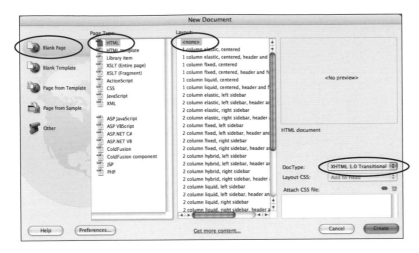

4 Select **Blank page** in the **Category** list. Select **HTML** in the **Page Type** list and **<none>** in the **Layout** list. Choose **XHTML 1.0 Transitional** in the **DocType (DTD)** pop-up menu, and click **Create**.

Dreamweaver CS3 creates a new, blank HTML/XHTML document.

These options instruct Dreamweaver CS3 to create a basic HTML page. Only the New Document dialog box lets you choose a specific DOCTYPE (**DOC**ument **TYPE**) for a new document; the Welcome Screen doesn't offer this option. Sure, you can add a DOCTYPE later (you will learn how to do this in Chapter 12, *"Using XHTML"*), but why not do it the correct way right from the start? You'll most likely stick with XHTML 1.0 Transitional, which is the default and what you'll use throughout this book. But if you work on a site that requires a different DOCTYPE, you can specify the default for all new documents in the New Document category of the Dreamweaver CS3 preferences.

NOTE:

Using the New Document Dialog Box

The **New Document** dialog box gives you access to many templates, which help you create new pages in Dreamweaver CS3. These templates— sorted by category—give you the HTML code required to begin creating pages for specific pur- poses. For example, in the **Starter Page (Theme)** cat-

egory, found in the **Page from Sample** list, you'll find a number of site designs sorted by topic, such as Entertainment or Lodging. The templates save you time and get you started in the right direction. The **Page from Template** list is reserved for templates you create from scratch. You'll learn how to create templates in Chapter 16, *"Using Templates and Library Items."*

NOTE:

Choosing a DOCTYPE

The DOCTYPE tells the browser which version of HTML or XHTML it should use to render the page. In older browsers (Netscape 4 and the like), DOCTYPE was an unimportant part of the page. In modern browsers, the DOCTYPE you choose can determine how a page is rendered, which is why including a DOCTYPE at the top of every page is important.

Because XHTML is still being adopted across the Internet, you should probably still use the XHTML 1.0 Transitional DOCTYPE. This DOCTYPE includes support for older HTML attributes, such as table widths and targets on links, which lets you code newer documents using attributes from older specifications.

That's about all you need to know about DOCTYPEs for the moment. Just know you should have a DOCTYPE declaration at the top of every page in your site to ensure that browsers render each page in a predictable fashion.

Before you continue, you'll make sure this page is in fact being created with the XHTML Transitional DOCTYPE you chose. You can't tell by simply looking at the page in Design view. To find out what's really going on, you need to look at the raw code of the page.

5 Make sure the **Document** toolbar is visible. If it's not, choose **View > Toolbars > Document**. In the **Document** toolbar, click the **Code** button to change to **Code** view.

As you probably guessed, Code view displays only the code of your page. Some people find looking at all this code difficult or downright scary. Well, if you want to be a professional Web designer/developer, you really need to feel comfortable working with code and not limit yourself to just the visual editing environment of Dreamweaver CS3. Consider this lesson "Code 101."

Refer to the code in lines 1 through 3, which define the DOCTYPE. As you can see, the DOCTYPE is set to XHTML 1.0 Transitional, just as you specified in Step 4. This code tells the browser (and the rest of the curious world) that this page is an XHTML page and not an HTML page. As long as you see this code, you can be assured your page is considered a true XHTML page.

6 In the **Document** toolbar, click the **Design** button to return to the default **Design** view of your page.

Before you go on, it is important to save your file first. All the site management benefits introduced in Chapter 3, *"Managing Your Sites,"* depend on Dreamweaver CS3 knowing the physical location of your file. So, the program constantly notifies you if you are working on an unsaved document. Besides, no one wants to unexpectedly lose work, and this practice is good insurance against system crashes and power outages.

Tip: Anytime you see an asterisk (*) next to the file name of the page in the page's title bar, you know you have made changes to your page and haven't saved them yet.

---

7 Choose **File > Save** or press **Ctrl+S** (Windows) or **Cmd+S** (Mac) to open the **Save As** dialog box.

Because you're currently on the Chapter 4 site, Dreamweaver CS3 automatically chooses the file location based on the folder you specified during the site definition process (your root folder). In this case, it should default to the chap_04 folder. If it did not, just click the Site Root button to instantly navigate to your root folder. It's critically important for all your Web site's pages to be saved within your root folder. Otherwise, Dreamweaver will be unable to keep track of them.

---

8 Type **index.html** for the file name, and click **Save**. Leave the file open for the next exercise.

Understanding the Significance of Default Documents

You just created a document called **index.html**. What you may not appreciate is that this particular file name (along with a few others) has special significance. Most Web servers recognize the **index.html** (or **index.htm**) file as the default homepage. (You can use **.html** and **.html** interchangeably; Web servers recognize both as HTML pages.) If you type **www.google.com** in your browser, for example, what you will really see is **www. google.com/index.html**, even though you didn't type it that way. The Web server knows to open the **index.html** file automatically without requiring users to type the full URL (**U**niform **R**esource **L**ocator). Therefore, if you name the opening page of your Web site with the file name

index.html, the Web server will know to automatically display this file first.

This is why the file name **index.html** is so significant. It's also the reason most professional Web developers use it as the root file name, although on some servers a different name is used, such as **default.html**. What you may not realize is you are not limited to just one **index.html** file on your site. You can have an **index.html** file in each folder that represents a category for your site, such as **Company**, **Services**, **Store**, and **Products**. That way you can provide easy-to-remember URLs for people, such as **yoursite.com/services** or **yoursite.com/products**.

2 | Setting Page Titles

In this exercise, you'll learn how to set the page title of your documents. The page title appears at the top of your visitors' browsers and is also used for search engine listings and bookmark titles. Giving your page a good title is the first task you should perform before starting to work on the page.

---

1 You should still have the **index.html** file from Exercise 1 open. If not, complete Exercise 1, and then return to this exercise.

You can also double-click index.html in the Files panel to open it.

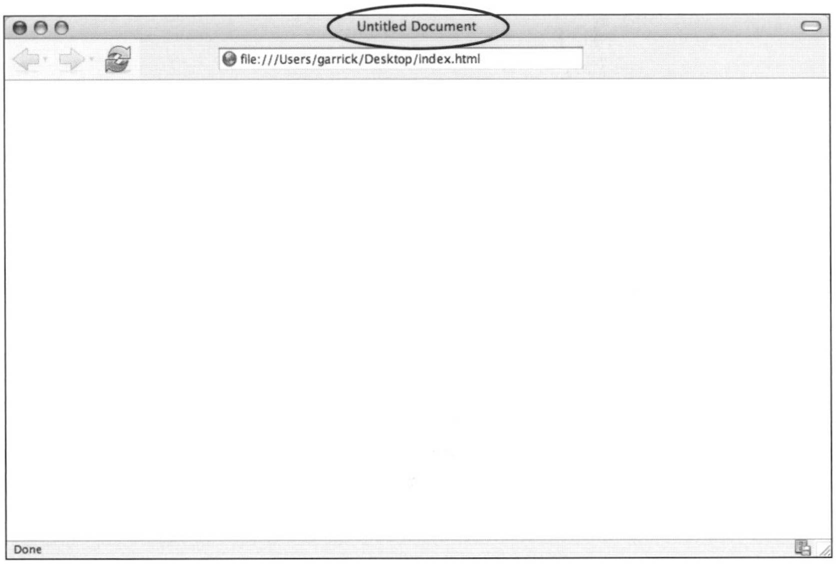

---

2 Press **F12** (Windows) or **Opt+F12** (Mac) to preview the page in your browser.

As shown in the illustration here, the title bar of the browser says *Untitled Document*, which is not very meaningful. When you create Web pages, you need to give your pages meaningful titles because search engines use the titles to provide information about the pages. A title is also used in your visitors' bookmarks or favorites to name the page, and it gives them an easy way to figure out which page of a site they're currently viewing.

---

3 Return to Dreamweaver CS3. If you look in the **Document** toolbar, you'll see **Untitled Document** in the **Title** field. Type **Welcome to Teacloud** in the **Title** field of the **Document** toolbar, and press **Enter** (Windows) or **Return** (Mac) to define a page title.

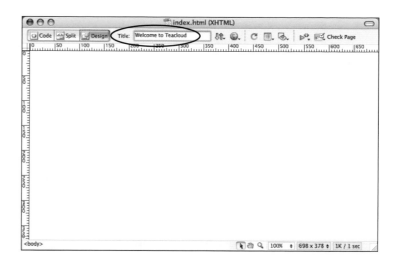

4 Press **F12** or **Opt+F12** to preview the file again, and you'll see that the title bar now shows **Welcome to Teacloud**.

Obviously, *Welcome to Teacloud* is a far more meaningful title than *Untitled Document*. It gives your viewers an idea of what's on the page and makes it easy for them to figure out which page they're viewing.

5 Save and close **index.html**.

NOTE:

File Names vs. Titles

As you create Web pages with Dreamweaver CS3, you will need to specify various names for your files, folders, sites, and so on. This might not seem tricky at first glance, but two different names are actually associated with XHTML files: the file name and the page title.

When you save a document, you will be assigning its file name. The file name must end with a valid document extension (**.htm** or **.html**). The other name associated with the document is the **page title**. In this exercise, you've assigned the page title **Welcome to Teacloud** to the file **index.html**.

File names absolutely cannot contain spaces or special characters; if they do, the browser may not be able to request the correct file from the server. Page titles, however, are meant for public consumption, so you should make them as descriptive as possible, and you're free to use spaces, capital letters, and proper spelling in grammar. Just don't go overboard and make them too long. Remember, when your visitors bookmark your page, its title shows up in their bookmarks menu, so ideally you should just use a brief, descriptive title for your page.

3 | Inserting Images

In this exercise, you'll learn how to insert images for the site's homepage image, logo, and navigation buttons.

---

1 In the **Files** panel, double-click **draft.html** to open it. Make sure the **Assets** panel is visible. If it's not, choose **Window > Assets**, or press **F11**.

Inserting images using the Assets panel ensures you are working with images only from within your local root folder. This is a good practice, because inserting images from outside your local root folder will cause problems when you try to upload your page to the Web server—the images won't appear!

NOTE:

Working with the Assets Panel

The **Assets** panel is an incredibly powerful and useful feature in Dreamweaver CS3; it's one of the panels you will use most often. The **Assets** panel maintains a listing of all the asset types (images, colors, links, movies, scripts, library items, and templates) within the current site. Each type of asset is separated into its own category so you can find what you are looking for quickly and easily. You can even designate an asset as a "favorite," which places the asset in the **Favorites** group—a customized asset group containing items you use most often. This feature is really powerful when you have hundreds or thousands of assets within your local root folder. That might sound like a lot of assets, but you'll be surprised how quickly they add up.

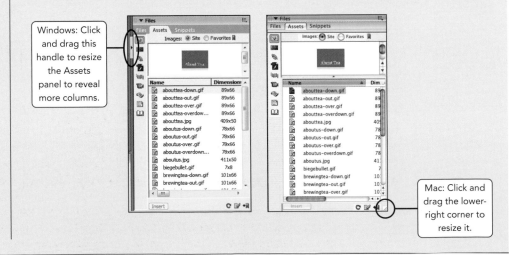

Windows: Click and drag this handle to resize the Assets panel to reveal more columns.

Mac: Click and drag the lower-right corner to resize it.

NOTE:

Working with the Assets Panel *continued*

The **Assets** panel is really small by default, and some of its features are hidden from view. In the illustrations shown here, you can see the **Images** group contains information about the file size, type, and path of the various images listed in the group. Each asset group has different columns relating to the specific type of assets. By default, the assets are listed in alphabetic order from A to Z. You can reverse the order by clicking the **Name** column at the top. In fact, you can rearrange all the columns in ascending or descending order by clicking the column names—another handy-dandy feature of the **Assets** panel.

The **Assets** panel con-textual menu lets you easily copy assets between the various sites you have defined. Using this menu, you can also refresh the list-ing, which is sometimes helpful when you add new assets to a site and Dreamweaver CS3 is already open.

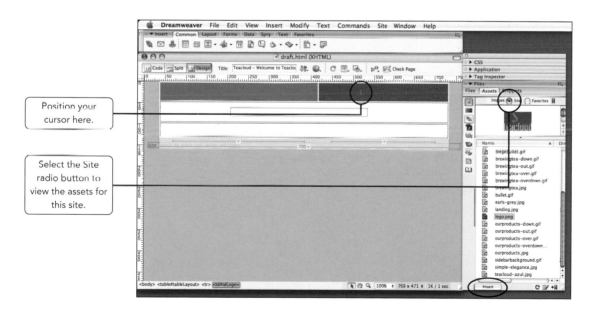

Position your cursor here.

Select the Site radio button to view the assets for this site.

2 In the **Document** window, position your cursor in the upper-right table cell. In the **Assets** panel, make sure the **Site** radio button is selected, and select **logo.png**. Click the **Insert** button at the bottom of the panel to insert **logo.png** into the table cell. When the **Image Tag Accessibility Attributes** dialog box appears, type **Teacloud Logo** in the **Alternate text** field, and click **OK**.

When you're finished, the teacloud logo populates the upper-right table cell of the page. Next, you'll apply the skills you learned and fill the rest of the page with images.

3 In the **Document** window, position your cursor in the upper-left table cell. In the **Assets** panel, select **aboutus-out.gif**. Click **Insert** to insert the selected image into the page. When the **Image Tag Accessibility Attributes** dialog box appears, type **About Us** in the **Alternate text** field, and click **OK**.

4 In the **Document** window, click to the right of **aboutus-out.gif** to deselect it. In the **Assets** panel, select **ourproducts-out.gif**. Click **Insert** to insert the selected image into the page. When the **Image Tag Accessibility Attributes** dialog box appears, type **Our Products** in the **Alternate text** field, and click **OK**.

5 In the **Document** window, click to the right of **ourproducts-out.gif** to deselect it. In the **Assets** panel, select **abouttea-out.gif**. Click **Insert** to insert the selected image into the page. When the **Image Tag Accessibility Attributes** dialog box appears, type **About Tea** in the **Alternate text** field, and click **OK**.

6 In the **Document** window, click to the right of **abouttea-out.gif** to deselect it. In the **Assets** panel, select **brewingtea-out.gif**. Click **Insert** to insert the selected image into the page. When the **Image Tag Accessibility Attributes** dialog box appears, type **Brewing Tea** in the **Alternate text** field, and click **OK**.

7 Position your cursor inside the dotted lines in the center of the page. In the **Assets** panel, select **landing.jpg**. Click **Insert** to insert the selected image into the page. When the **Image Tag Accessibility Attributes** dialog box appears, type **Welcome to teacloud** in the **Alternate text** field, and click **OK**.

The illustration shown here displays what your page should look like at this point. Not too bad for a day's work, wouldn't you say? As you can see, Dreamweaver CS3 makes it really easy to insert images into your Web pages.

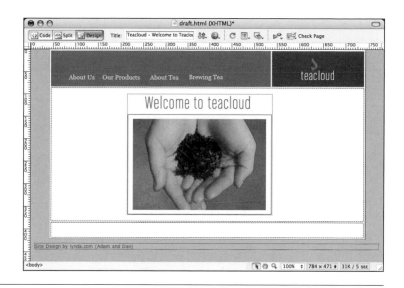

8 In the **Document** toolbar, click the **Code** button to change the page view to **Code** view.

Even though you've added only a few images to the page, you can see that quite a bit of code is required. Dreamweaver CS3 inserted an **<img>** tag for each of the images you inserted into the page. Imagine how long it would take you to type all that XHTML code in Notepad or TextEdit!

Get into the habit of looking at Code view for your page as often as possible. It's a great way to get more comfortable with what goes on behind the scenes in the XHTML code.

Note: If the code doesn't wrap to fit in the Document window, choose View > Code View Options > Word Wrap.

9 In the **Document** toolbar, click the **Design** button to return to the **Design** view. Save **draft.html**, and leave it open for the next exercise.

TIP:

Other Ways to Insert Images

In this exercise, you learned how to use the **Assets** panel to insert images into your page, which is the quickest and safest way to insert images into your page. Why? First, only images within your site are listed in the **Assets** panel. Second, by inserting images from within your site, you ensure Dreamweaver CS3 automatically creates the proper paths so everything works when you upload your page to a remote Web server. But the **Assets** panel isn't the only way to insert images in Dreamweaver CS3. Here are five other ways to insert images:

- Choose **Insert > Image**.

- In the **Insert** panel, click the **Image** button.

- Press **Ctrl+Alt+I** (Windows) or **Cmd+Opt+I** (Mac).

- Click and drag the image from the **Assets** panel to the page.

- Click and drag the image from the **Files** panel to the page.

As you become more comfortable with Dreamweaver CS3, you will find the method that fits best into your workflow.

4 | Inserting Text

Adding text to your Web page is simple in Dreamweaver CS3. Just like with your favorite word processor, you can simply start typing text, and the text will appear. In this exercise, you will add some text to the landing page you worked with in Exercise 3.

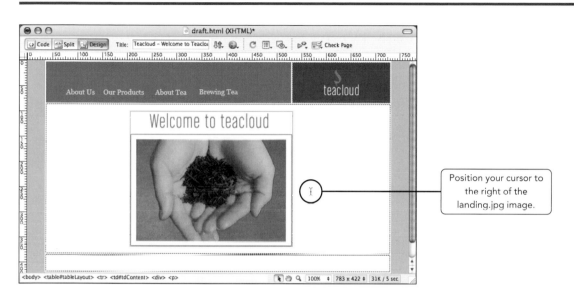

Position your cursor to the right of the landing.jpg image.

1 You should still have the **draft.html** file from Exercise 3 open. If not, complete Exercise 3, and then return to this exercise.

2 Click to the right of the **landing.jpg** file. Press **Enter** (Windows) or **Return** (Mac) to create a paragraph break, and type the following text:

Brewing the finest loose-leaf tea nature has to offer. We bring exotic and tantalizing teas from the fields to your cup. For over 15 years, Teacloud has elevated the tea drinking experience and has provided tea lovers around the world with unsurpassed quality.

3 Press **Enter** (Windows) or **Return** (Mac) to create another paragraph break, and type the following text:

Please explore the rest of our site to learn more about the wonderful history, flavor, and fragrance of tea.

Your page should now match the page shown in the illustration here. Wondering why you didn't need to specify your fonts and font sizes? This page uses CSS to define the presentation of the page, and I've already taken care of all of that for you. You'll learn more about CSS in Chapter 6, *"Working with Cascading Style Sheets,"* and more about typography in Chapter 7, *"Working with Typography."*

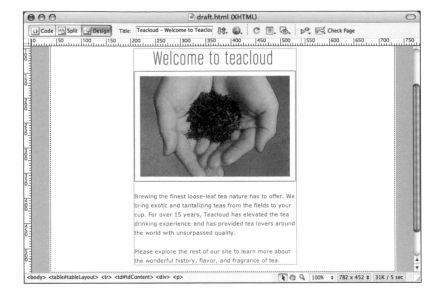

Next you'll add some text navigation to the bottom of the page.

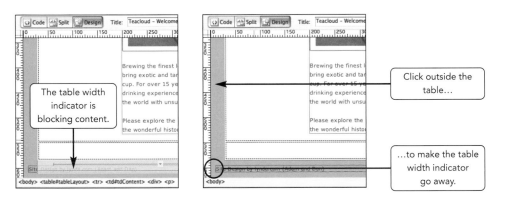

4 Position your cursor at the beginning of the text in the footer at the bottom of the page (where the **Site Design** credit appears). If the table width indicators are hiding the footer from you, click outside the table to remove the table width indicators, and then click in the footer.

5 Press **Shift+Enter** (Windows) or **Shift+Return** (Mac) to add a new line break, and then press the **up arrow** key to move your cursor up to the new line that was just inserted.

6 Type the following text on the new line to add some extra text navigation to the page (press **Shift+backslash** to add the pipe symbols):

About Us | Our Products | About Tea | Brewing Tea

The pipe symbol (|) is an effective and common way to separate characters in navigation bars.

Your page should now match the page shown in the illustration here.

---

7 Save **draft.html**, and leave it open for the next exercise.

Paragraph Breaks vs. Line Breaks

In the previous exercise, each time you pressed **Enter** (Windows) or **Return** (Mac), Dreamweaver CS3 skipped down the page two lines. Pressing this key inserts a single paragraph break (one line of blank space between paragraphs). The XHTML tag for a paragraph break is **<p>**. This is useful when you want to increase the space between paragraphs. However, sometimes you may want to go to the line directly below the one you are working on without introducing extra space. Pressing **Shift+Enter** (Windows) or **Shift+Return** (Mac) inserts a line break instead. The XHTML tag for a line break is **
. Knowing the difference between a **<p> tag and a **
** tag will give you more control over the spacing between lines of text.

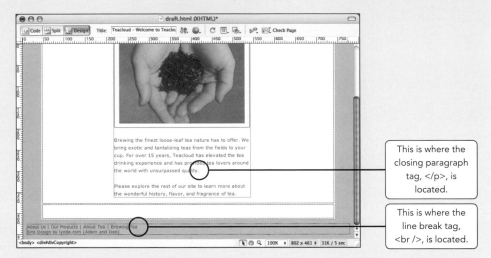

This is where the closing paragraph tag, </p>, is located.

This is where the line break tag, <br />, is located.

The paragraph tag, **<p>**, creates an extra blank line between the closing paragraph tag, **</p>**, and the next line of content. The line break tag, **
**, places content on the very next line.

The illustration here shows what the closing paragraph **</p>** and the line break **
** tags look like in the XHTML code.

5 | Aligning Text and Images

Now that you have added some images and text to your page, it's time to learn how to align them. This section shows you how to use the **Property inspector** to center and justify text and images. Keep in mind that this is the first alignment technique you are learning, and you will learn many other alignment techniques throughout this book.

1 You should still have the **draft.html** file from Exercise 4 open. If not, complete Exercise 4, and then return to this exercise. Place your cursor in the footer at the bottom of the page.

Note: If the table width indicators are hiding the footer, click outside the table to get rid of them.

2 In the **Property inspector**, click the **Align Center** button to snap the text to the center of the screen.

As you can see, the navigation text you created in Exercise 3, which was originally aligned to the left, is now aligned in the center of the page. The Site Design credits have been aligned as well, because even though they appear on a separate line from the navigation text, Dreamweaver still considers the two lines to be part of the same paragraph, and you can't have multiple alignments within a single paragraph.

Next, you'll align the text for the navigation buttons at the top. Remember, though, the navigation buttons aren't text like the navigation at the bottom—they are a series of images you inserted in Exercise 3.

3 Place your cursor anywhere in the upper-left table cell containing the navigation buttons. In the **Property inspector**, click the **Align Center** button.

The navigation buttons are now centered. As you can see, you can use the same technique to align images as you do to align text.

4 In the **Document** toolbar, click the **Code** button to view the code for this page.

Notice Dreamweaver added **<div>** tags with **align="center"** attributes around the footer and the navigation images. This tag and attribute instruct Dreamweaver to align the text and images in the center, overriding the default alignment of the tag (which is left-aligned).

In addition to aligning left and center, you can also justify text. The text below the image in the middle of the page would look best justified so the right edge of the text lines up nicely with the right edge of the image above it. You'll learn how in the next steps.

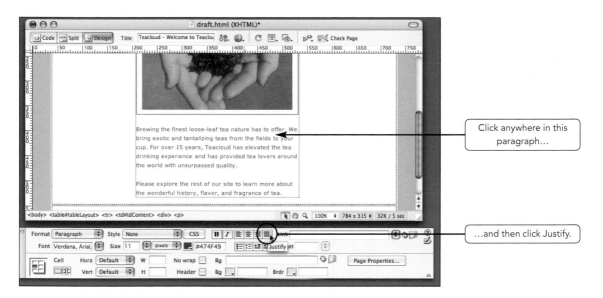

Brewing the finest loose-leaf tea nature has to offer. We bring exotic and tantalizing teas from the fields to your cup. For over 15 years, Teacloud has elevated the tea drinking experience and has provided tea lovers around the world with unsurpassed quality.

Please explore the rest of our site to learn more about the wonderful history, flavor, and fragrance of tea.

Click anywhere in this paragraph…

…and then click Justify.

5 In the **Document** toolbar, click the **Design** button to switch back to **Design** view. Click in the first paragraph below the image, and click the **Justify** button in the **Property inspector**.

Wondering why only the first paragraph changed? Dreamweaver CS3 applies alignment attributes to single paragraphs of text. Next, you'll justify the second paragraph of text. If you want to change the alignment of more than one paragraph at the same time, you can click and drag to highlight multiple paragraphs and then set the alignment properties in the Property inspector.

6 Position your cursor anywhere in the text of the second paragraph, and click **Justify**.

As you can see, both paragraphs of text are now justified, so the edges line up perfectly with the edges of the image. Very nice!

Although you can use more efficient ways to align text (which you'll learn about later in this book), this is a great example of how quickly you can manipulate image and text alignment in Dreamweaver CS3.

7 Save **draft.html**, and leave it open for the next exercise.

6 | Creating Links with Images and Text

Linking pages and sites is what makes the Web what it is. After all, what good is a page that doesn't link to somewhere else or doesn't have any other page linking to it? This exercise shows you how to set up links using the **Property inspector** in Dreamweaver CS3.

1 You should still have the **draft.html** file from Exercise 5 open. If not, complete Exercise 5, and then return to this exercise. Click to select the **aboutus-out.gif** (About Us) image.

2 In the **Property inspector**, click the **Browse for File** icon next to the **Link** field to open the **Select File** dialog box.

Note: If your Property inspector is smaller than what is shown in the illustration here, click the arrow icon in the lower-right corner to expand it.

3 Browse to the **chap_04/html** folder. Select **aboutus.html**, and click **OK** (Windows) or **Choose** (Mac).

Congratulations, you have just created your first relative image link—you linked the About Us button to the aboutus.html page in the html folder. Why is the link relative? As you learned in Chapter 3, *"Managing Your Sites,"* relative links point to files within the same site, not to an external Web site.

4 Select the **ourproducts-out.gif** (Our Products) image.

---

5 In the **Property inspector**, click the **Browse for File** icon next to the **Link** field to open the **Select File** dialog box.

---

6 Browse to the **chap_04/html** folder. Select **ourproducts.html**, and click **OK** (Windows) or **Choose** (Mac).

You just linked the Our Products button to the ourproducts.html page in the html folder.

---

7 Repeat Steps 4, 5, and 6 to link the **About Tea** button to the **html/abouttea.html** page and the **Brewing Tea** button to the **html/brewingtea.html** page.

You have just successfully added links to the images on this page!

---

8 If you want to preview the links in a browser, save the page, press **F12** (Windows) or **Opt+F12** (Mac), and click any of the images. Position your cursor over one of the navigation buttons. Notice the cursor changes to the hand icon, indicating it is a link.

Next, you will create links using text. The process is almost identical, except you will be selecting text instead of images.

9 Return to Dreamweaver. Click and drag to select the words **About Us** at the bottom of the page.

---

10 In the **Property inspector**, click the **Browse for File** icon next to the **Link** field to open the **Select File** dialog box.

---

11 Browse to the **chap_04/html** folder. Select **aboutus.html**, and click **OK** (Windows) or **Choose** (Mac).

---

12 Repeat Steps 9, 10, and 11 to link the **Our Products** text to the **html/ourproducts.html** page, the **About Tea** text to the **html/abouttea.html** page, and the **Brewing Tea** text to the **html/brewingtea.html page**.

Wondering why the color of the links didn't change color? The style sheet applied to this page defines what color the links should be. You'll learn all about style sheets in Chapter 6, *"Working with Cascading Style Sheets."*

---

13 Click and drag to select the **lynda.com** text at the bottom of the page.

14 In the **Link** field in the **Property inspector**, type **http://www.lynda.com**, and press **Enter** (Windows) or **Return** (Mac).

Congratulations, you just created your first absolute link. It's an absolute link because it begins with an http header and includes the full address. As you know from Chapter 3, *" Managing Your Sites,"* any time you link to an external Web site, you must use an absolute link.

---

15 Press **F12** (Windows) or **Opt+F12** (Mac) to preview the page in a browser so you can test the links you created in this exercise. (The pages you linked to are all blank right now—you're just testing to make sure the links themselves work.) When you're finished, close the browser, and return to Dreamweaver CS3.

---

16 Save **draft.html**, and leave it open for the next exercise.

Inserting <meta> Tags

One of the big challenges of Web design (aside from designing and building a Web site) is letting the search engines know your site exists. Getting your site listed requires two steps: First, you have to list it with all the search engines out there, and second, you need to insert **<meta>** tags into your XHTML so the search engines can find and correctly index your site. Many search engines send **robots** (also called **spiders**) to search the Web for content. When you insert certain **<meta>** tags into your document, you make it much easier for a search engine's robots to understand how to categorize your site. This exercise shows you how to add **<meta>** tags with specific attributes so you can make your Web page more search-engine friendly.

1 You should still have the **draft.html** file from Exercise 6 open. If not, complete Exercise 6, and then return to this exercise. Choose **Insert > HTML > Head Tags > Keywords** to open the **Keywords** dialog box.

Keywords reflect the content of specific pages. They're used by some (but not all) search engines to help provide accurate search results. You should always use short, relevant keywords and phrases to describe the content of the page.

2 Type **Tea, Brewing, Kettles, Teapots**, and click **OK**.

When you define keywords for your Web pages, think about what keywords a user might type into a search engine to find your site.

3 Choose **Insert > HTML > Head Tags > Description** to open the **Description** dialog box.

Some search engines use the description to describe the contents of a particular page in search listings.

4 Type **Teacloud brews the finest loose-leaf tea nature has to offer. We bring exotic and tantalizing teas from the fields to your cup.** Click **OK**.

```
1    <!DOCTYPE html PUBLIC "-//W3C//DTD XHTML 1.0 Transitional//EN"
2    "http://www.w3.org/TR/xhtml1/DTD/xhtml1-transitional.dtd">
     <html xmlns="http://www.w3.org/1999/xhtml">
3    <head>
4    <meta http-equiv="Content-Type" content="text/html; charset=iso-8859-1" />
5    <title>Teacloud - Welcome to Teacloud</title>
6    <link href="assets/styles.css" rel="stylesheet" type="text/css" />
7    <meta name="Keywords" content="Tea, Brewing, Kettles, Teapots" />
8    <meta name="Description" content="Teacloud brews the finest loose-leaf tea nature has to offer. We bring exotic and
     tantalizing teas from the fields to your cup." />
9    </head>
10
11   <body>
12   <table width="700" align="center" id="tableLayout">
13     <tr>
14       <td id="tdNavigation"><div align="center"><a href="html/aboutus.html"><img src=
     "assets/images/navigation/aboutus-out.gif" alt="About Us" width="78" height="66" /></a><a href="html/ourproducts.html"
     ><img src="assets/images/navigation/ourproducts-out.gif" alt="Our Products" width="100" height="66" /></a><img src=
     "assets/images/navigation/abouttea-out.gif" alt="About Tea" width="89" height="66" /><img src=
     "assets/images/navigation/brewingtea-out.gif" alt="Brewing tea" width="101" height="66" /></div></td>
15     <td id="tdLogo"><img src="assets/images/logo.png" alt="Teacloud Logo" width="70" height="50" /></td>
16     </tr>
17     <tr>
18       <td colspan="2" id="tdContent"><div style="width: 325px; margin: auto;">
19         <p><img src="assets/images/landing.jpg" alt="Welcome to Teacloud" width="325" height="267" /></p>
20         <p align="justify">Brewing the finest loose-leaf tea nature has to offer. We bring exotic and tantalizing
     teas from the fields to your cup. For over 15 years, Teacloud has elevated the tea drinking experience and has
     provided tea lovers around the world with unsurpassed quality.</p>
```

`<head>`   `32K / 5 sec`

5 In the **Document** toolbar, click the **Code** button to view the code in this document.

Notice the **<meta>** information in the **<head>** tag? Visitors to your site won't be able to see the **<meta>** tag information because it's visible only in the XHTML code. It's a part of authoring the page, but it has nothing to do with appearance and everything to do with helping search engines find and properly rank your site.

---

6 Close **draft.html**. You don't need to save your changes.

Onward ho! You just built a page, set links, and added **<meta>** tags all in one chapter. Future chapters will reveal even more powers of Dreamweaver CS3, so keep reading!

WARNING:

Keywords and Descriptions

Keywords are `<meta>` tag values that specify certain words to help Internet search engines index your site. Many search engines limit the number of keywords you can use. Choose your words wisely, and use no more than 10 to 15 keywords that best describe the contents of your site.

Descriptions are `<meta>` tag values that also help Internet search engines index your site. Some search engines will use the description you create to describe your site. Again, some search engines limit the number of characters indexed, so keep it short and simple! If you want more information about `<meta>` tags, check out these resources:

Web Developer: META Tag Resources:
http://webdeveloper.internet.com/html/html_metatag_res.html

Search Engine Watch:
http://searchenginewatch.com/webmasters/meta.html

Linking

You can create links in a few ways you haven't learned about yet. In this chapter, you'll learn about **Point to File**, which lets you point directly to the page you want to link to in the **Files** panel. Another type of link is an **e-mail link**. This special type of link launches your visitors' e-mail program and automatically enters a recipient address. Another link you'll learn about here is called a **named anchor**, which works in conjunction with links to let you jump to different sections of the same page. The final type of link this chapter demonstrates is a **file link**, which lets you link to files, such as PDF files, SIT and ZIP archives, and so on. If this all sounds abstract, dive into the chapter so you can get the hands-on experience that will make these new concepts understandable.

1 | Linking with Point to File

The **Point to File** feature is an alternate way to create links on your Web pages. This feature forces you to select files in your local root folder, eliminating the unwanted possibility of linking to files located outside your defined site. Here's how it's done.

---

1 If you haven't already done so, copy the **chap_05** folder from the **Dreamweaver HOT CD-ROM** to your desktop. Define your site as **Chapter 5** using the **chap_05** folder as the local root folder. Make sure the **Files** panel is open. If it's not, choose **Window > Files**, or press **F11**.

---

2 In the **Files** panel, double-click **index.html** to open it.

This file is complete but does not contain any links. You will create the links by using the Point to File feature in Dreamweaver CS3.

---

3 Click the **aboutus-out.gif** (About Us) image to select it.

Before you can create a link, you must first select the image or text you want to turn into a link.

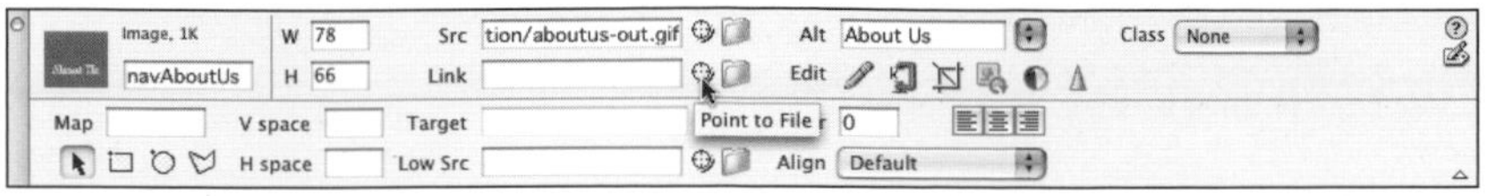

4 In the **Property inspector**, click and hold the **Point to File** icon next to the **Link** field.

When you click and hold the Point to File icon, the Link field populates with text, telling you to point to a file to create a link.

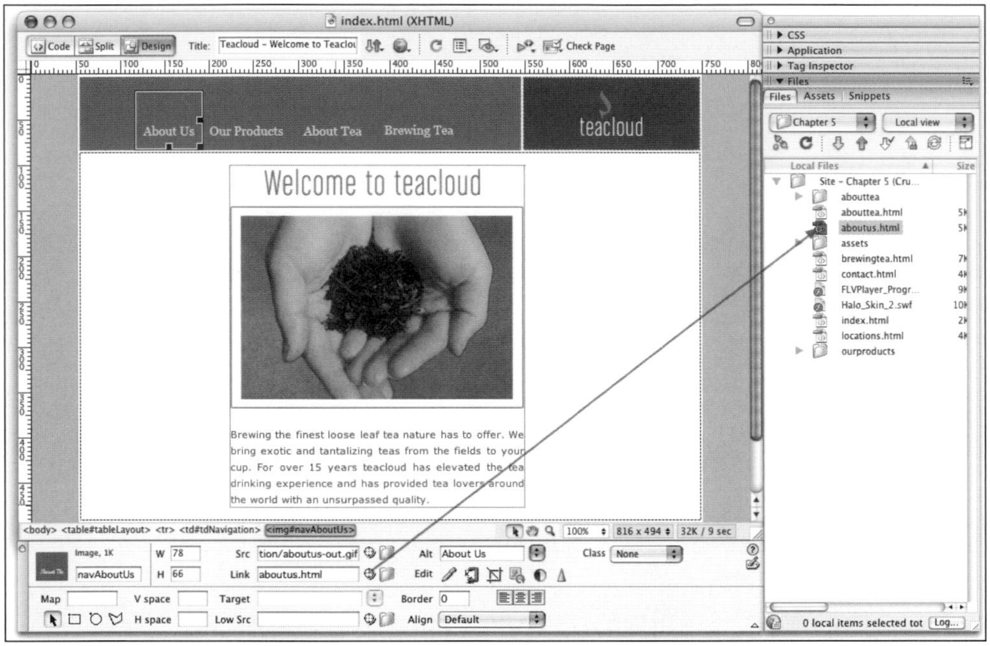

5 Click and drag the **Point to File** icon to the **aboutus.html** file in the **Files** panel, and release the mouse.

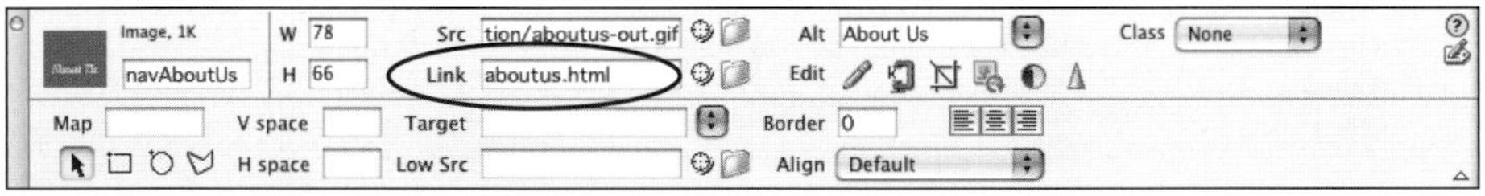

You've just successfully created a link to the aboutus.html file, as you can see in the Property inspector's Link field. This is a good place to look if you forget what file you linked to. The great aspect of using the Point to File technique is that there's no way to accidentally set the link to a misspelled or missing file.

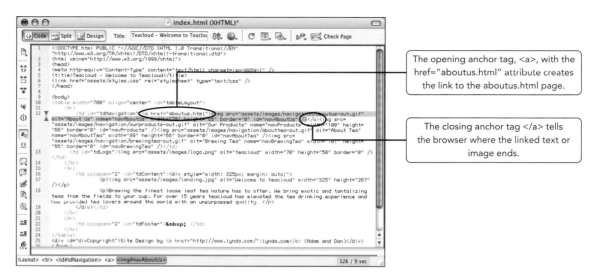

The opening anchor tag, <a>, with the href="aboutus.html" attribute creates the link to the aboutus.html page.

The closing anchor tag </a> tells the browser where the linked text or image ends.

6 In the **Document** toolbar, click the **Code** button to view the code for the **index.html** page. Some of the code may be highlighted because the **aboutus-out.gif** image is selected in **Design** view.

This automatic highlighting of selected objects is one of my favorite features in Dreamweaver CS3 because it lets you quickly see the relevant code for your selection in Design view. This feature will come in handy more and more as you continue to design pages.

Dreamweaver CS3 automatically inserted the code shown in the illustration here into the page automatically when you created a link to the aboutus.html page. It's nice to know that you don't have to type all of this (and type it correctly) each time you want to add something as simple as a link to your page.

TIP:

Learn As You Code

If you are new to HTML (**H**yper**T**ext **M**arkup **L**anguage) or XHTML (e**X**tensible **H**yper**T**ext **M**arkup **L**anguage), I strongly urge you to get into the habit of flipping back and forth between **Code** view and **Design** view (or use **Split** view) so you increase your exposure to the raw code behind the visual design of your page. Doing this lets you instantly see the new code that Dreamweaver CS3 creates as you perform various functions in **Design** view. Being comfortable looking at and editing code is essential to every Web designer's success because there *will* come a time when you need to make a tweak here and there in your code.

---

7 In the **Document** toolbar, click the **Design** button to return to **Design** view of the **index.html** page.

---

8 Select the **ourproducts-out.gif** (Our Products) image.

---

2 On the left side of the page, click the image placeholder next to **Teacloud Azul**.

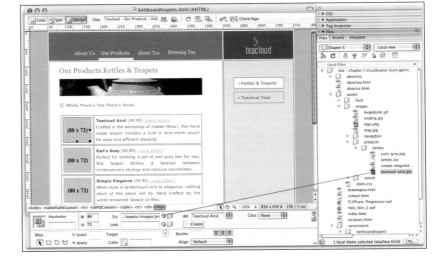

3 In the **Property inspector**, click the **Point to File** icon next to the **Src** option, and drag it over the **Files** panel. Hold the icon over the **assets** folder to expand it, and then hold the icon over the **images** folder, then the **products** folder, and finally the **kettles** folder to expand it so you can select one of the images inside. (Don't let go of that mouse yet!)

4 Position the icon over the **teacloud-azul.jpg** image, and release the mouse to replace the placeholder with **teacloud-azul.jpg**.

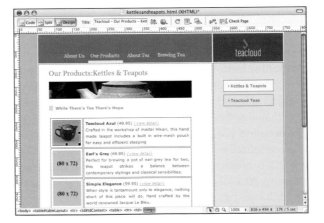

Notice the placeholder has been replaced with the selected image.

5 Click to select the image placeholder below the image you just replaced.

6 In the **Property inspector**, click the **Point to File** icon next to the **Src** option. Drag it over **earls-grey.jpg**, and release the mouse to replace the placeholder with **earls-grey.jpg**.

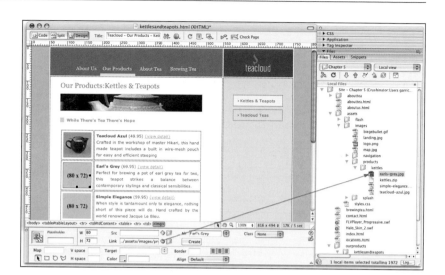

Notice the second placeholder has now been replaced with the image.

7 Repeat Steps 5 and 6 to replace the next placeholder with **simple-elegance.jpg**.

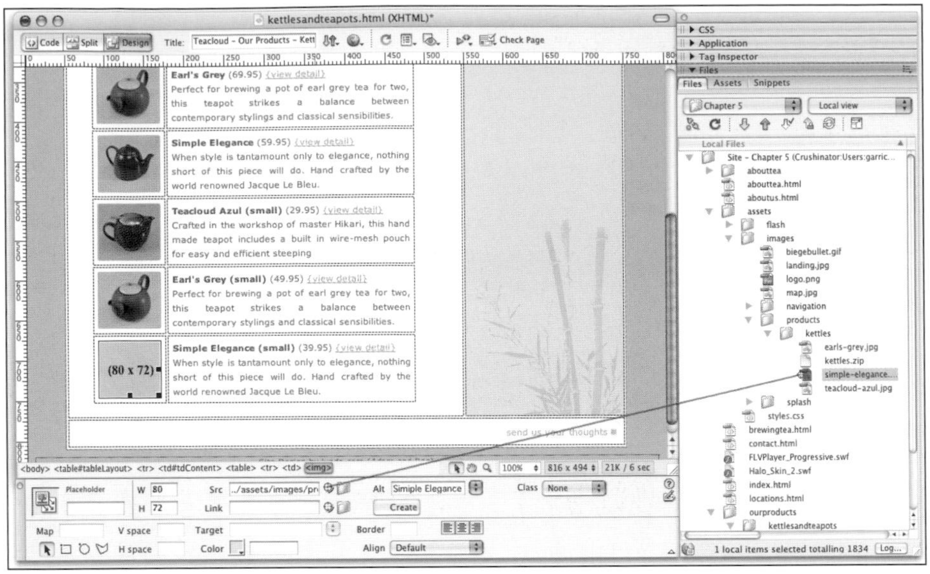

8 For a little extra practice, perform the same steps for the next three placeholders so that the "small" version of each teapot uses the same photo as their larger siblings. They're the same as the first three images, but a little target practice never hurt anybody.

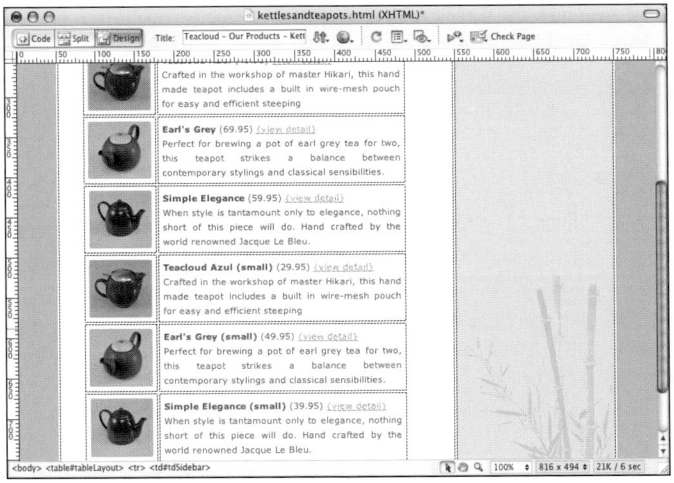

When you're finished, your file should match the illustration shown here.

9 Save and close **kettlesandteapots.html**. You'll use this file again in Exercise 5 of this chapter.

3 | Creating E-mail Links

An e-mail link automatically launches a user's default e-mail application and inserts the recipient's address into the **To** field. This process is convenient and doesn't require users to remember or copy and paste complex and lengthy e-mail addresses. This exercise shows you how to create an e-mail link.

1 In the **Files** panel, double-click **contact.html** to open it.

This file contains descriptions of the different Teacloud customer service departments. Each department has its own e-mail address for customers to contact them. You will create links to those e-mail addresses in this exercise.

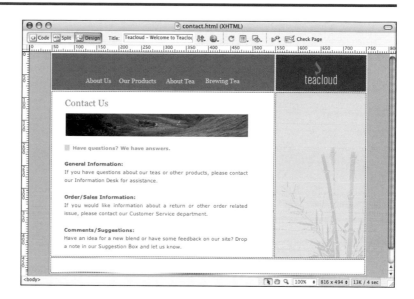

2 Click and drag to select the **Information Desk** text in the **General Information** section.

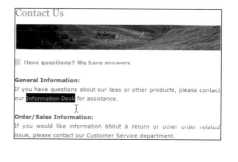

3 In the **Common** group of the **Insert** bar, click the **Email Link** icon to open the **Email Link** dialog box.

4 Notice the **Text** field automatically populates using your selected text. In the **E-Mail** field, type **info@teacloud.com**. Click **OK**.

Email Link

Text:	Information Desk
E-Mail:	info@teacloud.com

OK
Cancel
Help

---

5 Click the e-mail link you just created.

Format [Paragraph] Style [None] [CSS] **B** *I* ≡ ≡ ≡ Link [mailto:info@teacloud.com]
Font [Verdana, Arial,] Size [11] [pixels] #C89D5A ≡ ≡ ≡ ≡ Target
Cell Horz [Default] W No wrap Bg Page Properties...
Vert [Default] H Header Bg Brdr

In the Property inspector, notice the Link field reads mailto:info@teacloud.com. This is the correct format for creating e-mail links.

---

6 In the **Document** toolbar, click the **Code** button to view the code for this page.

The highlighted code shown in the illustration here was added when you created the e-mail link. Notice the similarity between an e-mail link and the other links you created in Exercise 1. They both start and end with the anchor tag, **<a>**, and they both use the **href** attribute.

contact.html (XHTML)*

◎ Code ◎ Split ◎ Design Title: Teacloud — Welcome to Teaclou ⓘ ⓘ C ▤ ⓘ ⓘ ⓘ Check Page

```
src="assets/images/navigation/ourproducts-out.gif" alt="Our Products" name="navProducts" width="100" height="66" border="0"
id="navProducts" /></a><a href="aboutttea.html" onmouseover=
"MM_swapImage('navAboutTea','','assets/images/navigation/aboutttea-over.gif',1)" onmouseout="MM_swapImgRestore()"><img src=
"assets/images/navigation/aboutttea-out.gif" alt="About Tea" name="navAboutTea" width="89" height="66" border="0" id=
"navAboutTea" /></a><a href="brewingtea.html" onmouseover=
"MM_swapImage('navBrewingTea','','assets/images/navigation/brewingtea-over.gif',1)" onmouseout="MM_swapImgRestore()"><img
src="assets/images/navigation/brewingtea-out.gif" alt="Brewing Tea" name="navBrewingTea" width="101" height="66" border="0"
id="navBrewingTea" /></a></td>
38       <td id="tdLogo"><a href="index.html"><img src="assets/images/logo.png" alt="teacloud" width="70" height="50" border
="0" /></a></td>
39       </tr>
40       <tr>
41       <td id="tdContent"><h1>Contact Us </h1>
42       <p><img src="assets/images/splash/aboutus.jpg" alt="asdf" width="411" height="58" /></p>
43       <h2>Have questions? We have answers. </h2>
44       <p><strong>General Information:</strong><br />
45       If you have questions about our teas or other products, please contact our <a href="mailto:info@teacloud.com">
46 ▲ Information Desk</a> for assistance. </p>
47       <p><strong>Order/Sales Information:</strong><br />
48       If you would like information about a return or other order related issue, please contact our Customer Service
department. </p>
49       <p><strong>Comments/Suggestions:</strong><br />
50       Have an idea for a new blend or have some feedback on our site? Drop a note in our Suggestion Box and let us know. </p>
51       </td>
52       <td id="tdSidebar"> </td>
53       </tr>
54       <tr>
55       <td colspan="2" id="tdFooter">  </td>
56       </tr>
```

<body> <table#tableLayout> <tr> <td#tdContent> <p> <a>   13K / 4 sec

---

7 Click the **Design** button to return to **Design** view for this page. Click and drag to select the **Customer Service department** text in the **Order/Sales Information** section.

Order/Sales Information:
If you would like information about a return or other order related issue, please contact our Customer Service department

---

8 Choose **Insert > Email Link** to open the **Email Link** dialog box.

As you can see, there are several ways to create e-mail links—using the Insert bar as you did in Step 3 and using the menu as you're doing in this step.

---

9 Notice the text you selected appears in the **Text** field. In the **E-Mail** field, type **cs@teacloud.com**. Click **OK**.

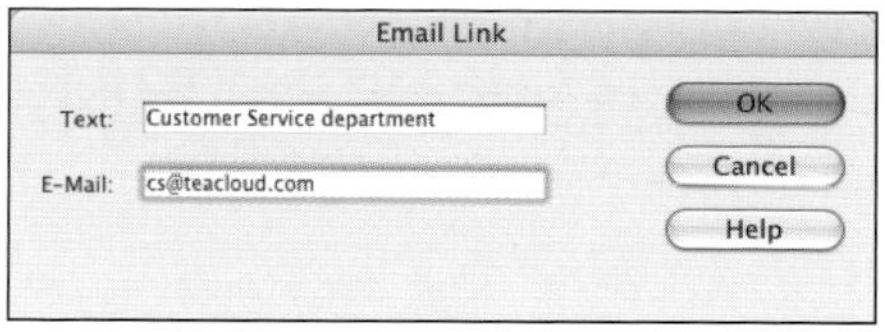

Note: Because Dreamweaver automatically inserts any e-mail address you used in the previous steps, info@teacloud.com will automatically appear in the E-Mail field when you open in the Email Link dialog box. Not to worry—you can simply type another e-mail address in the E-Mail field to specify a different e-mail address.

Next, you'll learn how to create an e-mail link without using the Email Link dialog box.

---

10 Click and drag to select the **Suggestion Box** text in the **Comments/Suggestions** section.

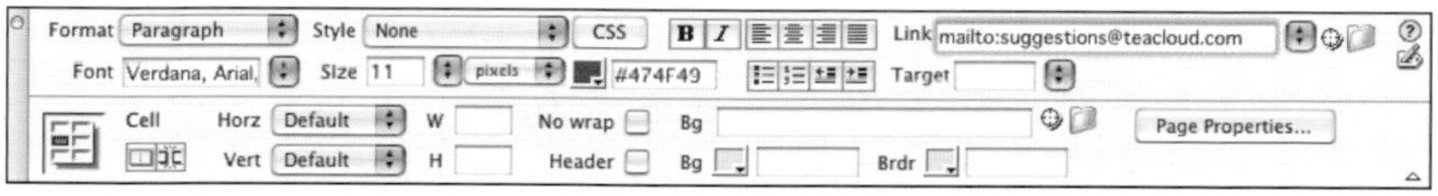

11 In the **Property inspector**, type **mailto:suggestions@teacloud.com** in the **Link** field, and press **Enter** (Windows) or **Return** (Mac) to create an e-mail link from the selected text.

You see, there's yet another way to do the same operation. As you build your skills in Dreamweaver CS3, you'll develop your own preferences for creating e-mail links, just as you will develop your own preferences for assigning links.

---

12 Press **F12** (Windows) or **Opt+F12** (Mac) to preview this page in a browser. Click each of the e-mail links to make sure they work. If you have a mail program installed on your computer, each one should open and create a new e-mail message for you.

---

13 Close **contact.html**. Save the page if prompted to do so.

WARNING:

Browser E-mail Settings

Not all site visitors use a standard e-mail program such as Microsoft Outlook or Apple Mail. Many visitors use Web-based e-mail programs such as Hotmail or Gmail. If visitors using a Web-based e-mail program click an e-mail link, they will get an error message asking them to set up an e-mail account using a standard e-mail program. You can't do a whole lot about this, so you might want to include the e-mail address directly on the page (or simply use the e-mail address on the page as the link) so visitors can copy and paste the address into their e-mail programs.

4 | Creating Named Anchors

Named anchors are a special type of link that let users jump to a specific section of a document. These links are particularly useful if you have a large amount of text on a single page that requires your visitors to scroll up and down through the document. Named anchors have two components—the anchor and the link. Working together, they make it easy to jump to specific areas of your page. This exercise shows you how to set up named anchors.

1 In the **Files** panel, double-click **teacloudteas.html** in the **ourproducts** folder to open it. This file has a long list of teas separated by type. Scroll down to the bottom of the page to get a better idea of exactly how long this page really is.

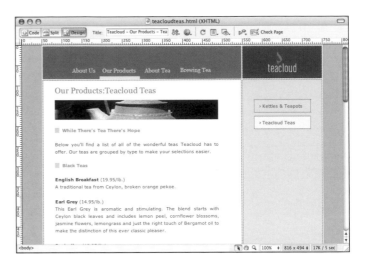

As you can imagine, searching through a lengthy page to find the information you need can be tedious, and sometimes visitors to your site may not even realize you have additional content they're interested in near the bottom of the page. To help ease this annoyance (and make sure visitors get all the juicy bits from your site), use named anchors to link to specific locations on the same page.

2 Click to the right of the **Black Teas** text to position your cursor there.

First you'll learn how to wrap a named anchor around the text so users can easily jump to the Black Teas section farther down the page.

3 In the **Common** group of the **Insert** bar, click the **Named Anchor** button to open the **Named Anchor** dialog box.

4 Type **blackteas** in the **Anchor name** field, and click **OK**.

Tip: When you create anchor names, follow a few simple guidelines: Use simple names without spaces or special characters, and don't use a number as the first character. Starting the anchor name with a number or including special characters or spaces can cause a browser to completely ignore the anchor.

Notice a small yellow anchor marker appears on your page where you insert the named anchor tag (although it currently looks blue because it's still selected). Don't worry, no one but you will ever see the named anchor icon; it's there for your benefit as you create these types of links. When you preview the page in a browser, you will not see the icon.

Note: If you don't see the named anchor icon, choose View > Visual Aids, and make sure Invisible Elements is selected.

Tip: If you ever want to change the name you specified for a named anchor, click the yellow anchor marker and type a new name in the Name field of the Property inspector.

---

5 Scroll down the page until you find the **Green Teas** text. Click to position your cursor to the right of it.

You'll insert another named anchor here so users can easily jump to the Green Teas section of the page.

---

6 Choose **Insert > Named Anchor** to open the **Named Anchor** dialog box. Type **greenteas** in the **Anchor name** field, and click **OK**.

As you can see, you can create named anchors in Dreamweaver CS3 in several ways. You can use the Insert menu, as you did here, or you can use the Named Anchor button in the Insert panel as you did in Step 3.

---

7 Scroll farther down the page, and find the **Oolong Teas** text. Click to the right of the text, and choose **Insert > Named Anchor** to open the **Named Anchor** dialog box. Type **oolongteas** in the **Anchor name** field, and click **OK**.

Tip: Dreamweaver CS3 also has a handy keyboard shortcut for inserting named anchors—Ctrl+Alt+A (Windows) or Opt+Cmd+A (Mac). If you're creating a lot of named anchors, you'll find this keyboard shortcut very helpful.

You're halfway done. Now that you've created named anchors, all that's left to do is to create links to them.

---

8 Scroll to the top of the page. Position your cursor at the end of the last sentence in the first paragraph, and type **Feel free to browse our Black, Green, and Oolong teas.**

---

9 Click and drag to highlight the word **Black** in the line of text you typed in Step 8. In the **Property inspector**, click and drag the **Point to File** icon to the anchor marker after the **Black Teas** text. When you release the mouse, you'll automatically create the link between the text you highlighted and the **blackteas** named anchor you created in Steps 3 and 4.

Notice the link field in the Property inspector has a number sign (#) before the anchor name. Links to named anchors always begin with # to identify the link as a named anchor.

---

10 Double-click the word **Green** in the text you typed in Step 8. In the **Property inspector**, click and drag the **Point to File** icon to the anchor marker after the **Green Teas** text. (If you can't see the anchor, just hold the cursor below the bottom of the document, and Dreamweaver will scroll the document for you.) When you release the mouse, you'll automatically create the link between the text you highlighted and the **greenteas** named anchor.

---

11 Using the same technique, create a link from the **Oolong Teas** text to the **oolongteas** named anchor.

---

12 Press **F12** (Windows) or **Opt+F12** (Mac) to preview the page in a browser. Click each of the links at the top to see how the named anchors work.

As you can see, named anchors are a nice way to jump to different sections within a single page. But wouldn't it also be nice if you had links to a named anchor that would take you back to the top of the page from anywhere else on the page? You'll learn how in the next few steps.

---

13 Close the browser and return to Dreamweaver CS3. Click the upper-left corner of the document (to the left of the table containing all the content for the page) to position your cursor at the beginning of the document.

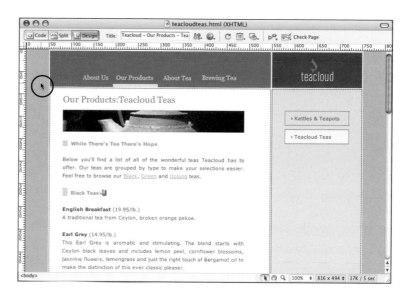

14 Choose **Insert > Named Anchor** to open the **Named Anchor** dialog box. Type **top** in the **Anchor name** field, and click **OK**.

You now have a yellow anchor marker at the top of the page.

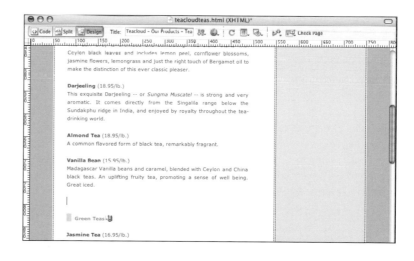

15 Scroll down the page until you find the **Vanilla Bean** text. Position your cursor at the end of the description, and press **Enter** (Windows) or **Return** (Mac) to create a new paragraph.

16 In the **Common** group of the **Insert** bar, click the **Hyperlink** button to open the **Hyperlink** dialog box.

Using the Hyperlink dialog box is yet another way to link to named anchors (or to link to any other page, for that matter). Earlier in this exercise, you used the Point to File icon. The Hyperlink dialog box achieves the same result. As you've learned throughout this book, Dreamweaver CS3 offers many ways to accomplish the same task.

17 Type **Top of page** in the **Text** field. Choose **#top** in the **Link** pop-up menu, and click **OK**.

Because the Hyperlink dialog box lists all the named anchors in the current document, you can easily link directly to them.

18 Using the techniques you learned in Steps 15, 16, and 17, create two more "top of page" links for the **Green Teas** and **Oolong Teas** paragraphs.

Adding these links will make it easy for visitors to move quickly between the different tea varieties, since they can click a link to jump directly to the section they want.

19 Press **F12** (Windows) or **Opt+F12** (Mac) to preview the page in a browser, and try clicking all the links.

As you click each link, the browser will automatically scroll to the position of the anchor you clicked.

Tip: You can use your browser's Back button to return to the link you clicked to go to the named anchor, even though it's on the same page.

20 Return to Dreamweaver CS3. Save and close **teacloudteas.html**.

VIDEO: | **anchors.mov**

To learn more about creating named anchors, check out **anchors.mov** in the **videos** folder on the **Dreamweaver HOT CD-ROM**.

---

5 | Linking to Files

In addition to creating links to XHTML pages, you may occasionally need to link to a file. For example, maybe you have a PDF (**P**ortable **D**ocument **F**ormat) brochure for visitors to download, or perhaps you want to let them download an entire folder of stuffed or zipped images. The possibilities are endless. The good news is that linking to files is just as easy as linking to other XHTML pages. This exercise shows you how.

1 In the **Files** panel, double-click **kettlesandteapots.html** in the **ourproducts** folder to open it. If you completed Exercise 2, the file should match the illustration here. If you haven't completed Exercise 2, not to worry, you can still follow along with the exercise. You'll just see place-holder graphics instead of the teapot images on the left side of the page.

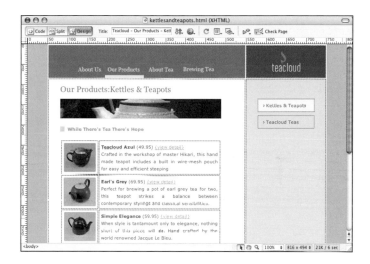

This page contains a table with information about some of the kettles and teapots available from teacloud.com. You'll create a link to a PDF file that contains similar information to what you see at the site. PDFs are a perfect format for printing.

2 At the top of the page, position your cursor after **While There's Tea There's Hope**, and press **Enter** (Windows) or **Return** (Mac) to create a new paragraph.

3 Type the text **View a PDF version of our Kettles & Teapots brochure**.

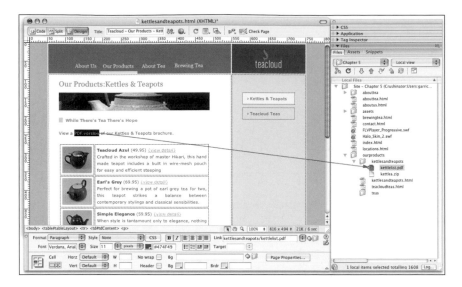

4 Click and drag to highlight the **PDF version** text you created in Step 3. Hold down the **Shift** key, and click and drag the highlighted text to the **kettlelist.pdf** file, which is located in the **ourproducts** folder in the **kettlesandteapots** folder. If the folders are not expanded, pause as you drag over each folder to expand the contents of the folder.

By holding the Shift key, you're using the Point to File linking method, which is identical to the one you learned earlier in this chapter, only you aren't using the Property inspector.

5 Press **F12** (Windows) or **Opt+F12** (Mac) to preview this page in a browser. Click the link to the PDF file.

Clicking a link that points to a PDF file automatically launches the Adobe Reader plug-in if it's installed in your browser. If it's not installed and you get an error or if the browser asks you where you want to download the file when you click the link, you'll need to download Adobe Reader from www.adobe.com/reader (it's free). You should also consider adding a link to the Adobe Reader download area to your page so users can download the plug-in if they don't already have it installed.

TIP:

Creating PDF Files

In this exercise, you have learned how to create and view a link to a PDF file, but you did not learn how to create the PDF file itself. Creating PDF files is a pretty easy process; you just need the right software.

If you think you'll create PDF files often, you might want to purchase the full version of Adobe Acrobat. Adobe Acrobat is a PDF authoring tool that lets you create PDF files from almost any application.

You can create PDF files online for free at Adobe's Web site at **http://createpdf.adobe.com**.

For Mac OS X users, you can create PDFs from any application. Here's how:

1. Choose **File > Print** to open the **Print** dialog box.

2. Choose **Save as PDF** in the **PDF** button pop-up menu (Mac OS X 10.4 Tiger), or click the **Save as PDF** button (Mac OS X 10.3 Panther) at the bottom of the **Print** dialog box, to open the **Save** dialog box.

3. Choose a location, and type a file name in the **Save** dialog box. Click **Save**.

In the following steps, you will learn how to create a link to a file of compressed images. Using a compressed file format lets you transfer large amounts of data, such as images, with a smaller file size. Two of the most common formats are SIT (StuffIt) files for the Mac and ZIP files for both the Mac and Windows. For this exercise, you'll use ZIP files, but the same concepts apply when you're working with SIT files.

6 Position your cursor at the end of the **View a PDF version of our Kettles & Teapots brochure** text you added earlier in this exercise. Press **Shift+Enter** (Windows) or **Shift+Return** (Mac) to create a new line break. Type **Download images of all our teapots in a zip file.**

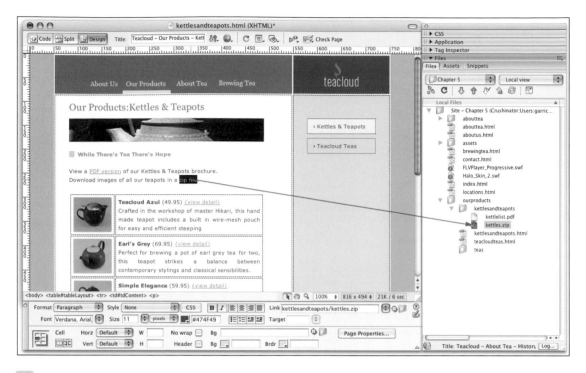

7 Click and drag to select the words **zip file**. Using any of the linking methods you learned in this chapter, create a link to the **kettles.zip** file in the **kettlesandteapots** folder.

---

8 Save the page and press **F12** (Windows) or **Opt+F12** (Mac) to preview the page in a browser. Click the **zip file** link. Depending on which browser you're using, either you'll automatically be prompted to save the file on your hard drive or the ZIP file will simply open since it's located locally on your computer. (Visitors to your site will be prompted to save the save.) Click **Cancel** to abort the download.

---

9 Save and close **kettlesandteapots.html**.

In this chapter, you learned how to link to files in a variety of ways. You can use the Point to File feature in the Property inspector, browse for files directly, or use the Hyperlink dialog box to create an entire link in one shot. In the next chapter, you'll begin learning about Cascading Style Sheets, the basis for any good site design.

Creating ZIP Files

When you have a large file or a collection of files you want to share for download, compress the files so the download goes as quickly and smoothly as possible. Both Windows Vista and Mac OS X natively support opening and creating ZIP files. Here's how:

Windows: Right-click the file or folder of files you want to compress. Choose **Send To > Compressed (zipped) folder in** the contextual menu. Name the file when prompted to do so.

Mac: Right-click the file or folder of files you want to compress, and choose **Create Archive of** in the contextual menu. You may rename the zipped file if you need to do so.

image_maps.mov

One type of linking not covered in this chapter is image maps. Image maps let you link to multiple locations from a single image. For more information about how to create image maps, check out **image_maps.mov** in the **videos** folder on the **Dreamweaver HOT CD-ROM**.

Working with Cascading Style Sheets

The **CSS** standard defined by the W3C lets you separate the structure of your page from the presentation. As a result, you can develop an XHTML document containing no information about colors, fonts, font sizes, or even where elements should be positioned. The rules defined in a CSS file handle all the presentation information.

Why would you want to do this? If, for example, you want all the text in your document to be blue and all the headlines to be green, with standard HTML you would have to go through the elements on the page one by one and assign those colors to the text using **<font>** tags, which can clutter up your pages. Using style sheets, you can redefine all the elements in the entire document (or an entire Web site) to turn blue with just one CSS rule and then perform the same single step for the headlines to turn green.

CSS also offers more control over type and other elements on your page than XHTML does. For instance, with CSS you can create rollovers that would ordinarily require a bunch of images and JavaScript—you'll get a chance to do just that in the last exercise of this chapter. You can even use CSS to lay out entire Web pages. CSS has come a long way, and with much improved browser support today, you should definitely be using CSS on all your Web pages.

Understanding the CSS Specifications

The W3C has released several recommendations for Cascading Style Sheets: CSS 1, CSS 2, and CSS 3. The CSS 1 recommendation was formalized December 17, 1996, and revised on January 11, 1999. It contains about 50 properties. The CSS 2 recommendation was formalized on May 12, 1998. It contains about 120 properties, including those from the CSS 1 recommendation. The CSS 3 specification isn't yet finished, and most browsers won't support the new properties created in the specification. You'll be using CSS 2 throughout this book, which is well supported by modern browsers and degrades quite gracefully in older browsers, meaning it won't cause an error even if it doesn't display as you'd like.

If you're interested, take the time to read the CSS 2 recommendations to learn what's possible with CSS, review the CSS code examples, and learn about compatibility issues. However, I should warn you that these documents are very technical and make for boring reading. If you prefer something a bit more digestible, you should invest in a good CSS book, such as *Eric Meyer on CSS* and *CSS Web Site Design Hands-On Training*, both written by Eric Meyer.

You can find the CSS 2 recommendations online at **www.w3.org/Style/CSS/**.

Understanding the Cascading Part of Style Sheets

The term *cascading* in Cascading Style Sheets refers to how browsers interpret your style sheet. When you use multiple style sheets (such as inline and external, which you'll learn about later in this chapter), conflicts can arise, and the browser has to know which style sheet to honor. So, **cascading** refers to which rules the browser follows when it encounters conflicting CSS information. The rules are complex, and describing them here would require more space than we have room for in this book. If you are interested in learning more about the rules for the cascading structure, visit **www.w3.org/TR/CSS21/cascade.html#cascade**. Understanding the cascade and specificity (how specific a rule is) can be a complicated and daunting subject. You'll get to work with it on a minimal basis in this book, but it's a subject well worth digging deeper into when you have the time.

Exploring the Anatomy of a Style Sheet

The anatomy of a style sheet includes some terminology that is likely new to you, such as *declarations* and *selectors*. Here are some examples of how these terms relate to style sheet programming.

At the very core of CSS are **rules**. Here is an example of a simple CSS rule:

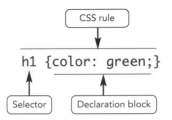

Rules consist of two parts: the **selector** and the **declaration block**. In this example, the **h1** (the Heading 1 tag) is the selector—it selects the **<h1>** elements on the page. The information contained in the brackets is the declaration—it declares how the selector styles elements on a page. In this example, the selector selects all the Heading 1

elements on the page and declares the color of each as green, as specified in the declaration block.

A declaration block can contain multiple declarations, each consisting of two parts: a property and a value, followed by a semicolon. Notice a colon separates the property from the value.

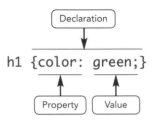

The **property** identifies what to change, such as color, and the **value** instructs the browser how to change it. In this example, the property identifies the **color** of the **<h1>** tag as the property to be changed, and the value instructs the browser to change the color to **green**.

This example is simple but shows you the three basic parts of any CSS rule: the selector, the declaration block, and a series of declarations consisting of properties and values. You can add as many declarations in a declaration block as you want. Here are some more complex rules that set all the properties for the **<h1>** tag in the Teacloud site.

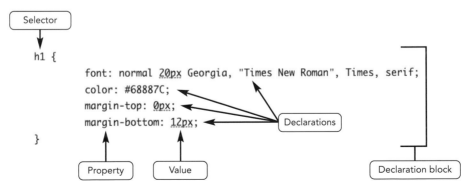

Even though the rules are far more complex, they still have the same basic parts: the selector, the declaration block, and the declarations. The declaration block simply has more declarations defined than the previous example. Notice that a semicolon separates each declaration. And though it's helpful to use line breaks to separate the declarations, they're not required. You could have all your declarations on the same line as long as they're separated by semicolons.

1 | Understanding CSS and Page Properties

This exercise gives you a gentle introduction to CSS in Dreamweaver CS3. Although this exercise covers a lot of information, you will see how you can use CSS almost transparently to control the basic formatting of a Web page. For example, by simply setting the various page properties, Dreamweaver CS3 automatically creates an embedded style sheet to handle formatting tasks, such as setting page background colors, font types and sizes, and page margins. As you will see in this exercise, it's easy to separate the structure of a page from its presentation with CSS.

1 If you haven't already done so, copy the **chap_06** folder from the **Dreamweaver HOT CD-ROM** to your desktop. Define your site as **Chapter 6** using the **chap_06** folder as the local root folder. Make sure the **Files** panel is open. If it's not, choose **Window > Files**.

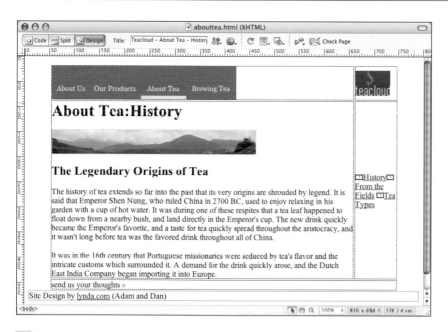

2 In the **Files** panel, double-click **abouttea.html** in the **chap_06** folder to open it.

This page contains the layout for the Teacloud site, but no other formatting, such as fonts, font color, background color, link color, or heading color, has been applied to the elements on the page. Unfortunately, this makes for a less than inspiring visual appeal. Not to worry—in this exercise, you'll change these attributes using CSS.

Be Sure to Use CSS Formatting

Because CSS is the recommended method for styling your Web pages, Dreamweaver CS3 creates internal style sheets anytime you format text or change page properties (rather than writing the page's code using the older method of HTML formatting). Dreamweaver writes CSS by default, but it's worth double-checking your Dreamweaver settings at this point before moving on in the exercise.

Choose **Edit > Preferences** (Windows) or **Dreamweaver > Preferences** (Mac), and in the **General** category, make sure **Use CSS instead of HTML tags** is selected. With this option deselected, Dreamweaver will style your pages with HTML formatting, and you won't be able to follow the exercises in this chapter.

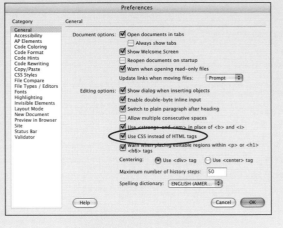

3 In the **Property inspector**, click the **Page Properties** button or choose **Modify > Page Properties** to open the **Page Properties** dialog box.

Before you start poking around the various Page Properties options, you need to understand exactly what you are about to do here. To the casual eye, it looks like you are doing nothing more than setting some basic formatting options, such as background color, text color, background image, and so on. But, in fact, you are doing much more. By setting the page properties in this dialog box, you are asking Dreamweaver CS3 to create an embedded style sheet and apply those styles to the various elements on the page.

Remember—an embedded style sheet sets options for the entire page. For example, if you choose a font list in this window (which you'll do in the next step), such as Verdana, Arial, Helvetica, or sans-serif, that font list will become the default font for all the text on your page. As you are about to see, with just a few clicks of the mouse you can create a rather complex and visually pleasing internal style sheet.

4 In the **Category** list, select **Appearance**. Choose **Verdana, Arial, Helvetica, sans-serif** in the **Page font** pop-up menu.

Specifying a page font determines the default font for the text on the page.

5 Type **11** in the **Size** field, and make sure **pixels** is selected in the **Size** pop-up menu, as shown in the illustration here.

Size sets the default size of the text on your page: 11 pixels is a nice size for most large bodies of onscreen text.

6 Type **#474F49**, which is the hexadecimal value for a dark green, in the **Text color** field. Type **#DEC2C2**, which is a light grayish color, in the **Background color** field.

7 Type **0** in the **Left margin**, **Right margin**, **Top margin**, and **Bottom margin** fields. Make sure **pixels** is selected in each pop-up menu, as shown in the illustration here.

By default, there is always a slight empty margin between a Web page's content and the borders of the browser window. Setting the margins to 0 ensures the page is flush with all four edges of the browser.

Tip: If you want to preview the changes you've made, click Apply. This lets you see the changes to your page without closing the Page Properties dialog box.

Now that you've finished specifying the Appearance attributes, next you'll set attributes for Links.

8 In the **Category** list, select **Links**, which opens the properties that allow you to control how links on your Web page appear and behave.

9 Type **#C89D5A** in the **Link color** field, **#9F7535** in the **Rollover links** field, **#CFA970** in the **Visited links field**, and **#474F49** in the **Active links** field.

Link color specifies the color for all unvisited links on the page. Visited links specifies the color for any link a user has visited. Rollover links changes the link color when a user positions (or **hovers**, in CSS-speak) the cursor over the link. Active links changes the link color as users click a link (with the mouse depressed), so it is less important than the Link color and Visited links settings.

---

10 Choose **Hide underline on rollover** in the **Underline style** pop-up menu.

Underline style lets you control what happens to the line underneath the links when your visitors position the cursor over the links on a page. By default, this option is set to Always underline, which causes the underline to be visible at all times. As you can probably guess, Hide underline on rollover, which you specified here, hides the underline when users position the cursor over a link.

Now that you've finished specifying the Link attributes, next you'll set attributes for Headings.

---

11 In the **Category** list, select **Headings**. Choose **Georgia, Times New Roman, Times, serif** in the **Heading font** pop-up menu. Type **20** in the **Heading 1** field, make sure **pixels** is selected in the **Size** pop-up menu, and type **#68887C** in the **Heading 1 Color** field. Type **11** in the **Heading 2** field, make sure **pixels** is selected in the **Size** pop-up menu, and type **#949D87** in the **Heading 2 Color** field.

These options set the font, font size, and color for all headings in the document. Headings help identify and separate different areas of text on a page. As a result, you want to specify fonts and font sizes that are different but still complementary to the ones you specified for the body text in the Appearance pane.

---

12 Click **OK** to accept these settings, and close the **Page Properties** dialog box.

As you can see, the options you specified in the Page Properties dialog box have been applied to the abouttea.html page. With just a few clicks, you now have the basic formatting for your page. It's not much to look at yet, but don't worry, you have still have lots to do.

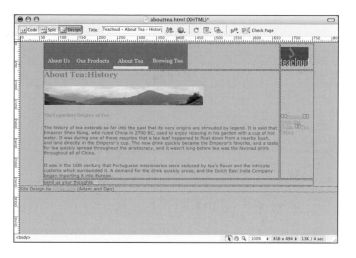

13 Save the page and press **F12** (Windows) or **Opt+F12** (Mac) to preview the page in a browser. Although Dreamweaver CS3 does a great job rendering CSS code in **Design** view, it cannot render some features, such as the rollover link color and underline effects, so it's always a good idea to check your work in a real browser. Position your cursor over the text links to observe the rollover link effect. When you are done marveling at your hard work, exit the browser, and return to Dreamweaver CS3.

Even though you may not have been thinking about it or even aware of it, Dreamweaver CS3 was building an embedded CSS style sheet as you changed the various page properties. Heck, you didn't even have to do anything except pick a few colors and options. This is a great example of how Dreamweaver CS3 encourages you to use CSS to control the formatting and presentation of your Web pages.

14 In the **Document** toolbar, click the **Code** button to display the code for this page. If you have to, scroll to the top of the page (about line 32) so you can locate the embedded CSS code. Take a moment to read through the CSS code that was generated. You should be able to easily point out the various selectors and declaration blocks.

Dreamweaver CS3 created all of this code automatically, and because it was placed in the **<head>** tag of this document and affects only the formatting of this one document, it is referred to as an **embedded** style sheet. You'll learn

about different types of style sheets, including embedded, inline, and external, later in this chapter.

15 In the **Document** toolbar, click the **Design** button to return to the visual editing environment.

There you go—you have made it through your first CSS lesson, and you didn't even have to type a single line of code—sweet!

16 Save **abouttea.html**, and leave it open for the next exercise.

Although this exercise was a great introduction to CSS in Dreamweaver CS3, there is one potentially serious problem with using this workflow. Using CSS to set the page properties is great, but it forces you to create an embedded style sheet, which prohibits you from utilizing one of the most powerful features of CSS: applying the same styles to multiple pages.

But don't worry—there's an easy solution! If you want all the pages in your site to use the same page formatting options you set up in this exercise, you should use an external style sheet. Why? Well, then you need to define the CSS just once and can apply it to other pages via a linked external style sheet. Using the workflow in the previous exercise would require that you repeat this process for every page in your site, which is an inefficient way to work.

Therefore, the next exercise shows you how to export the CSS code from this page to an external style sheet and then apply that style sheet to other pages. This will give you a real-world look at how things should really be done and still let you use this convenient workflow to get there.

Using the Page Properties Dialog Box

The **Page Properties** dialog box does more than just set the colors of the links and text. The following handy chart explains all the properties you can set for a page:

	HTML/XHTML Page Properties	
Category	**Property**	**Description**
Appearance		
	Page font	Sets the font face for the entire document. All text in the page will be formatted with the font you choose here, unless you specifically set a selection of text to a different font.
	Size	Sets the default font size for the entire document.
	Text color	Sets the default text color for the entire document. The values can be in hexadecimal format or by name, such as red, white, and so on.
	Background color	Sets the background color of the document. The values can be in hexadecimal format or by name, such as red, white, and so on.
	Background image	Sets a background image for your Web page. A background image can be any GIF or JPEG file. If the image is smaller than the browser panel, it will repeat (**tile**) by default.
	Repeat	Determines whether the background image specified for the page should repeat in a fashion other than the default. You can specify that an image not repeat at all or that it repeat on either the X or Y axis of the document.
	Left margin	Sets the left margin value for the document.
	Top margin	Sets the top margin value for the document.
	Right margin	Sets the right margin value for the document.
	Bottom margin	Sets the bottom margin value for the document.
Links		
	Link font	Sets the default font for all links in the document. You should generally leave this set to (**Same as page font**). You can also specify whether links should be bold or italic.

continues on next page

HTML/XHTML Page Properties *(continued)*

Category	Property	Description
Links *(continued)*	**Size**	Sets the default size for all links in the document.
	Link color	Sets the color for links.
	Visited links	Specifies how the link will appear after a visitor has clicked it.
	Rollover links	Sets the color for links when the visitor's cursor is over the link.
	Active links	Specifies how the link will appear when someone clicks it.
	Underline style	Determines how underlines are handled for all links in the document.
Headings		
	Heading font	Sets the font face for all headings in the document.
	Heading 1–6	Sets the size and color for all headings in the document.
Title/Encoding		
	Title	Sets the title of your page that will appear in the title bar of the browser and when your page is bookmarked. This name can contain as many characters as you want, including special characters such as %, (, #, *, and !.
	Document Type (DTD)	Sets the document type for the current document.
	Encoding	Specifies the language for the characters and fonts used in the document.
	Unicode Normalization Form	Determines how Unicode characters are handled in UTF-8 documents. You can find out more about Unicode Normalization at **www.unicode.org/reports/tr15**.
Tracing Image		
	Tracing image	Creates guides to set up the layout of your page. Tracing images can be a GIF, JPEG, or PNG file.
	Transparency	Sets the transparency level of your tracing image.

Understanding the Types of Style Sheets

In the previous exercise, you created an embedded style sheet using the **Page Properties** dialog box in Dreamweaver CS3. This method is fine if you're working on a site with a single page, but chances are you're developing a number of pages that all need the same formatting. CSS offers three types of style sheets to style your documents, some more efficient than others. Knowing the difference between them is important so you can decide which one is best for your Web projects. The following chart outlines the different types of style sheets:

<table>
<tr><th colspan="2">Types of Style Sheets</th></tr>
<tr><th>Type</th><th>Description</th></tr>
<tr>
<td>Embedded</td>
<td>Embedded style sheets are an internal part of the HTML document. All the code is written in the <head> tag of the document and affects only this page. Some sample embedded CSS code looks like this:

```
<style type="text/css">
<!-
h1 {color: blue; font-family: Verdana;}
->
</style>
```

Embedded style sheets are useful if you want to apply styles to a single page only.</td>
</tr>
<tr>
<td>External (linked)</td>
<td>External style sheets, also referred to as linked style sheets, are the most powerful type of style sheet because you can use a single style sheet to format dozens, hundreds, and even hundreds of thousands of pages. If you make a change to the external style sheet, all the pages that link to the style sheet are instantly updated to reflect the new style(s). The contents of an external style sheet file look just like the contents of an embedded style sheet, except they are not part of the HTML page. Instead, they are stored in a separate file with a .css extension instead of an .html extension. The .css file simply contains a list of styles with no other XHTML code. Instead of embedding the code in the XHTML document, you make a link to the external CSS file. Here's an example:

```
<link rel="stylesheet" href="mystyles.css" type="text/css />
```
</td>
</tr>
<tr>
<td>Inline</td>
<td>Inline styles are useful when you want to override some other style definition applied by an embedded or external style sheet or when you have just one element in your site that's going to use this particular style and it doesn't need to be defined in your style sheet. Inline styles are similar to embedded styles, in that they are part of the XHTML document. However, they are written as an attribute of the tag you want to style. Here is an example of some sample code from an inline style:

```
<body>
<h1 style="color: orange; font-family: Verdana">This is some sample text.</h1>
</body>
</html>
```

Inline styles are much less powerful than embedded and external style sheets, because if you ever want to change the style, you will have to change it in every place the inline style appears in your document. Use inline styles for "one-off" styles that you won't use anywhere else in your entire site.</td>
</tr>
</table>

One of the most powerful features of CSS is linking a single external CSS file to multiple pages. This results in consistent formatting and an incredibly efficient and fast workflow. In the previous exercise, because of the Dreamweaver CS3 defaults, you were forced to create an embedded style sheet when you set the various page properties. In this exercise, you will learn how to export the CSS from that page to an external CSS file and then apply the external CSS file to multiple pages. This exercise clearly shows you just how powerful external style sheets and CSS can be.

1 You should still have the **abouttea.html** file from Exercise 1 open. If not, complete Exercise 1, and then return to this exercise.

If a page already contains an embedded style sheet, the process of converting it to an external style sheet is pretty straightforward. In previous versions of Dreamweaver, you had to export the embedded CSS information from the Web page to its own external CSS file, attach this new CSS file to the page, and then manually remove the originally embedded CSS information. Happily, Dreamweaver CS3 has made this process much simpler by handing the attaching and deleting of CSS for you. The next few steps walk you through this process.

2 Open the **CSS Styles** panel, or choose **Window > CSS Styles**. Make sure the **All** tab is selected, and open the **<style>** list. Here you can see a list of all the rules you created when you set up the page properties in the previous exercise.

For this exercise you'll export all these rules into an external style sheet.

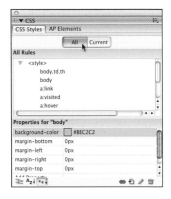

3 Select the first rule in the list (**body,td,th**). Then scroll down to the bottom of the list, hold **Shift** on your keyboard, and click the last rule (**h2**). Because you held down **Shift**, all the rules are now selected.

Now you need to tell Dreamweaver to place these rules in their own external style sheet.

4 **Right-click** any of the selected rules, and choose **Move CSS Rules** in the contextual menu.

Move To External Style Sheet

Move Rules To

○ Style sheet: _____ [⊕] (Browse...)

◉ A new style sheet...

(OK)
(Cancel)
(Help)

---

5 In the **Move To External Style Sheet** dialog box, select **A new style sheet**. Click **OK**.

You have the option of placing these styles in an existing style sheet, but since you don't have one, you'll create a new one.

---

6 In the **Save Style Sheet File As** dialog box, click **Site Root**, browse to the **assets** folder, and save the file as **styles.css**.

You can save this file anywhere within the local root folder for the site, but it helps to keep all your style sheets in one folder to keep things neat.

Save Style Sheet File As

Save As: styles.css

assets

Name	Date Modified
flash	11/1/05
images	11/1/05

URL: assets/styles.css

Relative to: Document

Change default Link Relative To in the site definition.

Select file name from: (Data Sources...) (Server...) (Site Root)

(New Folder) (Cancel) (Save)

7 After you click **Save**, notice that Dreamweaver has opened a new tab for the **styles.css** document. Select it, and you'll see it contains all the styles you created for the **abouttea.html** page in the previous exercise.

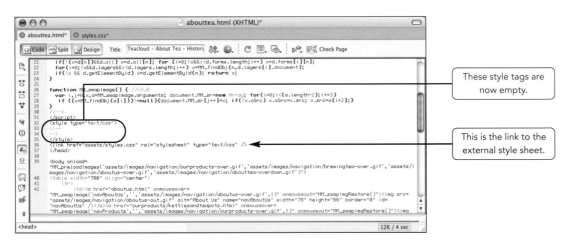

These style tags are now empty.

This is the link to the external style sheet.

8 Click the **abouttea.html** tab to return to that document. Then click the **Code** button in the **Document** toolbar to look at the page's code.

Notice that Dreamweaver automatically removed all the styles that had previously been embedded in this page (lines 32–35) and added a link to the external style sheet styles.css located in the assets folder.

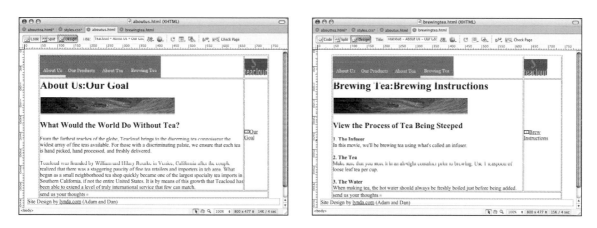

9 In the **CSS Styles** panel, notice that both **<style>** and **styles.css** are now listed. **<style>** is the reference to the previously embedded (but now empty) internal style sheet, while **styles.css** is the external style sheet you just created. Since you no longer need **<style>**, select it and click the **trash can** icon in the lower-right corner of the **CSS Styles** panel to delete it. Notice that the code for that embedded style sheet disappears from **Code** view. This isn't an essential step, but it does remove unnecessary code from your page.

---

10 Click the **Design** button in the document toolbar to return to **Design** view.

Next, you'll apply the styles.css external style sheet to other pages on the Teacloud site so you can see the true power of external style sheets.

11 In the **Files** panel, double-click to open **aboutus.html** and **brewingtea.html**.

These pages are seriously lacking in some formatting. However, because they are part of the same site as the aboutus.html page, you'll want to apply the same formatting to these pages so all the pages on the Teacloud site have a consistent appearance. In the next few steps, you'll do just that.

---

12 Make sure **aboutus.html** is the active document.

---

13 In the **CSS Styles** panel, click **Attach Style Sheet** to open the **Attach External Style Sheet** dialog box.

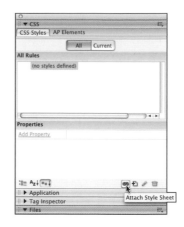

14 Click the **Browse** button, and locate **styles.css**, which you saved in the **assets** folder. Make sure the **Link** radio button is selected, and click **OK**.

With the external style sheet attached to the aboutus.html page, the page updates immediately and now perfectly matches the formatting of the aboutttea.html page. How cool—you just matched the formatting of the aboutttea.html page with the click of a button!

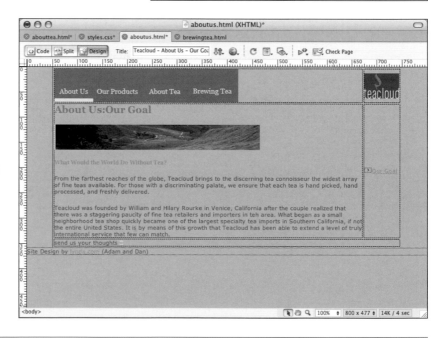

15 Click the tab for **brewingtea.html** to make it the active document, and then click the **Attach Style Sheet** button in the **CSS Styles** panel.

The Attach External Style Sheet dialog box remembers the most recently used external style sheet in the File/URL field, so all you have to do here is click OK.

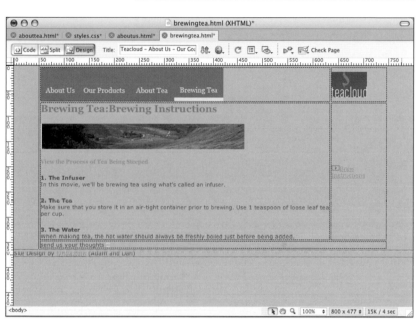

As you can see, once you create an external style sheet, it's really easy to apply the same formatting to multiple pages. In fact, you could format hundreds of pages in minutes by simply attaching the external style sheet to each of those pages.

In the last few steps of this exercise, you'll make a simple change to the external style sheet and observe how this change cascades over all the pages linked to it.

16 In the **CSS Styles** panel in *any* of the documents, click the **body** rule to select it. In the **Properties** pane in the **CSS Styles** panel, click the **color picker** next to **background-color**, and choose white, **#FFFFFF**. You'll immediately see the background color change to white in all the documents that link to the **styles.css** external style sheet.

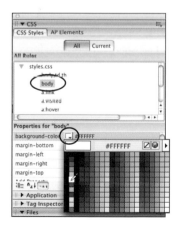

When you change a CSS rule in the CSS Styles panel from a page that links to the external style sheet, Dreamweaver CS3 actually changes the code in the external style sheet. By default, it will automatically open the file for you and make the change.

If you look at the top of the Document window, you'll see the styles.css tab is marked with an asterisk, which means the file has changed.

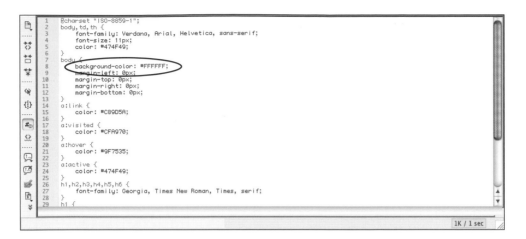

```
1    @charset "ISO-8859-1";
2    body, td, th {
3        font-family: Verdana, Arial, Helvetica, sans-serif;
4        font-size: 11px;
5        color: #474F49;
6    }
7    body {
8        background-color: #FFFFFF;
9        margin-left: 0px;
10       margin-top: 0px;
11       margin-right: 0px;
12       margin-bottom: 0px;
13   }
14   a:link {
15       color: #C89D5A;
16   }
17   a:visited {
18       color: #CFA970;
19   }
20   a:hover {
21       color: #9F7535;
22   }
23   a:active {
24       color: #474F49;
25   }
26   h1,h2,h3,h4,h5,h6 {
27       font-family: Georgia, Times New Roman, Times, serif;
28   }
29   h1 {
```

                                                              1K / 1 sec

17 Click the **styles.css** tab to switch to the CSS file. Scroll to the top, and you'll see that Dreamweaver CS3 changed the value for the **background-color** property to **#FFFFFF**.

---

18 Close **styles.css**. You don't need to save your changes. The background color reverts to the original gray color you chose in the previous exercise.

Now that you've closed styles.css without saving your changes, all the documents that are attached to this external style sheet have the gray background color restored. This is a great example of how powerful external style sheets can be. With one change, you affected the appearance of three pages. Had the styles.css external style sheet file been linked to 100 pages, then all 100 pages would have been updated. Very powerful indeed!

---

19 Save and close **aboutus.html** and **brewingtea.html**. Keep **abouttea.html** open for the next exercise.

Using the CSS Styles Panel

Let's take some time now to get more familiar with the **CSS Styles** panel, which is essentially the control center for all the CSS you apply to the pages in your site. The **CSS Styles** panel has two modes: **All** (which you've already used a bit) and **Current** (which you'll learn about in more detail later in this chapter).

The **All** mode shows you all the style sheets that are linked to or embedded in the current document. It groups the rules by the style sheet they're defined in so you see a folder-like structure of all your CSS rules. The following chart provides an overview of the options in the **All** mode in the **CSS Styles** panel, shown in the illustration here:

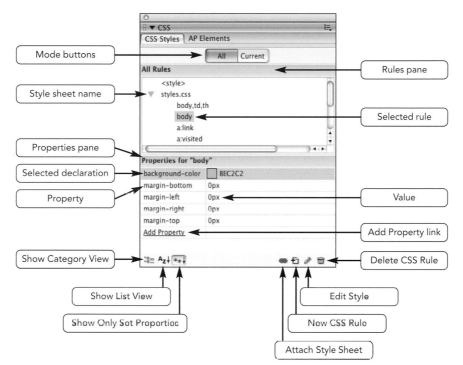

CSS Styles Panel All Mode	
Item	**Description**
Mode buttons	Allow you to switch between **All** mode and **Current** mode.
Rules pane	Contains all the CSS rules affecting the current document.
Style sheet name	Lists the style sheet affecting the currently selected document. You can click the **Expand/Collapse** button to show or hide all the rules for each style sheet.
Selected rule	Highlights the currently selected rule in gray. All the currently selected properties appear in the **Properties** pane.

continues on next page

CSS Styles Panel All Mode *(continued)*	
Item	**Description**
Properties pane	Shows all the declarations for the currently selected rule.
Selected declaration	Highlights the currently selected declaration in the **Properties** pane in gray.
Property	Contains all the properties for the currently selected rule.
Value	Contains all the matching values for the properties of the currently selected rule.
Add Property link	Adds a new declaration to the currently selected rule directly from the **CSS Styles** panel without having to go through the **CSS Rule** dialog boxes.
Show Category View	Changes the **Properties** pane so it shows every possible CSS property, grouped by category.
Show List View	Changes the **Properties** pane so that it shows every possible CSS property in an alphabetical list, with properties that already have a value listed at the top.
Show Only Set Properties	Shows only the properties with valid values for the current selection. (This is the default and is what you'll use throughout the book.)
Delete CSS Rule	Deletes the currently selected rule from the style sheet, removes the style sheet from the current document if the style sheet name is selected, or deletes the currently selected declaration from a CSS rule if a declaration is selected.
Edit Style	Opens the currently selected rule in the **CSS Rule Definition** dialog box.
New CSS Rule	Opens the **New CSS Rule** dialog box.
Attach Style Sheet	Attaches a style sheet to the current document.

The **Current** mode of the **CSS Styles** panel shows you all the rules that apply to the currently selected element in **Design** view. An element's style in a document may be affected by one rule or twenty, depending on how you have your styles defined. The **Current** mode of the **CSS Styles** panel makes it easy to see what rules affect which part of the document's display. The following chart provides an overview of the options in the **Current** mode in the **CSS Styles** panel, shown in the illustration on the next page.

This information is a lot to digest, and you shouldn't expect to grasp it all at once. As you go through the rest of the exercises in this book, you'll become more familiar and comfortable with the **CSS Styles** panel, which is an integral part of doing any design work in Dreamweaver CS3. The purpose of this information is to identify the elements that make up the **CSS Styles** panel so you're familiar with the terminology and controls as you work through the rest of the book.

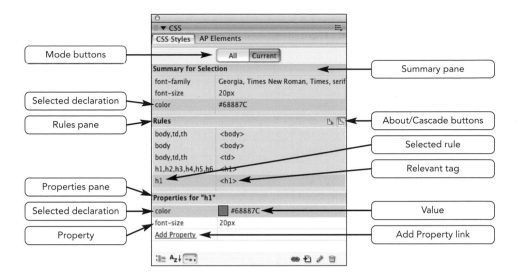

Mode buttons	
Summary pane	
Selected declaration	
Rules pane	
About/Cascade buttons	
Selected rule	
Relevant tag	
Properties pane	
Selected declaration	
Value	
Property	
Add Property link	

CSS Styles Panel Current Mode

Item	Description
Mode buttons	Lets you switch between **All** mode and **Current** mode.
Summary pane	Shows the end result of all the styles applied to the current selection.
Rules pane	Shows all the CSS rules affecting the current selection.
Selected declaration	Highlights the currently selected declaration in the **Summary** and **Properties** panes in gray.
About/Cascade buttons	Changes the display of the CSS **Styles** panel in **Current** mode. Choosing **About** shows a brief description of the currently selected declaration and states the rule that defines it. Choosing **Cascade** (the default and what you'll use throughout the book) shows everything, as shown in the illustration above.
Selected rule	Highlights the currently selected rule in gray. All its properties are then displayed in the **Properties** pane.
Relevant tag	Shows the tag whose rule affects the display of the current selection.
Properties pane	Shows all the declarations for the currently selected rule.
Property	Contains all the properties for the currently selected rule.
Value	Contains all the matching values for the properties of the currently selected rule.
Add Property link	Adds a new declaration to the currently selected rule directly from the **CSS Styles** panel without having to go through the **CSS Rule** dialog boxes.

Understanding CSS Selectors

Now that you're a bit more familiar with the **CSS Styles** panel and you've created some rules for a document (even though it was through the **Page Properties** dialog box), it's time to start creating your own selectors. Before you can do that, you need to learn a bit more about all the different types of selectors available.

A **selector** defines to what a particular declaration block should be applied. Quite a few CSS selectors are available, but you'll work with only the most commonly used selectors: classes, type selectors, ID selectors, and a few pseudo-classes. The following chart describes each of these selectors, and the next exercise shows how to use them:

Selector Types		
Selector	**Example**	**Use**
Type	`p {color: green;}`	Type selectors redefine all instances of a specific XHTML tag. For example, if you want to change the appearance of all the paragraphs in a document, you can create a type selector to change them all at once.
ID	`#myTag{color: green;}`	ID selectors redefine one specific element, with an ID that matches the selector. In this example, any tag with an **ID** attribute equal to **myTag** would be styled with a green color: **<div id="myTag">**.
Class	`.highlight {color: green;}`	Class selectors style any element with a **class** attribute that matches the selector. Class selectors are the easiest type of selector to start using, but be careful not to litter your document with selectors that may be better suited to ID or type selectors.
Pseudo-class	`a:hover {color: green;}`	Pseudo-class selectors are used to style an element when it's in a specific state. In this example, the rule will style an **<a>** tag when the user's cursor hovers over the link. Pseudo-classes are usually used to style links by changing the styling when a user interacts with a link.

Understanding Type Selectors

Type selectors are probably the most efficient way to declare CSS formatting rules. A type selector *redefines* how to render a particular XHTML tag. When I say "particular XHTML tag," I don't mean just one **<p>** tag on your page, but every single **<p>** tag on your page. One single type selector rule can affect thousands upon thousands of lines of code. These are mighty powerful indeed.

You may not realize it yet, but you've already written some CSS rules using type selectors. When you set the page font in the **Page Properties** dialog box, you were telling Dreamweaver CS3 to create type selectors for you. Dreamweaver CS3 created the following rules:

```
body,td,th {
   font-family: Verdana, Arial, Helvetica, sans-serif;
   font-size: 11px;
   color: #474F49;
}
body {
   background-color: #BEC2C2;
   margin-left: 0px;
   margin-top: 0px;
   margin-right: 0px;
   margin-bottom: 0px;
}
```

The first rule, which has the **body,td,th** selector, redefines the **<body>**, **<td>**, and **<th>** tags. Dreamweaver CS3 grouped the three tags so all three have the same styles applied to them. This rule introduces you to the concept of grouping selectors. You can group as many selectors as you'd like by separating the selectors with commas. Even though the **<td>** and **<th>** tags are in the **<body>** tag, some browsers don't apply font sizes to table cells and headers properly, so Dreamweaver redefines all three tags for you.

The second rule redefines only the **<body>** tag to have a background color of **#BEC2C2** and margins of **0** all the way around. That's all there is to using type selectors. It's an awfully simple but powerful concept to grasp.

3 | Creating Type Selectors

This exercise walks you through creating and editing several type selectors to fine-tune the formatting of the pages you worked on previously in this chapter. You'll move beyond the **Page Properties** dialog box to do some advanced formatting, and you'll get some face time with the **CSS Styles** panel so you can become more comfortable with how it behaves. Plus, you'll continue to explore the benefits of working with the external style sheet you attached in Exercise 2.

1 You should still have the **abouttea.html** file from Exercise 2 open. If not, complete Exercise 2, and then return to this exercise.

Although the formatting looks better than it did when you started in Exercise 1, it could still use some more fine-tuning to make it a little more visually appealing.

2 In the **CSS Styles** panel, click the **New CSS Rule** button to open the **New CSS Rule** dialog box.

First, you'll change the default style information for paragraph text in the document, specifically the line height (the space between the lines) and the alignment of the text. The New CSS Rule dialog box lets you create new CSS rules or redefine existing rules. In this case, you're redefining an existing tag—the paragraph tag. When you're doing anything other than simple text formatting, you need to use the New CSS Rule dialog box.

3 In the **Selector Type** section, select **Tag**. Type **p** in the **Tag** field. You're going to be adding this rule to the style sheet you created in the previous exercise, so make sure the **Define in** field is set to **styles.css**. Click **OK** to open the **CSS Rule Definition** dialog box.

The three options for Selector Type are here simply for convenience. The Class option adds a period to the beginning of anything you specify in the Name field to turn it into a class selector. The Tag option lets you type only tag names, and the Tag pop-up menu will list all XHTML tags. I prefer to select Advanced, which lets you type anything you want in the Selector field.

The CSS Rule Definition dialog box lets you set almost every possible CSS property for your new rule. Because the text on the site is a little on the small side, it will look better if the lines in each paragraph are spaced farther apart.

4 Type **1.7 em** in the **Line height** field. When you leave the field (by pressing **Tab** or clicking outside the field), Dreamweaver CS3 will change the **Line height** field to **1.7** and automatically select **ems**.

Note: Don't worry too much about font measurements at this point. In the next chapter, you'll learn all about the different font measurements.

5 In the **Category** list, select **Block**. Select **justify** in the **Text align** pop-up menu to justify all the paragraphs. Click **OK**.

styles.css has been opened and changed, but not a single line of code was changed in abouttea.html.

With the new CSS style added, all the paragraph tags have some extra space between each line, and the text is nicely justified. You should also note that the styles.css file has been opened for you and is marked with an asterisk on its tab, indicating it has changed. You should also see the new **p** rule in the CSS Styles panel.

Did you notice the abouttea.html tab at the top of the Document window is *not* marked as changed? Even though the appearance of the text on the page is markedly different, not a single line of code was changed in the file; only the style sheet you attached in Exercise 2 has changed. Again, this is the true benefit of working with CSS—the presentation is separate from the content. If you had other pages in the site using this style sheet, they would also update with each change.

Next, you'll make some changes to the headings used on the page. Although the **<h1>** tag looks fine in the serif font you specified in the Page Properties dialog box, the rest of the headings are smaller, and serif fonts can be difficult to read at smaller sizes.

6 **Right-click** the **h1,h2,h3,h4,h5,h6** rule in the **CSS Styles** panel, and choose **Delete** in the contextual menu.

Did you catch what just happened? The **h1,h2,h3,h4,h5,h6** rule declared the font for all headings should be Georgia, Times New Roman, Times, serif. Because you deleted the rule, all the headings are now styled with the font specified for the **<body>** tag, which is Verdana, Arial, Helvetica, sans-serif. By default, if you remove or choose not to specify a rule for the headings, the style sheet will use the same rule as the **<body>** tag if one is defined.

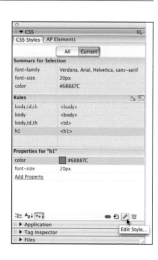

If you switch to the Current mode in the CSS Styles panel and place your cursor in the **<h1>** tag, you'll see the font is now Verdana, Arial, Helvetica, sans-serif. If you position your cursor over the font-family declaration in the Summary pane, you'll see the property is set in the **body,td,th** rule in styles.css. Now that's one handy panel.

To change the font for the headings below Heading 1, you had to remove the CSS rule for all headings, including Heading 1. What if you want Heading 1 to continue using the same font? Well, you can go back and change Heading 1, which you'll do in the next steps. Because all the headings were grouped in a single rule, changing that one rule changed the font for all the headings at the same time.

---

7 Select the **h1** rule from the **Rules** pane in the **CSS Styles** panel. Click the **Edit Style** button to open the **CSS Rule Definition** dialog box, which shows all the declarations for the rule.

8 Choose **Georgia, Times New Roman, Times, serif** in the **Font** pop-up menu, and click **OK**.

The **<h1>** tag is back to using a serif font, while the other headings continue to use the sans-serif font. Also note the abouttea.html file still hasn't changed a bit. All the editing you've done is part of the style sheet, not the abouttea.html file, which means if you had multiple pages linked to the style sheet, all the pages would update automatically. Once again, you're seeing firsthand the power and efficiency of using CSS to separate the presentation from the content of pages.

The last thing that's not quite right with this page is that the arrow images in the right side-bar have borders around them. Browsers, by default, add borders around any image tag that's located in an anchor tag (**<a>**). These images serve as anchors to navigate to other sections on the About Tea page. Without CSS, you'd have to edit each image individually and set its border to 0 in the Property inspector (which is how the navigation images are defined). Fortunately, there is an easier way—using a CSS rule.

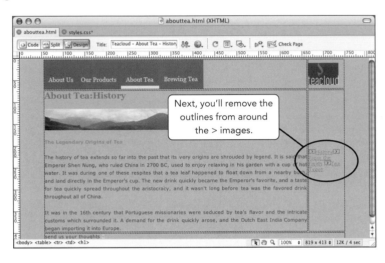

9 In the **CSS Styles** panel, click the **New CSS Rule** button to open the **New CSS Rule** dialog box.

10 In the **New CSS Rule** dialog box, select **Advanced** in the **Selector Type** section. In the **Selector** field, type **a img**. Make sure the **Define in** field is set to **styles.css**. Click **OK**.

You've just created a descendent selector. A **descendent selector** contains any number of regular selectors separated by spaces. What this particular rule means is "find any **img** tag that's a *descendent* of (or inside of) an **a (link)** tag." Any image that is inside a link in the document will be affected by the rule you're about to create.

11 In the **CSS Rule Definition** dialog box, select **Border** in the **Category** list, and type **0 pixels** in the **Width** field. Leave the **Same for all** box selected to set all the borders for the image to **0**, and click **OK**. You can leave the **Style** and **Color** blank.

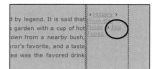

The borders are now gone from the images in the sidebar. Do I need to even mention abouttea.html still hasn't changed? Just as with the other steps in this exercise, the changes you made are to the style sheet, not to abouttea.html, which means the change would automatically update in any other file to which the style sheet was linked.

The last rule you'll edit is the h2 rule. To set the **<h2>** tags off a bit more, it would be nice to have a colored box next to each **<h2>**. You can do this with an image, but you'd need to add that image in front of every single **<h2>** tag in the site. How about using a border instead?

12 Click anywhere in the **<h2>** tag (the **The Legendary Origins of Tea** text) on the page, and select the **h2** rule in the **CSS Styles** panel.

13 Click the **Add Property** link, and choose **border-left-color** in the pop-up menu.

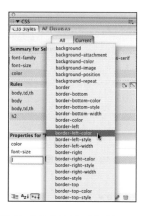

14 Click the **color picker**. Position your cursor over the color swatch for the **color** property. The pointer automatically changes to the eye-dropper. Click the color swatch to sample the color—**#949D87**.

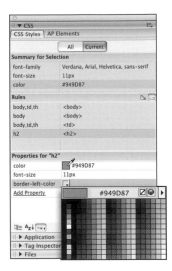

15 Click the **Add Property** link, and choose **border-left-width** in the pop-up menu. Type **11px** for the value.

16 Click the **Add Property** link, choose **border-left-style** in the pop-up menu, and choose **solid**.

17 Click the **Add Property** link one more time, choose **padding-left** in the pop-up menu, and type **7px**.

When all is said and done, you should have four new declarations in the CSS Styles panel, and the **<h2>** tag now has a nice square "bullet" next to it, all without adding an image to the page and (do I really need to say it?) without changing abouttea.html. The changes are all part of the style sheet.

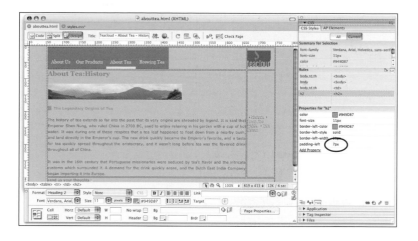

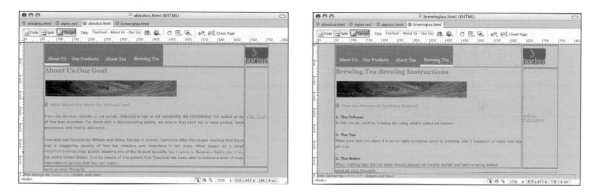

18 In the **Files** panel, double-click **aboutus.html** and **brewingtea.html** to open both files.

Notice the changes you made throughout this exercise are reflected in these pages as well. In Exercise 2, you linked the same style sheet to abouttea.html as well as the two files you opened here. Because the changes you made in this exercise were to the style sheet, not abouttea.html, the changes were automatically applied to aboutus.html and brewingtea.html. Are you seeing the power of CSS?

In this exercise, you learned how to modify CSS rules using type selectors. The next exercise walks you through setting up ID selectors.

19 Close **aboutus.html** and **brewingtea.html**. Since you didn't actually change anything in the file, leave **abouttea.html** open for the next exercise. Save **styles.css**, and leave it open for the next exercise as well.

Understanding ID Selectors

There will come a time when you want to style one specific element on a group of pages, such as a navigation bar, a background color, a logo, or even a footer that's displayed on every page of the site. This one element should be treated differently than anything else in the site. Your immediate solution would probably be to create a class selector and apply that class to the footer in each page. A more elegant (and semantically correct) approach is to give that element a unique ID and then style just that specific element. The more specific you are with your rules, the less likely you are to have issues with something getting incorrectly styled. Take this example:

```css
#divCopyright {
  font-size: 10px;
  margin: 1em;
  text-align: center;
}
```

The number symbol (#) identifies this selector as an ID selector. The text following the number symbol is the ID of the element that should be styled. So, the following **<div>** would have a font size of 10 pixels and a margin of 1 em, and it would be centered:

<div id="divCopyright">This is the site Copyright</div>

No other element in the page will have this same style applied to it, since ID selectors should be unique in each document. You should never have more than one element with the same ID. Although it's possible it will work, and the browser won't crash on you, it's technically incorrect.

4 | Creating ID Selectors

ID selectors are one of the most powerful tools available when you're working on the layout of your pages. They let you target specific areas of your page for styling. This exercise shows you how to set the necessary IDs on the elements you want to style as well as define the ID selectors to do the actual styling.

1 You should still have the **abouttea.html** page from Exercise 3 open. If not, complete Exercise 3, and then return to this exercise.

In this exercise, you'll style each of the table cells for the layout. Each table cell will have an ID that uniquely identifies it on the page, and then each table cell will get its own style. This ensures only one specific element gets styled.

2 To begin using ID selectors, you need to add some IDs to the document. Click anywhere in the table on the page, and then click the **<table>** tag in the **Tag Selector**.

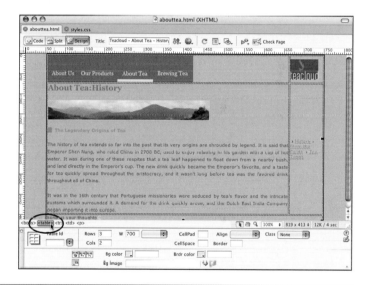

3 In the Property inspector, type **tableLayout** in the **Table Id** field.

The Table Id pop-up menu identifies all the ID selectors defined in the style sheet, which is helpful because if you create your ID selectors first, you can simply choose them in the pop-up menu. Since ID selectors are case-sensitive, choosing them in the pop-up menu means you don't have to worry about typing them incorrectly.

Naming ID Selectors

As a general rule, it's best to name your ID selectors with the tag first and then with the purpose for that particular tag. In the previous step, you named the table that contains the layout for the entire page, so **tableLayout** is a descriptive and useful name for the selector. Using descriptive names makes it easy to tell which styles affect which elements just by looking at the style sheet itself.

4 In the **CSS Styles** panel, click the **New CSS Rule** button to open the **New CSS Rule** dialog box.

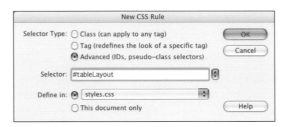

5 Make sure the settings match the ones shown in the illustration here, and click **OK** to open the **CSS Rule Definition** dialog box.

Because you had an element with an ID of tableLayout currently selected in the document, Dreamweaver CS3 automatically added the ID selector to the Selector field. You can change the selector if necessary, but in this case Dreamweaver CS3 got it right.

6 In the **Category** list, select **Background**. Type **#FFFFFF** in the **Background color** field. In the **Category** list, select the **Border** category. Deselect the **Same for all** option for **Style**, **Width**, and **Color**. Type **solid**, **1 pixels**, and **#B0B0B0** for the **Right** and **Left** borders. Click **OK** to add the new rule.

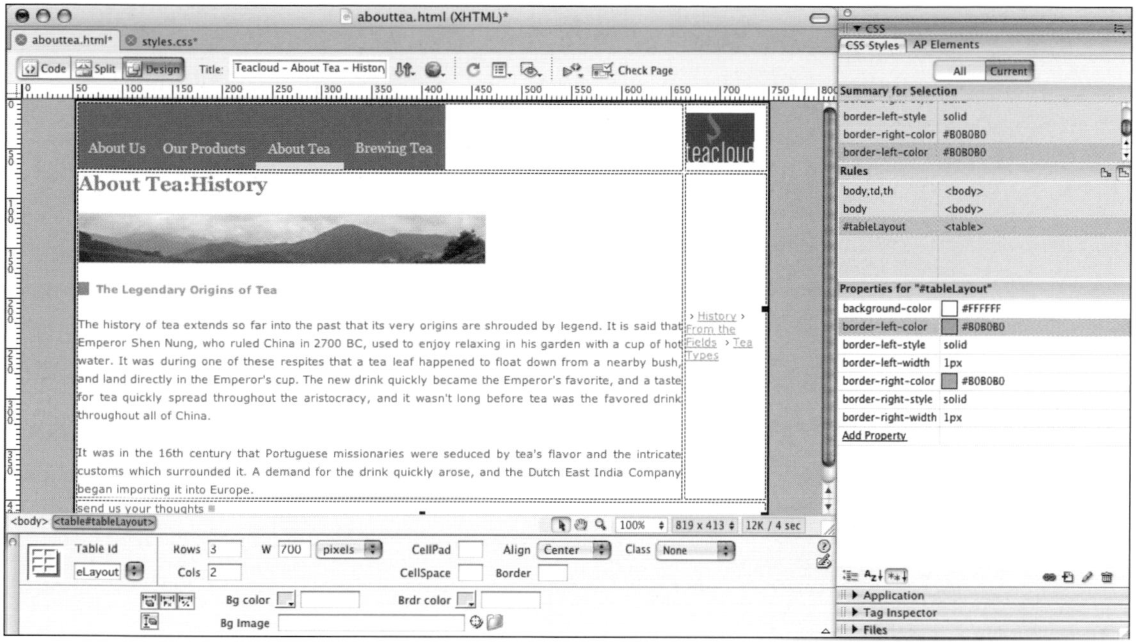

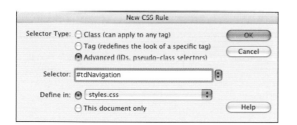

You just created an ID selector to change the background of the page from gray to white, which radically transforms and improves the appearance of the site. The #tableLayout selector you just created affects only the element with that specific ID — in this case the background color for the table.

Next, you'll make some changes to the styling of the navigation bar at the top of the page. You'll define this style in the opposite order you defined the style for the background color; you'll create the ID selector first and then apply it to the table cell.

---

7 In the **CSS Styles** panel, click the **New CSS Rule** button to open the **New CSS Rule** dialog box.

---

8 In the **Selector Type** section, select **Advanced**. Type **#tdNavigation** in the **Selector** field, and make sure the **Define in** field is set to **styles.css**. Click **OK** to open the **CSS Rule Definition** dialog box.

---

9 In the **Category** list, select **Background**, and type **#6E7970** in the **Background color** field. In the **Category** list, select **Block**, and select **Center** in the **Text align** pop-up menu. In the **Category** list, select **Box**. Deselect the **Same for all** box in the **Padding** section, and type **0** in the **Bottom** field. Click **OK**.

The 0 bottom padding ensures the navigation images are flush with the bottom of the table cell. You'll learn more about dealing with table margins and padding in Chapter 8, *"Working with Tables."*

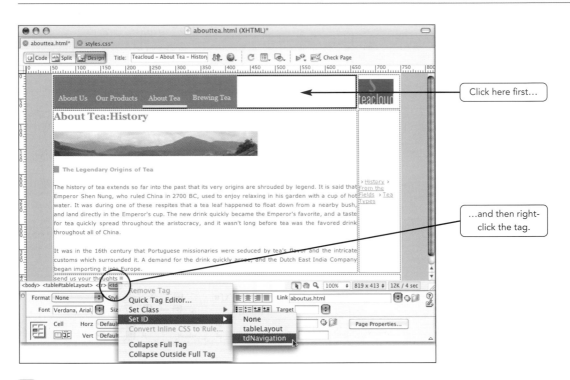

10 In the **Document** window, click anywhere inside the table cell containing the navigation. In the **Tag Selector**, **right-click** the **<td>** tag. Choose **Set ID > tdNavigation** in the contextual menu, and watch what happens to the table cell.

That's just another way to make sure the IDs on your XHTML elements actually match the ID selectors in your CSS file. There isn't always a way to set an ID from the Property inspector like you can with **<table>** tags, so using the contextual menu in the Tag Selector can save you a lot of time and headaches trying to figure out why an element isn't getting styled correctly when you may have just got the capitalization wrong.

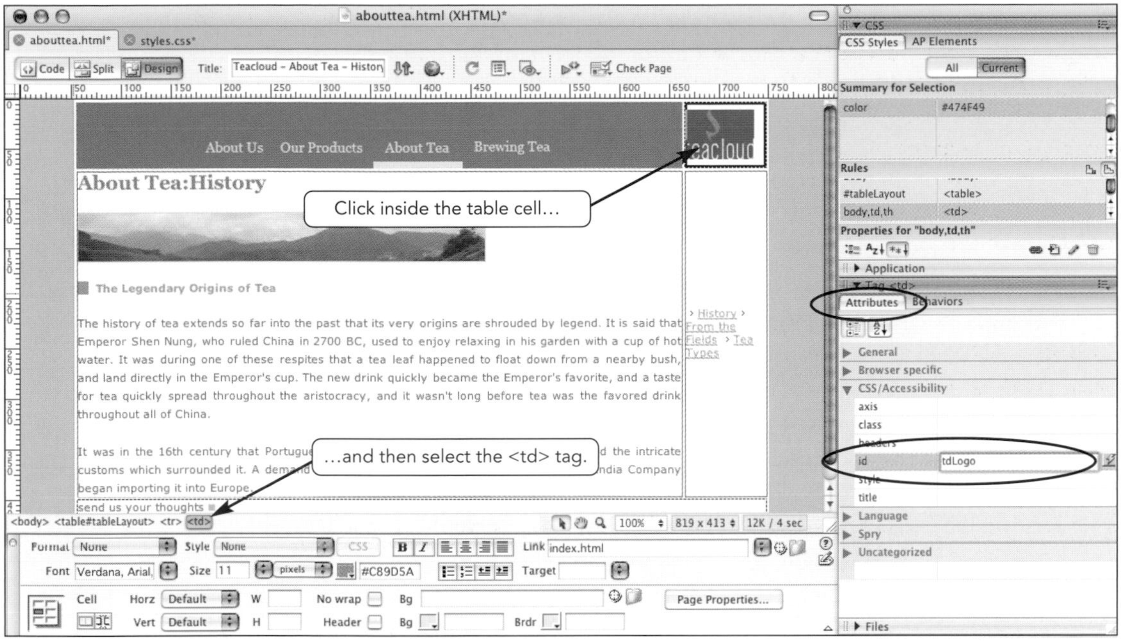

11 Click in the table cell containing the **Teacloud** logo. Select the **<td>** tag in the **Tag Selector**, and then choose **Window > Tag Inspector** to open the **Tag inspector**.

The Tag inspector lets you see (and edit) all the attributes of a particular XHTML tag. Since there is no way to assign an ID to a table cell from the Property inspector, you're going to use the Tag inspector to do it this time.

---

12 In the **Tag inspector**, make sure the **Attributes** tab is selected. Click to the right of the **id** attribute, type **tdLogo**, and press **Enter** (Windows) or **Return** (Mac).

---

13 In the **CSS Styles** panel, click the **New CSS Rule** button to open the **New CSS Rule** dialog box. In the **Selector Type** section, select **Advanced**. Type **#tdLogo** in the **Selector** field, and make sure the **Define in** field is set to **styles.css**. Click **OK** to open the **CSS Rule Definition** dialog box.

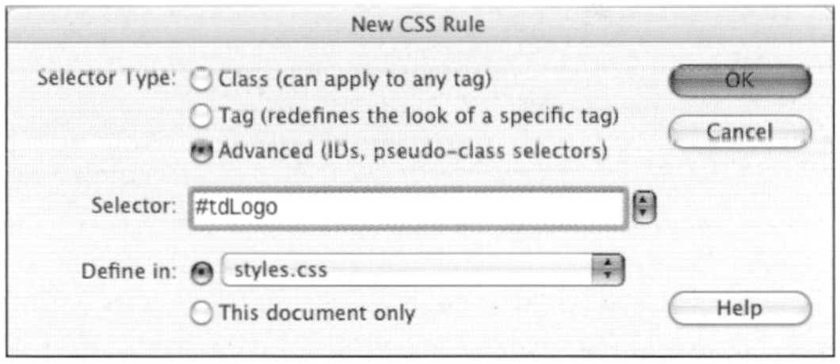

14 In the **Category** list, select **Background**, and type **#474F49** in the **Background color** field. In the **Category** list, select **Block**, and choose **Center** in the **Text align** pop-up menu. In the **Category** list, select **Box**, and set **Width** to **140 pixels**. Click **OK**.

The `text-align` property aligns everything in the element to which the style is applied. When the rule is applied to a table cell (as it is in this case), all elements in that table cell will be centered. The `text-align` property isn't just for text.

The table cell containing the logo now has the same background color as the logo image, and the logo is nicely centered in the table cell.

The last table cell you're going to style is the sidebar on the right side.

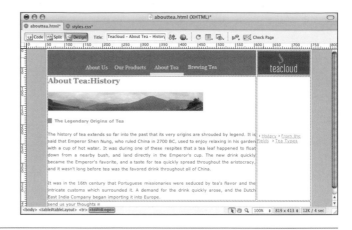

15 Click in the table cell below the **Teacloud** logo, and select the **<td>** tag in the **Tag Selector**.

16 In the **Attributes** tab of the **Tag** panel, set **id** to **tdSidebar**.

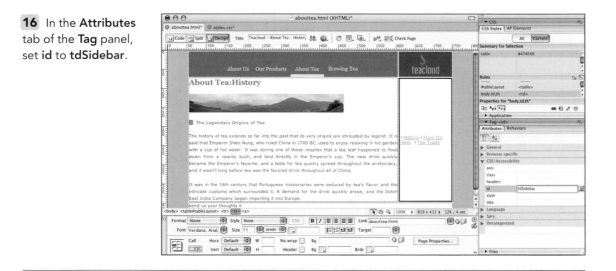

17 In the **CSS Styles** panel, click the **New CSS Rule** button to open the **New CSS Rule** dialog box.

18 In the **Selector Type** section, select **Advanced**. Type **#tdSidebar** in the **Selector** field, and make sure the **Define in** field is set to **styles.css**. Click **OK** to open the **CSS Rule Definition** dialog box.

19 In the **Category** list, select **Background**, and type **#E3E5DC** in the **Background color** field. Click **Browse** for the **Background Image**, and select the **sidebarbackground.gif** file in the **assets/images/ navigation** folder. Choose **no-repeat** in the **Repeat** pop-up menu. Choose **bottom** in the **Vertical position** pop-up menu. In the **Category** list, select **Block**, and choose **top** in the **Vertical alignment** pop-up menu to ensure the content is always aligned with the top of the table cell.

Setting the background image to no-repeat and aligning it to the bottom of the sidebar ensures the image doesn't repeat at all in the table cell and that it always displays at the bottom of the sidebar table cell.

---

20 Click **OK** to create the new style.

---

21 Save the page, and press **F12** (Windows) or **Opt+F12** (Mac) to view the page in a browser. Dreamweaver prompts you to save the CSS file that's attached to this page. Because you made changes to **styles.css**, Dreamweaver has to save the file before the browser can properly render the page. Click **Yes** to save the changes.

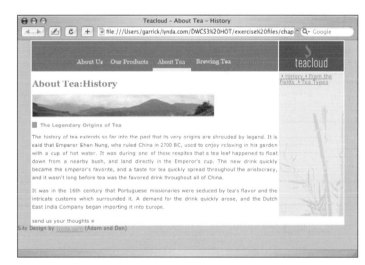

The page is starting to look pretty good at this point. All the table cells are properly styled using a minimum of CSS rules. Giving each of the table cells an ID ensures they're the only table cells affected by the new styles.

This exercise showed you how to specify ID selectors to affect a specific element on the page. You won't be finishing the entire page at this point—you'll have time for that in Chapter 8, "*Working with Tables.*" Now it's time to cover class selectors.

---

22 Return to Dreamweaver CS3. Keep **abouttea.html** and **styles.css** open for the next exercise.

VIDEO: | **id_selectors.mov**

For more information about ID selectors, check out **id_selectors.mov** in the **videos** folder on the **Dreamweaver HOT CD-ROM**.

Understanding Class Selectors

The class selector lets you specify a custom selector name and apply that style to an XHTML element using the `class` attribute. A class selector should start with a period (.) and be followed by the class name, which can't contain any special characters or spaces and can't start with a number. Here's an example of a class selector:

```
.smallprint {font-size: 10px;}
```

You could apply this rule to a paragraph with the following code:

```
<p class="smallprint">This is some small text.</p>
```

You could also apply the rule to a **<div>** or a table cell **<td>** just as easily:

```
<div class="smallprint">This is also some small text.</div>
```

Class selectors can also start with a tag name if the class should be applied only to particular elements. Let's assume you want small print text in paragraphs to be 10 pixels, but you want small print in **<div>** tags to be 12 pixels. You would use the following class selectors:

```
p.smallprint {font-size: 10px;}
div.smallprint {font-size: 12px;}
```

Using these two class selectors, any paragraph with a `class` attribute of `smallprint` will be 10 pixels, and any **<div>** with a `class` attribute of `smallprint` will be 12 pixels.

Class selectors are one of the easiest selectors to wrap your head around, and at first glance they seem like an easy and efficient way to start formatting a page, and that's how most people get started. But I caution you to take it easy with class selectors. It's entirely possible to become "class-happy," applying classes all over your page to get the formatting you desire. Although this seems like a good idea in the beginning, it can often lead to pages that are difficult to manage and update. A common mistake is to define a class for the body text of a document and then apply that class to every **<p>** tag on the page. Many new CSS users end up with something like this:

```
<p class="bodytext">A paragraph with lots of text…</p>
<p class="bodytext">Another paragraph with lots of text…</p>
<p class="bodytext">Yet another paragraph with lots of text…</p>
<p class="bodytext">The last paragraph with lots of text…</p>
<p class="smallprint">A paragraph with small text</p>
```

This accomplishes little in the way of separating out presentation information, because every paragraph has to be told how it should be styled. It's far more efficient to simply redefine the **<p>** tag using a type selector, which you learned about earlier. So be careful with your classes, and try to use them as a last resort. Use classes for exceptions to the other CSS rules you define. This code looks much more efficient and easy to read:

```
<p>A paragraph with lots of text…</p>
<p>Another paragraph with lots of text…</p>
<p>Yet another paragraph with lots of text…</p>
<p>The last paragraph with lots of text…</p>
<p class="smallprint">A paragraph with small text</p>
```

5 | Creating Class Selectors

Class selectors are probably the most common selector (and the most often abused). They let you define a class that you can apply to multiple elements using a **class** attribute on the XHTML tag. This exercise shows you how to create and apply class selectors in Dreamweaver CS3.

---

1 You should still have the **abouttea.html** file from Exercise 4 open. If not, complete Exercise 4, and then return to this exercise.

As a general rule, sites tend to have their copyrights and less important text in a smaller font than the rest of the site. Therefore, you'll create a class to make text smaller on the site.

---

2 In the **CSS Styles** panel, click the **New CSS Rule** button to open the **New CSS Rule** dialog box.

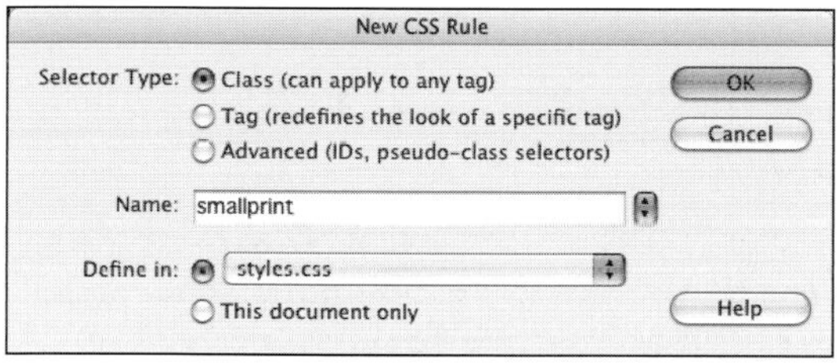

---

3 In the **Selector Type** section, select **Class**. Type **smallprint** in the **Name** field, and make sure the **Define in** field is set to **styles.css**. Click **OK**.

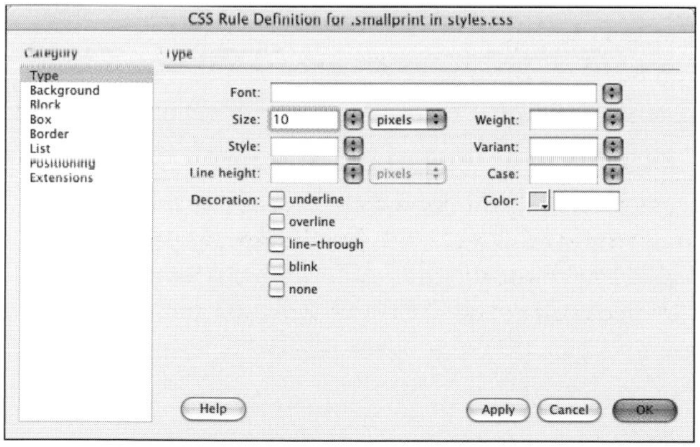

---

4 In the **CSS Rule Definition** dialog box, set **Size** to **10 pixels**, and click **OK**.

---

5 If you didn't already have it open, **styles.css** will open. It will be marked with an asterisk to indicate that the document has changed. Switch to the **All** mode in the **CSS Styles** panel. Scroll to the bottom of the **Rules** pane, and you'll see the new class selector has been added to the style sheet.

6 Click in the table cell at the bottom of the layout containing the text **send us your thoughts**. In the **Property inspector**, choose **smallprint** in the **Style** pop-up menu.

When your cursor is in a tag and there is no text selected, the Property inspector will apply the class to the first tag it finds. If you have a block of text selected and choose a style from the Property inspector, Dreamweaver will wrap the selected text with a **<span>** tag with the class applied to it.

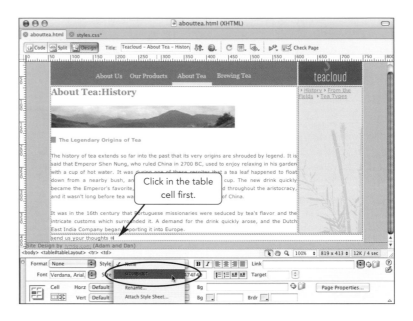

NOTE:

Span, the All-Purpose Container

The **<span>** tag is a generic container that doesn't have any default styling. It's used to wrap text or other objects with a tag that can be easily styled. It's easy to get carried away with **<span>** tags, and Dreamweaver sometimes makes it a little too easy by wrapping just about anything in a **<span>**. Pay careful attention to what Dreamweaver is doing, and try to avoid the **<span>** tags by applying classes to tags that are already on the page (such as the **<td>** to which you just applied a class).

You should notice Dreamweaver has added the **class** attribute to the **<td>** tag and the Tag Selector now shows the **smallprint** class applied. The *send us your thoughts* text is also just a tad bit smaller.

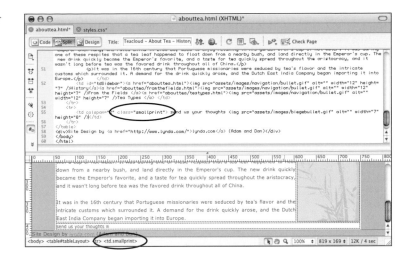

7 If you can't see the text at the bottom of the screen because of the table width indicators, choose **View > Visual Aids > Table Widths** to turn them off. Click in the **Site Design by lynda.com** text. **Right-click** (Windows) or **Ctrl-click** (Mac) the **<div>** tag in the **Tag Selector**, and choose **Set Class > smallprint** in the contextual menu.

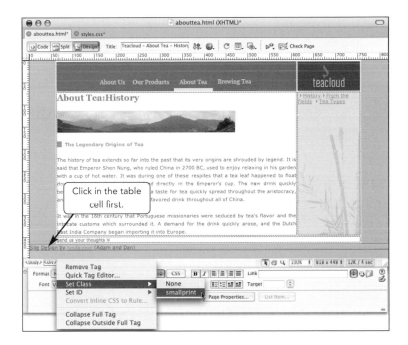

Click in the table cell first.

8 The **Site Design by lynda.com** text is now 10 pixels as well. Unfortunately, it doesn't look very good aligned to the left of the screen. You need to create a new rule to center any text in a **<div>** tag that has a **class** of **smallprint**. In the **CSS Styles** panel, click the **New CSS Rule** button to open the **New CSS Rule** dialog box.

9 In the **New CSS Rule** dialog box, select **Advanced** in the **Selector Type** section. Type **div.smallprint** in the **Selector** field. Make sure **styles.css** is selected in the **Define in** field. Click **OK** to open the **CSS Rule Definition** dialog box.

10 In the **CSS Rule Definition** dialog box, select **Block** in the **Category** list, and choose **Center** in the **Text align** pop-up menu. Click **OK** to create the style.

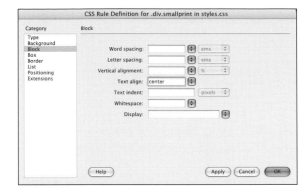

You should now see the new `div.smallprint` class in the Rules pane in the CSS Styles panel. The text in the `<div>` is now centered. You've just created a complex CSS class selector that states that any `<div>` tag with a `smallprint` class should not only be 10 pixels tall but should also be centered.

11 Save **abouttea.html** and **styles.css**, and leave them open for the next exercise.

Pseudo-Class Selectors

The last type of selector you'll learn about is a pseudo-class. A **pseudo-class** describes the *state* of a particular element and isn't based on something that can be determined by looking at the source code of a document. Pseudo-classes are tacked onto the end of other selector types to assign a style that happens only when an object is in a certain state. The most common pseudo-classes, and the ones you'll use more often than any other, are **:link**, **:visited**, **:hover**, and **:active**. These pseudo-classes are most often applied to links, or **<a>** tags. A common rule using a pseudo-class is to remove underlines from links when a user holds the cursor over the link. Dreamweaver CS3 automatically wrote a rule for this when you used the **Page Properties** dialog box and chose **Hide underline on rollover** in Exercise 1:

```
a:hover {
  text-decoration: none;
  color: #9F7535;
}
```

This rule redefines the **<a>** tag using a type selector, but because it has the **:hover** pseudo-class on the end, the rule is activated only when the user's cursor hovers over the link. Here's a description of the four pseudo-classes you'll be using most often:

Common Pseudo-Classes	
Pseudo-Class	**Description**
:link	This style is applied to elements that have not yet been visited.
:visited	This style is applied to elements that have been visited.
:hover	This style is applied when the element is underneath the user's cursor.
:active	This style is applied when the user clicks, or activates, the element.

TIP:

LoVe HAte Relationship

Generally speaking, you should apply pseudo-class selectors in a specific order to ensure links display properly. The mnemonic LoVe HAte can help you remember to define them in the following order: **:link**, **:visited**, **:hover**, and then **:active**. Because of the cascading nature of style sheets, these classes will be applied to elements in the order in which they are defined.

6 | Creating CSS Rollovers with Pseudo-Classes

Pseudo-class selectors are one of the more powerful selectors. Not only can they style an element, but they can change an element's style based on user interaction. In this exercise, you'll learn how to create some sophisticated navigation using nothing but a few pseudo-class selectors.

1 You should still have the **abouttea.html** page from Exercise 5 open. If not, complete Exercise 5, and then return to this exercise.

If you were watching closely in the previous chapters, you would have noticed the sidebar navigation was far more attractive than what is in the current chapter. In this exercise, you'll style the links in the sidebar to make them match what you've seen in the other chapters.

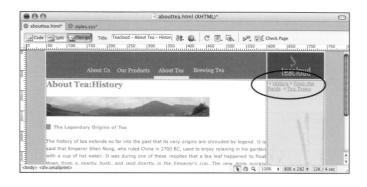

2 The first thing to do is give the links their default style. In the **CSS Styles** panel, click the **New CSS Rule** button to open the **New CSS Rule** dialog box.

3 In the **Selector Type** section, select **Advanced**. Type **#tdSidebar a** in the **Selector** field, and make sure the **Define in** field is set to **styles.css**. Click **OK**.

Notice you're creating another descendent selector, just like you did in Exercise 3 when you defined a border for all images in an anchor. In this rule, you're selecting all anchors in the sidebar table cell.

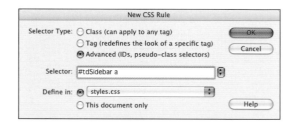

4 In the **CSS Rule Definition** dialog box, select **Type** in the **Category** list, and select the **none** check box. Type **#474F49** in the **Color** field.

Choosing none for the text decoration ensures that the links in the sidebar don't have underlines.

Block Level Elements vs. Inline Elements

One of the most powerful capabilities of CSS is to change the way an element is treated by browsers. We're not talking about just changing colors but actually changing the fashion in which an element is handled. There are two types of elements: block and inline.

Block-level elements "reserve space," which means that with a block-level element, nothing can sit to the left or right of the element, because it reserves that space for itself. In the previous step, you defined the anchor tag as a block-level element so that each anchor would reserve the space to the left and right of it and each element stacks up nicely below the one before it.

Inline elements don't reserve any more space than it takes to display them. Other inline elements line up nicely to the left and right of other inline elements, and they display in a line, just like a row of text.

5 In the **Category** list, select **Block**, and choose **block** in the **Display** pop-up menu.

Setting the links to be block-level elements ensures that each anchor reserves space in the document and all the anchors will be on their own lines, stacked up on top of each other. If the anchors were left as inline elements, they would all line up in a row, which isn't the effect you want.

CSS Rule Definition for #tdSidebar a in styles.css

Category	Box
Type	
Background	
Block	
Box	Width: ▢ pix... ⬍ Float: ⬍
Border	Height: ▢ pix... ⬍ Clear: ⬍
List	
Positioning	Padding ☑ Same for all Margin ☑ Same for all
Extensions	Top: 8 ⬍ pix... ⬍ Top: 10 ⬍ pix... ⬍
	Right: 8 ⬍ pix... ⬍ Right: 10 ⬍ pix... ⬍
	Bottom: 8 ⬍ pix... ⬍ Bottom: 10 ⬍ pix... ⬍
	Left: 8 ⬍ pix... ⬍ Left: 10 ⬍ pix... ⬍

(Help)   (Apply) (Cancel) (OK)

---

6 In the **Category** list, select **Box**, and type **8** in the **Padding Top** field. Leave the **Same for all** box selected to ensure that all sides of the anchor have the same padding. Type **10** in the **Margin Top** field, and leave the **Same for all** box selected.

Setting a value for the padding adds some space around the text inside the anchor, which will make it look more like a button. Adding a margin around each anchor ensures they're nicely spaced out and their borders (which you'll add next) butt up against each other.

7 In the **Category** list, select **Border**. Deselect all the **Same for all** boxes, and choose **solid** in the **Style Top** and **Style Bottom** pop-up menus. Type **1px** in the **Width Top** and **Width Bottom** fields. Type **#CED2B6** in the **Color Top** and **Color Bottom** fields. Click **OK** to add the rule to your document.

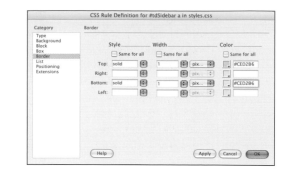

The border settings add a top and bottom border to each link in the sidebar, which adds some visual separation between the buttons and lets the user know where the **hot spots** are (where they're able to click).

When the first rule is complete, the buttons in the sidebar look fantastic. Each of the links is surrounded by a dotted line because Dreamweaver CS3 now sees them as block-level elements. When you preview the page in your browser (almost there, I promise), you won't see the dotted line around the links.

8 In the **CSS Styles** panel, click the **New CSS Rule** button. In the **New CSS Rule** dialog box, select **Advanced** in the **Selector Type** section. Type **#tdSidebar a:hover** in the **Selector** field. Make sure the **Define in** field is set to **styles.css**. Click **OK**.

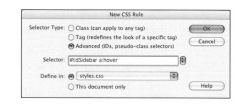

This rule, which includes the :hover pseudo-class, will change the background color of the links when the user hovers the cursor over the link.

9 In the **CSS Rule Definition** dialog box, select **Background** in the **Category** list. Type **#FBFCF9** in the **Background color** field. Click **OK**.

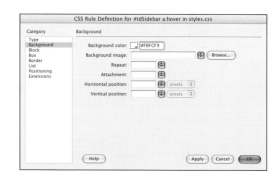

10 Press **F12** (Windows) or **Opt+F12** (Mac) to preview the page in your browser, and when prompted, save all the necessary documents. Position your cursor over each of the links, and you'll see the background color change for each link. (You may have to click the **Refresh** or **Reload** button in your browser to see the changes.)

That's all there is to CSS rollovers. The process is simple, but the payback is amazing. You can create complicated navigation without using a single image, which cuts down on bandwidth and page load time and also makes your pages much easier to maintain. If you decide to add a new link or change the text of a link, or even change the background color of the mouseover effect, there's no need to create or edit image files.

TIP:

Ask the SelectOracle

One of the most confusing parts of working with CSS is figuring out what those darned selectors actually mean. Well, the easiest way is to simply ask the SelectOracle. You can type any number of selectors or type the full URL (**U**niform **R**esource **L**ocator) to a CSS file online into the SelectOracle, and it will give you a plain English (or Spanish) description of exactly what that selector matches.

You can find the SelectOracle at **http://gallery.theopalgroup.com/selectoracle/**. It's the first place to turn when you're looking at a site that's doing something you don't quite understand or when you need to write a particularly complex rule and can't seem to get it right on your own.

I covered a lot of material in this chapter, and I hope I've stretched your brain a bit. You should now have a pretty good understanding of how to apply styles to your pages and how to work with the powerful CSS Styles panel. In the next chapter, you'll expand your CSS knowledge and learn how to do more with the typography of your site.

Again, multiply that by 20 pages in a site, and you have a couple of hours of work ahead of you manually changing **<font>** tags, double-checking to make sure everything is correct, and generally working up an ulcer. Imagine several clients with a penchant for changing their minds, and you'll soon be at the funny farm.

Let's look at the same problem, but let's solve it with CSS. Here's our XHTML code:

```
<p>This is a paragraph full of text.</p>
<p>This is another paragraph full of text.</p>
```

First, notice the code is much easier to read than the code samples shown previously with the **<font>** tag. It's not cluttered up with display information, but it also doesn't have any formatting. You can add that formatting by creating a new CSS rule that redefines how all **<p>** tags should be rendered by the browser. Here's what the code looks like:

```
<style type="text/css">
p {
    font-family: Verdana, Arial, Helvetica,
sans-serif;
}
</style>
<p>This is a paragraph full of text.</p>
<p>This is another paragraph full of text.</p>
```

As you can see, this code sample is much easier to read than the **<font>** mess you saw first. Now if your client with the commitment problem comes back with the same request, "Make it Georgia and red!"—no problem, just change that one rule:

```
<style type="text/css">
p {
    font-family: Georgia, "Times New Roman",
Times, serif;
    color: #FF0000;
}
</style>
<p>This is a paragraph full of text.</p>
<p>This is another paragraph full of text.</p>
```

As you can see, that single change modified the font for every **<p>** tag on the entire page. If that style declaration were in an external file attached to every page in your site (which you learned about in the previous chapter), you'd have to change only the font and color for **<p>** tags in *one* spot. Think of all the money you'd save on antacids!

Using Valid XHTML Typographic Elements

With all the hubbub surrounding the use (or mis-use) of the **<font>** tag combined with all kinds of conflicting information on the Web, I figure it's a good idea to present the following chart with some of the more common XHTML 1.0 elements relating to Web typography. The purpose of this chart is to identify the XHTML elements relating specifically to typography, not to list all the elements that will work in modern and older browsers. These elements identify the structure of the text on the page, though some browsers will apply some default formatting to the elements. By using only these XHTML elements to control the type in your pages, you will ensure that your pages are XHTML compliant and that you truly separate the structure of your page from its presentation.

XHTML 1.0 Typographic Elements	
XHTML Element	**Description**
<p>	The paragraph tag defines paragraphs on a Web page. You will get to work with the paragraph tag in Exercise 1 of this chapter.
<h1> through **<h6>**	The heading tags define various levels of importance on a page and have a range from 1 to 6, with 1 being the most important. You will learn more about heading elements in the "The Importance of Headings" sidebar later in this chapter.
<ul>	The unordered list tag creates lists with bullets (or other characters). You will get to work with lists in Exercise 5.
<ol>	The ordered list tag creates lists with numbers (or other characters) that follow an ascending order. You will get to work with lists in Exercise 5.
<li>	The list item tag defines items within an ordered or unordered list.
<dl>	The definition list tag identifies a list of words that are being defined, much like you would find in an ordinary dictionary.
<dt>	The definition term tag identifies a word that is going to be defined on a page. This is similar to looking up a specific word in a dictionary.
<dd>	The define definition tag identifies text that is being used to define the word within a definition term element. This would be similar to identifying the definition in a dictionary.
<hr />	The horizontal rule tag adds a horizontal divider on a page.
<pre>	The preformatted tag adds text to a page that maintains the exact formatting applied in **Code** view. Text within this tag can contain as many spaces or tabs as desired and is typically formatted using a monospaced font, such as Courier.

continues on next page

XHTML 1.0 Typographic Elements *(continued)*	
XHTML Element	**Description**
`<em>`	The emphasis tag adds importance to text on a page. Most browsers render text wrapped with `<em>` tags as italic by default. Although this sounds like it's affecting presentation, it's really identifying text that will be read with emphasis by screen reader programs for those who are sight-impaired.
`<strong>`	The strong element adds importance to text on a page. Most browsers make text wrapped with `<strong>` tags bold by default.

Please remember that this chart is not complete and represents only the XHTML 1.0 elements you will encounter most often. For a complete listing of all valid XHTML 1.0 elements, please visit the following links:

XHTML 1.0—Transitional:
www.w3.org/TR/xhtml1/DTD/xhtml1-transitional.dtd

W3 Schools:
www.w3schools.com/xhtml/xhtml_reference.asp

XHTML 1.0—Frameset:
www.w3.org/TR/xhtml1/DTD/xhtml1-frameset.dtd

XHTML 1.0—Strict:
www.w3.org/TR/xhtml1/DTD/xhtml1-strict.dtd

1 | Formatting Text with the Property Inspector

In this exercise, you will learn how to format text by modifying the typeface, size, and color. When you change font styling with the **Property inspector**, Dreamweaver CS3 writes a series of styles for you so you don't have to define any CSS styles. As you will see, creating and formatting text with Dreamweaver CS3 is just as easy as working with any word processing application.

---

1 If you haven't already done so, copy the **chap_07** folder from the **Dreamweaver HOT CD-ROM** to your desktop. Define your site as **Chapter 7** using the **chap_07** folder as the local root folder. Make sure the **Files** panel is open. If it's not, choose **Window > Files**.

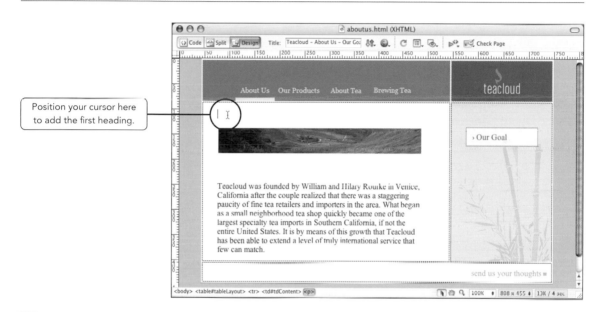

Position your cursor here to add the first heading.

2 In the **Files** panel, double-click **aboutus.html** to open it. Position your cursor above the image in the center of the page, and type **About Us: Our Goal**.

This is a version of the About Us page used throughout this book, but it's missing a few key pieces of text, which you'll add throughout this exercise.

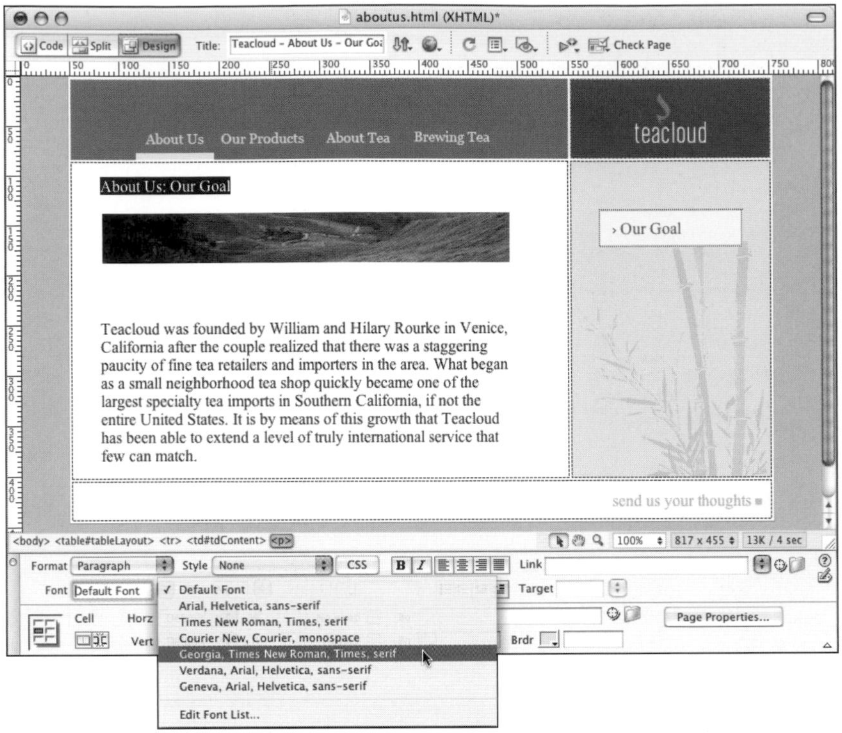

3 Click and drag to select the text you just typed. In the **Property inspector**, choose **Georgia, Times New Roman, Times, serif** in the **Font** pop-up menu.

Unless you have the Georgia font installed on your computer, you probably didn't notice any change at all, because the font was already styled with Times New Roman to start.

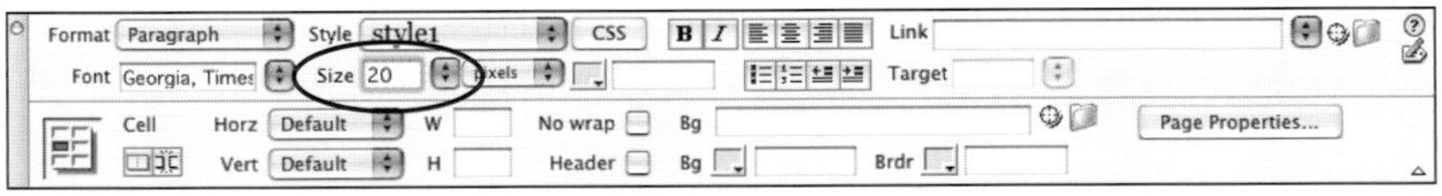

4 With the text still selected, type **20** in the **Size** field. The pop-up menu next to **Size** will then show **pixels**, which means the text is set to be 20 pixels tall. Press **Enter** (Windows) or **Return** (Mac) to commit your changes.

5 With the text *still* selected, type **#68887C** in the **Color** field, and then switch to **Code** view.

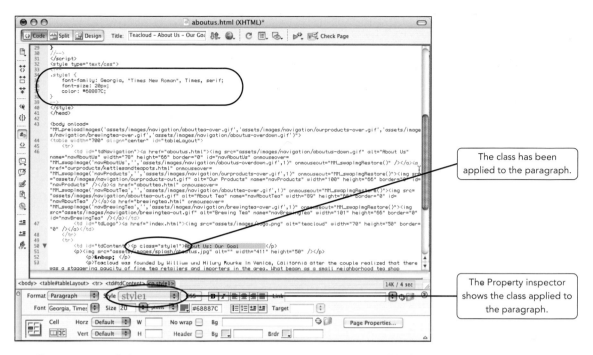

The class has been applied to the paragraph.

The Property inspector shows the class applied to the paragraph.

You'll notice several changes to your page. First, Dreamweaver CS3 added a **<style>** tag with a class defining the formatting you just specified. That class has also been applied to the **<p>** tag surrounding the *About Us: Our Goal* text. And finally, the Property inspector now shows style1 has been applied to the text.

6 Switch back to **Design** view. This text seems to hold some special meaning to this page—it's the first item on the page, and it's larger than the remaining text in order to stand out. This text seems like a good candidate for a heading. With your cursor anywhere in the block of text, choose **Heading 1** in the **Format** pop-up menu in the **Property inspector**.

The text is now tagged with an **<h1>** tag instead of a **<p>** tag, indicating the text is a heading, not just regular paragraph text.

NOTE:

The Importance of Headings

In the previous step, you formatted some text using headings. The tags look like this: **<h1>**. They range from 1 to 6 and change the size of the text they're wrapped around. Most browsers will display them in a decreasing font size as the numbers get larger. (An **<h1>** tag is rendered larger than an **<h2>**, and so on.)

Headings don't just make text larger; they also serve an important and useful purpose: giving your pages *structure*, which accomplishes several goals:

- **Readability:** Headings make the page easier to read by breaking content into smaller, digestible pieces. People reading online are more likely to skim through a long page of text than to read an entire article line by line. Providing occasional headings makes it easier for viewers to get right to the text they want.

- **Accessibility:** If sight-impaired users access your Web page, they might not "see" your Web page but will instead have a reading device "read" it aloud. Screen readers can use heading tags to make it much easier for visually impaired people to navigate through a Web page. You might not imagine that your site has much of a sight-impaired audience and perhaps do not think this information applies to your site design strategy. In many cases, however, making your site accessible is not an option but a requirement—especially if you work for a company or organization that must meet Section 508 accessibility standards (**www.section508.gov**).

- **Findability:** (OK, that's not really a word, but you know what I mean.) Search engines love headings because they represent text of some increased importance. If something is a heading, it must be relevant to what immediately follows it, so search engines will give more weight to text in a heading than they will to text in the rest of a document. So, make your headings useful and relevant, and the search engines will love you.

My advice is to use heading tags instead of increased font sizes for headlines. Give your page structure in order to make it meaningful.

---

7 By default, heading tags are bold, but for the Teacloud layout, this particular heading shouldn't be. If the **CSS Styles** panel isn't already open, choose **Window > CSS Styles** to open it, and make sure the **All** mode radio button is selected. Here you can see both the attached external style sheet (**styles.css**) and the internal style sheet you just created containing **.style1**. Collapse **styles.css**, and expand **<style>**.

If you need a quick refresher on the CSS Styles panel, review the section called "Using the CSS Styles Panel" on page 119 in Chapter 6, *"Working with Cascading Style Sheets."*

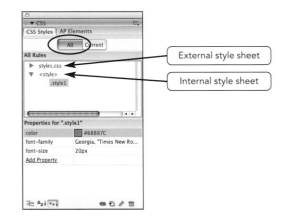

External style sheet

Internal style sheet

8 With **.style1** selected, click the **Edit Style** button. The **CSS Rule Definition** dialog box appears.

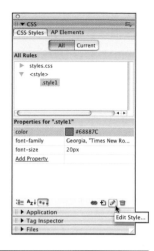

9 Choose **normal** in the **Weight** pop-up menu, and click **OK**.

You just changed the style definition for the class applied to the **<h1>** tag.

What you've just done is technically all right, but anytime you want an **<h1>** tag to look like the one you just set up, you need to apply the **style1** class to it. If you have 50 **<h1>** tags in your site, you need to apply the class to every single one of them. It's far better to use a type selector to redefine how all the **<h1>** tags are displayed; you just have to update the type selector, and all 50 **<h1>** tags will update automatically. Using a type selector in this case is far more efficient.

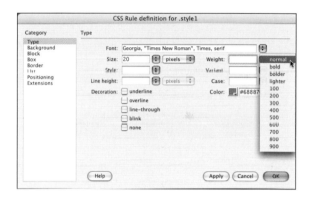

10 The only way to change a CSS selector from one type to another is to switch to **Code** view and change it manually. In the **Document** toolbar, click the **Code** button to switch to **Code** view.

11 Scroll up to line 34 (or thereabouts), and find the **.style1** CSS rule. Highlight the text **.style1**, press **Delete** to remove the selector, and then type **h1** in its place.

When you're finished, the CSS rule should look like the code shown in the illustration here.

Replace the .style1 class with an h1 type selector.

```
30    //-
31    </script>
32    <style type="text/css">
33    <!--
34    h1 {
35        font-family: Georgia, "Times New Roman", Times, serif;
36        font-size: 20px;
37        color: #68887C;
38        font-weight: normal;
39    }
40    -->
41    </style>
42    </head>
```

12 Switch back to **Design** view. Notice the text looks the same. The rule still applies to the **<h1>**. It's just using a type selector instead of a class selector. Now you can remove the class. Place your cursor anywhere in the **<h1>** tag, and choose **None** in the **Style** pop-up menu in the **Property inspector**. (It's possible that **None** may already be selected, in which case you don't need to perform this step.)

13 Place your cursor in the blank space below the image on the page, and type the eternal question on everyone's mind: **What Would the World Do Without Tea?**

14 With your cursor still in that paragraph, press **Ctrl+2** (Windows) or **Cmd+2** (Mac) to wrap the text in an **<h2>** tag instead of a **<p>** tag.

That makes the text a little too big for this design. You'll fix this with a style.

15 In the **CSS Styles** panel, click the **New CSS Rule** button. In the **New CSS Rule** dialog box, select **Tag** for **Selector Type**, and type **h2** in the **Tag** field. You'll add this new style to the attached external style sheet, so make sure **styles.css** is selected in the **Define in** list, and click **OK**.

16 In the **Type** category of the **CSS Rule Definition** dialog box, set **Size** to **11 pixels**, choose **bold** in the **Weight** pop-up menu, and type **#949D87** in the **Color** field. Click **OK** to add the style to **styles.css**.

You're almost there. The last task to get all the type correct is to redefine the font family for the body of the document. The **<h2>** tag you created and the paragraph below it don't look great in the default serif font. Notice styles.css has also been opened for you since changes have been made to the file.

17 In the **CSS Styles** panel, click the **New CSS Rule** button. In the **New CSS Rule** dialog box, select **Tag** for **Selector Type**, and type **body** in the **Tag** field. Make sure **styles.css** is selected in the **Define in** list, and click **OK**.

Redefining the style of the **<body>** tag affects everything in the entire document. This is a great way to set some default styles for every element on the page; then you need to code only for the *exceptions*, such as changing the font face for the **<h1>** tag or the font size of the **<h2>** tag.

18 In the **CSS Rule Definition** dialog box, choose **Verdana, Arial, Helvetica, sans-serif** in the **Font** list, and set **Size** to **11 pixels**. Click **OK** to add the new rule.

The page is definitely looking better. However, the page doesn't have quite enough white space, so things still look cramped. In the next exercise, you'll learn how to use margins, padding, and line height to improve the readability of your pages.

19 Save your changes, and keep **aboutus.html** open for the next exercise.

This exercise showed you how to use the Property inspector to apply font settings to the text on your page and how to define the default font style for the entire document the "right" way. Unfortunately, the Property inspector has the tendency to create class-happy pages, which makes your projects harder to manage in the long term, so throughout the rest of this chapter you'll be using the CSS Styles panel to create your styles.

What Measurement Should You Use?

If you've played with the **CSS Rule Definition** dialog box at all, you probably noticed you can use a few different units of measurement for sizing text, some of which you'll use on a daily basis and others of which you'll probably never touch in your design career. The following chart describes each of the measurement units:

CSS Measurement Units	
Measurement Unit	**Description**
Screen measurements	
pixels	This refers to the actual pixels of the device viewing the content. If a font size is set to 12 pixels, its height will be 12 pixels on the device viewing the content. Pixel measurements are the most reliable for getting consistent sizes between different operating systems and devices.
ems	The em size is a relative measurement, which means it can change based on the context in which it's used. One em is equal to the current size of the text. If you set a font to **1.5** ems, the font will be 1.5 times its default size, whether that's generated by another CSS rule or the browser default.
exs	The exs measurement is similar to the em, but its height is based on the height of the lowercase x in the current font. I've never had a use for this measurement.
%	Percentage measurements will render the same as em measurements. If you set a font size to **150%**, it will be rendered 1.5 times its default size, whether that's generated by another CSS rule or the browser default.
Print measurements	
points	Point measurements are used for printing, and each point is equal to 1/72 of an inch.
in, cm, mm	You can also size print content by inches, centimeters, and millimeters.
picas	A pica is equal to 12 points.

Well, now that you know what the different CSS measurements are, which one should you use? That depends completely on what you're after as a designer. Pixel measurements give you the most control over how your text will appear, but if you're serving your site to a Windows majority using Internet Explorer, you're taking away some of their choices. If your site has font sizes set in pixels, it's impossible for a Web user to resize the text on your page. Most designers' initial reaction to that is "Great! I don't want them destroying my layout by resizing the text anyway." Unfortunately, many people have pretty bad eyesight, and some sites are simply unusable if the font is too small, so allowing users to increase the font size helps them get the information they need. All other browsers I'm aware of allow a user to resize the text regardless of the font size used, but Internet Explorer is still the majority.

So, what measurements do you use? As a general rule, you might consider setting a default font size for the body of your document in ems and then size everything based on that default measurement. So, the rule for the body of the document would be something like this:

```
body {
   font-size: 0.8em;
}
```

That rule sets all the text on the entire page to 0.8 em. Then all further measurements are based on that measure, so an **h1** would be styled like this:

```
h1{
   font-size: 1.5em;
}
```

Using ems allows you to have fine control over your sizes but still lets your visitors resize their text. To avoid confusion and skip the whole "which to use" discussion, you'll primarily use pixels to size the text throughout this book. As you become more familiar with CSS and start developing your own development style, pick what works best for you and your visitors.

EXERCISE

2 | Managing White Space with Margins, Padding, and Line Height

If I could give you only one piece of advice for styling your text, it's "use white space." The Web is full of text, and much of the time it isn't very easy on the eyes. Reading text on a screen is far more difficult than reading it on paper, so you should take a tip from professional print designers and use lots of white space in order to make your pages easier to read, especially if you're presenting large blocks of text. In this exercise, you'll learn how to manage the white space of your text using margins, padding, and line height.

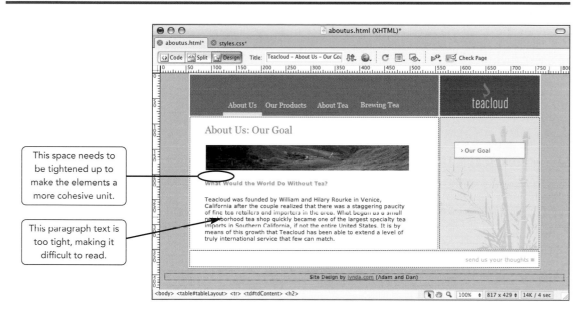

1 You should still have the **aboutus.html** file from Exercise 1 open. If not, complete Exercise 1, and then return to this exercise.

In this exercise, you'll tighten up the space around the headings and create more space between the text in the paragraphs.

2 The first task is to adjust the line height of the paragraphs on the page. In the **CSS Styles** panel, click the **New CSS Rule** button to create a new rule.

3 In the **New CSS Rule** dialog box, select **Tag** for **Selector Type**, type **p** in the **Tag** field, and click **OK**.

4 In the **Type** category of the **CSS Rule Definition** dialog box, set **Line height** to **1.7 ems**, and click **OK** to add the new rule.

The line height makes an immediate difference in the display of the page. The text in the paragraph now has more space between the lines of text, which makes it easier for a reader to scan from line to line without getting lost.

Now it's time to tighten up the space between the **<h1>** tag and the image immediately following it by changing the margins on the **<h1>** tag.

5 In the **CSS Styles** panel, select the **h1** rule, and click the **Edit Style** button to open the **CSS Rule Definition** dialog box.

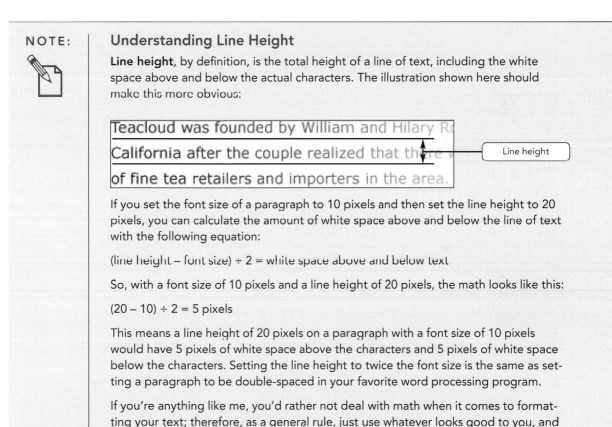

NOTE:

Understanding Line Height

Line height, by definition, is the total height of a line of text, including the white space above and below the actual characters. The illustration shown here should make this more obvious:

If you set the font size of a paragraph to 10 pixels and then set the line height to 20 pixels, you can calculate the amount of white space above and below the line of text with the following equation:

(line height – font size) ÷ 2 = white space above and below text

So, with a font size of 10 pixels and a line height of 20 pixels, the math looks like this:

(20 – 10) ÷ 2 = 5 pixels

This means a line height of 20 pixels on a paragraph with a font size of 10 pixels would have 5 pixels of white space above the characters and 5 pixels of white space below the characters. Setting the line height to twice the font size is the same as setting a paragraph to be double-spaced in your favorite word processing program.

If you're anything like me, you'd rather not deal with math when it comes to formatting your text; therefore, as a general rule, just use whatever looks good to you, and skip the math altogether. The mathematical rules simply make it a little easier to understand what's happening when you format your sites.

6 In the **CSS Rule Definition** dialog box, select **Box** in the **Category** list. You want to change only the space below the **<h1>** tag, so deselect the **Same for all** check box in the **Margin** section, and set **Bottom** to **12 pixels**. Click **OK** to apply the rule.

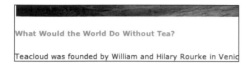

The last change made to the h1 rule didn't affect the display of the document at all. The reason that nothing changed is because of the way margins are calculated.

NOTE:

Understanding How Margins Are Calculated

The last change you made to the **h1** rule didn't affect the display of the document because of the way margins are calculated. Every element on the page has a margin, and text elements (headings and paragraphs) have built-in margins. Two adjacent elements share their margins, and the larger of the two margins is used to separate the two elements. Take the **<h1>** tag on the page and the following image (which is in a **<p>** tag) as an example:

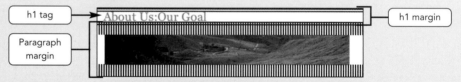

The **<h1>** tag has 12 pixels of bottom margin, shown by the horizontal lines above and below it. The paragraph containing the image has a default margin of about 20 pixels, shown by the vertical lines, which is roughly twice the font size of the paragraph. I say "about 20 pixels" because this is the browser default margin that's being drawn, which can be quite different between browsers. When the browser decides how far to space the two elements apart, it **collapses** the margins, placing them on top of each other so that the space between the two elements is equal to the *larger* of the two margins. In the page you're working on, the larger margin on the **<p>** tag is the one that's honored, which is why there was no visual change to the display of the document when you set the bottom margin of the **<h1>** tag to 12 pixels; the **<p>** tag still had a margin greater than 12 pixels, so the **<p>** tag's margin was used to separate the two elements.

7 To finish collapsing the space between the header and paragraph, double-click the **p** rule in the **CSS Styles** panel to edit it. In the **CSS Rule Definition** dialog box, select **Box** in the **Category** list. In the **Margin** section, set **Top** to **0 pixels**. Click **OK** to apply the rule.

Now that the top margin of all **<p>** tags is set to 0, the **<h1>** tag and the following paragraph are spaced 12 pixels apart. Because of the collapsing margin calculations, the browser determines that 12 is greater than 0, so it sets the margin between the two elements to 12 pixels.

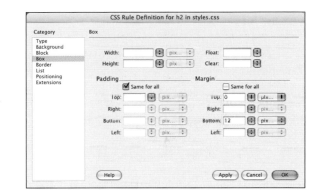

8 To tighten up the space around the **<h2>** tag, double-click the **h2** rule in the **CSS Styles** panel to edit it. In the **CSS Rule Definition** dialog box, select **Box** in the **Category** list. In the **Margin** section, set **Top** to **0 pixels**, and set **Bottom** to **12 pixels**. Click **OK** to apply the rule.

The page is looking pretty good now. The headers are spaced nicely around the image, and the paragraph of text is much easier to read with the line height. The last task is to differentiate the **<h2>** tag by adding a small colored border on the left side of the text. Adding the border will simulate the appearance of a square and will help make the heading stand out from the rest of the text. Sound strange? Follow the next few steps, and you'll see what a useful trick this is!

9 Double-click the **h2** rule in the **CSS Styles** panel again to open the **CSS Rule Definition** dialog box. Select **Border** in the **Category** list, and deselect **Same for all** in the **Style**, **Width**, and **Color** sections. Choose **solid** in the **Left** pop-up menu, and set **Size** to **11 pixels**. Type **#D7DACE** in the **Color** field. When you're finished, make sure your settings match the ones shown in the illustration here. Click **OK** to apply the rule.

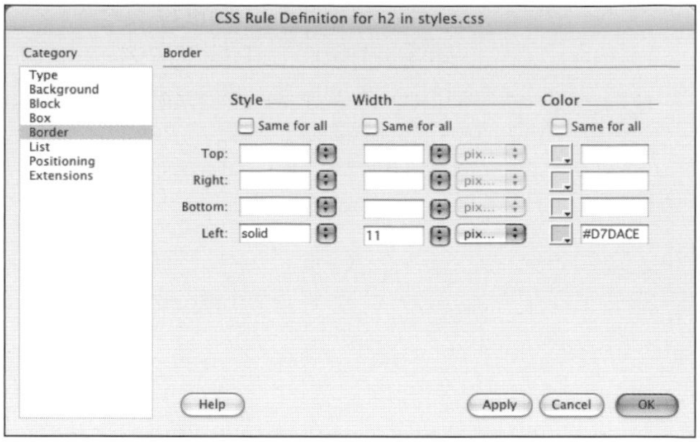

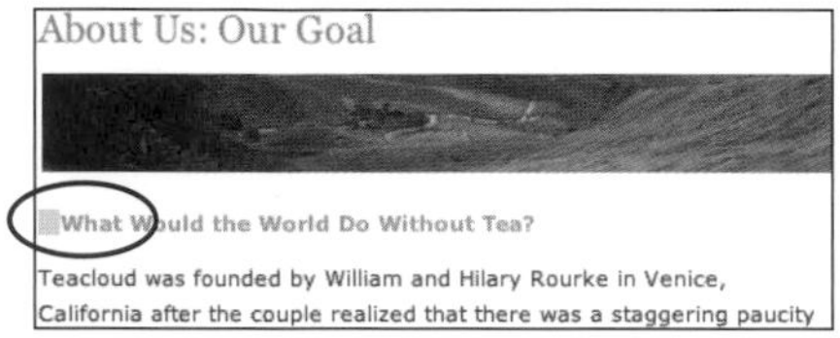

The **<h2>** now has a border to the left of it, which looks like a square icon. Pretty cool trick, huh? Unfortunately, it's *still* not looking quite right—the border is right up against the first letter of the **<h2>** tag, which makes things a little crowded. Not to worry, you can get rid of the crowding in the **<h2>** tag by adding some padding.

10 Double-click the **h2** rule in the **Styles** panel one last time, and select **Box** in the **Category** list. Deselect the **Same for all** box in the **Padding** section, and set **Left** to **7 pixels**. Click **OK** to apply the rule.

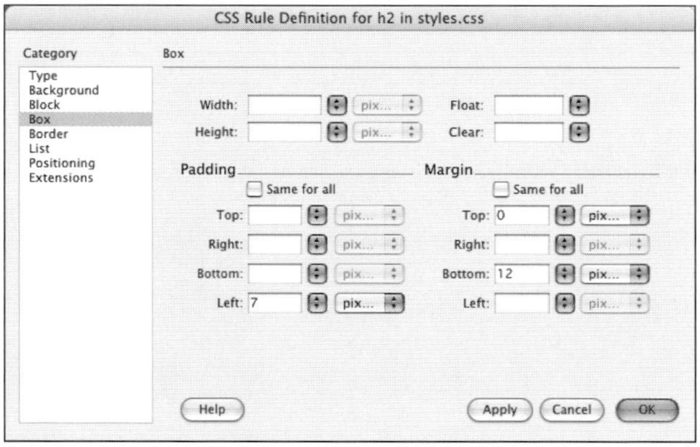

With the 7-pixel padding added, the border on the **<h2>** tag is nicely separated from the text.

Understanding Padding

Margins control the space outside a block of text; **padding** controls the spacing inside a block of text. In the illustration here, you can see the anatomy of a block of text (or as the CSS specification likes to call it, a **box**).

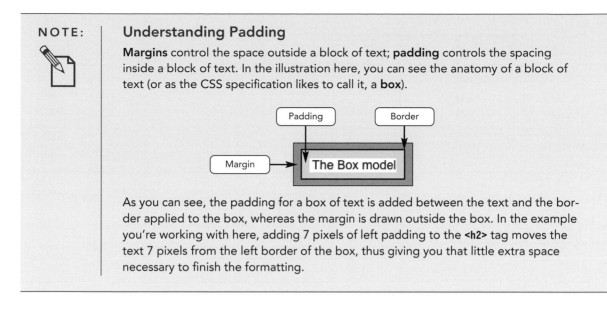

As you can see, the padding for a box of text is added between the text and the border applied to the box, whereas the margin is drawn outside the box. In the example you're working with here, adding 7 pixels of left padding to the **<h2>** tag moves the text 7 pixels from the left border of the box, thus giving you that little extra space necessary to finish the formatting.

11 Save and close **aboutus.html**, as well as **styles.css** if it's open.

In this exercise, you learned how to use line height, margins, and padding to control the white space in your documents. Properly managing your white space can greatly increase the readability (and usability) of your Web sites.

3 | Using Font Lists

Now that you've played with setting font faces, you may be wondering why you're limited by the default font choices Dreamweaver offers. Dreamweaver CS3 offers the most common collection of fonts that users viewing your site will have installed on their computers. In this exercise, you will learn how to add and modify the font lists that come with Dreamweaver CS3. You will learn how to modify what typefaces are in the existing font lists and how to create your own custom font list.

---

1 In the **Files** panel, double-click **fontlists.html** to open it.

This page lists the default font lists provided by Dreamweaver CS3. The last paragraph, however, isn't a standard Dreamweaver CS3 font list. In this exercise, you'll learn how to create this font list.

> fontlists.html (XHTML)
>
> Code · Split · Design   Title: Untitled Document   Check Page
>
> This is the Arial, Helvetica, sans-serif font list
>
> This is the Times New Roman, Times, serif font list
>
> This is the Courier New, Courier, mono font list
>
> This is the Georgia, Times New Roman, Times, serif font list
>
> This is the Verdana, Arial, Helvetica, sans-serif font list
>
> This is the Geneva, Arial, Helvetica, sans-serif font list
>
> This is the Tahoma, Verdana, Arial, Helvetica, sans-serif font list
>
> `<body> <p.style1>`   100% ÷   649 x 318 ÷   2K / 1 sec

NOTE: | ## How Font Lists Work

Font lists are a useful way of ensuring the text on your Web page is viewed the way you intended. When visitors load a Web page, the browser searches for each font in the list until it finds one that is installed. Once the browser finds a font in the list, it will use that font to display the text on the Web page. For example, if you apply the `"Arial, Helvetica, sans-serif"` font list to a piece of text, the browser will try to use Arial first to display text. If your visitor doesn't have Arial installed, the browser will then try to display Helvetica. If the browser cannot find Helvetica, it will display the default sans-serif font on the user's computer. The goal of font lists is to create sets of fonts that have similar structure and characteristics, so the contents of your Web pages appear the same from viewer to viewer.

---

2 Place your cursor anywhere in the document. In the **Property inspector**, choose **Edit Font List** in the **Font** pop-up menu to open the **Edit Font List** dialog box.

The Edit Font List dialog box lets you create and edit existing font lists, which you'll learn how to do in the following steps.

---

3 In the **Available fonts** list (which lists all the fonts installed on your computer), select **Tahoma**, and click the **<<** button to add it to the **Chosen fonts** list.

Note: If you don't have Tahoma installed on your local machine, it won't be in the list. Don't worry if it's not there; just type the font name in the field below the Available fonts list. This field lets you to add fonts that you don't actually have installed on your local machine.

4 In the **Available fonts** list, select **Verdana**, and click the **<<** button to add the font to the **Chosen fonts** list.

NOTE:

Add Them Right the First Time

Unfortunately, there's no easy way to change the order of the fonts in a font list without removing everything and starting over. So, make sure you plan the order in which you're going to add the fonts, or you'll have to start over if you get it wrong.

5 In the **Available fonts** list, select **Arial**, and click the **<<** button to add it to the **Chosen fonts** list.

6 In the **Available fonts** list, select **Helvetica**, and click the **<<** button to add it to the **Chosen fonts** list.

Tip: You can press H to jump to the font names that begin with *H*.

7 Finally, at the bottom of the **Available fonts** list, select **sans-serif**, and click the **<<** button to add it to the **Chosen fonts** list.

8 When you're all done, the **Edit Font List** dialog box should match the illustration shown here. Click **OK** to add the new list to the existing font lists.

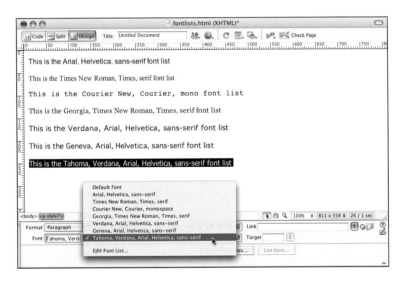

TIP:

Always Provide an Alternative

You should always have a generic font type as the last item in your font list. If users don't have any of the fonts in the list, they'll at least see a font of the type you want. Valid generic font types are as follows: cursive, fantasy, monospace, sans-serif, and serif.

9 Highlight the **This is the Tahoma, Verdana, Arial, Helvetica, sans-serif font list** text in the document. In the **Property inspector**, choose the **Tahoma, Verdana, Arial, Helvetica, sans-serif** font list in the **Font** pop-up menu.

Notice the text automatically changes to reflect the font choice you just made. This exercise gives you an example of how these font lists will display on your computer. What you see might appear differently in other people's browsers, because they might have different fonts installed on their computers than you do, so the second, third, or even fourth font on the list might be displayed instead of the first one.

10 Close **fontlists.html**. You don't need to save your changes.

4 | Aligning Text

In this exercise, you will learn how to align text on the page. You have four options for aligning text: **Left Align**, **Center Align**, **Right Align**, and **Justify**. You have some extra options when you align text next to images, which you will also explore in this exercise.

---

1 In the **Files** panel, double-click **brewingtea.html** to open it.

Notice the text on the page is aligned to the left. This is the default alignment setting for text.

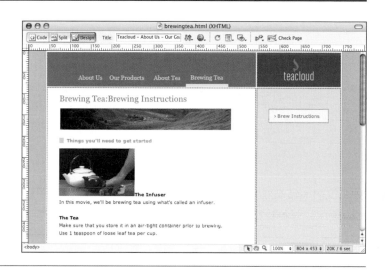

---

2 Click anywhere in the line of text that reads **Brewing Tea: Brewing Instructions**.

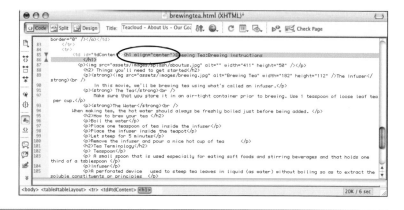

---

3 In the **Property inspector**, click the **Align Center** button to center your text on the page.

Clicking the Align Center button in the Property inspector added the `align` attribute to the `<h1>` tag. Although this is all right for single elements, if you want all `<h1>` tags to be centered, you should edit the **h1** rule in the CSS Styles panel and set the Text Align property to the desired alignment.

4 In the **Property inspector**, click the **Align Right**, **Justified**, and **Align Left** buttons to see how each of them affects the alignment of this line of text.

5 Click the photo of the teapot and the hand reaching for the tea infuser to select it. Take a look at the contents of the **Align** pop-up menu.

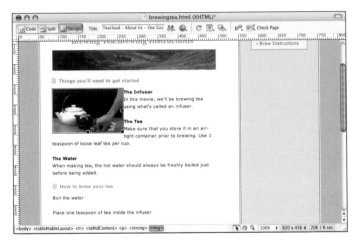

Notice when you select an image to align with type, different alignment options are available in the Property inspector. The alignment options in this menu are exclusively for aligning text next to an image.

6 In the **Property inspector**, choose **Left** in the **Align** pop-up menu.

Notice the text moves to the top-right of the image. The image has been "floated" to the left, so the text flows along the right side of the image.

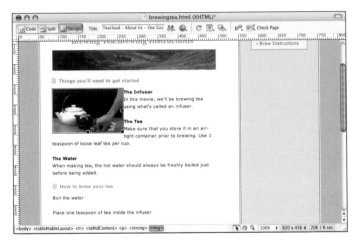

7 With the image still selected, choose **Right** in the **Align** pop-up menu.

Now that the image is aligned to the right, the text flows nicely down the left side of the image. This lets you make better use of the space on your page and add some visual interest to your text. Just remember the text will be on the opposite side of the image's alignment. This means if you align an image to the left, the text will flow to the right; if you align an image to the right, the text will flow to the left.

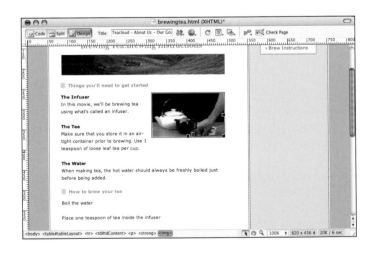

Aligning Text and Images

Dreamweaver CS3 offers many alignment options for text and images. The following chart defines all the alignment terms:

XHTML Text and Image Alignment Options	
Alignment	**Description**
Default	Varies between browsers but usually uses **Bottom** alignment as the default
Baseline	Aligns the baseline of the text to the bottom of the image
Bottom	Aligns the baseline of the text to the bottom of the image (same as **Baseline**)
Absolute Bottom	Aligns text, including descenders (letters such as *g* and *j*), to the bottom of the image
Top	Aligns the image to the tallest part of the object (image or text)
TextTop	Aligns the image with the tallest character in the line of text
Middle	Aligns the baseline of the text to the middle of the image
Absolute Middle	Aligns the middle of the text to the middle of the image
Left	Left-aligns the image and wraps text to the right
Right	Right-aligns the image and wraps text to the left

8 Save **brewingtea.html**, and leave it open for the next exercise.

Chapter 7 : **Working with Typography** | **177**

Using Ordered, Unordered, and Definition Lists

In this exercise, you will learn how to create a variety of lists—an ordered list, an unordered list, and a definition list. You can generate these lists from existing text or from scratch, and as a general rule they behave just like a list in a word processing application.

---

1 You should still have the **brewingtea.html** file from Exercise 4 open. If not, complete Exercise 4, and then return to this exercise.

---

2 Click and drag to highlight the text beneath the **Things you'll need...** heading.

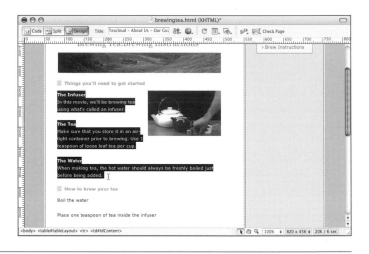

---

3 In the **Property inspector**, click the **Unordered List** button.

You just created an unordered list. Unordered lists are great for items that don't require a specific order.

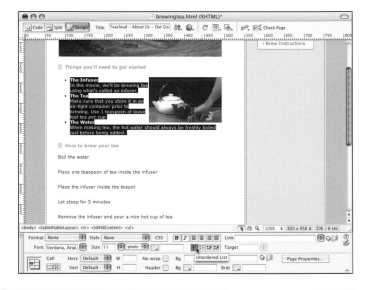

---

4 Click and drag to highlight the text beneath the **How to brew...** heading.

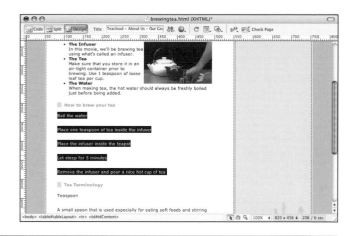

5 Choose **Text > List > Ordered List**, or click the **Ordered List** button in the **Property inspector**.

You just created an ordered list using numbers to number each item in the list. Use ordered lists when your list requires a specific order. In this case, users should follow the steps in numerical order to make a tasty cup of tea.

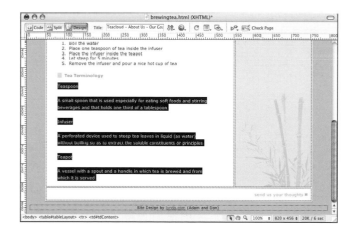

6 Click and drag to highlight the text beneath the **Tea Terminology** heading.

7 Choose **Text > List > Definition List**.

You just created a definition list. Definition lists are great for giving people more information about a particular term. The use of a definition list makes it obvious which text goes with which item.

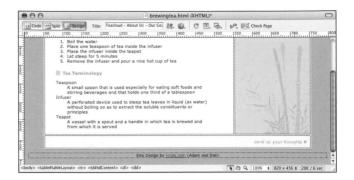

NOTE:

What's in a List?

The previous steps were pretty short and simple. However, what goes on behind the scenes is a bit more involved. When you define a list, Dreamweaver CS3 wraps each selection in a tag that defines the list and then wraps each item in the list with tags showing that they're each a member of the list. Take the **How to brew your tea** list as an example. Before you defined it as an ordered list, the code looked like this:

```
<p>Boil the water</p>
<p>Place one teaspoon of tea inside the infuser</p>
<p>Place the infuser inside the teapot</p>
<p>Let steep for 5 minutes</p>
<p>Remove the infuser and pour a nice hot cup of tea</p>
```

After you change it to an ordered list, the code looks like this:

```
<ol>
    <li>Boil the water</li>
    <li>Place one teaspoon of tea inside the infuser</li>
    <li>Place the infuser inside the teapot</li>
    <li>Let steep for 5 minutes</li>
    <li>Remove the infuser and pour a nice hot cup of tea </li>
</ol>
```

In this code, the **<ol>** tag tells the browser that what's inside those **<ol>** tags is in fact a list. Each item in the list is wrapped with an **<li>** tag, which defines it as a list item.

The benefit of this structure is that if you want to change the **How to brew your tea** list to an unordered list, which shows bullets instead of numbers, you simply change the **<ol>** tag to a **<ul>** tag, and it will automatically change the unordered list to an ordered list.

---

8 Save and close **brewingtea.html**.

In this exercise, you learned how to create the most basic of lists. Lists are an *incredibly* powerful way of organizing information, and the brief overview you've received here doesn't really do them justice. Because they're so powerful, they can also be quite difficult to wrap your head around. If you'd like, do some of your own research to learn more about how to use host lists. For more information, check out Listamatic at http://css.maxdesign.com.au/listamatic/.

What Is Flash Text?

It's pretty hard to be involved in Web design today and not hear the word *Flash*. It has become widely adopted in the Web design industry as an alternative or adjunct to XHTML formatting. Adobe Flash CS3 is a vector-based drawing, animation, interactivity, and application development program. You can use it to create something as simple as a button for a Web page or as complex as an entire video game that can be played on the Web. Flash uses a proprietary file format called SWF (pronounced "swiff"). Flash content that gets uploaded to the Web always ends in the **.swf** suffix.

To view Flash content on the Web, you must have the Flash Player installed in your browser. If you don't have this plug-in, you can download it for free at **www.adobe.com/products/flashplayer/**, though the majority of browsers have some version of Flash already installed.

The Flash Text feature in Dreamweaver CS3 lets you create text and text rollovers for your Web pages, using any font on your system, in the SWF file format. Flash Text is a great feature for creating text rollovers and small lines of text, such as headlines for your body text, because it lets you use exactly the font you want without worrying whether visitors viewing the site have that font installed on their computers. As a result, you can have full control over the appearance of the text. Unfortunately, Flash Text is not searchable by search engines, and as a result, you should not use it for large bodies of text. Before you move on to the next exercise and learn the nuances of Flash Text, here's a handy chart outlining some of the pros and cons of this feature:

Using Flash Text

Pros	Explanation
Font integrity	With Flash Text, you can use any font installed on your system, and the visitors to your page don't need to have that font installed, as they do with regular XHTML text. This feature gives you much more flexibility when you are designing your pages.
Text rollovers	Creating text rollovers usually requires you to use a separate image-editing program to create the necessary images. With Flash Text, you can create text rollovers without ever leaving Dreamweaver CS3.

Cons	Explanation
Plug-in required	To be viewed properly, all Flash content on the Web requires a plug-in. Flash Text is no different and requires that the Flash plug-in be installed in the browser.
Not accessible	Flash, as a general rule, is not accessible. Individuals with disabilities have a hard time dealing with Flash content because browsers don't know what's inside Flash files, so they can't let users know where buttons and text exist. Recent versions of Flash have improved this problem, but there's still a long way to go. If you're concerned about accessibility, you should use Flash Text only for items that aren't integral to the functionality of your site.

Creating Flash Text

In this exercise, you'll create Flash Text, which lets you use any font you want without worrying whether the visitors to your site will have it installed on their computers. It also lets you easily create rollovers without using any JavaScript. It's really easy to learn and use—read on and try it out to see what I mean!

---

1 In the **Files** panel, double-click **index.html** to open it.

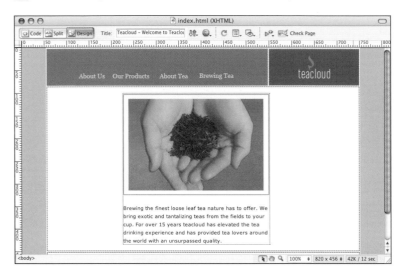

This page is almost identical to the index.html files in other exercises, except it's missing the *Welcome to teacloud* text above the image. You're going to create that text using Flash Text.

---

2 Click the hand image to select it, and press the **left arrow** key to move the cursor before the image.

---

3 Choose **Insert > Media > Flash Text** to open the **Insert Flash Text** dialog box.

Note: You can also insert Flash Text using the Media button in the Common group of the Insert bar.

---

4 Choose a font for your text in the **Font** pop-up menu. Type **30** in the **Size** field to set the size of your text in points.

I am using a font called Eurostile. If you don't have Eurostile installed, use whatever font you have available. Just pick something other than the standard fonts you saw in Exercise 3 so you can truly see that you can pick any font you want for Flash Text.

---

5 Click the **color picker**. Position your cursor over the gray background in the navigation bar. Notice the cursor changes to the eyedropper, indicating you can sample color. Click to sample color from the gray area.

> Click to sample the dark navigation background color.

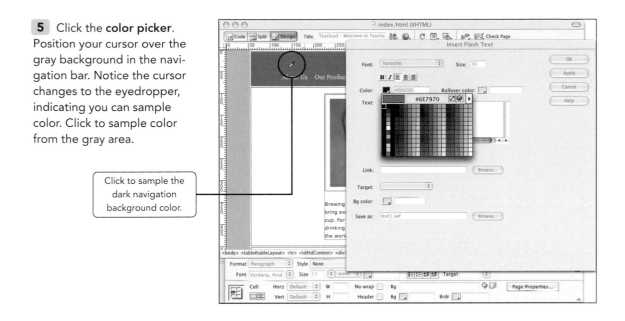

6 Click the **Rollover color picker** box. Position your cursor over the dark gray background behind the **Teacloud** logo. Click to sample color from the dark gray area.

Setting this color will automatically create a rollover effect for the Flash Text.

7 In the **Text** field, type **Welcome to teacloud**.

By default, the Show Font check box is selected, giving you a preview of the text in the font you selected.

Note: This dialog box will not give you a preview of the size you specified; you can see the actual size only in the document itself.

8 Type **#FFFFFF** in the **Bg Color** field to set the background color to white.

9 In the **Save as** field, type **welcome.swf**. Click **OK** to open the **Flash Accessibility Attributes** dialog box.

Insert Flash Text

Font:	Eurostile	Size: 30
	B *I* ≡ ≡ ≡	
Color:	▣ #6E7970	Rollover color: ▣ #474F49
Text:	Welcome to teacloud	
	☑ Show font	
Link:		Browse...
Target:		
Bg color:	▣ #FFFFFF	
Save as:	welcome.swf	Browse...

OK · Apply · Cancel · Help

10 Type **Welcome to teacloud** in the **Title** field, and click **OK**.

At a minimum, you should always add a title to the Flash Text so visitors who don't have the Flash Player installed can see what the Flash Text should be.

Flash Accessibility Attributes

Title: Welcome to teacloud
Access key: [ ] Tab index: [ ]

OK · Cancel · Help

If you don't want to enter this information when inserting objects, change the Accessibility preferences.

When you're finished, your page should match the illustration here.

As you can see, you just successfully added a *Welcome to teacloud* title using Flash Text. Next, you'll learn how to preview the Flash Text.

| **Adobe Dreamweaver CS3** : H·O·T

Flash Text	W 268	File welcome.swf		Edit...	Class None	
	H 26			Reset size		
V space	Quality High	Align Default	Play			
H space	Scale Default (Show ;)	Bg #FFFFFF	Parameters...			

11 With the **Flash Text** selected, click the **Play** button in the **Property inspector**. Move your cursor over the **Flash Text** to preview the rollover effect. Click the **Stop** button to turn off the preview.

12 Press **F12** (Windows) or **Opt+F12** (Mac) to preview your page in a browser. Save all files when prompted. Take a look at the Flash Text. Position your cursor over the text to see the rollover.

Note: If you're using Internet Explorer, you may find that it's set to block Flash content. If this is the case, click Allow Blocked Content.

You should see your *Welcome to teacloud* text in the font you specified. When you move your cursor over the text, it will change to the darker color you specified in the Flash Text dialog box.

13 Return to Dreamweaver CS3. Save and close **index.html**.

TIP:

Preview All Flash

You can quickly and easily way preview all the Flash content on your pages by simply pressing **Ctrl+Alt+Shift+P** (Windows) or **Shift+Opt+Cmd+P** (Mac). You will get an instant preview of all the Flash files on your page.

In this chapter, you learned about the basics of typography. A lot of this was a review from Chapter 6, *"Working with Cascading Style Sheets,"* but you should have picked up some new tips for your text-formatting arsenal, including how to take care of that all-important white space in your documents. In the next chapter, you'll learn how to work with tables, which you've been dabbling with throughout the entire book as you worked through the exercises. Now it's finally time to get serious with them.

8

Working with Tables

For many years, tables have been the de facto way to create the layout for Web pages. Despite never being intended for this purpose, tables control the layout on many Web sites to this day. Tables consist of rows and columns that intersect to create cells and were originally designed to give Web designers a way to display and organize charts and data. The authors of the original HTML (**H**yper**T**ext **M**arkup **L**anguage) specifications who created tables for the Web did not predict developers would use tables to build entire layouts instead of just displaying text and numbers. You'll learn about both uses for tables: a formatting device for data and a layout device for custom positioning of various page elements. Though CSS (**C**ascading **S**tyle **S**heets) offers new (and more semantically correct) ways to lay out your sites, which you'll learn about in Chapter 9, *"Using Layout Tools,"* tables still serve a real need for quick and easy layouts that display well across multiple browsers.

This chapter shows you how to create custom tables, insert rows and columns, manipulate borders, and handle formatting and sorting tasks. You will also learn how to use tables to align and position images. Tables are a critical item in your Web design toolbox, and Adobe Dreamweaver CS3 gives you great control and techniques for mastering them.

What Is a Table?

A table is a highly versatile feature in XHTML (eXtensible HyperText Markup Language). It can be useful for organizing data or positioning page elements. What does a table look like in Dreamweaver CS3? It comprises a combination of XHTML tags.

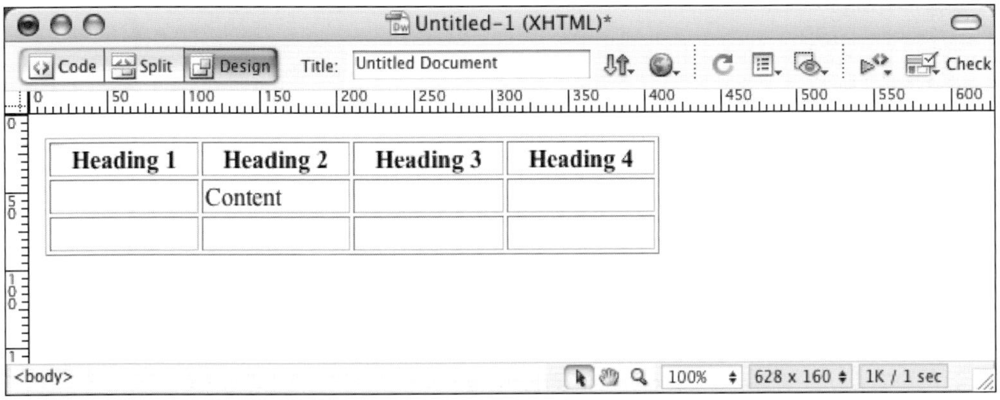

A basic table in Dreamweaver CS3. This table consists of four columns and three rows.

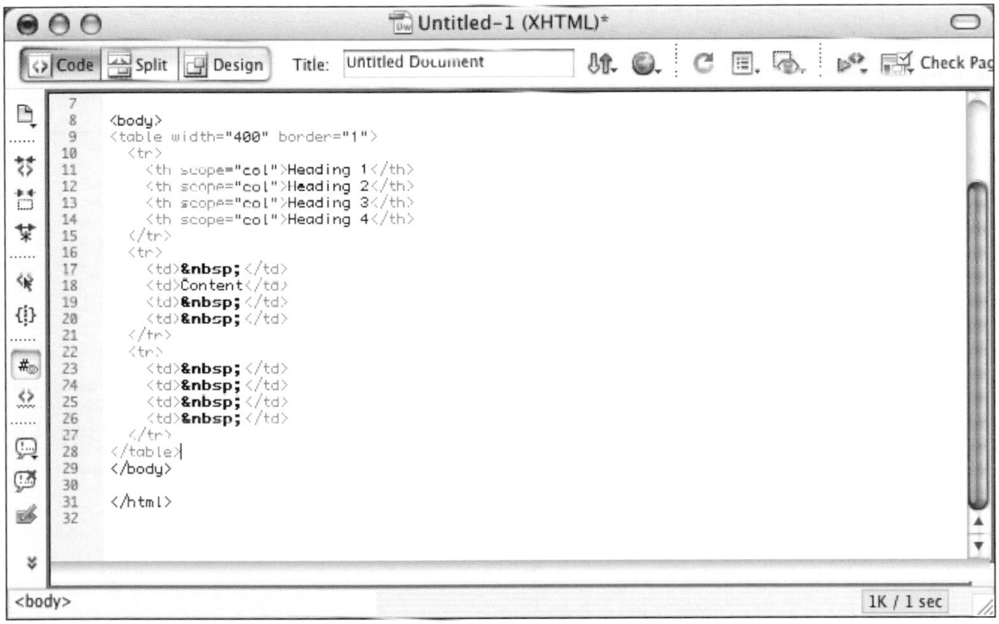

Here's the XHTML code for the table. Tables always begin with a **<table>** tag. The **width** and **border** elements are attributes of the **<table>** tag. The **<tr>** tags define the start and end of each table row, and the **<td>** and **<th>** tags define each table cell.

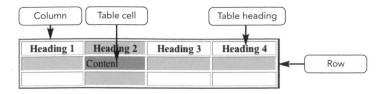

A table contains rows, columns, and cells. Each row in the table is defined by a **<tr>** (**t**able **r**ow) tag. Each **<tr>** tag can have any number of **<td>** (**t**able **d**ata) and **<th>** (**t**able **h**eader) tags, which define the table cells. The browser will line up each of the cells in the table rows in order to create the table columns; you don't have to define table columns with XHTML tags.

The **<th>** tag defines a special kind of table cell: a table header. You should use table headers in the first row of a table to define the contents of that column. Screen readers and other software used by visually impaired visitors can tell the difference between a header and a regular table cell and can give the user more information about the table they're "seeing."

More tags are related to tables than mentioned here, but you won't be using them all in this book. Here's a chart of the most common table tags:

Table Tags	
Tag	**Use**
<table>	The **<table>** tag determines the start and end of a table. You can specify the entire width of the table, whether the table has a border, and the spacing to place between table cells.
<caption>	The **<caption>** tag places a text heading above the table, which labels the table for reference. For instance, a table containing a third-quarter financial report might have a caption of *Q3 Financials*.
<tr>	The **<tr>** tag defines the start and end of a table row.
<th>	The **<th>** tag defines a table header, which acts as a label for a group of table cells, whether they're in a row or a column.
<td>	The **<td>** tag defines a standard table cell.

1 | Creating and Adding Content to a Table

What better way to get started with tables than by creating one from scratch? This exercise shows you how to create and add data to a table from scratch. You will learn to work with a combination of the **Insert Table** object, the **Modify > Table** menu, and the **Property inspector**. You'll also build a simple listing table for the Teacloud teapot collection.

---

1 If you haven't already done so, copy the **chap_08** folder from the **Dreamweaver HOT CD-ROM** to your desktop. Define your site as **Chapter 8** using the **chap_08** folder as the local root folder. Make sure the **Files** panel is open. If it's not, choose **Window > Files**.

---

2 In the **Files** panel, **right-click** the local root folder, and choose **New File** in the contextual menu to create a new document. Save it as **teapots.html**. In the **Files** panel, double-click the file you just created to open it. Set the title of the document by typing **Teacloud Teapots** in the **Title** field of the **Document** toolbar. Lastly, choose **View > Visual Aids**, and make sure **Table Widths** is selected.

3 In the **Common** group of the **Insert** bar, click the **Table** button or choose **Insert > Table** to open the **Table** dialog box.

Using the Table dialog box, you can create and format a table exactly how you want it from the beginning. The most important sections are Table size and Header, which control how many rows and columns the table has, how wide it is, how thick the borders are, how table cell spacing is handled, and which rows or columns contain `<th>` tags. The Accessibility section lets you add a caption for the table, as well as a complete summary of what the table contains (which is not displayed in the browser). You'll certainly become more familiar with this dialog box as you work with tables more and more.

The table you'll create in this exercise will have information for three products, including a photo, a description, and a price, so you need four rows (don't forget the header row) and three columns.

4 Type **4** in the **Rows** field, type **3** in the **Columns** field, click **Top** in the **Headers** section, and type **Teacloud Teapots** in the **Caption** field. Click **OK** to create the table using the criteria you specified.

Your first exposure to tables doesn't look very exciting, does it? When you completed the Table dialog box, you didn't supply any value for the width of the table, so Dreamweaver CS3 collapses the table to the smallest size necessary to fit its contents. Since this table doesn't yet have any contents, it has been collapsed. The dotted lines you see around each cell are just table border guides; they won't be visible in a browser.

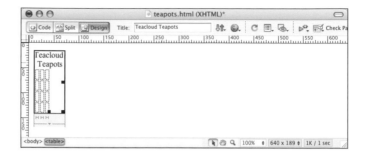

5 To make the table easier to work with, press **F6** or choose **View > Table Mode > Expanded Tables Mode**. The **Getting Started in Expanded Tables Mode** dialog box will appear if this is the first time you've used this mode. Select the **Don't show me this message again** check box, and click **OK**.

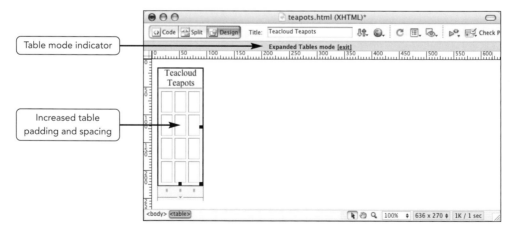

Expanded Tables mode increased the cell padding and cell spacing of the table (which you'll learn about in a bit), which makes it easier to select the table cells and insert content. The table mode indicator at the top of the document lets you know which table mode you're in, and it provides a link to exit Expanded Tables mode.

Understanding Table Modes

Dreamweaver CS3 has three table modes: **Standard** mode (default), **Expanded Tables** mode, and **Layout** mode. You can switch between these various modes by choosing **View > Table Mode** and selecting the appropriate mode. Throughout this chapter, you will work mostly in **Standard** mode. In the next chapter, you will get a chance to work with the **Layout** mode. **Expanded Tables** mode is similar to **Standard** mode except extra cell padding and table borders are used to make table editing easier.

6 Position your cursor in the first table cell in the upper-left corner, and type **Photo**. Press the **Tab** key to move the cursor to the next table cell, and type **Description**. Press **Tab** once more, and type **Price** in the last cell in the first row.

Moving Through Tables

The **Tab** key lets you to quickly move through a table, both forward and backward. Pressing the **Tab** key moves your cursor to the next cell in the table, even if it's in the next row. Pressing **Shift+Tab** moves your cursor to the previous cell. If you're in the very last cell of the table and press the **Tab** key, a new row is added to the bottom of the table, and your cursor will be placed in the first cell of the new row.

7 Now that you have some content to hold the table cells open, click the **exit** link in the table mode indicator to get out of **Expanded Tables** mode.

8 Position your cursor in the first cell in the **Photo** column. Choose **Insert > Image**. Browse to **assets/ images/products/kettles**, select the **teacloud-azul.jpg** image, and click **OK** (Windows) or **Choose** (Mac). If the **Image Tag Accessibility Attributes** dialog box opens, type **Teacloud Azul** in the **Alternate text** field, and click **OK**. (Whether or not the Image Tag Accessibility dialog box opens depends on your Accessibility preference settings. See Chapter 18, "*Understanding Accessibility,*" for more information.)

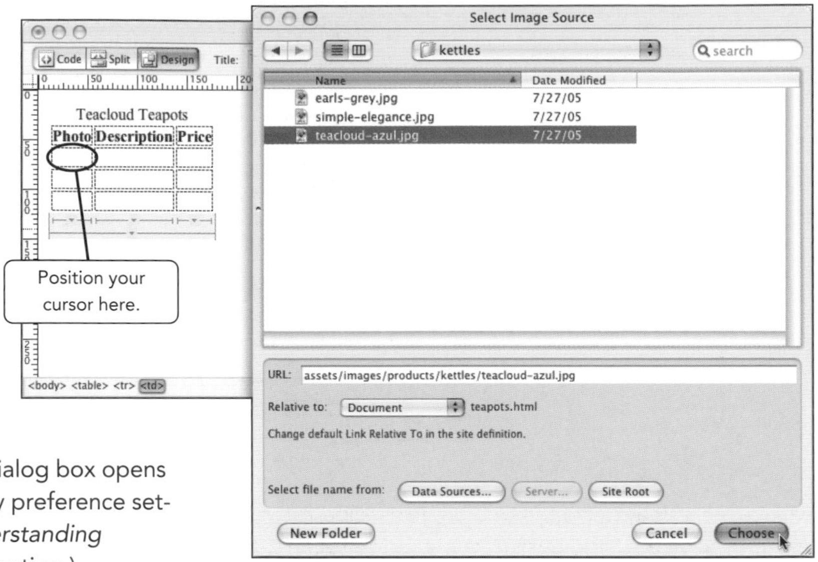

This is what your table should look like with the new image inserted.

---

9 Press **Tab** to move the cursor to the **Description** cell, and type the following text (pressing **Shift+Enter** [Windows] or **Shift+Return** [Mac] to add a line break between the teapot name and its description):

Teacloud Azul
Crafted in the workshop of master Hikari, this handmade teapot includes a built-in wire-mesh pouch for easy and efficient steeping.

If the text starts to get cramped while you're typing, simply click anywhere outside the table cell, or press F5, to refresh the Design view. Dreamweaver CS3 holds off updating tables as you type in order to apply the text to the page faster.

---

10 Press **Tab** again, and type **$49.95** in the **Price** column.

You've now finished adding your first row of table data.

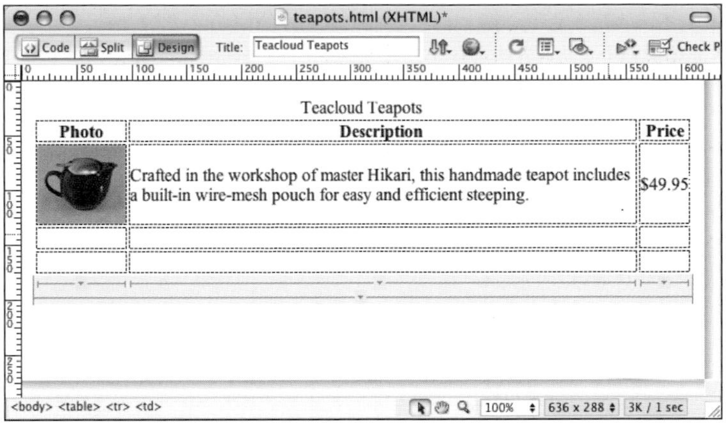

11 Now it's time to complete the information for the next two teapots. Press **Tab** to move your cursor to the **Photo** cell in the third row. Using the techniques you learned in Step 8, insert the **earls-grey.jpg** image from the **assets/images/products/kettles** folder. If the **Image Tag Accessibility** dialog box appears, type **Earl's Grey** for the alternate text, and click **OK**.

12 Press **Tab**, and type the following text in the **Description** column (pressing **Shift+Enter** [Windows] or **Shift+Return** [Mac] to add a line break between the teapot name and its description):

Earl's Grey
Perfect for brewing a pot of Earl Grey tea for two, this teapot strikes a balance between contemporary stylings and classical sensibilities.

13 Finally, press **Tab**, and type **$69.95** in the **Price** column.

The table is starting to look a little better now that it has content. One more row to go!

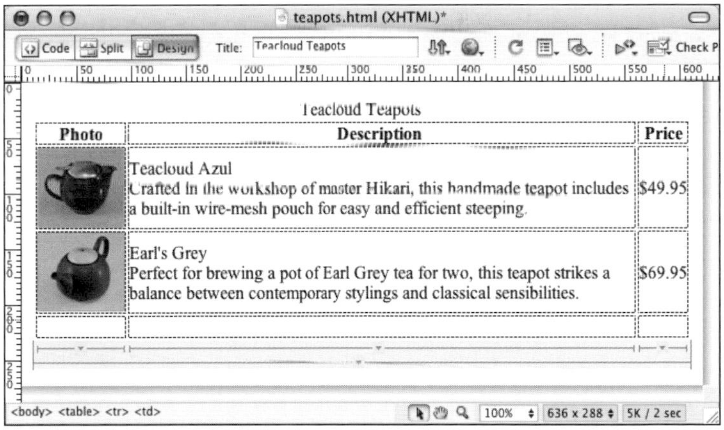

14 Press **Tab** to move your cursor to the **Photo** cell in the fourth row. Insert the **simple-elegance.jpg** image from the **assets/images/products/kettles** folder. If the **Image Tag Accessibility** dialog box appears, type **Simple Elegance** for the alternate text, and click **OK**.

---

15 Press **Tab**, and type the following in the **Description** column (pressing **Shift+Enter** [Windows] or **Shift+Return** [Mac] to add a line break between the teapot name and its description):

Simple Elegance
When style is tantamount only to elegance, nothing short of this piece will do. Hand-crafted by the world-renowned Jacque Le Bleu.

---

16 Press **Tab**, and type **$59.95** in the **Price** column.

The table is finally complete and nicely laid out in columns and rows.

In this exercise, you learned how to insert a table into the document and navigate through the table cells. The next exercise will teach you how to manipulate the display of your tables.

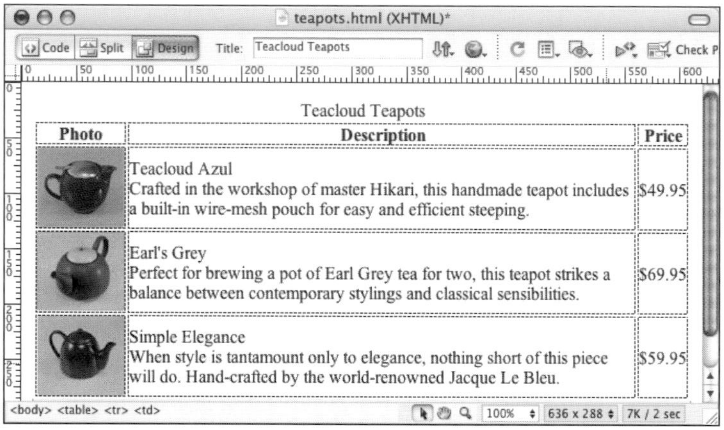

---

17 Save **teapots.html**, and leave it open for the next exercise.

---

2 Changing the Border of a Table with XHTML

This exercise helps you build your table-formatting skills using the table you created in Exercise 1. It also alerts you to a common XHTML problem relating to empty table cells. You see, even if a table cell is empty, you have to put something in it to preserve the table formatting. That "something" can be a single-pixel transparent GIF, which is a small image file set to be fully transparent (making it invisible), or preferably just a nonbreaking space. Either the transparent GIF or the nonbreaking space can serve as a placeholder to keep the table formatting from collapsing with empty cells.

1 You should still have the **teapots.html** file from Exercise 1 open. If not, complete Exercise 1, and then return to this exercise.

2 Press **F12** (Windows) or **Opt+F12** (Mac) to preview the file in your browser.

Notice how the dotted lines don't appear in the browser? In this file, you haven't set the border yet, so it defaults to 0. Also, the table displayed in the browser doesn't have any borders to separate the content.

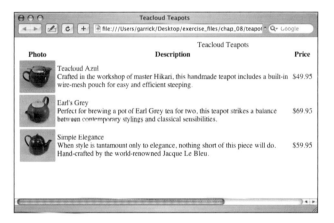

3 Return to Dreamweaver CS3. Select the entire table by moving your cursor over the edge of the table until you see a thin red outline and the cursor changes to show a small table. With the red line visible, click to select the table and the table width bar at the bottom of the table.

Note: You can also select a table by using the Tag Selector at the lower left of the Document window. Here's how: Click anywhere in the table. You should see the tag **<table>** appear in the Tag Selector. Click it to select the table.

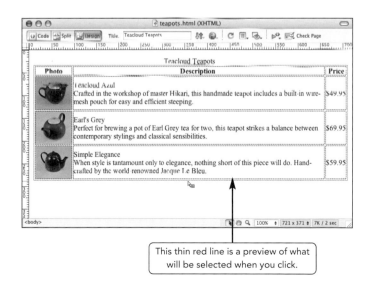

This thin red line is a preview of what will be selected when you click.

When the table is selected, you'll see a thick black line around the outside of the table.

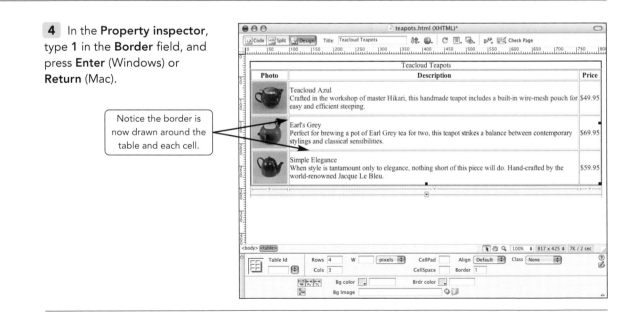

NOTE:

Selecting Table Elements

Selecting tables, rows, and columns is a simple task in Dreamweaver CS3. As you move your cursor over the table, rows, and cells, a thin red outline will appear as your cursor moves over the edge of each element. This red line is a preview of what will be selected if you click. If you don't like red, you can change this color in **Preferences** by choosing **Edit > Preferences > Highlighting** (Windows) or **Dreamweaver > Preferences > Highlighting** (Mac).

4 In the **Property inspector**, type **1** in the **Border** field, and press **Enter** (Windows) or **Return** (Mac).

Notice the border is now drawn around the table and each cell.

5 Save the page, and press **F12** (Windows) or **Opt+F12** (Mac) to preview the results in a browser.

Notice how the border value affected the appearance? Borders are one of the most basic controls you have over the appearance of tables. It's not the prettiest border in the world, though, so in the next exercise you'll learn how to use CSS to spiff it up.

6 It's fairly obvious that the first column of the table contains a photo, so the heading in that first column is pretty redundant. Position your cursor over the **Photo** text, hold down **Ctrl** (Windows) or **Cmd** (Mac), and click the table cell to select the entire cell.

You'll notice the cursor changes to show a small box (representing a single table cell), and the table cell has a red outline to indicate that clicking will select the entire table cell.

7 Press **Delete** to delete the text in the table cell.

8 In the **Document** toolbar, click the **Code** button to display the code for this page.

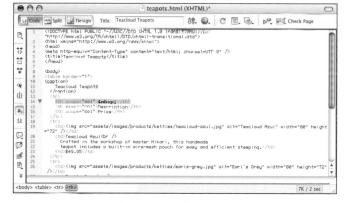

This is the code required to display the table you just modified. Notice the first <th> element contains a nonbreaking space element ( ), even though you just deleted the *Photo* text from the table cell. Dreamweaver CS3 automatically inserts the ** ** element into every empty table cell, whether it's a newly created cell or one that has been emptied by having its content removed. Some browsers require that every cell contain some content; cells that don't contain content will collapse, and borders around those cells won't be displayed—Internet Explorer is one of the largest culprits here. The nonbreaking space is the perfect solution because it qualifies as content to the browser and is invisible to the person viewing your page, so nobody ever knows it's there (except the browser, of course). The next few steps will show you why this is important.

Scope Attributes

You may have noticed the **<th>** tag has a **scope** attribute applied to it. Dreamweaver automatically adds the **scope** attributes if you specify headers when the table is created. The **scope** attribute tells screen readers and other accessibility devices what the **<th>** tag applies to either a column (**scope="col"**) or a row (**scope="row"**).

9 While still in **Code** view, delete ** ** from the **<th>** tag so that the table cell is completely empty.

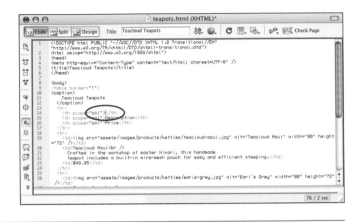

10 Switch back to **Design** view.

Notice the upper-left table cell now has a dashed border around it instead of a solid border.

11 Save the page, and press **F12** (Windows) or **Opt+F12** (Mac) to preview the page.

Depending on which browser you're using, you may not notice any difference in the upper-left cell. Both Firefox and Safari render the empty cell properly. But in Internet Explorer, notice the upper-left cell no longer has a border around it. Without a nonbreaking space, Internet Explorer will not properly render the table cell.

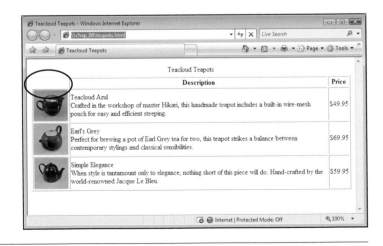

12 Return to Dreamweaver CS3, and make sure your cursor is still in the **<th>** tag. Choose **Insert > HTML > Special Characters > Non Breaking Space**, or press **Ctrl+Shift+spacebar** (Windows) or **Cmd+Shift+spacebar** (Mac) to replace the nonbreaking space you deleted previously. Save the page, and press **F12** (Windows) or **Opt+F12** (Mac) to preview the page again, just to make sure everything is OK.

Your page should now look the same as it did in Step 5 of this exercise.

WARNING:	**Special Characters Warning**
	If you receive a warning stating that special characters may not appear in all browsers, click OK. The nonbreaking space is actually an encoded character and will display just fine in any browser.

---

13 Save **teapots.html**, and leave it open for the next exercise.

In this exercise, you learned how to apply a border to a table using the standard attributes of the **<table>** tag. In the next exercise, you'll learn how to take finer control of your table borders using CSS.

3 | Changing the Border of a Table with CSS

The previous exercise showed you how to create a border on a table using standard XHTML attributes. Although the border is functional, it's certainly not very easy on the eyes. This exercise will show you how to use CSS to take control of your table borders, allowing you to create fine line borders of any color.

1 You should still have the **teapots.html** page from Exercise 2 open. If not, complete Exercise 2, and then return to this exercise.

The borders on the table—created with standard XHTML attributes—aren't very visually pleasing.

2 Select the table by clicking the **<table>** tag in the **Tag Selector** or by clicking the edge of the table (remember to wait until you see the red border).

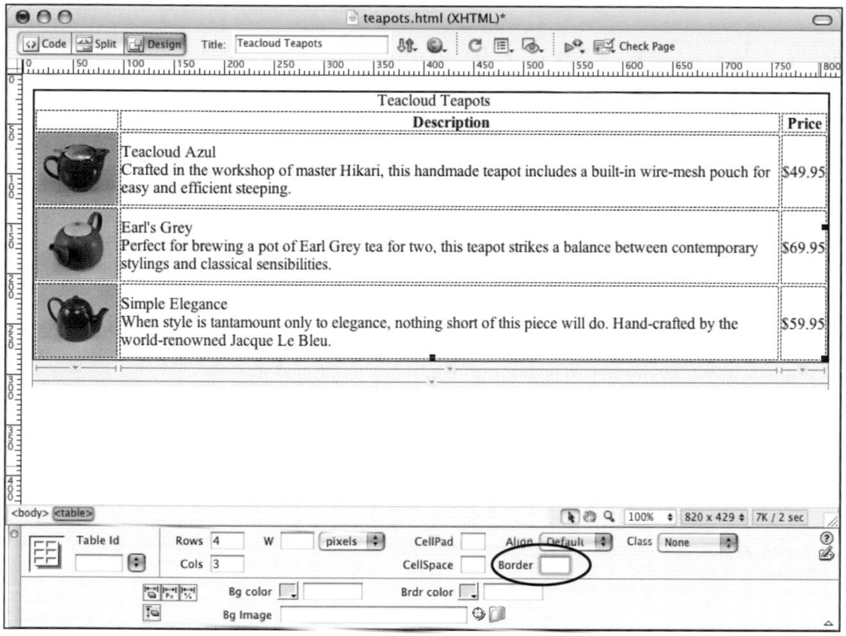

3 In the **Property inspector**, delete the value in the **Border** field, and press **Enter** (Windows) or **Return** (Mac) to commit the changes.

Now it's time to start setting borders with CSS.

4 In the **CSS Styles** panel, click the **New CSS Rule** button. Select **Tag** in the **Selector Type** section, choose **table** in the **Tag** pop-up menu, and select **This document only** in the **Define in** section. Click **OK** to start defining the rule.

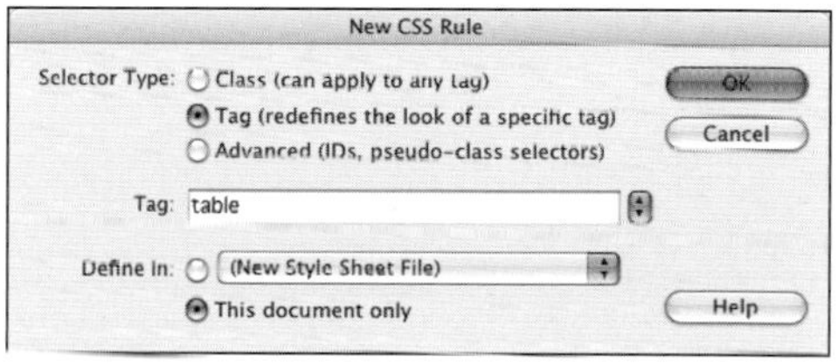

5 Select **Border** in the **Category** list. Leave the **Same for all** options selected. Choose **solid** in the **Top** pop-up menu in the **Style** column, and set **Width** to **1 pixels**. Type **#000000** in the **Color** field. Click **OK** to create and apply the rule. Save the page, and press **F12** (Windows) or **Opt+F12** (Mac) to preview this style in your browser.

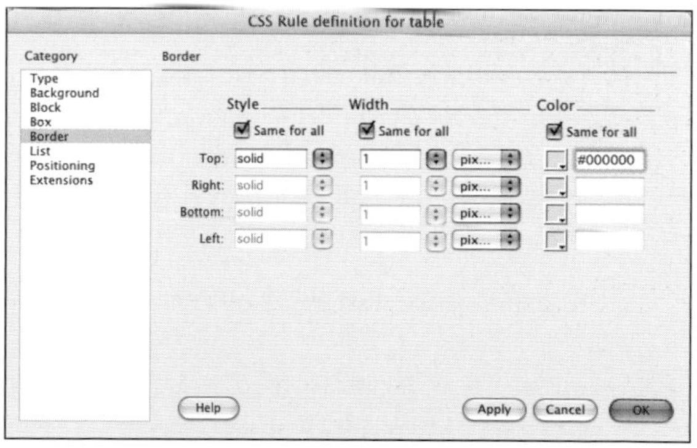

You should now see a thin black border around the table on the page. You were probably expecting borders around all the table cells, but the rule you created applies *only* to the **<table>** tag. The **<table>** tag affects only the border around the perimeter of the table. To apply the same borders to the entire table, including the dividing lines between the cells, you must redefine the styles for the **<table>**, **<th>**, and **<td>** tags. You'll learn how in the next steps.

6 Return to Dreamweaver, select the table rule in the **CSS Styles** panel, and click the **Delete** button to remove the rule you just created. Then click the **New CSS Rule** button.

7 In the **New CSS Rule** dialog box, select **Advanced** in the **Selector Type** section, and type **table, th, td** in the **Selector** field. Leave **Define in** set to **This document only**. Click **OK** to define the style.

In this case, you're using a group of selectors to define not only the **<table>** tag but the **<th>** and **<td>** tags as well.

8 In the **CSS Rule Definition** dialog box, select **Border** in the **Category** list. Leave the **Same for all** options selected. Choose **solid** in the **Top** pop-up menu, and set **Width** to **1 pixels**. Type **#000000** in the **Color** field. Click **OK** to create and apply the rule.

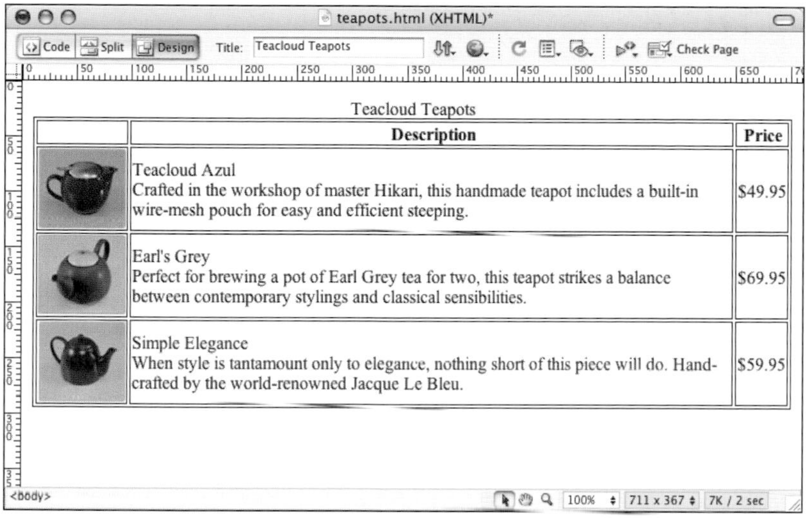

This looks a little more like it, but there's some space showing between each table cell.

9 Save the page, and press **F12** (Windows) or **Opt+F12** (Mac) to preview your page in the browser.

As you can see, the same space appears between the table borders. By default, table cells have some spacing around them, which is similar to the margins around paragraphs. To fix this problem, you'll need to add another property to the CSS rule that's not in the CSS Rule Definition dialog box like all the other border settings.

10 Return to Dreamweaver. In the **CSS Styles** panel, click the **table, th, td** rule to select it. Click the **Add Property** link.

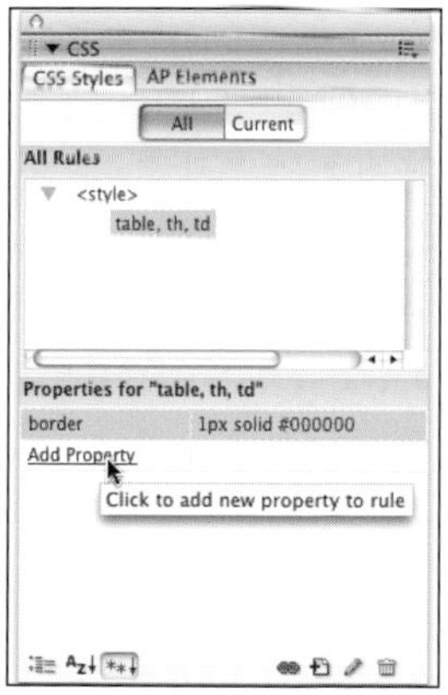

11 Type **border-collapse** in the field. Click in the second column, and choose **collapse** in the **Value** pop-up menu.

Design view updates automatically. Unfortunately, nothing changed. This view does not support the **border-collapse** attribute, so it still shows the table borders separated.

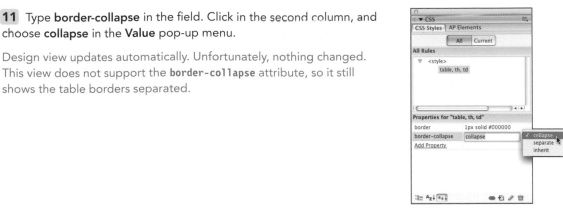

12 Save the page, and press **F12** (Windows) or **Opt+F12** (Mac) to preview your page in the browser.

	Teacloud Teapots	
	Description	**Price**
	Teacloud Azul Crafted in the workshop of master Hikari, this handmade teapot includes a built-in wire-mesh pouch for easy and efficient steeping.	$49.95
	Earl's Grey Perfect for brewing a pot of Earl Grey tea for two, this teapot strikes a balance between contemporary stylings and classical sensibilities.	$69.95
	Simple Elegance When style is tantamount only to elegance, nothing short of this piece will do. Hand-crafted by the world-renowned Jacque Le Bleu.	$59.95

The borders are now nice and tight. You'll probably agree this is a much better look than the bulky beveled borders the XHTML **border** attribute provided.

13 Save **teapots.html**, and leave it open for the next exercise.

In this exercise, you learned how to add table rows to your table using CSS instead of XHTML. CSS gives you a much finer level of control over your table borders. In the next exercise, you'll start adding color to the table.

EXERCISE

4 | Adding Color to Tables

Next on the list of table-building skills is learning how to apply color formatting. When it comes to coloring your tables, you may use the automatic color features or set whatever custom colors you desire. In this exercise, you will learn how to manually apply color to the background of tables, columns, rows, and cells by using the **Property inspector**, and, of course, you'll learn some CSS as well.

1 You should still have the **teapots.html** page from Exercise 3 open. If not, complete Exercise 3, and then return to this exercise.

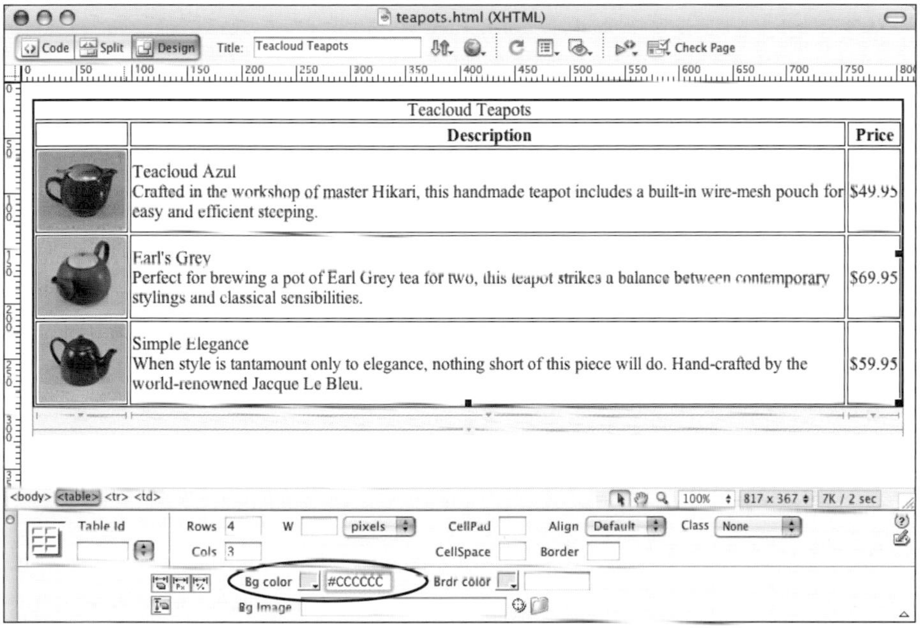

2 To begin coloring the table, select the entire table by clicking anywhere in the table and then clicking the **<table>** tag in the **Tag Selector**. In the **Property inspector**, type **#CCCCCC** in the **Bg color** field to set the background color for the entire table.

As you can see, the table background immediately changes to gray.

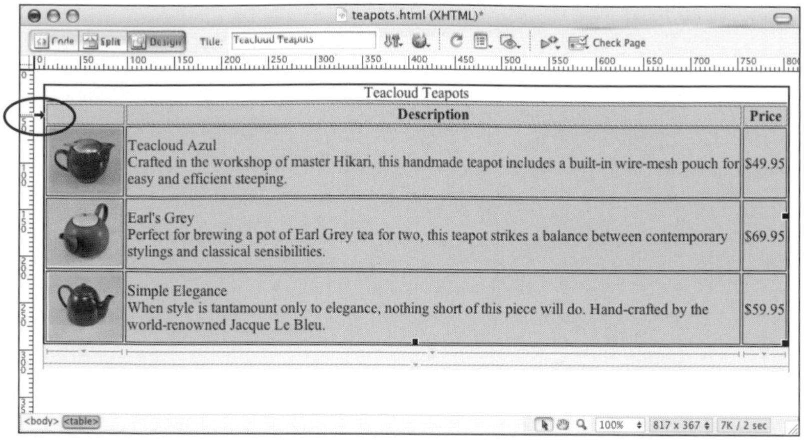

3 Move your cursor to the left of the upper-left table cell until it changes into a right-facing arrow. Click to select the first table row. You'll know the row is selected when you see the thin red line.

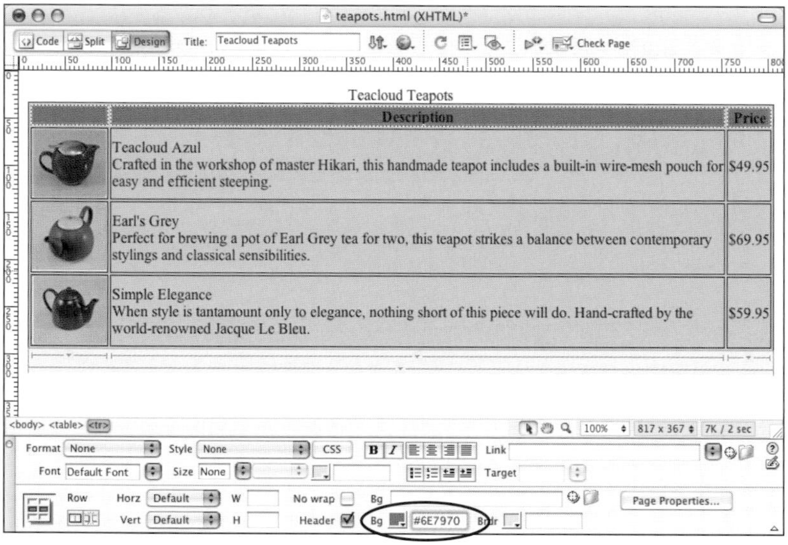

4 In the **Property inspector**, type **#6E7970** in the **Bg** color field, and press **Enter** (Windows) or **Return** (Mac) to commit the changes. The background color of the header row instantly changes.

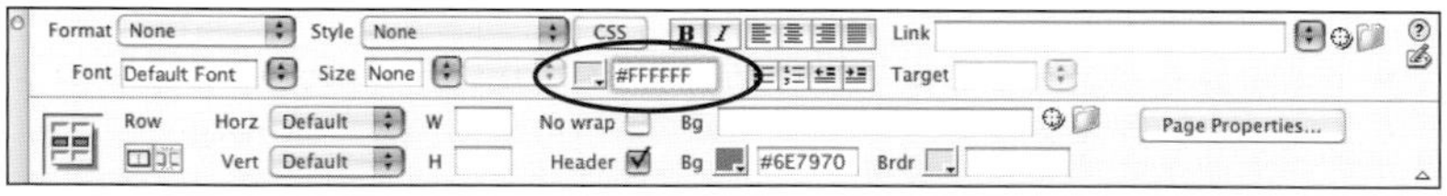

5 The black headings are now a little difficult to read over the dark background color. In the **Property inspector**, type **#FFFFFF** in the **Font Color** field, and press **Enter** (Windows) or **Return** (Mac) to commit the changes.

6 To make the rows of the table stand out a little more, it's always nice to use alternating row colors. Select the third row of the table, which contains the Earl's Grey teapot. In the **Property inspector**, type #FBFCF9 in the **Bg** field, and press **Enter** (Windows) or **Return** (Mac) to commit the changes.

This is the new code for your table. You can see that the **<table>** tag has a **bgcolor** attribute, each of the **<th>** tags now has a **<span>** tag wrapped around the text (even the empty table cell), and the third row also has a **bgcolor** attribute.

You've now seen how to work with colors using XHTML attributes, but your deep inner geek can't stand to see XHTML attributes where you can use CSS instead. So, it's time to start over with this table and do the same formatting using CSS. This will allow you finer control over the colors and make it easy to style hundreds of tables with the same colors by using an external style sheet. Using CSS to style tables has all the benefits of styling regular text that you learned about in previous chapters.

7 Save and close **teapots.html**, and then open **css-teapots.html** using the **Files** panel. This file has the same table and formatting your page had at the beginning of this exercise.

Notice the file looks the same as it did when you opened the other file in Step 1. First you'll set the background color for the table.

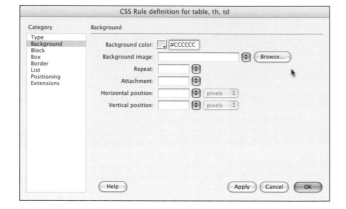

8 In the **CSS Styles** panel, double-click the **table, th, td** rule to open the **CSS Rule Definition** dialog box. Select **Background** in the **Category** list, and type **#CCCCCC** in the **Background color** field. Click **OK** to update the rule.

Next you'll create a new rule for the **<th>** tag.

9 In the CSS Styles panel, click the New CSS Rule button. In the New CSS Rule dialog box, select **Tag** in the **Selector Type** section, type **th** in the **Tag** field, and leave **Define in** set to **This document only**. Click **OK**.

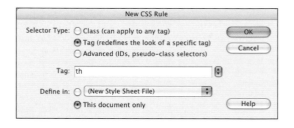

10 In the **CSS Rule Definition** dialog box, select **Type** in the **Category** list. Type **#FFFFFF** in the **Color** field. Select **Background** in the **Category** list, and type **#6E7970** in the **Background color** field. Click **OK** to apply the rule.

In this step, you're using the "cascade" of Cascading Style Sheets to override the color of the **<th>** tag defined in the **table, th, td** rule. Because you defined the th rule after the **table, th, td** rule, it's lower in the cascade, so it takes precedence, and the **<th>** tag will have a background color of #6E7970.

From a display perspective, there's no difference in the look of the CSS-styled table versus the HTML-styled table. If you look at the code, though, there has not been any change to the `<table>` or `<th>` tags, just a few new styles.

The last task you need to do is set the alternating row color, which you'll do next.

11 In the **CSS Styles** panel, click the **New CSS Rule** button. In the **New CSS Rule** dialog box, select **Advanced** in the **Selector Type** section, type **tr.altRow td** in the **Selector** field, and leave **Define in** set to **This document only**. Click **OK**.

This new rule will be applied to a table row. The new rule, `tr.altRow td`, states that any `<td>` tag inside a `<tr>` tag with a class of `altRow` will be styled using this new rule.

12 In the **CSS Rule Definition** dialog box, select **Background** in the **Category** list. Type **#FBFCF9** in the **Background color** field. Click **OK** to add the new rule.

13 Select the table row containing the Earl's Grey teapot. In the **Property inspector**, choose **.altRow** in the **Style** pop-up menu.

The table now looks exactly as it did when you styled it using the Property inspector. However, you've made minimal changes to the table at this point, only adding a simple class to control the alternating row color. If you decide to change the color of the headings or the color of the alternating row color, you could now change it in one place. Imagine a site with dozens of tables that need to be styled, and you'll probably agree that going the CSS route is definitely preferred.

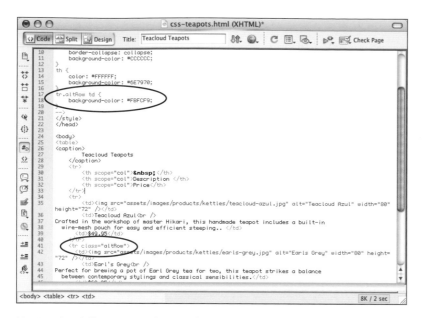

```
        border-collapse: collapse;
        background-color: #CCCCCC;
}
th {
        color: #FFFFFF;
        background-color: #6E7970;
}

tr.altRow td {
        background-color: #FBFCF9;
}

-->
</style>
</head>

<body>
<table>
<caption>
            Teacloud Teapots
        </caption>
    <tr>
        <th scope="col">  </th>
        <th scope="col">Description </th>
        <th scope="col">Price</th>
    </tr>
    <tr>
        <td><img src="assets/images/products/kettles/teacloud-azul.jpg" alt="Teacloud Azul" width="80"
height="72" /></td>
        <td>Teacloud Azul<br />
Crafted in the workshop of master Hikari, this handmade teapot includes a built-in
    wire-mesh pouch for easy and efficient steeping.. </td>
        <td>$49.95</td>
    </tr>
    <tr class="altRow">
        <td><img src="assets/images/products/kettles/earls-grey.jpg" alt="Earls Grey" width="80" height=
"72" /></td>
        <td>Earl's Grey<br />
Perfect for brewing a pot of Earl Grey tea for two, this teapot strikes a balance
    between contemporary stylings and classical sensibilities.</td>
```

`<body> <table> <tr> <td>`   `8K / 2 sec`

Notice the differences in the CSS-based code compared to the code you created previously in this exercise. The code has a few new CSS rules, but the table code hasn't changed at all, except for the class now applied to the Earl's Grey table row. The **<th>** tags are much more efficient using this method, because you don't have to apply a bunch of **<span>** tags to change the color of the text. The code is far cleaner and easier to maintain using CSS to format your tables.

---

14 Save **css-teapots.html**, and leave it open for the next exercise.

In this exercise, you learned how to change the colors of your table, both with XHTML and with CSS. In the next exercise, you'll learn how to change the alignment of the text and images in the table cells.

Adobe Dreamweaver CS3 : H·O·T

5 | Aligning Table Content

Tables handle alignment a little differently than other XHTML tags. You can use the standard alignment buttons in the **Property inspector** to align something in a table cell, but it's usually a better idea to let the table cell actually handle the alignment. This exercise will show you how to change the alignment of table cells.

1 You should still have the **css-teapots.html** page from Exercise 4 open. If not, complete Exercise 4, and then return to this exercise.

By default, content in table cells is centered vertically inside the cell, which 99 percent of the time is not what you'll want for your tables. Changing this behavior is pretty simple.

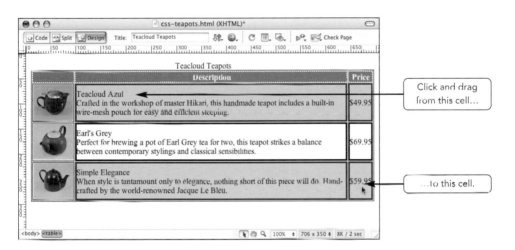

2 Click and drag from in the **Description** column for **Teacloud Azul** to the **Price** column for **Simple Elegance** to select all six table cells.

3 In the **Property inspector**, choose **Top** in the **Vert** pop-up menu (which handles vertical alignment).

The contents of the selected cells move to the top of the table cell so that it lines up nicely. You can also see that a **valign** attribute has been added to the **<td>** tags, with a value of **top**. This is how XHTML handles table cell alignment. As usual, it's time to give this a try with CSS.

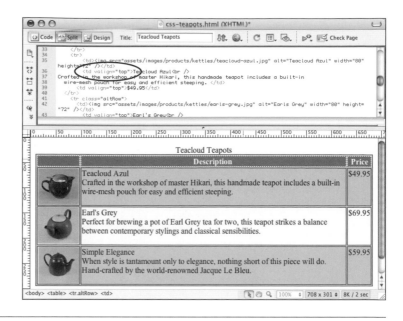

4 Choose **Edit > Undo** to undo the table alignment changes. You're going to set the same alignment using CSS this time. In the **CSS Styles** panel, click the **New CSS Rule** button. In the **New CSS Rule** dialog box, select **Advanced** in the **Selector Type** section, type **th, td** in the **Selector** field, and leave **Define in** set to **This document only**. Click **OK** to define the rule.

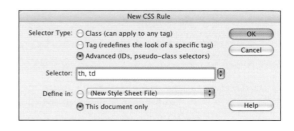

5 In the **CSS Rule Definition** dialog box, select **Block** in the **Category** list, and set the **Vertical alignment** property to **top**. Click **OK** to apply the rule.

The table doesn't look any different than it did when you used the table cell's **valign** attribute. However, using CSS to control the cell alignment means that the alignment applies to *every* cell of the table so that you don't have to manually set the alignment on every table cell.

6 It's time to do some horizontal alignment. Change the price of the Simple Elegance teapot to **$159.95**.

Notice the prices are lined up along the left side of the table cell. As a general rule, prices should line up on their decimal places (by aligning them to the right) so they're easier to read.

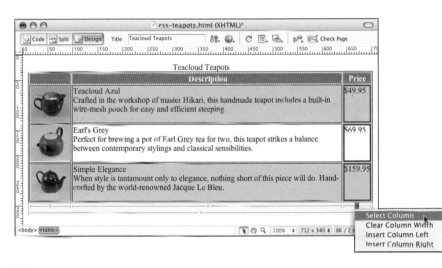

7 If you can't see the column header menus below the table, choose **View > Visual Aids > Table Widths**. At the bottom of the **Price** column, click the small triangle to open the column header menu, and choose **Select Column**.

8 In the **Property inspector**, choose **Right** in the **Horz** pop-up menu.

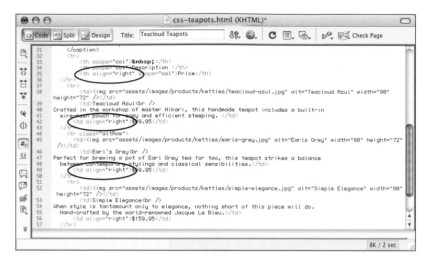

The Price column is now nicely aligned to the right. If you take a look at the code, you'll see an `align` attribute added to each table cell with a value of `right`. But, you guessed it—it's time to do the same thing with CSS.

---

9 Choose **Edit > Undo** or select the price column again, and choose **Default** in the **Horz** pop-up menu to remove the changes you just made.

NOTE:

Table and Column Header Menus

When you select a table in Dreamweaver CS3, you'll notice a bunch of green lines and little arrows at the bottom of the table and each of the columns. These **column header** menus give you quick access to some table features. The options on the bottommost menu affect the *entire* table, such as clearing all heights and widths, making all widths consistent, and even hiding the table widths.

The column header menus for the individual columns offer different options, such as clearing the width of an entire column and inserting a new column to the right or left. These menus are visible only in the Dreamweaver CS3 interface and never in a browser. If you deselect the table, the menus will disappear. **Note:** You can turn off the column header menus by choosing **View > Visual Aids > Table Widths**.

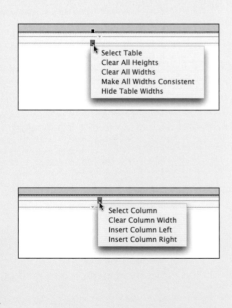

10 In the **CSS Styles** panel, click the **New CSS Rule** button. You're going to define a class that will be applied to any table cell you want to right-align. In the **New CSS Rule** dialog box, select **Class** in the **Selector Type** section, type **.rightAlign** in the **Name** field, and leave **Define in** set to **This document only**. Click **OK** to define the rule.

11 In the **CSS Definition** dialog box, select **Block** in the **Category** list, and choose **right** in the **Text align** pop-up menu. Click **OK** to apply the rule.

12 Select the **Price** column again. In the **Property inspector**, choose **rightAlign** in the **Style** pop-up menu.

Once again, the table looks the same, but you're now using a method that's far easier to maintain than a bunch of XHTML attributes on your table.

The next task is to get the content away from the edges of the table a bit. Having the text too close to the borders often makes it difficult to read.

13 In the **CSS Styles** panel, double-click the **th, td** rule to edit it.

14 In the **CSS Rules Definition** dialog box, select **Box** in the **Category** list. Type **5** in the **Padding** field, and click **OK** to apply the rule (leave **Same for All** checked).

NOTE: | **Table Cell Padding**

Cell padding in tables works just like padding on standard typographic elements, which you learned about in Chapter 7, *"Working with Typography."* Padding is added to the inside of the table cell, and it controls the distance of the text from the border.

---

15 Save the page, and press **F12** (Windows) or **Opt+F12** (Mac) to preview the page in a browser.

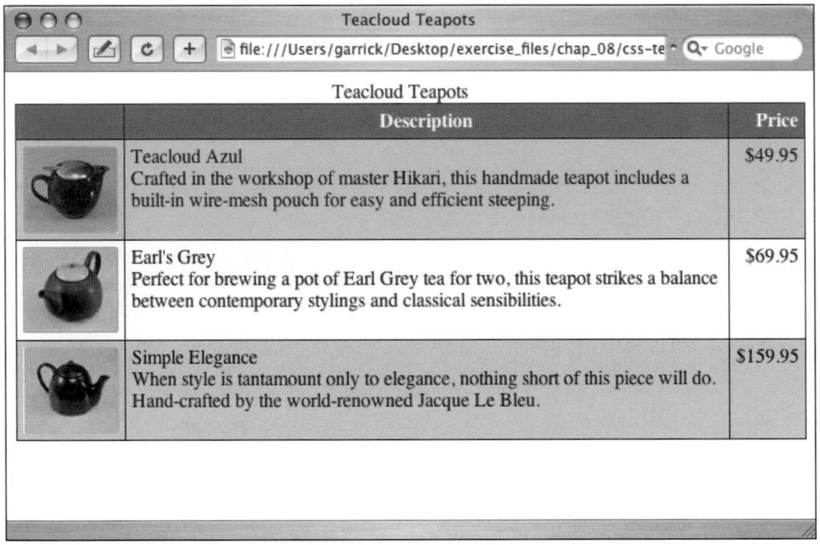

The table looks much better now that you've taken care of the alignment and the text has a little more room to breathe in the table cells.

---

16 Save **css-teapots.html**, and leave it open for the next exercise.

---

6 | Sorting a Table

Way back in Dreamweaver 2.0, Macromedia introduced the capability to sort table content both alphabetically and numerically. Before this feature existed, if you wanted to sort a table, you had to copy and paste each row or column manually. Thankfully, sorting table content is only a simple dialog box away.

1 You should still have the **css-teapots.html** page from Exercise 5 open. If not, complete Exercise 5, and then return to this exercise.

2 Make sure your cursor is somewhere in the table. Choose **Commands > Sort Table** to open the **Sort Table** dialog box.

3 Choose **Column 2** in the **Sort by** pop-up menu, and choose **Alphabetically** and **Ascending** in the **Order** pop-up menus. Click **OK**.

As you can see, the table contents have been sorted according to the product names. The images and prices stayed with their appropriate descriptions, and the alternating row colors were maintained.

Next, you'll sort the table by price (most expensive first).

4 With the table still selected, choose **Commands > Sort Table** to open the **Sort Table** dialog box.

5 Choose **Column 3** in the **Sort by** pop-up menu, and choose **Numerically** and **Descending** in the **Order** pop-up menus. Click **OK**.

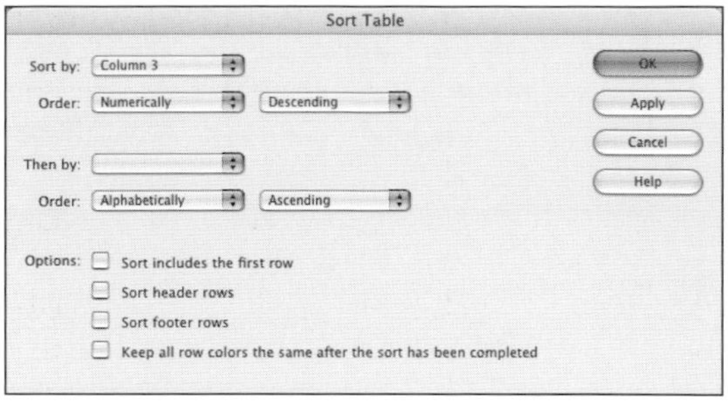

As you can see, the table is now sorted by price, with the most expensive item first.

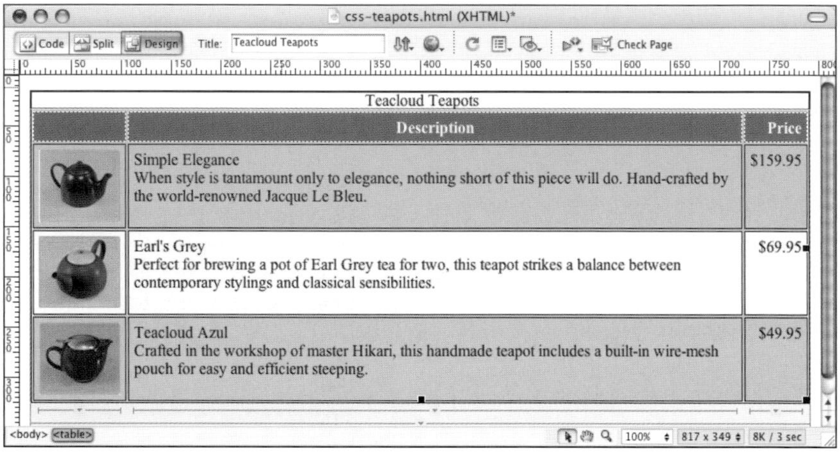

6 Save **css-teapots.html**, and leave it open for the next exercise.

Adobe Dreamweaver CS3 : H·O·T

Sort Table Command Options

The **Sort Table** dialog box has a variety of options to help you modify the appearance of tables. See the following chart for an explanation of all its features:

Sorting Features	
Feature	**Definition**
Sort by	Use this option to select which column you want to use to sort the table.
Order	Use these two pop-up menus to choose **Alphabetically** or **Numerically** and **Ascending** or **Descending**.
Then by	Use this option to sort multiple columns in your table.
Sort includes the first row	If this box is selected, the first row in your table will be sorted. This option is off by default because most often the first row is used as a header for the table, which you'll want to keep at the top of the table.
Sort header rows	If this box is selected, all the rows in the table's headers (if any) will be sorted using the same criteria as the body rows.
Sort footer rows	If this box is selected, all the rows in the table's footers section (if any) will be sorted using the same criteria as the body rows.
Keep all row colors the same after the sort has been completed	If this box is selected, all the row colors will remain associated with their content, even if the rows are rearranged after the sorting is completed. Leave this box deselected to keep alternating table row colors in their rightful place.

When you created the table for this exercise, you didn't explicitly declare any width for the table, so the browser determines the width for you by stretching out the table as wide as it can in order to accommodate the table's content. As a result, your tables will change based on the size of the browser window. Although many times this functionality is what you're looking for, other times you'll want to specify the exact width. In this exercise, you'll learn how to take control of your table widths by specifying widths in both pixels and percentages. You'll learn about controlling table size with pixels first, and then after that you'll switch to percentages.

1 You should still have the **css-teapots.html** site from Exercise 6 open. If not, complete Exercise 6, and then return to this exercise.

First, you'll set the table width to 500 pixels, which means no matter what size your browser is, the table will always remain fixed at 500 pixels wide.

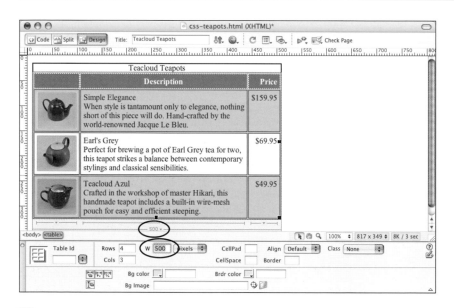

2 Select the entire table. In the **Property inspector**, type **500** in the **W** (width) field, and press **Enter** (Windows) or **Return** (Mac) to commit your changes to the table.

After you change the table width, the table column header at the bottom of the table shows the width of the entire table. With the column headers, you can easily see your column and table widths without selecting the appropriate cell or table and checking the Property inspector.

With a fixed table width of 500 pixels, the Price column is a bit narrow. Next you'll make it wider to give it a bit more space.

3 Position your cursor over the divider between the **Description** and **Price** columns, and click and drag to resize the columns. Make the **Price** field about **70** pixels, and then release the mouse.

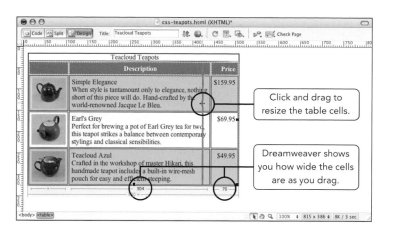

Click and drag to resize the table cells.

Dreamweaver shows you how wide the cells are as you drag.

Clicking and dragging the column widths is a quick and easy way to adjust pixel-based column widths. Dreamweaver CS3 will set the width of the columns on either side of the line you're dragging.

The table widths at the bottom of the table give you more information than you probably suspected. If, for whatever reason, Dreamweaver can't draw the table cell at the width you specified, it will display the width that's specified in the XHTML and then the width that it's actually rendered in parentheses.

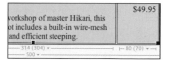

Next you'll learn how to create percentage-based table widths. You can use the table column header menu to quickly remove all the sizing information from the table.

NOTE:

Calculating Table Cell Widths

Having rendered table cell widths that aren't the same as the widths in the XHTML isn't always a bad thing. In Step 3 of this exercise, Dreamweaver tells you that the table cells are being drawn 58 pixels wide, even though you specified that the cell should be 70 pixels wide. Let's do a little math to figure out why this is happening.

If you recall in previous exercises, you added 5 pixels of padding to the **<th>** and **<td>** tags using CSS. When padding is added to a table cell, it's added all the way around. So, Dreamweaver added 5 pixels of padding to the left of the table cell and 5 pixels to the right of the table cell for a total of 10 pixels of padding as far as the width of the cell goes. You also added a border around the table cells. A border on the left and one on the right adds up to 2 pixels. Let's use this formula to calculate the width:

Cell width – (left padding + right padding + left border + right border) = actual width

If you use the values you defined in the CSS, the formula looks like this:

$70 – (5 + 5 + 1 + 1) = 58$

So, the effective width of the contents of the table cells turns out to be 58, just like Dreamweaver CS3 said. If, for whatever reason, you had content that was wider than the table cell, such as an extra-large image that stretched out the table cell, Dreamweaver CS3 would list the larger table cell size in parentheses to let you know your table is getting stretched out.

That's just one more thing Dreamweaver CS3 does to make your table-formatting life easier.

4 Click the column header menu for the table width, and choose **Clear All Widths**.

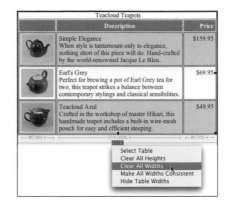

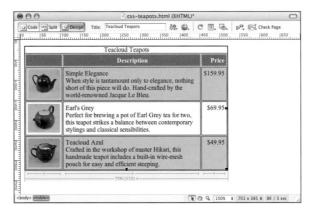

5 With the table still selected, type **75%** in the **W** field in the **Property inspector**.

Percentage width tables can be handy if you're trying to create a fluid layout, which adjusts with the visitor's browser window. If your layout is flexible enough, it will display nicely on any screen resolution.

The table width markers work essentially the same for percentage-based table widths. The percentage is listed, and then the actual rendered width of the table or table cell is listed in parentheses. Yours may not match the illustration depending on how wide your document window is.

6 Click and drag the divider between the **Description** and **Price** columns to **70** pixels again.

Notice that all the table cells received a percentage width this time. Dreamweaver CS3 knew that the table itself was set to a percentage, so it set each of the columns to be a percentage as well.

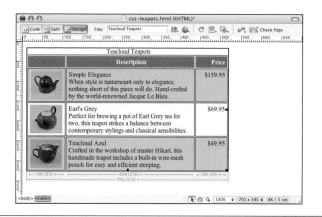

7 Save the page, and press **F12** (Windows) or **Opt+F12** (Mac) to preview the page in your browser. Click and drag to change the browser width to see the table flex.

Because all the table cells have percentage widths, every table cell changes width as you resize the browser window. Even the photo column is resized, which isn't desirable in this particular layout.

Because you probably don't want to have the photo column of the table resize with the browser width, you can set that column to use a pixel-based width instead of a percentage width. To do so, you'll need to clear the width from the other two columns and type an inline style into your page's code.

8 Return to Dreamweaver. Click the column headers for the **Description and Price** columns, and select **Clear Column Width** for both.

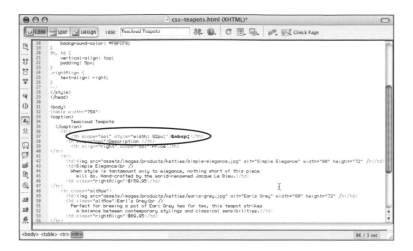

9 Click the top-left cell, and switch to **Code** view. Your cursor should be flashing in the first **th** tag. Click after **scope="col"** in this line, and type **style="width: 92px;"**.

Only one cell in any column needs a width in order to force the entire column to have that same width. You specified the value 92 because the images are each 80 pixels wide. Add 10 pixels of padding and 2 pixels for borders, and you get 92 pixels.

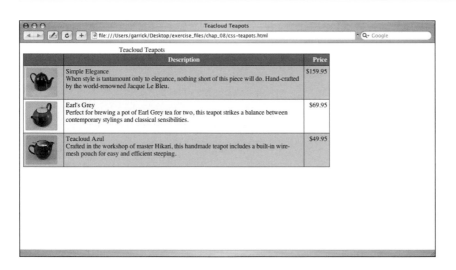

10 Switch back to **Design** view. Save the page, and press **F12** (Windows) or **Opt+F12** (Mac) to preview the page in your browser. Resize the browser a few times, and you'll see that although the table resized with the browser, the first column stays rock solid at 92 pixels wide.

11 Close **css-teapots.html**.

8 | Creating Rounded-Corner Tables

Tables, like most things on the Web, are square. Images are square, frames are square, the browser window is square, and CSS uses the "box model"; everything about how the Web is constructed consists of boxes. It's no wonder Web designers are always looking for ways to make things look less square. It's impossible for a table to have rounded corners, plain and simple. The nature of the Web is boxes, and you'll most likely never get away from that. So instead, in this exercise, you'll use images to give the user the illusion of rounded table corners.

---

1 In the **Files** panel, double-click **rounded.html** to open it.

This file has just a bit of text and an image that you'll place in a table with rounded corners.

---

2 Place your cursor at the beginning of the document, and choose **Insert > Table**. In the **Table** dialog box, type **3** in the **Rows** field, type **3** in the **Columns** field, and set **Table width** to **400 pixels**. Type **0** for **Border thickness**, **Cell padding**, and **Cell spacing**. In the **Header** section, click **None**. Click **OK**.

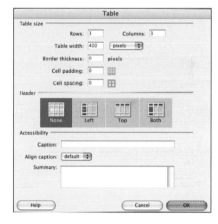

Notice the table already has a light gray background color. I took the liberty of defining a style to redefine the table's background color for you.

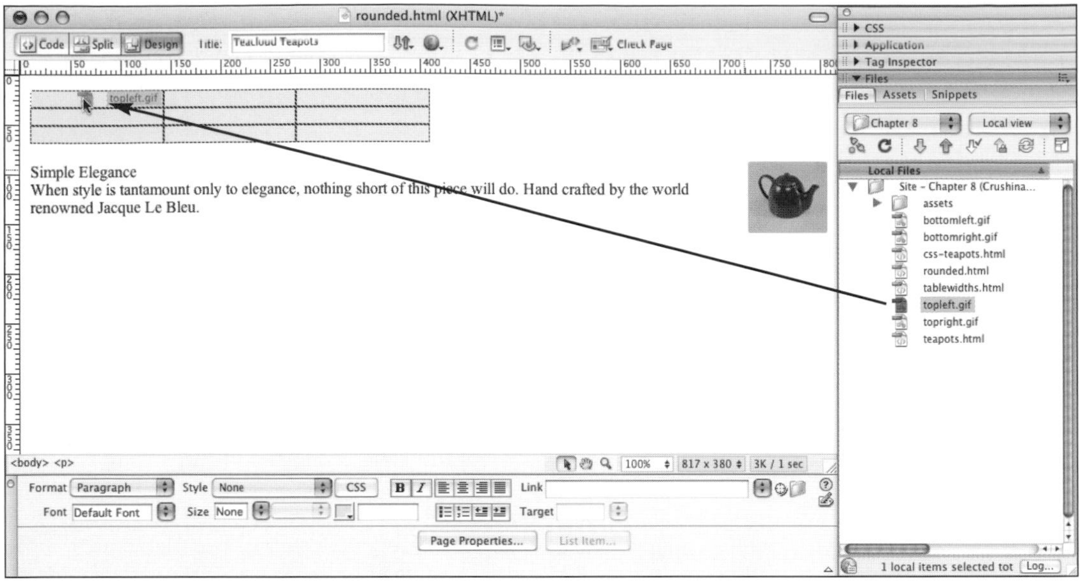

3 Click and drag the **topleft.gif** file from the root of your site to the upper-left table cell. If the **Image Tag Accessibility Attributes** dialog box appears, choose **<empty>** in the **Alternate text** pop-up menu, and click **OK**.

You can see that the image inserted into the upper-left corner of the table has the same background color as the table, and it has a white matte around it to match the page background color.

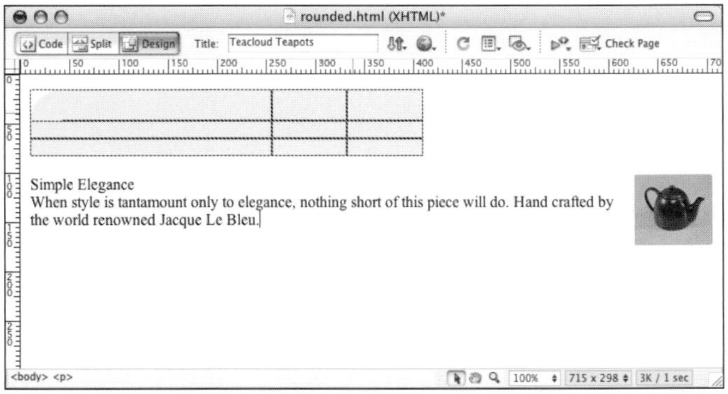

4 Click and drag the **topright.gif** file from the root of your site to the upper-right table cell. If the **Image Tag Accessibility Attributes** dialog box appears, choose **<empty>** in the **Alternate text** pop-up menu, and click **OK**.

5 Click and drag the **bottomleft.gif** file from the root of your site to the lower-left table cell. If the **Image Tag Accessibility Attributes** dialog box appears, choose **<empty>** in the **Alternate text** pop-up menu, and click **OK**.

6 Click and drag the **bottomright.gif** file from the root of your site to the lower-right table cell. If the **Image Tag Accessibility Attributes** dialog box appears, choose **<empty>** in the **Alternate text** pop-up menu, and click **OK**.

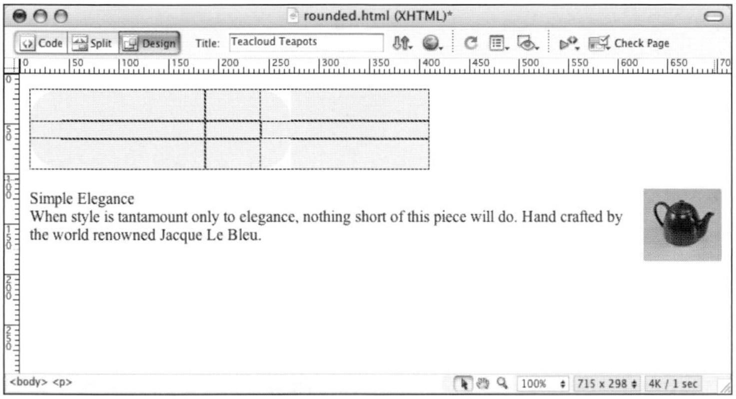

With all the images inserted, you can see how things are coming together. Unfortunately, the images aren't being rendered like they should be because of the lack of widths on the table cells.

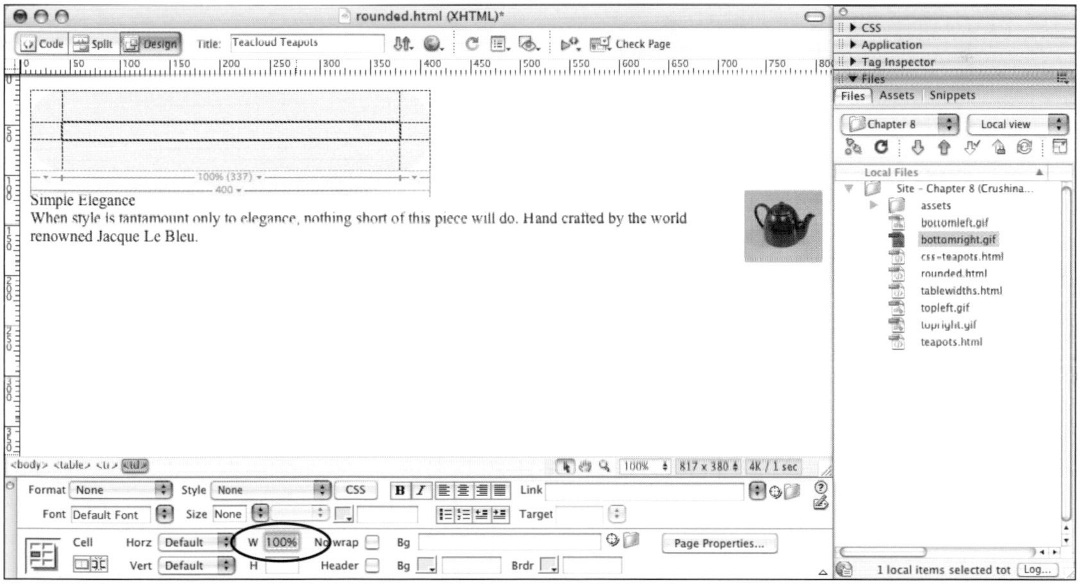

7 Click in the top-middle table cell, and type **100%** in the **W** field in the **Property inspector**.

Setting the width of the center column to 100% means the center column will take up as much space as it can, forcing the first and third columns to collapse tightly around the contents of their cells.

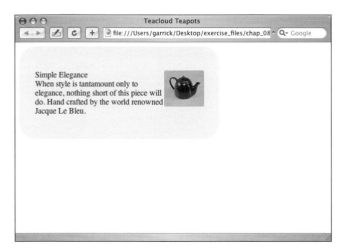

8 Click in the text at the bottom of the page, and select the **<p>** tag in the **Tag Selector**. Once the contents of the paragraph are highlighted, click and drag the entire paragraph to the center table cell.

9 Save the page, and press **F12** (Windows) or **Opt+F12** (Mac) to preview the file in your browser.

You now have a table with nicely rounded corners. All the table cells collapse tightly around the four corner images.

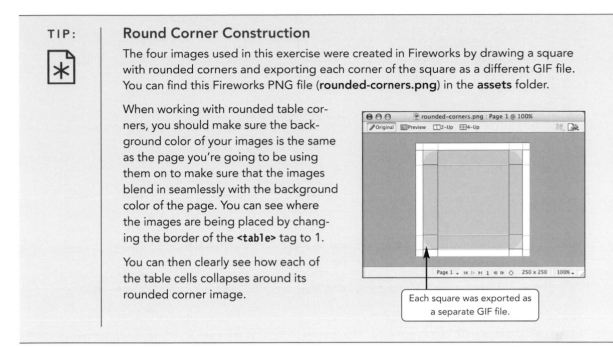
Round Corner Construction

The four images used in this exercise were created in Fireworks by drawing a square with rounded corners and exporting each corner of the square as a different GIF file. You can find this Fireworks PNG file (**rounded-corners.png**) in the **assets** folder.

When working with rounded table corners, you should make sure the background color of your images is the same as the page you're going to be using them on to make sure that the images blend in seamlessly with the background color of the page. You can see where the images are being placed by changing the border of the **<table>** tag to 1.

You can then clearly see how each of the table cells collapses around its rounded corner image.

Each square was exported as a separate GIF file.

10 Close **rounded.html**.

In this chapter, you learned how to create and edit tables, as well as how to format them using both XHTML and CSS. You also learned how to align text neatly and how insert images into a table to eliminate some of the boxiness inherent in Web design. Tables will be a part of your daily development, so it definitely pays to spend some time learning the intricacies of table manipulation. In the next chapter, you'll learn more about laying out entire Web pages, including more fun with tables.

Using Layout Tools

In regular page layout programs such as Adobe InDesign and QuarkXPress, most people take it for granted that they can move blocks of text and images almost anywhere on the screen. Unfortunately, standard XHTML (e**X**tensible **H**yper**T**ext **M**arkup **L**anguage) doesn't contain any tags that let you position elements easily. You've learned how you can use tables to position your elements both horizontally and vertically on your Web pages with table settings, but creating a basic table still doesn't give you the precision you get in traditional print layout programs. This problem has caused considerable frustration among Web page designers.

Fortunately, Adobe Dreamweaver CS3 has built-in functions to help you work in a visual mode to create precise alignment for your text and images. You'll learn how to align your images using tracing images and AP Divs, which you can then convert into tables that can be viewed on nearly any browser. In addition, Dreamweaver CS3 has an another layout feature called **layout cells**, which give you the freedom of absolute positioning while still conforming to XHTML table guidelines. In this chapter, you'll learn several techniques that let you position elements anywhere on a Web page. After completing these exercises, you can decide for yourself which method you prefer when building your own pages.

Using Tracing Images, AP Divs, and Tables for Layout

The following chart outlines the concepts behind tracing images, AP Divs, and tables, which you will learn about in the upcoming exercises:

Tracing Images, AP Divs, and Tables Defined	
Item	**Definition**
Tracing image	An image (GIF, JPEG, or PNG) that you can load into the background of **Design** view in Dreamweaver to serve as a reference for layout. Consider this the blueprint you follow to build your pages.
AP Div	**A**bsolutely **P**ositioned `<div>` tags. You can place them anywhere on the page, and they are completely self-contained. They aren't affected by other elements, and they don't affect the position of other elements on the page. AP Divs were called **layers** in previous versions of Dreamweaver.
Table	Tables can hold images and text in place, but they are not intuitive or flexible when it comes to positioning them on the screen. However, Dreamweaver CS3 offers some helpful features that give you more flexibility, including innovative table-drawing tools, and the capability to convert AP Divs to tables.

1 | Applying a Tracing Image

Imagine you have mocked up a wonderful layout for a Web page in Adobe Photoshop, Adobe Fireworks, Adobe Illustrator, or any drawing or painting program of your choice. The next step is getting the layout into Dreamweaver CS3. **Tracing images** let you import an image of that layout (as a GIF, JPEG, or PNG) and place it in the background of your page; you can then use it as a reference to align your XHTML elements perfectly. In this exercise, you will learn how to apply a tracing image to your Web page, as well as how to change its transparency and position on the page.

1 If you haven't already done so, copy the **chap_09** folder from the **Dreamweaver HOT CD-ROM** to your desktop. Define your site as **Chapter 9** using the **chap_09** folder as the local root folder. Make sure the **Files** panel is open. If it's not, choose **Window > Files**.

2 In the **Files** panel, double-click **index.html** to open it. This page is empty except that its title is **Welcome to Teacloud**. Choose **Modify > Page Properties** to open the **Page Properties** dialog box. Select **Tracing Image** in the **Category** list.

3 Click **Browse**.

4 Browse to the **assets** folder, and select **landing.gif** inside it. Click **OK**.

5 Leave the **Transparency** slider at **100%**. Click **OK** to close the **Page Properties** dialog box.

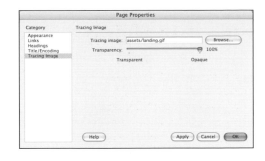

Your page, with the tracing image applied, should look like the illustration shown here. You inserted the image at 100% opacity using the Page Properties dialog box, which makes it opaque.

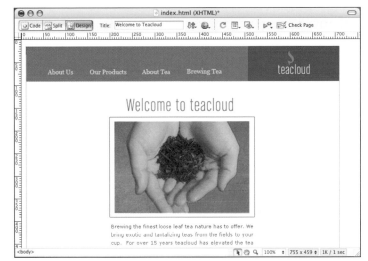

NOTE:

Browser Offset

The white space you see above and to the left of the tracing image is the result of Dreamweaver CS3 honoring the default margins that browsers add to your documents. By default this offset is X:10 Y:15, which means the image is offset 10 pixels from the top and 15 pixels from the left of the document. You can modify this offset by choosing **View > Tracing Image > Adjust Position**.

Dreamweaver CS3 offsets tracing images from the upper-left corner to emulate an offset that exists in browsers. You can get rid of this offset by setting the margin settings in the **Page Properties** dialog box. You'll want to leave the offset alone—it represents what will happen in a browser. If you haven't accounted for this offset in the design of your tracing image, I suggest you don't change this setting.

6 Save the page, and press **F12** (Windows) or **Opt+F12** (Mac) to preview this page in a browser.

Notice that the page appears completely blank. The tracing image appears only in Dreamweaver CS3, and it won't be visible to your user.

7 Return to Dreamweaver CS3. Choose **Modify > Page Properties** to access the tracing image settings again.

8 Drag the **Transparency** slider to **50%**, and click **OK**.

With the opacity reduced, it's much easier to use the tracing image as a guide because it doesn't compete with the foreground images and text.

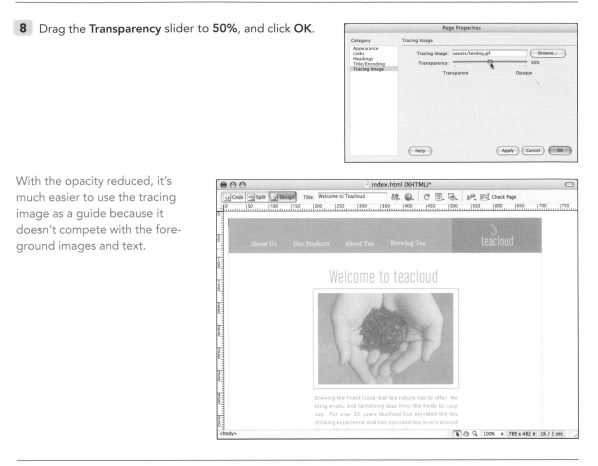

9 Save **index.html**, and leave it open for the next exercise.

N O T E : | **Tracing Image and Background Images**

Once you apply a tracing image to your page, it will hide any background images applied to the document while you are editing the document in Dreamweaver CS3. However, if you view the page containing the tracing image in a browser, the background image will be visible, and the tracing image will not. In other words, tracing images are visible to you only while you're working in Dreamweaver CS3.

2 | Adding AP Divs

In previous chapters, you placed artwork and text directly on your page or in tables. With that method, you can right-, left-, or center-align elements, and that's the end of the story. This is frustrating because it would be much easier if you could stick that artwork or text anywhere you wanted on the page and have it stay there. AP Divs are your friends because you can position them anywhere without restriction. Rather than simply placing artwork and text on a page, as you have been doing so far, you can put your content into AP Divs and move them anywhere you want, even using the new guides in Dreamweaver CS3 to make sure everything is lined up nice and neat. In this exercise, you will learn how to create AP Divs on your page and insert images and text in them.

1 You should still have the **index.html** file from Exercise 1 open. If not, complete Exercise 1, and then return to this exercise.

2 Choose **Insert > Layout Objects > AP Div**.

You just inserted your first AP Div, which you can make any size you like and drag to anywhere you want.

3 Position your cursor over the **handle** (the box on the upper left of the AP Div), and click and drag to move the AP Div so the upper-left corner aligns with the **teacloud** logo in the tracing image. Using the **resizing handles**, resize the AP Div so it fits around the edges of that image.

NOTE:

The Zoom Tool

If you have a hard time getting your AP Divs lined up just right (and we never get them right the first time), Dreamweaver CS3 now lets you zoom in **Design** view. All you need to do is click the magnifying glass icon in the **Tag Selector** and then click and drag a box around the area into which you want to zoom.

The pop-up menu next to the magnifying glass offers you a quick way to zoom to a predefined percentage or just to get back to the 100% view.

Note: Be sure to click the **Select** (arrow) tool when you're done using the **Zoom** tool.

4 Click in the AP Div, and choose **Insert > Image**. Browse to **assets/images**, and select the **logo.png** file. Click **OK** (Windows) or **Choose** (Mac). If the **Image Tag Accessibility Attributes** dialog box appears, type **Teacloud Logo** in the **Alternate text** field, and click **OK**.

An image is now in the AP Div. Notice how this image is darker, whereas the tracing image is screened back? That's because you set the tracing image's opacity to 50% in the previous exercise, which makes it easy to distinguish between the tracing image and the actual content on the page.

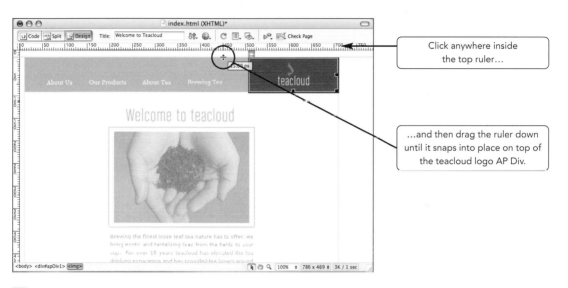

Click anywhere inside the top ruler…

…and then drag the ruler down until it snaps into place on top of the teacloud logo AP Div.

5 Next you're going to draw the AP Div for the navigation area, but to make sure everything gets lined up correctly, you'll use guides. To place a guide at the top of the **teacloud** logo AP Div, click in the ruler at the top of the document, and drag a guide to the top of the logo AP Div; it should snap nicely into place when you get close enough to the AP Div.

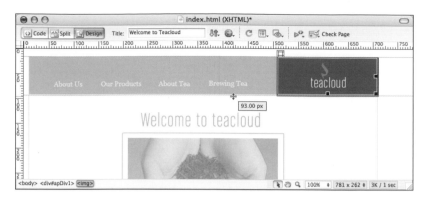

6 Do the same for the bottom of the **teacloud** logo: drag a guide from the top ruler until it snaps into place at the bottom of the AP Div.

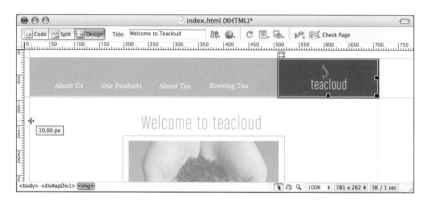

7 Finally, drag a guide from the left ruler so it lines up with the left of the navigation bar in the tracing image.

Now that you have guides for the navigation AP Div, it will be a "snap," quite literally, to draw the navigation AP Div. As you draw an AP Div, your cursor will snap to each of the guides to ensure you get the AP Div in just the right spot.

8 In the **Layout** group of the **Insert** bar, click the **Draw AP Div** object.

This is just another way to place an AP Div object on your page. This allows you to manually draw an AP Div, rather than having a presized AP Div appear on your page, like you did when you chose Insert > Layout Objects > AP Div.

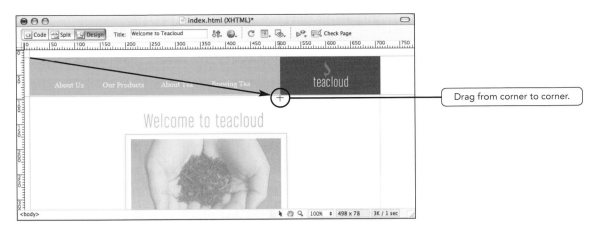

Drag from corner to corner.

9 Before you draw the AP Div, choose **View > Guides > Lock Guides** so you don't accidentally move a guide while you're working. Also make sure **Snap To Guides** is checked. With the **Draw AP Div** tool selected, draw an AP Div around the navigation area of the tracing image.

10 Using **Insert > Image** each time, insert **about us-out.gif**, **ourproducts-out.gif**, **abouttea-out.gif**, and **brewingtea-out.gif** from the **assets/images/ navigation** folder into the new AP Div you just created. If the **Image Tag Accessibility Attributes** dialog box appears, type an appropriate description in the **Alternate text** field for each image, and click **OK**.

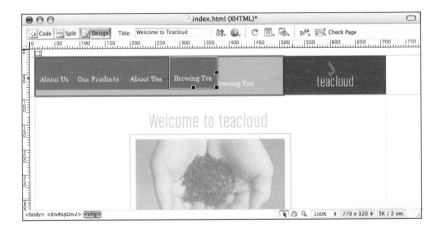

Unfortunately, this AP Div doesn't have any styling that defines how the images should be aligned in the AP Div. In the next step, you'll specify how everything should be aligned.

11 Open the **CSS Styles** panel by choosing **Window > CSS Styles**. Switch to the **All** mode of the panel, and expand the **<style>** group.

Notice there are two styles in here that you didn't write. Each time you insert or draw an AP Div, Dreamweaver automatically gives the AP Div a name and creates a style, which defines how to position the AP Div on the page. This is beneficial because it gives you a quick and easy hook into the AP Divs you just created.

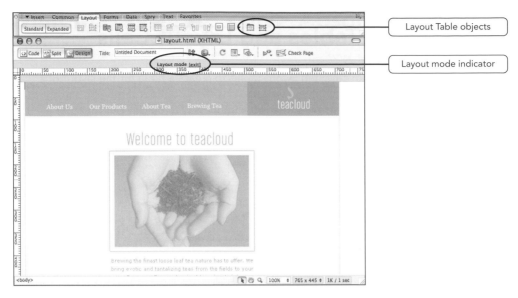

Layout Table objects

Layout mode indicator

You'll notice several changes when you switch to Layout mode. You'll see a gray border above and below the top ruler, as well as an exit link to get out of Layout mode. You should also notice a few new objects available in the Insert bar, which you'll use to begin drawing your tables.

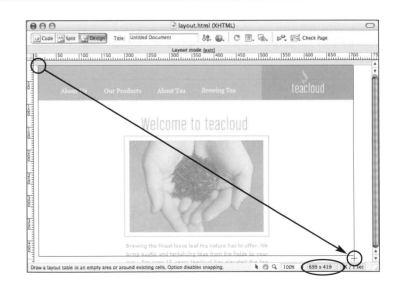

Draw Layout Table

3 In the **Insert** bar, click the **Draw Layout Table** object so you can begin drawing a table.

---

4 In **Design** view, click and drag to draw the table, as shown in the illustration here. Keep an eye on the dimensions in the **status bar**, setting the width of the table to be **700 pixels**. The height value doesn't have to be exact for this exercise.

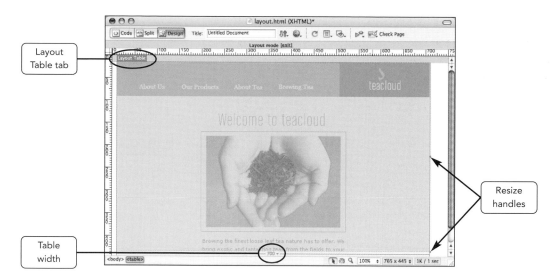

Layout Table tab

Resize handles

Table width

After drawing the table border, Dreamweaver CS3 adds a gray translucent background where the table should be and adds a Layout Table tab to the top of the table so you know what you're working with. You should also notice resize handles all the way around the table and that the table width is displayed at the bottom of the table.

Draw Layout Cell

5 Now it's time to draw the actual table cells. In the **Insert** bar, click the **Draw Layout Cell** object, which lets you draw individual cells in the table.

6 Starting in the upper-left corner of the layout table, draw a table cell the size of the navigation bar, which should be 496 pixels by 76 pixels.

You can check to see how large the cells are as you draw them by watching the status bar.

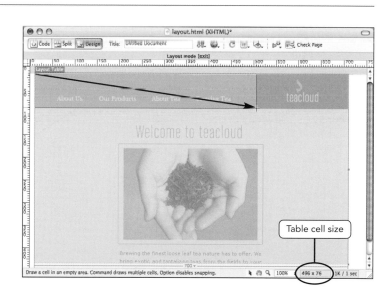

Table cell size

7 Click the **Draw Layout Cell** object again, and beginning in the upper-right corner of the last cell you drew, draw a table cell covering the **teacloud** logo, which should be 204 pixels by 76 pixels. Because you're drawing to the edge of the table, it will snap to the edge of the table border.

8 Click the **Draw Layout Cell** object again, and draw a table cell to hold the **Welcome to teacloud** image, which should be 324 pixels by 320 pixels.

Don't worry if you don't get it just right the first time—you can always adjust the table cells using the resize handles or adjust the width manually through the code or Property inspector.

When you're finished drawing the layout cells, the contents of the layout.html file should match the illustration shown here.

Drawing Multiple Layout Cells

As you work with the layout cells feature, you'll often find yourself creating multiple cells, one after another. However, each time you draw a cell, you need to reselect the **Draw Layout Cell** object before you can create another one. This can get annoying and slow down your workflow quite a bit. If you hold down **Ctrl** (Windows) or **Opt** (Mac) while you draw a layout cell, you can draw as many cells as you want without having to reselect the object each time.

9 It's now time to fill the table with content. Using the method of your choice, insert **aboutus-out.gif**, **ourproducts-out.gif**, **abouttea-out.gif**, and **brewingtea-out.gif** from the **assets/images/navigation** folder into the upper-left table cell. If the **Image Tag Accessibility Attributes** dialog box appears, type an appropriate description in the **Alternate text** field for each image, and click **OK**.

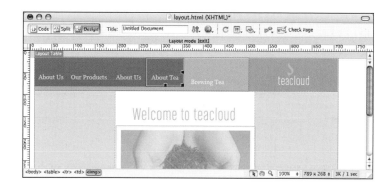

10 Click the edge of the table cell to select it. In the **Property inspector**, choose **Center** in the **Horz** pop-up menu, and choose **Bottom** in the **Vert** pop-up menu. Type **#6E7970** in the **Bg** field to set the background color of the table cell.

Notice the Property inspector is a little different for table cells when you're in Layout mode versus Standard mode, which you used in Chapter 8, *"Working with Tables."*

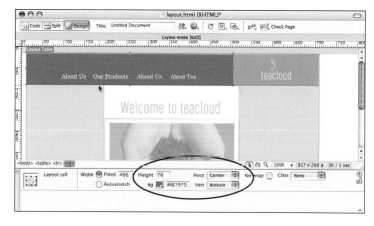

You get a few extra options, and quite a few (background image, header options, and so on) have been removed. For this reason, it's not really possible to work only in Layout mode since you don't get access to all the table and table cell properties.

11 Insert the **logo.png** image from the **assets/images** folder in the upper-right table cell. If the **Image Tag Accessibility Attributes** dialog box appears, type **Teacloud Logo** in the **Alternate text** field, and click **OK**.

12 Insert the **landing.jpg** image from the **assets/images** folder in the center table cell. If the **Image Tag Accessibility Attributes** dialog box appears, type **Welcome to Teacloud** for **Alternate text**, and click **OK**.

Unfortunately, the image isn't lining up nicely with the tracing image. You'll need to adjust the center table cell to bring the image down in line with the tracing image.

13 Click the border of the center table cell to select it, and click and drag the top-center resizing handle to bring the top of the image down in line with the tracing image.

Again, don't worry about getting it right on the first try; just keep adjusting until you get the image where you want it.

---

14 Save the page, and press **F12** (Windows) or **Opt+F12** (Mac) to preview the file in your browser.

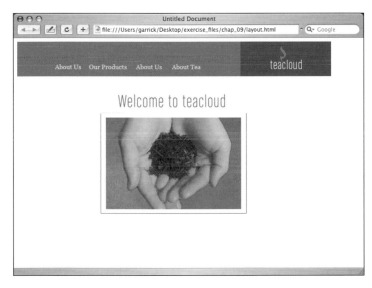

Everything is now right where you placed it in Layout mode. In the next exercise, you'll start working with table and cell widths in Layout mode.

---

15 Save **layout.html**, and leave it open for the next exercise.

---

4 | Working with Layout Table Widths

Although it may not seem like something as simple as setting table widths deserves an exercise all its own, table widths are handled a little differently in Layout mode than in **Standard** mode (which you used in Chapter 8, *"Working with Tables"*). In this exercise, you'll work with autostretch layout cells and learn how to manage the ebb and flow of your table cells in percentage-based layouts.

1 You should still have the **layout.html** file from Exercise 3 open. If not, complete Exercise 3, and then return to this exercise.

2 Select the navigation table cell. In the **Property inspector**, select the **Autostretch** radio button.

Setting this table cell to Autostretch means that as the browser window expands and contracts, the navigation table cell will always fill up as much of the available width as it can.

3 When the **Choose Spacer Image** dialog box appears, select the **Create a spacer image file** option to instruct Dreamweaver CS3 to create a single-pixel transparent GIF file. Click **OK**.

4 In the **Save Spacer Image File As** dialog box, browse to the **assets/images** folder, and click **Save**. The file will be named **spacer.gif** automatically.

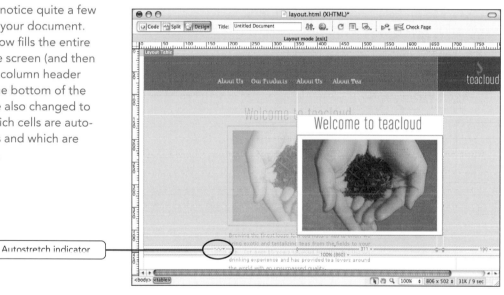

You should notice quite a few changes to your document. The table now fills the entire width of the screen (and then some). The column header menus at the bottom of the screen have also changed to indicate which cells are auto-stretch cells and which are fixed width.

Autostretch indicator

NOTE:

Understanding Spacer GIF Options

To prevent the table from collapsing in some browsers, Dreamweaver CS3 will insert an invisible GIF in the cells without content. If you're not overly concerned with older browsers, you can choose **Don't use spacer images for autostretch tables** in the **Choose Spacer Image** dialog box, but you may end up with odd results in some table layouts.

Understanding the Anatomy of Layout Cells

Notice the bottoms of the cells have changed. The following chart explains what each of these visual cues mean:

Layout Cell Display	
Item	**Description**
——— 244 ▾ ———	A layout cell with a numeric value displayed at the bottom means the cell has a specific width value set in pixels. You can change this value with the resize handles or in the Property inspector.
═══ 244 ▾ ═══	A layout cell with a numeric value and thick double lines indicates the cell is set to a specific pixel value and also contains a spacer GIF. This occurs when another column has been set to Autostretch.
——— ⩗▾ ———	A layout cell with a little squiggle at the bottom indicates the column has been set to Autostretch, which means it will stretch to fill the remaining horizontal space in the browser window. You can change this setting to a fixed-pixel value in the Property inspector.

5 Save the page, and press **F12** (Windows) or **Opt+F12** (Mac) to preview the page in your browser.

Resize the browser, and you'll see the navigation always fills the available width. However, the Welcome to teacloud graphic doesn't stay centered in the document. To get things to stretch the way they should, you need to do a little more work.

6 Return to Dreamweaver CS3. Select the center table cell, and click and drag the left and right resize handles to make the center table cell as wide as the entire table.

Resize handles

Drag both resize handles to the edges of the table.

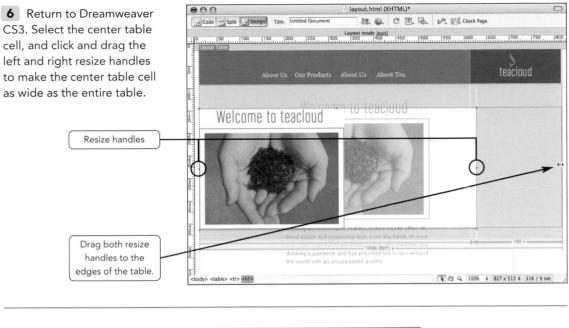

7 With the table cell still selected, choose **Center** in the **Horz** pop-up menu in the **Property inspector**.

8 Save the page, and press **F12** (Windows) or **Opt+F12** (Mac) to preview your page in the browser again.

Now, no matter how much you resize the browser window, the navigation always stays where it's supposed to be, and the Welcome to teacloud image is locked into the center of the page.

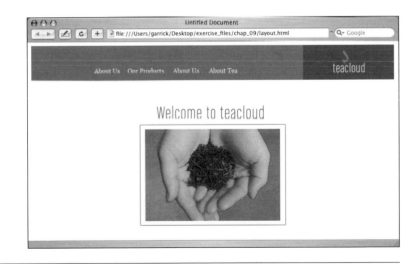

9 Click the **exit** link to leave **Layout** mode.

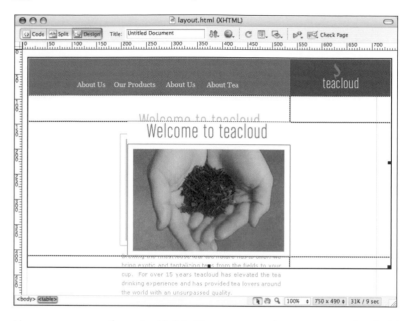

Here you can see the actual table Dreamweaver has constructed to hold your design in place. Figuring out how to create a table like this yourself can be difficult and time-consuming, especially when you need to determine which cells are going to contain transparent GIFs, which cells are going to merge with other cells, and so on. But all you had to do was switch to Layout mode, draw a layout table and some layout cells, and add your content. Dreamweaver handled all the dirty work.

---

10 Save and close **layout.html**.

You're all finished with another chapter. In this chapter, you learned how to draw and manipulate AP Divs, how to use the Zoom tool and guides to make it easy to draw your AP Divs, and how to use Layout mode to quickly develop complicated table structures.

10

Designing for Devices

In the past, if someone was looking at your site, you knew they were looking at it on a computer. They had at least a 15-inch monitor and were using one of four or five browsers. They used a Mac or Windows computer, and that was it. As a result, it was "easy" to develop a site to fit these parameters. As the world becomes more connected, users are accessing the Internet with smaller and more diverse devices. Your site may be accessed by a Mac, a Windows-based computer, a PDA (**P**ersonal **D**igital **A**ssistant), a cell phone, or even a refrigerator (no, we're not kidding). This change in the Internet landscape is just now starting to creep into the everyday life of a Web designer. As this trend continues, you'll need to design for devices other than computers.

In this chapter, you'll learn how to use CSS (**C**ascading **S**tyle **S**heets) to design for a printer by creating a print media style sheet; after all, a printer is just another device you can accommodate through your designs. Once you learn how to use a CSS-media style sheet for one type of device, you can apply the principles you've learned to other media style sheets and devices; you just need to learn which rules and concepts work on the type of device for which you're designing. Finally, you'll take a tour of the new Adobe Device Central, which lets you see how your Web pages will look on various portable devices.

What's a Device?

A **device** (in Web terms) is any electronic widget with which a user views a Web page. This can be a computer (the default device we all design for), a PDA (such as a Palm or Pocket PC), a cell phone, a TV, or the printer attached to your computer at home. CSS provides the flexibility to render pages differently depending on the type of device that's accessing a particular Web page. The following chart shows all the device types CSS supports:

SS Media Types	
Media Type	**Description**
all	Used as the default media type by CSS if nothing else is specified. As a result, any device accessing the site will use this style sheet to render the contents of the page.
braille	Used for Braille tactile feedback devices.
embossed	Used for Braille printers.
handheld	Used for handheld devices, such as PDAs and cell phones.
print	Used for printing and print previews.
projection	Used for projectors.
screen	Used for computer displays.
speech	Used for speech synthesizers. There is a complete section of the CSS specification intended for aural representation of data.
tty	Used for Teletypes and other devices intended for the hearing impaired.
tv	Used for television displays, such as Microsoft's WebTV.

Attaching a Printer-Friendly Style Sheet

The easiest device to design for is the printer. Nearly everyone has one, and to see what your page will look like on a printer, you simply need to use your browser's **Print Preview** options. In this exercise, you'll link your page to a print-media style sheet so users can effectively print the Teacloud site.

---

1 If you haven't already done so, copy the **chap_10** folder from the **Dreamweaver HOT CD-ROM** to your desktop. Define your site as **Chapter 10** using the **chap_10** folder as the local root folder. Make sure the **Files** panel is open. If it's not, choose **Window > Files**.

2 In the **Files** panel, double-click **abouttea.html** to open it. Press **F12** (Windows) or **Opt+F12** (Mac) to preview the file in your browser.

---

3 If you're using Firefox or Internet Explorer, choose **File > Print Preview**. If you're using Safari, choose **File > Print**, and click **Preview**.

Drawer Previous Next Page Back/Forward Zoom In Zoom Out Tool Mode

Teacloud – About Tea – History

About Us   Our Products   About Tea   Brewing Tea

teacloud

About Tea:History

> History

> From the Fields

> Tea Types

The Legendary Origins of Tea

The history of tea extends so far into the past that its very origins are shrouded by legend. It is said that Emperor Shen Nung, who ruled China in 2700 BC, used to enjoy relaxing in his garden with a cup of hot water. It was during one of these respites that a tea leaf happened to float down from a nearby bush, and land directly in the Emperor's cup. The new drink quickly became the Emperor's favorite, and a taste for tea quickly spread throughout the aristocracy, and it wasn't long before tea was the favored drink throughout all of China.

It was in the 16th century that Portuguese missionaries were seduced by tea's flavor and the intricate customs which surrounded it. A demand for the drink quickly arose, and the Dutch East India Company began

☐ Soft Proof   Print   Cancel

As you can see, the printed version of this page isn't very compelling. The navigation doesn't serve any use to your visitors when the page prints, and the logo looks terrible without its background color.

4 Return to Dreamweaver CS3. If it's not already open, open the **CSS Styles** panel by choosing **Window > CSS Styles**. Click the **Attach Style Sheet** button to attach a new style sheet.

I've created a blank style sheet file for you (print.css) that you'll attach. There aren't any styles defined, but you'll need to follow a few extra steps to make sure the style sheet is attached correctly.

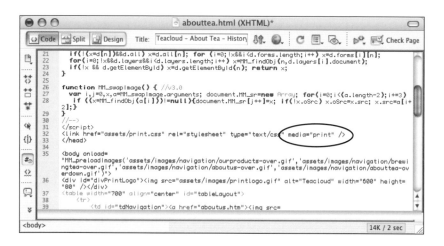

5 In the **Attach External Style Sheet** dialog box, click the **Browse** button, and locate the **print.css** file in the **assets** folder. Select **Link** as the **Add as** option, choose **print** in the **Media** pop-up menu, and click **OK**.

6 Switch to **Code** view. Scroll up to line 32, and find the **<link>** tag that attaches the **print.css** file.

Notice the **<link>** tag has a **media** attribute of **print**. Adding the **media** attribute declares the style sheet should be used only for a specific type of media; in this case, that's print.

7 Save **abouttea.html**, and leave it open for the next exercise, where you'll actually start creating the print styles.

2 | Styling for Print

Now that you've attached a print-media style sheet to your page, it's time to start creating the rules. Dreamweaver's **Style Rendering** toolbar makes it easy to design for devices, including printers, by allowing you to switch back and forth between style sheets when working in **Design** view. As you'll see, the **Style Rendering** toolbar has some quirks, but this exercise gives you an idea of what to expect as you style your pages.

---

1 You should still have the **abouttea.html** file from Exercise 1 open. If not, complete Exercise 1, and then return to this exercise. Make sure you're working in **Design** view.

---

2 If it's not already open, open the **CSS Styles** panel by choosing **Window > CSS Styles**. Click the **New CSS Rule** button to open the **New CSS Rule** dialog box.

First you'll hide the navigation table cell.

---

3 In the **New CSS Rule** dialog box, select **Advanced** for **Selector Type**, and type **#tdNavigation** in the **Selector** field to create a CSS rule that applies only to the navigation table cell. (I've already tagged the navigation cell with the **#tdNavigation** ID selector.) In the **Define in** pop-up menu, choose **print.css**, and click **OK** to open the **CSS Rule Definition** dialog box.

Choosing print.css ensures this change will apply only to the print-media style sheet, not to the main style sheet, so these changes will affect the site only when users choose to print the contents of a page.

---

4 In the **CSS Rule Definition** dialog box, select **Block** in the **Category** list, and set the **Display** property to **none**. Click **OK** to create the rule.

Setting the Display property to none will essentially "turn off" the navigation, so it does not display when users print the page.

---

5 You won't see any change in **Design** view. Save the page, and press **F12** (Windows) or **Opt+F12** (Mac) to preview the page in your browser. Again, you don't see any changes. Open **Print Preview**. If you're using Firefox or Internet Explorer, choose **File > Print Preview**. If you're using Safari, choose **File > Print**, and click **Preview**.

The display of the print version isn't quite what we were after yet. The navigation is now hidden, but the logo still needs some work. You should have noticed, however, that the navigation displayed just fine when viewing the page in the browser; it disappeared only when you chose Print Preview. Again, the changes you made are only to the print-media style sheet.

---

6 Return to Dreamweaver CS3, and switch to the **print.css** file. Now you'll add the selectors to ensure that the logo, the side navigation, and the footer of the page should also be hidden when this page is printed, since there's no real need for any of those items to appear on a printed page. Change the

#tdNavigation rule to **#tdNavigation, #tdLogo, #tdSidebar, #tdFooter** by simply typing the new selectors in the CSS file. When you're finished, your CSS file should look like the illustration shown here.

Changing the rule to include the additional table cells ensures they're also hidden when users attempt to print the page.

7 Save **print.css**, switch back to **abouttea.html**, and press **F12** (Windows) or **Opt+F12** (Mac) to preview the file again. If you're using Firefox or Internet Explorer, choose **File > Print Preview**. If you're using Safari, choose **File > Print**, and click **Preview**.

Now this page looks much more like it was intended to be printed rather than simply looking like a printed Web page.

As you can imagine, the process of editing a style sheet, saving the document, opening it in the browser, and opening the browser's Print Preview can be tedious. The Style Rendering toolbar makes this a far less painful process.

The Style Rendering toolbar

8 Return to Dreamweaver CS3. Choose **View > Toolbars > Style Rendering** to open the **Style Rendering** toolbar.

Understanding the Style Rendering Toolbar

The **Style Rendering** toolbar lets you switch the display to different media style sheets directly in **Design** view. Each of the buttons in the **Style Rendering** toolbar relates to a specific media type.

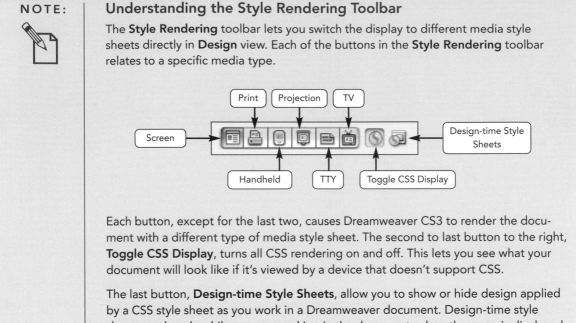

Each button, except for the last two, causes Dreamweaver CS3 to render the document with a different type of media style sheet. The second to last button to the right, **Toggle CSS Display**, turns all CSS rendering on and off. This lets you see what your document will look like if it's viewed by a device that doesn't support CSS.

The last button, **Design-time Style Sheets**, allow you to show or hide design applied by a CSS style sheet as you work in a Dreamweaver document. Design-time style sheets apply only while you are working in the document; when the page is displayed in a browser, only the styles that are actually attached to or embedded in the document appear.

Although style rendering in Dreamweaver CS3 for other media types isn't perfect (which you'll discover in a moment), it definitely helps you get close to your final design when designing a particular media style sheet.

9 In the **Style Rendering** toolbar, click the **Render Print Media Type** button, if it's not already selected.

Unfortunately, the `display:none` style on table cells happens to be one of the styles Dreamweaver CS3 fails to render, so at this point the Style Rendering toolbar isn't terribly exciting.

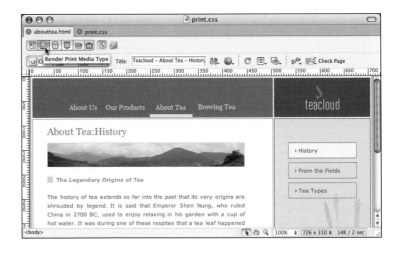

If you take a peek at the code of about-tea.html, you'll notice a `<div>` that's hidden. This `<div>` contains a logo specifically for printing, but its `display` property is set to `none` in the styles.css file, which is used for the screen. Next, you'll add a version of the teacloud logo that will appear only when the page is printed.

10 In the **CSS Styles** panel, click the **New CSS Rule** button so you can define a rule to display the print logo.

11 In the **New CSS Rule** dialog box, select **Advanced** for **Selector Type**, and type **#divPrintLogo** in the **Selector** field. In the **Define in** pop-up menu, choose **print.css**. Click **OK**.

12 In the **CSS Rule Definition** dialog box, select **Block** in the **Category** list. Set the **Text align** property to **center**, and set the **Display** property to **block**. Click **OK**.

The styles.css file sets the display property of `divPrintLogo` to `none`, which hides it from the browser. Setting the Display property to `block` in the print style sheet ensures the image displays when users print the page.

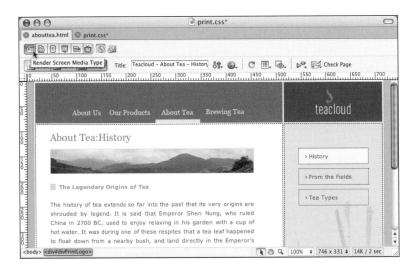

Now that the print logo **<div>** has been set to display as a block, and it shows up in Design view because Print is still selected in the Style Rendering toolbar.

13 In the **Style Rendering** toolbar, click the **Render Screen Media Type** button. The print logo disappears again.

Now that you're showing the screen media style sheet, the print logo is hidden. The **display:none** rule in the style.css file now takes precedence over the **display:block** style you added to print.css.

14 Press **F12** (Windows) or **Opt+F12** (Mac) one last time to preview the page in your browser. Save any files you're prompted to save. The browser now shows the design as it has always been. If you're using Firefox or Internet Explorer, choose **File > Print Preview**. If you're using Safari, choose **File > Print**, and click **Preview**.

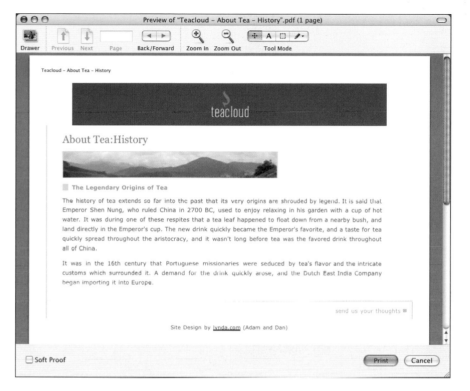

Notice the new print logo displayed with the navigation stripped from the document, just as intended. As you can see, using CSS and the Style Rendering toolbar in Dreamweaver CS3 makes it easy to design for different devices. Although you learned how to design for a printer in this exercise, you can apply the skills you learned when designing for any device, including PDAs, cell phones, and so on.

---

15 Return to Dreamweaver CS3, and leave **abouttea.html** open for the next exercise.

---

3 | Accessing Adobe Device Central

One of the main problems with designing for different devices is that to get an accurate rendering of the style sheet you're creating, you really should have the device for which you're designing. For example, if you're designing a site that's intended to be viewed on a cell phone or a PDA, you should have the phone or PDA you're designing for to really see what your Web page is going to look like on that particular device. But it's pretty unrealistic and impractical to obtain all the hundreds of possible devices your visitors might use to view your Web page.

Fortunately, Adobe has taken a major step forward in helping designers see what their pages might look like on different devices, with a new application called Device Central. Device Central comes bundled in all versions of the CS3 suite as well as with Dreamweaver CS3, so you already have a copy installed on your computer. In this exercise, you'll take a quick look at how Device Central can help you see what your Web pages will look like on several different devices.

1 You should still have the **abouttea.html** file from Exercise 2 open. If not, open it.

2 Choose **File > Preview in Browser > Device Central** to open Device Central.

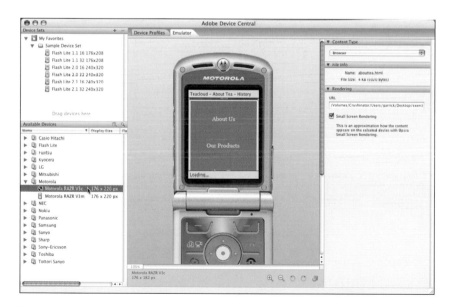

In Device Central, you can see an emulation of what the abouttea.html page will look like on a cell phone, as shown in the illustration here. And you can select from dozens of phones and devices.

3 In the **Available Devices** pane, double-click **Motorola**, and double-click **Motorola RAZR V3c**.

The emulator now shows what the page will look like on the RAZR phone. But you're not limited to just looking at the picture in the emulator. You can scroll through your page, check to see whether behaviors such as rollovers work in that particular device, and even click links.

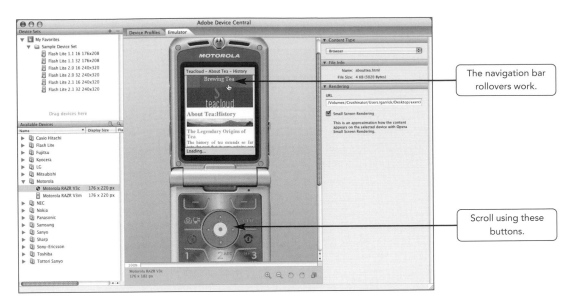

The navigation bar rollovers work.

Scroll using these buttons.

4 Use the navigation buttons on the RAZR to scroll down through your page and examine it. Position your cursor over some of the navigation items, and notice that the rollovers work on this device.

5 Take some time to double-click some of the other devices to check out how **about-tea.html** will be rendered. Note that the **Available Devices** pane lists each device's screen resolution, which can be particularly useful if you're targeting a specific device and want to make sure your page will fit properly on its screen.

Adobe is constantly adding new devices to Device Central. To make sure you have the most current collection of virtual devices, choose Devices > Check for Device Updates. You'll be taken to Device Central Online, where you'll be able to download the latest device profiles from Adobe.

6 When you're done checking out devices, quit Device Central, and return to Dreamweaver.

---

7 Save and close all open documents in Dreamweaver.

This chapter showed you how to specify a print-media style sheet, as well as how to use the Style Rendering toolbar to turn individual style sheets on and off. Unfortunately, Dreamweaver CS3's rendering of other media styles isn't an exact science, but as you begin to learn more about the inner workings of Dreamweaver CS3 and the limitations of the devices you're designing for, using the Style Rendering toolbar will speed up your development immensely. In the next chapter, you'll learn how to create rollovers and navigation bars to spice up your sites.

11

Adding Rollover Images

One of the key challenges in Web development is to produce artwork that clearly communicates how to navigate through your site. **Rollover graphics**, which change when the visitor's cursor moves over them, are great for adding visual cues that ensure your audience knows an image has special meaning or that it is a link. Rollovers are also great if you have limited space, because you can put extra information within the changing graphic. For example, you can make a button that says *Services*, and when a visitor places the cursor over the word, it can change to list the services you offer.

What you might not realize is that rollovers aren't just XHTML (e**X**tensible **H**yper**T**ext **M**arkup **L**anguage). Instead, rollovers are a combination of XHTML and JavaScript. JavaScript allows you to manipulate the user's browser to perform actions not possible with simple XHTML code.

Adobe Dreamweaver CS3 automatically writes all the necessary JavaScript code without ever having to write the scripts or even understand how they are constructed. Once you get more familiar with JavaScript, you'll most likely continue using the rollover capabilities in Dreamweaver CS3 because it can save days of programming work. For this reason, the Dreamweaver CS3 rollover feature is helpful to both designers and programmers.

Following Rollover Rules

Although this book provides many exercises that teach you how to implement rollovers, it is my hope you'll move beyond the exercises to create your own custom rollover graphics once you get the hang of this feature. If you plan to make your own rollovers from scratch, you should be aware of a few important concepts.

Rollovers require a minimum of two graphics—an **off** state (also called an **out** state) and an **on** state (also called an **over** state). Because this is a book about Dreamweaver CS3, it doesn't cover how to make the graphic component of rollovers. You would need an imaging program, such as Adobe Fireworks or Adobe Photoshop, to make the images. You'll learn more about creating graphics in Fireworks in Chapter 15, *"Editing Images."*

If you are going to make your own rollover graphics in an image editor, one important rule to understand is that the graphics for the off state and on state for each of your rollover images must have the same dimensions, or they might look distorted. If you have two different-sized pieces of artwork, then JavaScript will scale both to the same width and height, causing distortion. For this reason, all the images provided in this chapter's exercises share the same dimensions.

1 | Creating a Simple Rollover

This exercise shows you how to create a simple rollover. These types of rollovers involve two pieces of artwork. The first graphic—the original, or out, state—appears on the screen initially; the second graphic—the over state—appears when a user moves the cursor over it. In JavaScript terminology, this is called a **swap image**. But you will not be writing any JavaScript from scratch because Dreamweaver CS3 makes creating a simple rollover as easy as a few button clicks.

---

1 If you haven't already done so, copy the **chap_11** folder from the **Dreamweaver HOT CD-ROM** to your desktop. Define your site as **Chapter 11** using the **chap_11** folder as the local root folder.

The original state before the cursor moves over the graphic in the browser.

The over state after the cursor moves over the graphic in the browser.

The two images shown in the illustration here are what you'll be using to create the rollovers in this exercise. You'll insert the image on the left directly into the page, and the image on the right is what will be displayed when the user moves the cursor over the image.

---

2 In the **Files** panel, double-click **index.html** to open it.

This is the same design you've been using throughout the book, but I've removed the navigation from the top of the page. You'll get to add that navigation in the following steps.

---

3 Click in the table cell in the upper left of the page.

This is where you'll insert the navigation buttons, which will include rollovers with over states.

Click in this table cell.

---

4 In the **Common** group of the **Insert bar**, choose **Rollover Image** in the **Image** pop-up menu to open the **Insert Rollover Image** dialog box.

5 Type **aboutus** in the **Image Name** field. For **Original image**, click **Browse**, and select **aboutus_out.gif**, which is located in the **assets/images/navigation** folder. For **Rollover image**, click **Browse**, and select **aboutus_over.gif**, which is located in the same folder. Type **About Us** in the **Alternate text** field. Type **aboutus.html** in the **When clicked, Go to URL** field. Click **OK**.

The image has been added to the page. If you click the image and look at the Tag Selector, you can see that the image has been wrapped in an **<a>** tag and that the image has been given the ID **aboutus**.

Understanding the Insert Rollover Image Options

The **Insert Rollover Image** dialog box contains a number of options, and you need to understand each option and its role when creating rollovers:

	Insert Rollover Image Options
Field	**Description**
Image name	The **Image name** field specifies the ID that will be applied to the `<img>` tag so the JavaScript code Dreamweaver CS3 inserts can properly identify the image. The image name should be alphanumeric with no special characters or spaces, and it should start with a letter, not a number.
Original image	The original image is the image that displays when the page first loads; it remains there until the visitor moves the cursor over the image.
Rollover image	The rollover image is the image that's displayed when the visitor moves the cursor over the original image. The original image is swapped out for the rollover image, which gives the illusion that the original image changed.
Preload rollover image	Select this box to ensure the rollover image graphic is loaded into the browser's memory as soon as the page loads. If this option isn't selected, the browser won't actually grab the rollover image from the server until after the visitor moves the cursor over the image. It's best to leave this option turned on; otherwise, there might be a visible delay between the time the visitor positions the mouse over the image and the time it actually changes to the over image.
Alternate text	This field adds the `alt` attribute to the image.
When clicked	This field specifies the location the users will be sent to when clicking the image. For example, if the rollover is for a navigation bar, insert the page you want to link to when users click the navigation button.

6 Save the page, and press **F12** (Windows) or **Opt+F12** (Mac) to preview the rollover. Position the cursor over the image you just inserted.

Notice as you move the cursor over the image, the corresponding over image appears.

7 Return to Dreamweaver CS3, and position your cursor directly after the **About Us** image. Choose **Insert > Image Objects > Rollover Image**.

8 In the **Insert Rollover Image** dialog box, type **ourproducts** in the **Image name** field. For **Original image**, click **Browse**, and select **ourproducts_out.gif**, which is located in the **assets/images/navigation** folder. For **Rollover image**, click **Browse**, and select **ourproducts_over.gif**, located in the same folder. Type **Our Products** in the **Alternate text** field. Leave the **When clicked, Go to URL** field blank. Click **OK**.

9 Use the techniques you learned in Steps 7 and 8 to create navigation buttons, complete with over states, for the **About Tea** and **Brewing Tea** buttons. You'll find their corresponding out and over images in the **assets/images/navigation** folder.

Null Links and Rollovers

You may have noticed when you inserted the previous three images that the **Link** field for the **<a>** tags was set to a number sign (#). Dreamweaver CS3 inserted this symbol in order to create a link, even though you didn't specify one.

This link is necessary for the JavaScript rollover to work correctly. Inserting a number sign in the **Link** field inserts a stand-in link that doesn't actually take the user anywhere. It simply acts as a placeholder so the user can see the rollover. Once the rest of the pages are in place, you can then link them to the correct page.

10 Save the page, and press **F12** (Windows) or **Opt+F12** (Mac) once more to preview all the rollovers.

Move your cursor over each of the buttons, and you'll see the over state displayed.

11 Save **index.html**, and leave it open for the next exercise.

NOTE: | **Inserting Rollovers**

As you'll see later in this chapter, you can insert rollovers in other ways. Using the **Insert Rollover** feature, either in the menu bar or in the **Insert** bar, is certainly the most efficient. In addition to inserting both image states, you also get to name the image, give it an **<alt>** tag, and set your link, all in one dialog box.

NOTE: | **Creating Animated Rollovers**

Throughout this chapter, you'll learn different methods to insert and work with rollovers. In addition to what you're learning here, you should experiment with rollovers to examine new ways users can interact with your pages. One such technique is an **animated rollover**. An animated rollover is the same as a static-image rollover, but it uses an animated GIF in one, or both, of the rollover states. Although this can add a nice touch to any page, you want to be careful not to overdo it. In the case of animated GIFs, a little goes a long way. If your animated GIF is set to **loop**—that is, play continuously—preloading the image is fine. If it is supposed to play only once, make sure the **Preload Rollover Image** check box is deselected when importing the image. If the animated GIF preloads, the animation will play when preloaded, and by the time your user ends up moving the cursor over the image, it will no longer animate!

2 | Creating Disjointed Rollovers

Disjointed rollovers aren't really as painful as they may sound. A **disjointed rollover** happens when you visitor moves the cursor over one image and another image on the page changes. The "disjoint" happens because you're affecting a different image than the one the visitor is interacting with. This exercise shows you how to create a disjointed rollover and introduces you to the **Swap Image** behavior, which was added for you automatically in the previous exercise.

---

1 You should still have the **index.html** file from Exercise 1 open. If not, complete Exercise 1, and then return to this exercise.

It's always nice to give users some additional information about where they're going to end up when they click a link. In the following steps, you'll add a bit of "hint" text for each of the navigation buttons on your page.

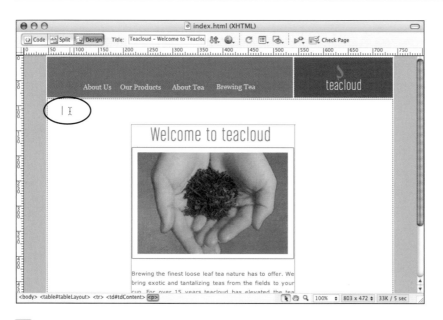

2 Position your cursor above the **Welcome to teacloud** image.

---

3 Choose **Insert > Image**, and browse to **blank.gif** in the **assets/images/hints** folder. If the **Image Tag Accessibility Attributes** dialog box appears when you insert the image, choose **<empty>** for **Alternate text**, and click **OK**.

It may not seem that you've done much at this point—you've just inserted a plain, blank image. However, this image will serve as the place-holder for the hint images you're about to add when your visitors move their cursors over each of the images in the navigation bar.

4 With the image still selected, type **hintimage** in the **ID** field of the **Property inspector**.

As mentioned in the previous exercise, each rollover image must have a valid ID for the JavaScript Dreamweaver CS3 inserts to find it.

These behaviors are applied to the <a> tag surrounding the image.

User actions that will trigger the behavior

Applied behaviors

5 Select the **About Us** image in the navigation bar, and switch to the **Behaviors** panel by choosing **Window > Behaviors**.

The Behaviors panel shows you each of the JavaScript behaviors attached to the selected element on the page. You can see that the About Us image has a Swap Image behavior and a Swap Image Restore behavior applied. The left column shows you the event the behavior is attached to; notice that it's actually applied to the **<a>** tag and not the **<img>** tag.

Now you'll add to these existing rollovers to create your disjointed rollovers.

6 Double-click the **Swap Image** behavior. This opens the **Swap Image** dialog box.

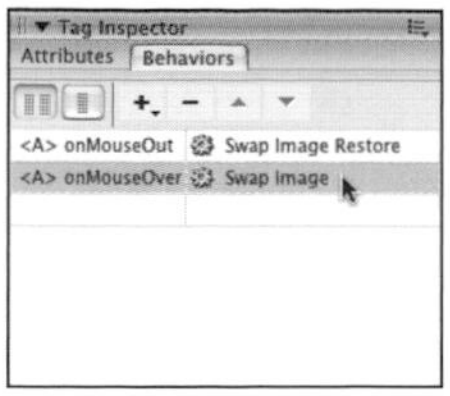

In here you can see the Swap Image behavior you applied in the previous exercise. If you select image "aboutus" in the Images list, you'll see that the Set source to field correctly indicates that the rollover image is aboutus-over.gif. Now you'll have an additional rollover occur when your visitors move their cursors over this image.

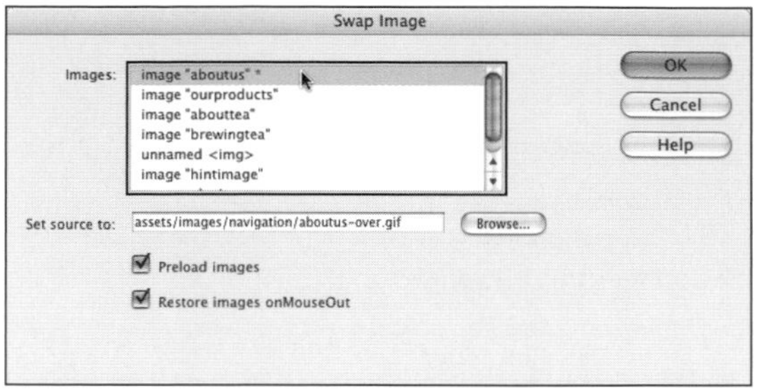

7 In the **Swap Image** dialog box, select **image "hintimage"** in the **Images** list. Click **Browse**, and select **aboutus.gif**, which is located in the **assets/images/hints** folder. An asterisk appears next to **hintimage** indicating that it now has a rollover behavior attached to it. Leave the **Preload images** and **Restore images onMouseOut** options selected, and click **OK**.

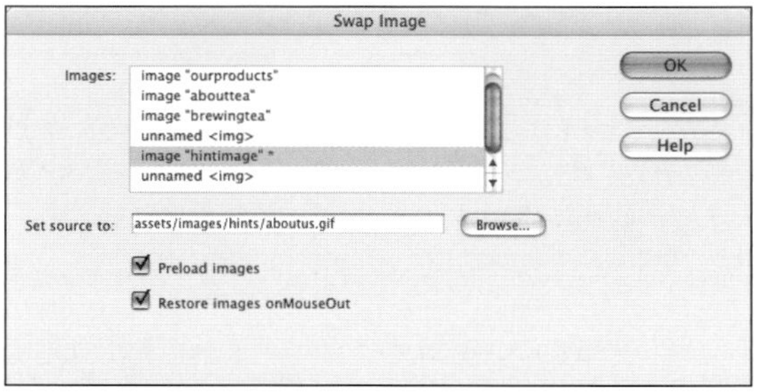

The Images list shows all the images on your page, even images without IDs. Any image without an ID shows as unnamed **<img>**. All images that have valid IDs are listed with their associated ID so you can easily find them. Leaving the two check boxes selected ensures the images get preloaded by the browser and that the image you're swapping is restored to its original state when the user moves the cursor away from the image (the Swap Image Restore behavior is added automatically).

8 Save the page, and press **F12** (Windows) or **Opt+F12** (Mac) to preview the page in your browser.

Notice that moving your cursor over the About Us image now produces two rollover effects: the aboutus image is being swapped, and the blank image is also being swapped for the aboutus text image. To the untrained eye, it may look like text is appearing out of nowhere, but you now know that a Swap Image behavior is actually occurring.

9 Close the browser window, and return to Dreamweaver.

Now you'll create the same effect for the Our Products navigation image.

10 Select the **Our Products** image, and in the **Behaviors** panel, double-click the **Swap Image** behavior.

Notice that the ourproducts image is already selected, and it has an asterisk next to it. Again, the asterisk indicates there is already a swap image for that particular image.

11 In the **Swap Image** dialog box, select **image "hintimage"** in the **Images** list. Click **Browse**, and select **ourproducts.gif**, which is located in the **assets/images/hints** folder. Click **OK**.

Now there is an asterisk next to both ourproducts and hintimage, which means the Swap Image behavior will now swap *two* images instead of one.

12 Use the techniques covered in Steps 10 and 11 to create the rollovers for the **About Tea** and **Brewing Tea** navigation images, setting **hintimage** to **abouttea.gif** and **brewingtea.gif**, which are both located in the **assets/images/hints** folder.

13 Now that you've updated all the **Swap Image** behaviors, save the page, and press **F12** (Windows) or **Opt+F12** (Mac) to preview your page in the browser. Each of the navigation images now shows a hint about what users will see when they click the button.

14 Save and close **index.html**.

VIDEO: | **disjointed_rollovers.mov**

Adding **Swap Image** behaviors can sometimes be a confusing prospect, because you're dealing with image IDs, multiple behaviors, and an oftentimes less-than-intuitive **Behaviors** panel. To learn more about **Swap Image** behaviors, check out **disjointed_rollovers.mov** in the **videos** folder on the **Dreamweaver HOT CD-ROM**.

EXERCISE 3 | Creating Navigation Bars with Multiple Rollover States

So far, you have created simple rollovers and disjointed rollovers. You have one more type of rollover to learn before you get to play with a bit of Flash—the navigation bar. A navigation bar allows each button to display four states: **up**, **over**, **down**, and **over while down**. Instead of working with two images for each rollover, this type of rollover requires you to work with four—one for each separate state. This might sound intimidating, but the Dreamweaver CS3 navigation bar feature makes it much easier than you might imagine.

| Out | Over | Down | Over while down |

1 To begin with, take a look at the **aboutus-out.gif**, **aboutus-over.gif**, **aboutus-down.gif**, and **aboutus-overdown.gif** images shown in the illustration here. Each of the navigation buttons has the same style of images, one for each of the states that will be defined using the Dreamweaver CS3 navigation bar feature.

NOTE:

Understanding Rollover States

Keeping track of the different types of rollover states can be a little tricky. The following chart outlines what each state means:

Rollover States	
State	**What It Does**
Up	The graphic that appears on the Web page when it is loaded. This is also referred to as the **out** or **off** state.
Over	The graphic that appears when the user's cursor moves over the image. Most often, this image will revert to the up state when the cursor is moved away from the image. This is sometimes referred to as the **on** state.
Down	The graphic that appears after the user clicks the over state.
Over while down	The graphic that appears when the user's cursor moves over the down state. It works just like the over state, except that it works on the down state only.

2 In the **Files** panel, double-click **aboutus.html** to open it.

This file is missing the navigation bar you set up in index.html. Instead of adding each image separately, you'll set up the entire navigation in one fell swoop.

---

3 Position your cursor in the cell in the upper-left corner of the page.

This is the cell where you'll insert the navigation bar, which will contain rollovers with multiple states.

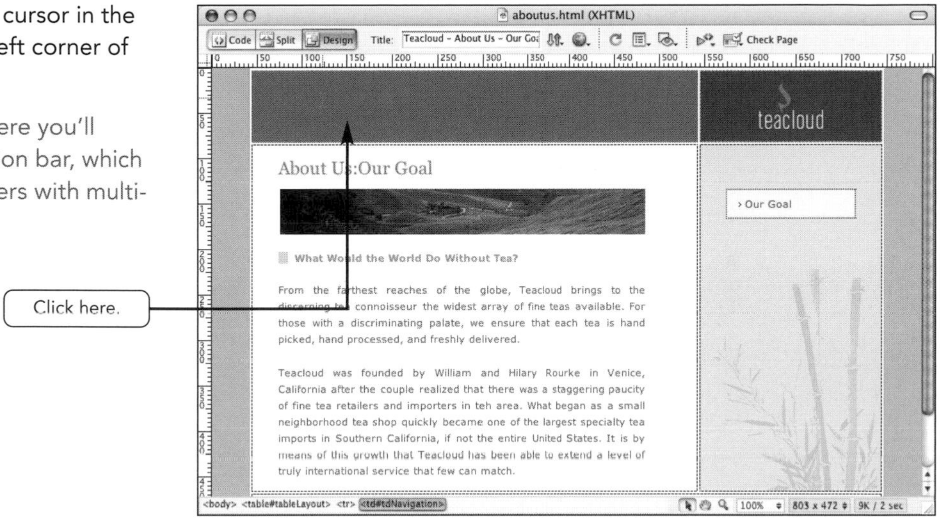

Click here.

---

4 Choose **Insert > Image Objects > Navigation Bar** to open the **Insert Navigation Bar** dialog box.

The Insert Navigation Bar dialog box can be a bit intimidating at first, but you'll get used to it quickly.

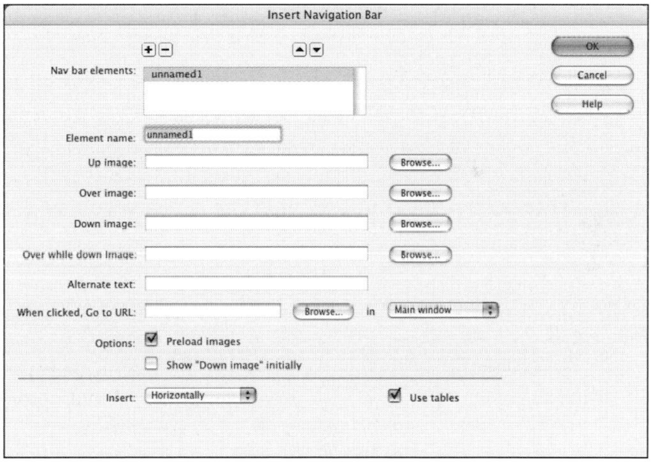

---

5 Type **aboutus** in the **Element name** field.

This is the same as the image name you provided when you used the Insert Rollover Image behavior in the previous exercise. This will be used as the ID for the **<img>** tag.

---

6 Click **Browse** next to the **Up image** field. Select the **aboutus-out.gif** file, which is located in the **assets/images/navigation** folder.

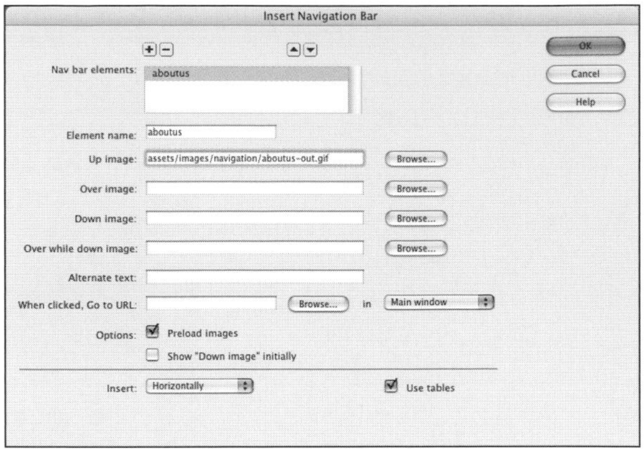

7 Click **Browse** next to the **Over image** field. Select the **aboutus-over.gif** file, which is located in the **assets/images/navigation** folder.

8 Click **Browse** next to the **Down image** field. Select the **aboutus-down.gif** file, which is located in the **assets/images/navigation** folder.

9 Click **Browse** next to the **Over while down image** field. Select the **aboutus-overdown.gif** file, which is located in the **assets/images/navigation** folder.

10 Type **About Us** in the **Alternate** text field.

11 Leave the **When clicked, Go to URL** field blank, since you're already on the **About Us** page.

12 Because you're adding this navigation bar to the **About Us** page, select the **Show "Down image" initially** check box.

13 Deselect the **Use tables** check box.

Leaving this box checked would place each of the navigation buttons in its own table cell; however, you don't need this option in this design.

When you're finished, the options in the Insert Navigation Bar dialog box should match the illustration shown here.

Note: If you accidentally press Enter or Return while working in the Insert Navigation Bar dialog box, the dialog box will close. To continue working on the navigation bar, choose Modify > Navigation Bar.

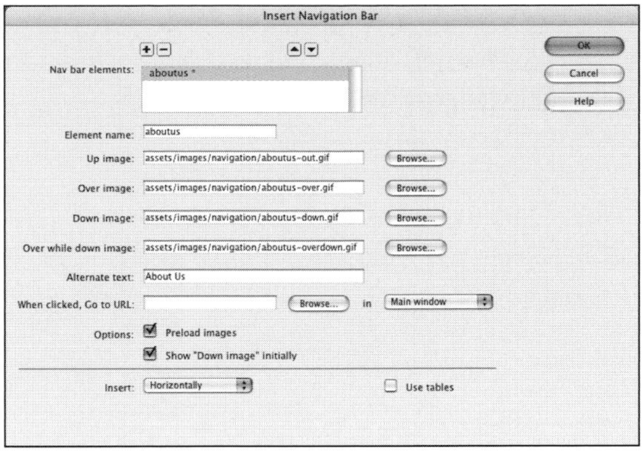

14 At the top of the **Insert Navigation Bar** dialog box, click the **+** to add the next image in the navigation bar. A new unnamed element is added to the **Nav bar elements** list.

15 In the **Insert Navigation Bar** dialog box, match the settings to the ones shown in the illustration here to create the rollover states for the **Our Products** image. Click the **Browse** button for the **When clicked, Go to URL** field to link this rollover to **ourproducts/kettlesandteapots.html**.

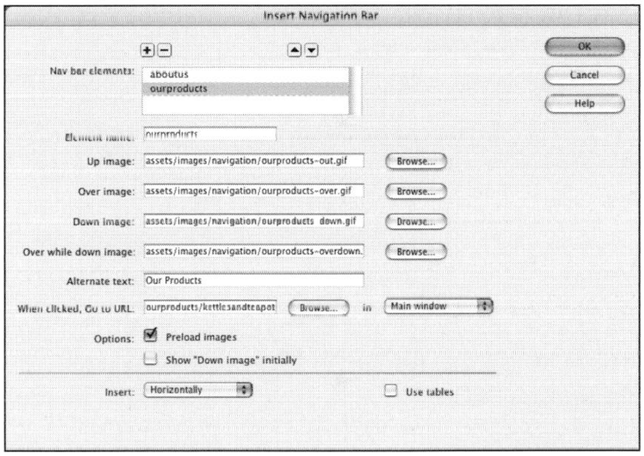

16 Click **+** to add the next image in the navigation bar. A new unnamed element is added to the **Nav bar elements** list. Match the settings to the ones shown in the illustration here to create the rollover states for the **About Tea** image. Link to **abouttea.html** in the **When clicked, Go to URL** field.

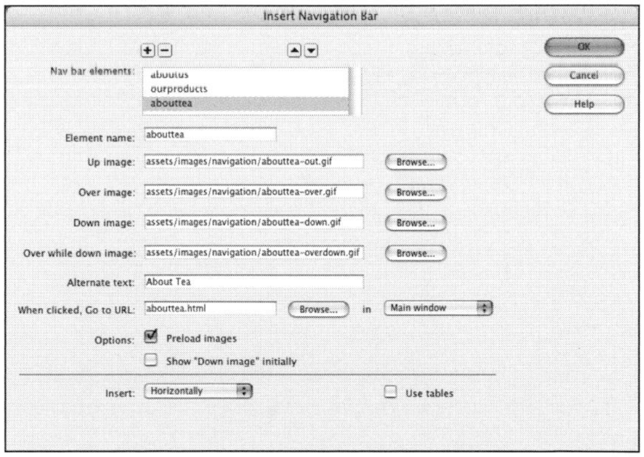

17 Click **+** to add the next image in the navigation bar. A new unnamed element is added to the **Nav bar elements** list. Match the settings to the ones shown in the illustration here to create the rollover states for the **Brewing Tea** image. Link to **brewingtea.html**.

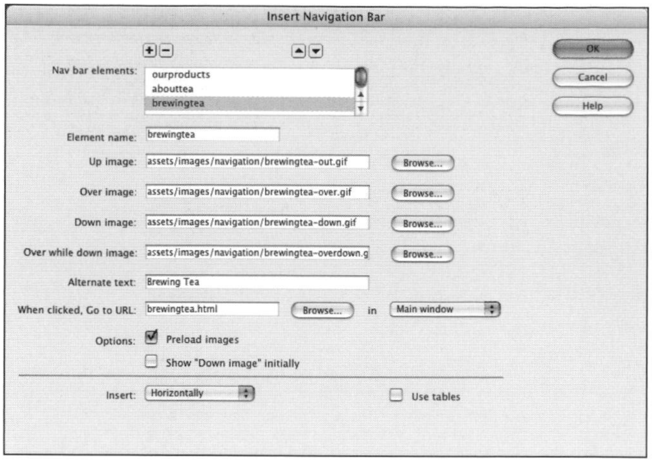

The dialog box should look like the illustration shown here when you're finished. Notice that the aboutus entry in the Nav bar elements list has an asterisk next to it, which tells you this particular element is set to show the down image initially. This gives you a quick indication of the state that each button will be in when the page loads.

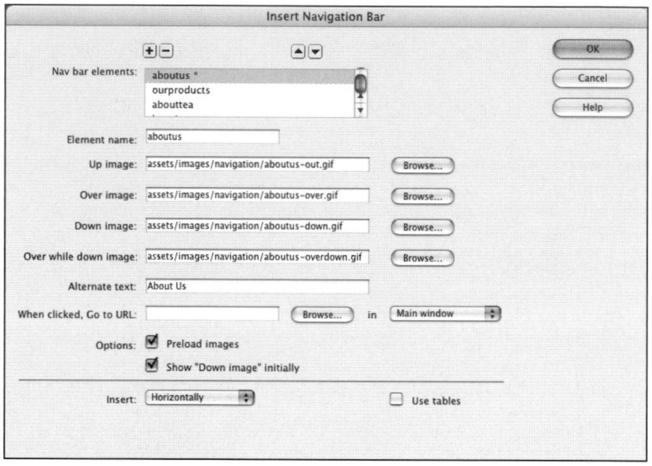

18 Click **OK** to close the **Insert Navigation Bar** dialog box.

Dreamweaver CS3 automatically inserts the images you specified and creates all the complex JavaScript necessary for the rollovers to function—all in about half a second.

19 Save the page, and press **F12** (Windows) or **Opt+F12** (Mac) to preview the page in the browser. Move your cursor over the buttons to see how they behave.

If you click any of the other navigation buttons, you'll find that those pages are missing the navigation bar. Luckily, Dreamweaver CS3 makes it easy to move your navigation bars from page to page.

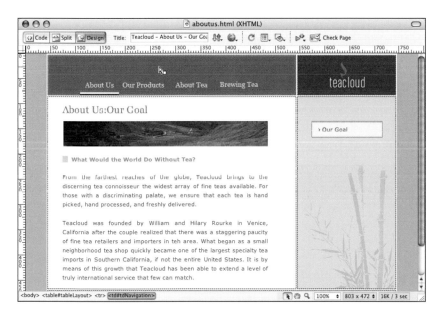

20 Return to Dreamweaver In **aboutus.html**, hold down **Ctrl** (Windows) or **Cmd** (Mac), and click the navigation table cell to select it. Choose **Edit > Copy** to copy the navigation bar to the **Clipboard**.

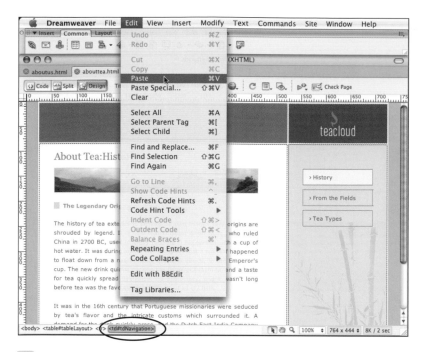

21 In the **Files** panel, double-click **abouttea.html** to open it. Click in the navigation table cell, and then click the **td#tdNavigation** tag selector to select the cell. Choose **Edit > Paste** to paste the navigation bar into the table cell.

The navigation bar is now inserted into abouttea.html, but the wrong image is in the down state.

22 Choose **Modify > Navigation Bar** to edit the navigation bar on the page.

23 With **aboutus** selected in the **Nav bar elements** list, set the **When clicked, Go to URL** field to **aboutus.html**, and deselect **Show "Down image" initially**.

24 Select **abouttea** in the **Nav bar elements** list, and select the **Show "Down image" initially** check box. Click **OK**.

25 Save the page, press **F12** (Windows) or **Opt I F12** (Mac) to preview the page in a browser, and then browse back and forth between **About Us** and **About Tea** to see how the states change for each of the images.

26 Return to Dreamweaver. Save and close all open files.

In this exercise, you learned how to use the Dreamweaver CS3 navigation bar behaviors to set up a complicated navigation bar on multiple pages. At this point, you're finished learning about standard rollover images, and in the next exercise you'll start inserting Flash Buttons directly in Dreamweaver CS3.

What Are Flash Buttons?

Dreamweaver CS3 lets you create **Flash Buttons**, which have similar characteristics to other rollovers you have worked with in this chapter. For example, Flash Buttons have an up state and over state, and you can set them to link to other pages. However, unlike with other buttons, you create them from within Dreamweaver CS3, which means you can quickly change them with just a few clicks, which can save time. You don't need to use an image editor such as Fireworks or Photoshop to work with Flash Buttons.

Creating Flash Buttons is fairly simple, as you will see in the next exercise. What is different is

that Dreamweaver CS3 creates the rollover in the SWF file format, instead of GIF or JPEG. In other exercises, you have simply worked with existing images designed in an image-editing program and set the behavior to write the necessary JavaScript to enact a rollover. With Flash Buttons, you create actual Adobe Flash files directly in Dreamweaver CS3, which can be incredibly convenient.

To view Flash content on the Web, you must have the Flash plug-in installed in your browser. If you don't have this plug-in, you can download it for free at **www.adobe.com/flashplayer**.

Creating Flash Buttons

Pros	Explanation
Font integrity	With Flash Buttons, you can use any font installed in your system, and the visitors to your page don't need to have that font installed. This gives you much more flexibility when you are designing your pages.
Easily updated	With just a few clicks, you can change the text and entire look of your Flash Buttons, which can save a lot of time when you need to make changes to your site.
Complex animations	Some of the Flash Buttons in Dreamweaver CS3 are animated, making it much quicker to add animated buttons to your page than you could easily achieve with animated GIF files.
Design consistency	Because you can set up a navigation system that uses Flash Buttons in minutes, it's easy to get a consistent look and feel to your site without spending a lot of time designing your own rollover graphics. This helps bring consistency to the overall design of your site.
Cons	**Explanation**
Plug-in required	Visitors need a plug-in to properly view Flash content on the Web. Flash Buttons are no different and require that the Flash plug-in be installed in the visitor's browser.
Limited linking	As you learned in Chapter 3, *"Managing Your Sites,"* site root relative links tell the browser to go to the root of the site and then find the page to which you're linking. Site root relative links don't work with Flash Buttons—only document relative links will work.
Fixed button sizes	Although Flash Buttons allow you to use any font installed in your system and choose the font size, the buttons themselves don't change to fit the text. Often you'll find your text too big for the button you've chosen. Usually a small modification to your text will make it fit, but you need to design with this in mind.

4 | Creating Flash Buttons

Flash Buttons are quick and easy to create and offer more variety than your plain vanilla image rollovers. This exercise shows you how to insert Flash Buttons into your site designs. Keep in mind, you may find Flash Buttons difficult to work with because the text you plan to use for the button may not fit.

---

1 In the **Files** panel, double-click **teacloudteas.html** in the **ourproducts** folder to open it.

This file is just like the ones you started with in earlier exercises—it's just missing its navigation bar.

---

2 Position your cursor in the empty navigation table cell.

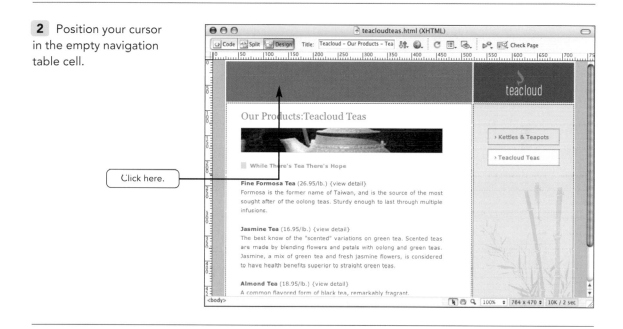

Click here.

---

3 In the **Common** group of the **Insert bar**, click the **Media** button, and choose **Flash Button** to open the **Insert Flash Button** dialog box.

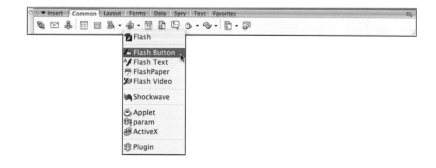

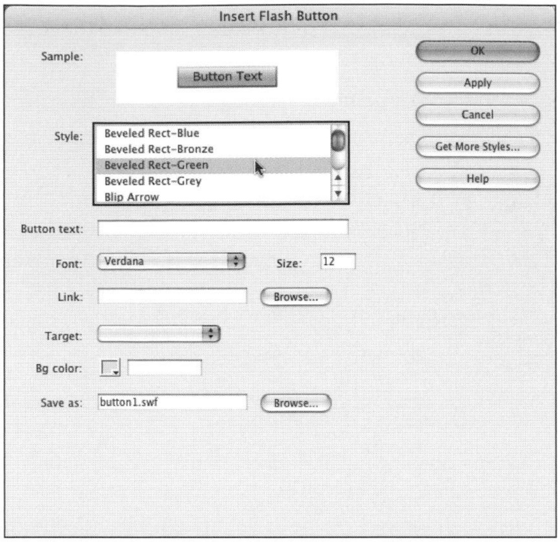

4 Select **Beveled Rect-Green** in the **Style** list.

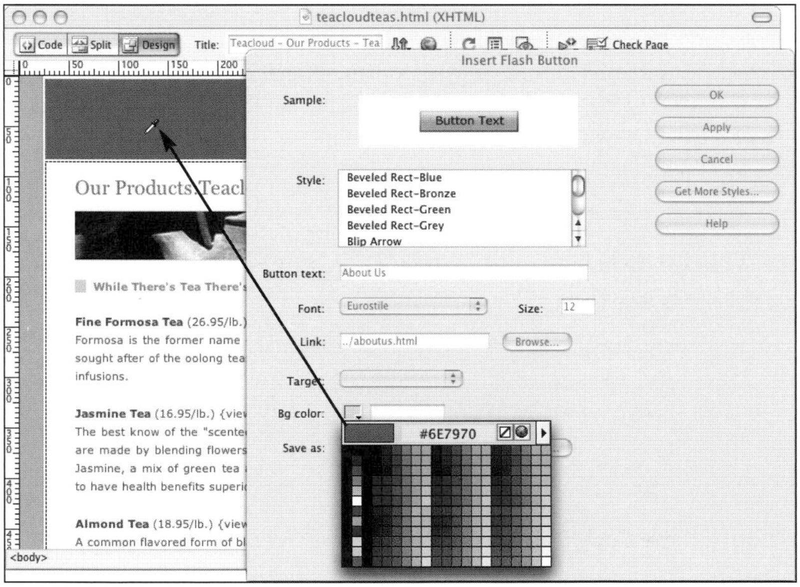

5 Type **About Us** in the **Button text** field, and choose a font you'd like to use in the **Font** pop-up menu. (In this case, we chose **Eurostile**.) Leave **Size** set to **12**. Click **Browse** next to the **Link** field, and select the **aboutus.html** file at the root of the site. Finally, click the **color picker**, and click to sample the background color of the navigation cell.

Always make sure you specify the background color the Flash movie is going to be on top of. Otherwise, you may end up with a white box around a button on top of a dark green background.

6 In the **Save as** field, keep the file name **button1.swf**. Click **OK**. If the **Flash Accessibility Attributes** dialog box appears, type **About Us** in the **Title** field, and click **OK**.

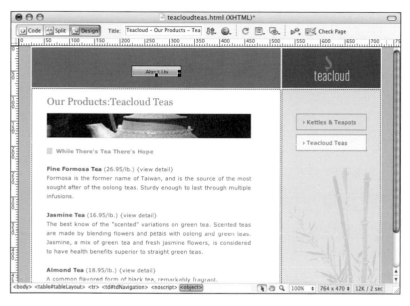

Your page should look like the illustration shown here with the Flash Button inserted. Notice it's not quite as elegant as the rollovers you worked with in the previous three exercises. When you work with Flash Buttons, you're limited to the predesigned buttons created by the designers at Adobe. As a result, the buttons don't look quite as much a part of the page design as they would if you designed them yourself or had a graphic designer create them for you.

---

7 With the **Flash Button** selected, click the **Play** button in the **Property inspector**, and then move your cursor over the Flash Button while in **Design** view in Dreamweaver CS3.

With the Flash Button playing in Design view, you can see the rollover state of the button. Click the button to get a glimpse of the down state. If you want to create the rest of the buttons, simply position your cursor after the About Us button, choose Insert > Media > Flash Button, and complete the dialog box for each of the other three buttons.

---

8 Save and close **teacloudteas.html**. If the **Copy Dependent Files** dialog box appears, click **OK** to dismiss it.

In this chapter, you learned about different types of rollovers. You learned how to create simple rollovers and disjointed rollovers, how to apply multiple rollovers to a single anchor, how to create complex navigation bars, and even how to insert Flash Buttons with just a few clicks. Mastering rollovers will give you a definite advantage when it comes to designing effective navigation. In the next chapter, you'll dig into the code behind all of the wonderful work Dreamweaver CS3 does for you, and you'll become intimately familiar with the Dreamweaver CS3 Code view.

12

Using XHTML

Beginners often wonder whether it's necessary to know XHTML (eXtensible HyperText Markup Language) to be a successful Web designer. Several years ago, the answer was a resounding "yes," because there were no alternatives to writing XHTML or HTML (HyperText Markup Language) to create Web pages. However, since the introduction of WYSIWYG (What You See Is What You Get) editors such as Adobe Dreamweaver CS3, Web developers are shielded from writing the markup and can create Web pages in a completely visual environment. However, it's still my belief that a basic understanding of XHTML is beneficial to *anyone* planning to work in this field professionally. This book doesn't teach XHTML, but you can teach it to yourself by looking at the markup while building pages visually within Dreamweaver.

Dreamweaver CS3 gives you three ways to view the **Document** window, combining the best of both the visual environment and the code environment. **Design** view is the visual WYSIWYG editing environment where you will do most of your work. **Code** view lets you use Dreamweaver CS3 like other full-featured text editors specializing in XHTML, such as BBEdit from Bare Bones Software or Macromedia HomeSite from Adobe. **Split** view lets you work with both the code and the visual elements of your page within the same **Document** window.

1 | Viewing the Markup

The Dreamweaver CS3 interface has three extremely useful buttons: the **Code** button, the **Split** button, and the **Design** button. The ability to toggle quickly between editing your code and working in the visual editing environment makes working with XHTML intuitive for anyone. If you're experienced with XHTML, you won't feel so far from home when using Dreamweaver CS3. If you're less familiar with markup, you'll find that you can watch Dreamweaver CS3 create the markup as you use the visual editing environment. Observing this process is actually a great way to learn good authoring techniques.

This exercise exposes you to all three views to show you how to edit your XHTML effectively. Even if you don't know a whole lot about XHTML, you should still work through this exercise.

---

1 If you haven't already done so, copy the **chap_12** folder from the **Dreamweaver HOT CD-ROM** to your desktop. Define your site as **Chapter 12** using the **chap_12** folder as the local root folder. Make sure the **Files** panel is open. If it's not, choose **Window > Files**.

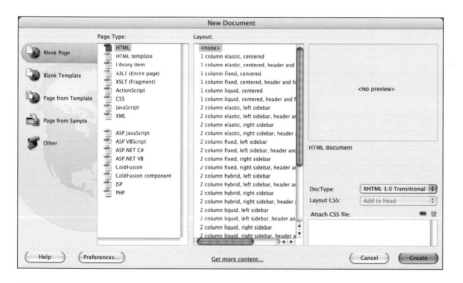

2 Create a new blank file by choosing **File > New**. Click **Blank Page**, select **HTML** in the **Page Type** list, and choose **<none>** in the **Layout** list. Make sure **XHTML 1.0 Transitional** is selected in the **DocType (DTD)** pop-up menu, and click **Create**.

---

3 Click the **Code View** button to view the XHTML in your **Document** window. Even though the page looks empty in **Design** view, some important XHTML already exists in **Code** view.

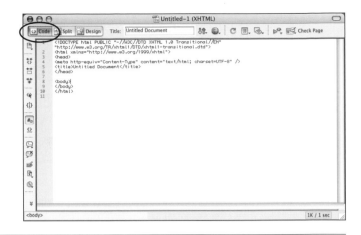

4 Click the **Design View** button to return to **Design** view.

As you can see, switching between these views is really easy.

5 Choose **Insert > Table** to open the **Table** dialog box. Make sure the settings match the ones shown in the illustration here, and then click **OK**.

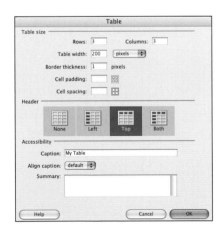

6 Click the **Code View** button.

You can see Dreamweaver has written a large amount of XHTML code for you. Because the table was selected in Design view, when you switched to Code view, all the necessary XHTML to create that table was also selected.

7 Click the **Split View** button to split your **Document** window so you can see the markup and the table on your page at the same time.

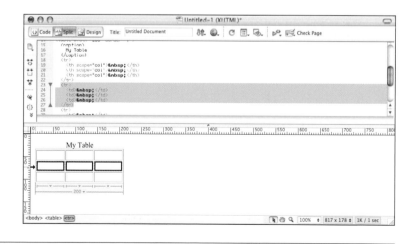

8 Position your cursor to the left of the second table row until it displays a right-facing arrow. Click to select the entire row.

Notice the relevant XHTML for that row is also selected. This level of visual feedback makes it easy to identify how the markup and the visual display are related.

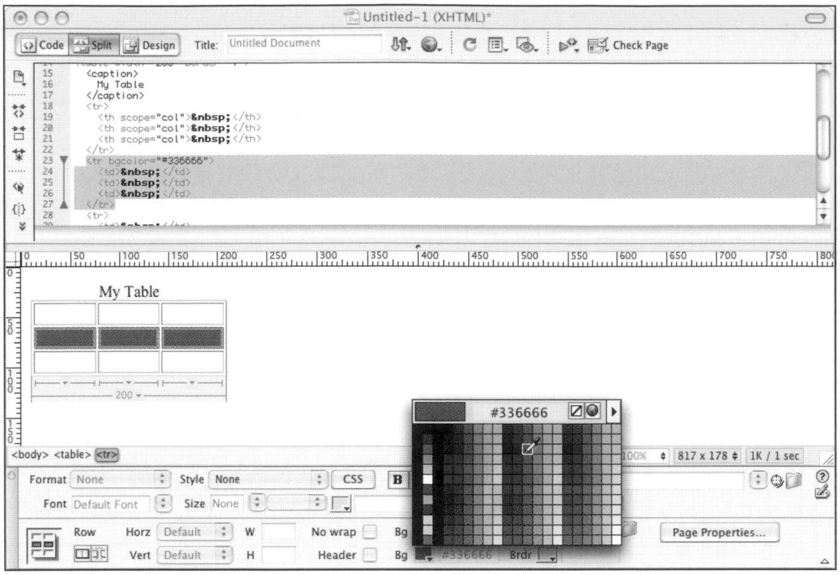

9 In the **Property inspector**, click the **color picker** for **Bg**, and choose any color you'd like for the background color of the selected row.

Notice how the background color was applied to the **<tr>** attribute rather than to each **<td>** tag? Applying the background attribute to one tag rather than three tags is an example of learning efficient coding.

Look at the Code pane in Split view. See how the XHTML is updated to reflect the changes you just made? This is a great way to learn XHTML. You can watch Dreamweaver CS3 generate the markup as you add, modify, and remove content from your page. Go ahead and make some more changes to your page, but stay in Split view so you can watch Dreamweaver CS3 create all the XHTML.

---

10 Choose **File > Save As**, type **xhtml.html** for the file name, and click **Save**. Leave the file open for the next exercise.

Reviewing Your Options in Code View

Several options are available to customize how you work in **Code** or **Split** view. The following chart outlines each of the selections in the **View options** menu. Note that these options are visible only when you're in **Code** or **Split** view.

Code and Split View Options	
Option	**Description**
Word Wrap	Wraps code within the window so you don't have to scroll to the left and right, making large amounts of code easier to see
Line Numbers	Adds line numbers along the left side of the window. This is especially helpful when you need to identify a specific line of code, such as when you're troubleshooting an XHTML error. The numbers won't appear in the final XHTML output; they're just there for your reference.
Hidden Characters	Shows all hidden characters in the document, including tabs, spaces, and line breaks. This makes it easier to identify where you might have any rogue characters affecting the display of your page.
Highlight Invalid Code	Highlights invalid HTML code in yellow. This is really helpful when you are looking for errors in your code. When bad code is selected, look in the **Property inspector** for ways to correct the problem.
Syntax Coloring	Color-codes parts of your XHTML based on your color preferences. This helps you quickly spot the different elements of code.
Auto Indent	Automatically indents code, which helps with readability.
Design View on Top	Inverts the positioning in the **Document** window. This option is available only in **Split** view.

The Code Inspector

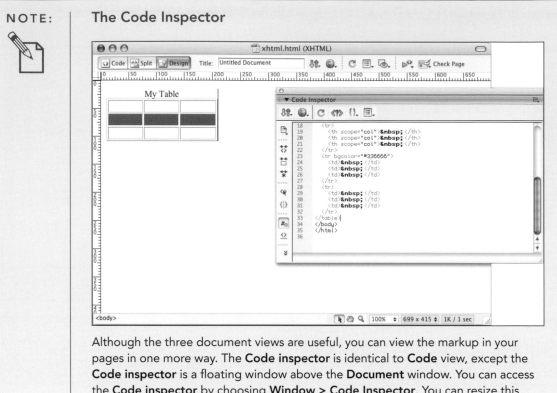

Although the three document views are useful, you can view the markup in your pages in one more way. The **Code inspector** is identical to **Code** view, except the **Code inspector** is a floating window above the **Document** window. You can access the **Code inspector** by choosing **Window > Code Inspector**. You can resize this floating window and move it around the screen without affecting the main **Document** window, which can be nice if you have a large monitor (or multiple monitors) and want to see the markup next to the visual editing environment.

2 | Editing in Code View

Now that you have an idea of how **Code** view works, you will learn how to use it to modify your page. In fact, if you wanted to build a page by hand, you could create your entire page in **Code** view.

In this exercise, you'll get more comfortable with code by using it to add and modify content on your page.

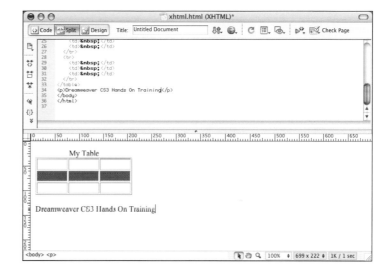

1 You should still have the **xhtml.html** file from Exercise 1 open. If not, complete Exercise 1, and then return to this exercise. Make sure you're in **Split** view so you can see both the **Code** and **Design** panes. In the **Design** pane, click anywhere below the table, and press **Enter** (Windows) or **Return** (Mac) to create a new paragraph. Type **Dreamweaver CS3 Hands On Training**. Look at the **Code** pane, and watch as your text is created.

2 In the **Code** pane, position your cursor before the word **Dreamweaver**, and type **Adobe**. When you are done typing, press **Ctrl+`** (that's the tilde symbol, to the left of the number 1 on your keyboard) to refresh the **Design** pane to see the change take effect.

3 In the **Design** pane, click and drag to highlight the text **Hands On Training**. With the words highlighted, click the **Bold** button in the **Property inspector**. Notice that the **<strong>** tags were added around the selected text in the **Code** pane.

4 In the **Code** pane, manually change the **<strong>** tags to **<em>** tags. The **<em>** tag will format the text in italics instead of bold, whereas the **<strong>** tag was used to bold the text.

You don't have to know HTML tags, such as **<strong>** and **<em>**, but if you do know them, you can type them right into the code just as you did here. However, it's easier to use the Property inspector for this type of formatting. This exercise is here simply to show you that you can edit the code directly if you want, which achieves the same result as if you had used the Property inspector.

Code Formatting Preferences

Dreamweaver CS3 gives you several ways to control the view and behavior of **Code** view. In **Preferences**, you can use the **Code Coloring**, **Code Format**, **Code Hints**, and **Code Rewriting** options to set everything from how the XHTML code appears to how it is formatted. So if you find yourself working in **Code** view a lot, be sure to look over these options.

5 Save and close **xhtml.html**.

You can begin to see how you can use the Design and Code views in tandem to create and modify your documents.

code_toolbar.mov

If you enjoy working with code, you'll really like Dreamweaver's **Code toolbar**. For a tour of the **Code toolbar**, check out **code_toolbar.mov** in the videos folder on the **Dreamweaver HOT CD-ROM**.

Using the Code Toolbar

If you're into working with code, the **Code** toolbar is one of the best features in Dreamweaver CS3. Once you become familiar with XHTML, and Web development in general, you'll most likely start spending more and more time in **Code** view, and the **Code** toolbar makes your life much easier by giving you quick access to the most common tasks you need to perform while working in **Code** view. The **Code** toolbar appears along the left side of the **Document** window when you're in **Code** view. The illustration shown here tells you what each button is, and the following chart describes what each button does.

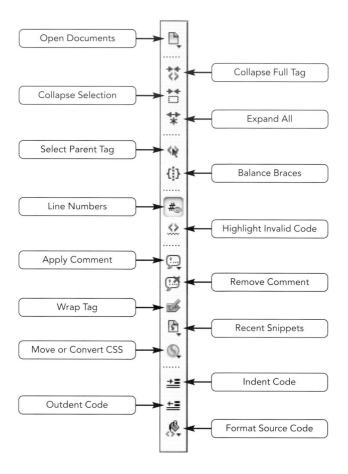

Open Documents

Collapse Full Tag

Collapse Selection

Expand All

Select Parent Tag

Balance Braces

Line Numbers

Highlight Invalid Code

Apply Comment

Remove Comment

Wrap Tag

Recent Snippets

Move or Convert CSS

Indent Code

Outdent Code

Format Source Code

Code Toolbar Functionality

Button	Description
Open Documents	Opens a pop-up menu, which lists the full file path of all open documents. If you're working on a large number of open documents, use this button to quickly find the document you need.
Collapse Full Tag	Collapses the entire tag currently containing the cursor. You'll learn more about this button in Exercise 3.
Collapse Selection	Collapses the currently highlighted selection. You'll learn more about this button in Exercise 3.
Expand All	Expands all currently collapsed blocks of code.
Select Parent Tag	Selects the parent tag of the current selection. For example, if your cursor is in a table cell, clicking this button will select the **<td>** tag. Clicking the button again will select the **<tr>** tag, which is the **<td>** tag's parent.
Balance Braces	Selects all the code between the enclosing parentheses, braces, or square brackets. If you have the code **(some text)** in your document and your cursor is between the words *some* and *text*, clicking this button will select the words *some text*. This function is particularly useful when working with JavaScript since it's dependent on where braces and parentheses start and end.
Line Numbers	Turns the line numbers on and off in **Code** view.
Highlight Invalid Code	Highlights any invalid XHTML in yellow so it's easy to find.
Apply Comment	Wraps the current selection in a comment or inserts a blank comment. You can apply multiple different comment styles from this button.
Remove Comment	Removes a comment wrapped around the current selection.
Wrap Tag	Opens the **Quick Tag Editor** in **Wrap Tag** mode, which you'll learn more about in Exercise 4.
Recent Snippets	Displays a list of recently used snippets. You'll learn more later in this chapter.
Move or Convert CSS	Lets you convert an inline CSS (**C**ascading **S**tyle **S**heet) rule to CSS rules or move embedded CSS into an external style sheet. You learned to move embedded CSS styles in Chapter 6, *"Working with Cascading Style Sheets."*
Indent Code	Adds a single tab to the beginning of each line in the current selection.
Outdent Code	Removes a single tab from the beginning of each line in the current selection.
Format Source Code	Reformats the source code of the current document, resetting all the tabs to make it easier to see the tags' nesting structure.

3 | Using Code Collapse

Once you start developing more complicated sites, the XHTML to create those sites also becomes more complicated. If you start working on dynamic sites using a server language such as ASP (**A**ctive **S**erver **P**ages), .NET, or ColdFusion, your code becomes even more complicated. You'll oftentimes need to examine multiple parts of a page at a time, but when your files start reaching more than 100 lines of code, referencing other parts of your page's code starts to become difficult because you have to constantly scroll back and forth to check the relevant lines. Dreamweaver CS3 can collapse blocks of code to get them out of your way, making it far easier to manage large files.

1 In the **Files** panel, double-click **abouttea.html** to open it. If you're not already in **Code** view, choose **View > Code**.

The first thing you'll probably notice is the JavaScript that Dreamweaver CS3 has inserted to handle the image rollovers for the navigation. This code starts at line 7 with an opening **<script>** tag and ends on line 32. Considering that Dreamweaver CS3 manages the JavaScript for you, you may prefer not to see it in your code.

2 Position your cursor anywhere in the **<script>** tag, and click the **Collapse Full Tag** button in the **Code** toolbar.

The Collapse Full Tag button in the Code toolbar collapses the entire tag currently surrounding the cursor. In this case, it will collapse the entire **<script>** tag.

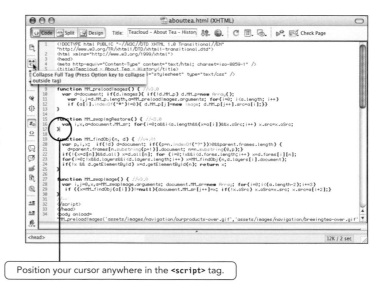

Position your cursor anywhere in the **<script>** tag.

After you collapse the `<script>` tag, it is displayed with a gray background and a plus sign (Windows) or a triangle (Mac) next to it. If you hold your cursor over the collapsed code, Dreamweaver CS3 shows you the first 10 lines of code in the collapsed area to give you an idea of what's inside.

3 Click the **plus** sign (Windows) or the **triangle** (Mac) to the left of the collapsed block, or double-click the collapsed block.

When you expand a block of code, Dreamweaver CS3 expands it and then immediately selects the entire block for you. This makes it easy to look in a block of collapsed code and then immediately collapse the code again.

4 With the `<script>` tag and its contents still selected, click either of the **minus** signs at the beginning and the end of the selected code (Windows), or click one of the **triangles** (Mac).

The code collapse indicators (the plus and minus signs or the triangles) will display anytime you make a selection in Code view in Dreamweaver CS3. This lets you collapse any piece of code on the page, whether it's a few words of text or an entire tag.

5 Scroll a little further down the page until you get to line 41, which is where the table cell containing all the content for the page is located.

When working on a site that has the design completed, you may care only about the content that's unique for the current page, which is almost always contained in either a single table or a `<div>` tag. You may find it helpful to collapse everything but the content area of the page to keep from getting distracted by all the code surrounding the section on which you need to work.

6 **Right-click** (Windows) or **Ctrl-click** (Mac) the **<td>** tag containing all the content for the page (line 41). In the contextual menu, choose **Selection > Collapse Outside Full Tag**.

You can also hold down Alt (Windows) or Opt (Mac) and click the Collapse Full Tag button in the Code toolbar if you prefer.

Now that you've collapsed everything outside the content table cell, you won't have any distractions while you're working on your code. Everything outside that **<td>** tag has been completely collapsed.

WARNING:

Code Collapse and Undo

When first working with code collapse, you might feel compelled to treat it like any other edit to your code—collapse a block of code, decide you really didn't want to, and press **Ctrl+Z** to undo the change. Unfortunately, attempting to undo a code collapse action doesn't work—you just end up undoing the last actual change to the code you made. If you're an undo-aholic, this is going to throw you the first few times, but once you get used to it, you'll remember to just double-click the collapsed block to expand it.

7 Switch to **Split** view.

You can see that the collapsed code is still completely rendered in Design view. Collapsing blocks of code doesn't have any effect on the display of the document in Design view.

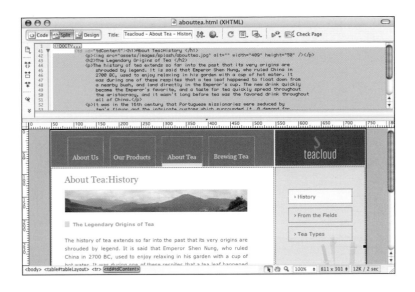

8 Switch back to **Code** view. If you've been collapsing a large number of code blocks, you might have some difficulty finding a line of code that could be causing a problem. To get rid of all collapsed blocks of code, click the **Expand All** button in the **Code** toolbar to expand every collapsed block of code in the document.

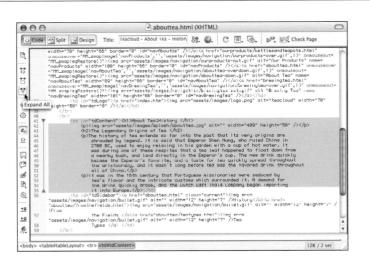

9 Close **abouttea.html**. You don't need to save your changes, because collapsing code doesn't have any effect on the actual code of your page, so there are no changes to save.

Tip: Code collapse doesn't forget. Dreamweaver CS3 will remember what blocks of code were collapsed in a document, even after you close it. If you reopen a document that had a block of code collapsed, that code will still be collapsed, which makes it easy to start right back where you left off.

4 | Using the Quick Tag Editor

The **Quick Tag Editor** gives you instant access to the XHTML on your page without requiring you to switch to **Code** view, which is great if you want to make a quick change to a tag or attribute. This exercise shows you how to use the **Quick Tag Editor** to quickly edit the XHTML behind your pages without leaving **Design** view.

---

1 In the **Files** panel, double-click **aboutus.html** to open it. Switch to **Design** view if necessary.

---

2 Position your cursor in the quote in the center of the page, and then select the **<p>** tag surrounding it in the **Tag Selector**.

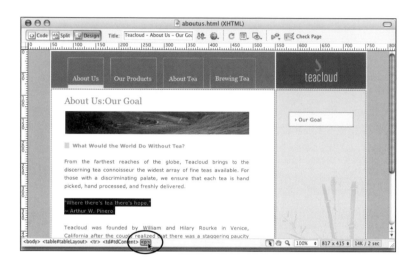

3 Press **Ctrl+T** (Windows) or **Cmd+T** (Mac) to open the **Quick Tag Editor**, which appears directly above the selected tag.

---

4 Press the **spacebar** to add a space after the **p**, type **style="background-color: #CCCCCC;"**, and press **Enter** (Windows) or **Return** (Mac) to commit the changes.

You just directly edited the **<p>** tag surrounding the quote without ever switching to Code view. There's more to the Quick Tag Editor, though.

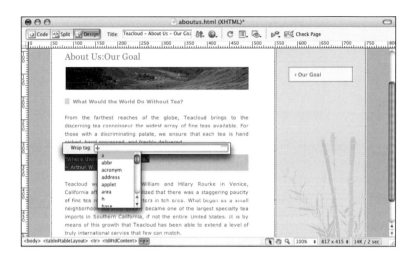

5 With the text still selected in **Design** view, press **Ctrl+T** (Windows) or **Cmd+T** (Mac) *twice* to set the **Quick Tag Editor** to **Wrap Tag** mode.

The Wrap Tag mode of the Quick Tag Editor lets you quickly wrap the current selection in another tag. In this case, you'll wrap the paragraph in a **<blockquote>** tag to indent the content.

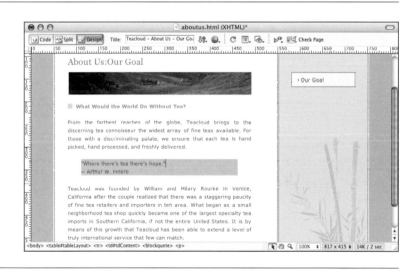

6 Type **blockquote** (or choose it in the tag list), and press **Enter** (Windows) or **Return** (Mac) to commit the changes.

In the Tag Selector, notice the **<p>** tag is now wrapped in a **<blockquote>** tag.

7 Save **aboutus.html**, and leave it open for the next exercise.

The Quick Tag Editor is a great tool if you want quick access to the XHTML. It's also useful if you're just starting out with editing code and you want to isolate only the code you want to change and prevent yourself from accidentally messing with unrelated code. As you just saw, you can make changes to the XHTML without ever leaving the visual environment.

5 | Using the Tag Editor and Tag Chooser

Another way to add markup to a document is to use the **Tag Editor** and **Tag Chooser**. The purpose of this exercise is to show you alternate ways to add and modify the markup code on your page. Whichever method you choose depends on what your workflow and personal preferences are.

---

1 You should still have the **aboutus.html** file from Exercise 4 open. If not, complete Exercise 4, and then return to this exercise.

---

2 Position your cursor at the beginning of the paragraph following the quote. In the **Tag Selector**, click the **<p>** tag, and press the **left arrow** key to move your cursor before the opening **<p>** tag of the paragraph.

It sometimes takes a bit of manipulation to get your cursor in the right spot when working in Design view. If you followed the steps correctly, your cursor should be at the beginning of the paragraph, and you *should not* see a **<p>** tag in the Tag Selector.

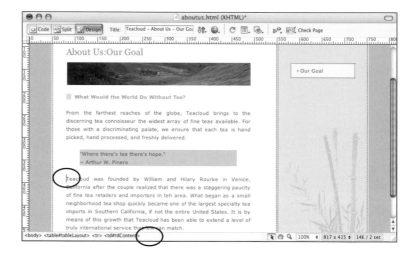

---

3 Choose **Insert > Tag** to open the **Tag Chooser**.

---

4 In the left pane, select **HTML tags**.

The right pane loads all the available XHTML tags.

---

5 Scroll down until you find **h2**. Select it, and click **Insert**.

6 The **Tag Editor** for the **h2** element opens. In the **Header** field, type **The Teacloud Founders**. To learn more about the tag you've chosen, click the **Tag info** triangle. Click **OK**.

7 In the **Tag Chooser**, click **Close** to close the dialog box.

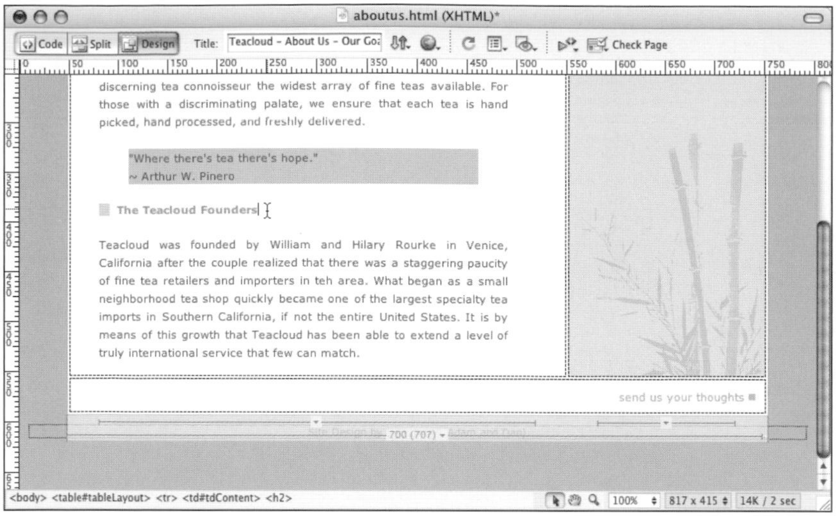

8 The **Document** window automatically goes to **Split** view, and the cursor's focus is in the **Code** pane. Click in the **Design** page, or click the **Design View** button in the **Document** toolbar to see the new **<h2>** tag added to the design.

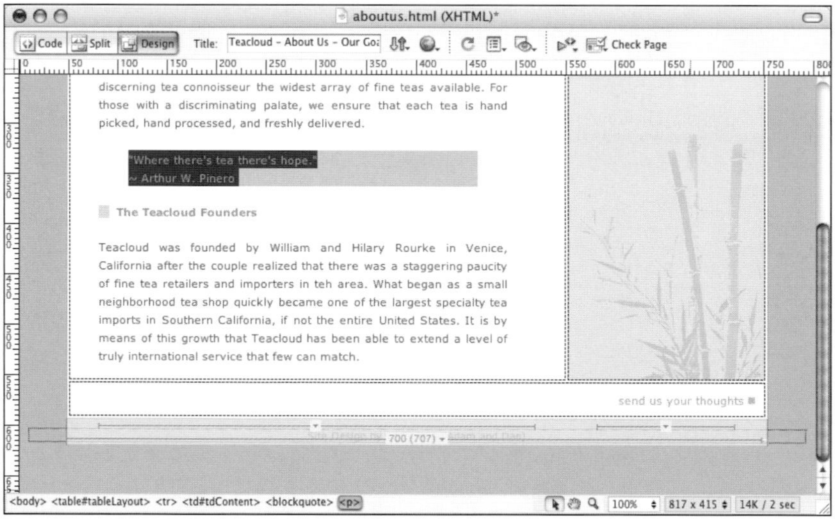

9 Click in the quote above the new **<h2>** tag, and select the **<p>** tag in the **Tag Selector**.

10 Choose **Modify > Edit Tag** to open the **Tag Editor** for the **<p>** tag.

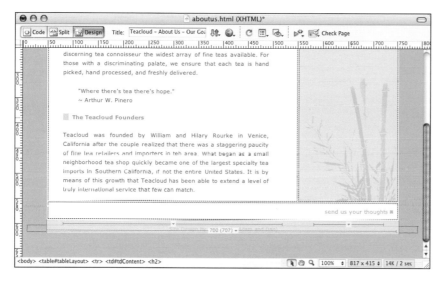

11 Select the **Style Sheet/Accessibility** category, and remove the background color property from the **Style** field. Click **OK**.

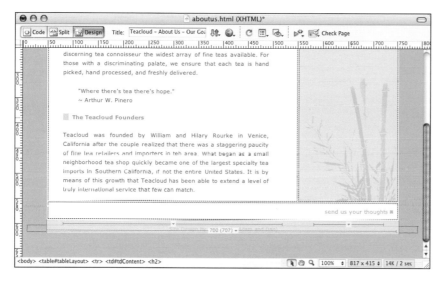

The changes in the Tag Editor are now reflected in Design view.

---

12 Save **aboutus.html**, and leave it open for the next exercise.

The Tag Chooser and Tag Editor are easy ways to edit the properties of a tag directly in Design view. Because all the attributes are nicely categorized, you can change what you need to without worrying about the necessary syntax.

Code Validation

Code validation is a way for you to ensure you're writing the correct code. Dreamweaver CS3 lets you validate your code against the XHTML specifications so that you can check your code for potential problems, which is helpful for two reasons. First, you'll find any errors you've made that could cause problems with your page, and second, you can ensure your documents conform to Web standards, which in turn means the markup you're using will work in the largest number of browsers possible. You can access the **Code Validator** by choosing **File > Validate > Markup** or by clicking the **Validate Markup** button in the **Document** toolbar. A listing of errors (if there are any) will appear in the **Results** panel, which identifies the problem and the exact line of markup where the error occurs.

The **Validator Preferences** let you choose how your markup is validated if there is no DOCTYPE associated with your page. For example, you might choose to use strict forms of HTML or XHTML, and you can set this up in the Dreamweaver CS3 **Preferences**. This flexibility makes the validation process more efficient by letting you exclude languages or language versions you're not using.

6 | Working with Snippets

Because no one can remember every piece of useful code they've ever used, Dreamweaver CS3 offers a way to store all those small bits of code you use every day, and they're called **snippets**. These are pieces of code (XHTML, JavaScript, CSS, server-side code, you name it) you can add to your documents with the click of a button. Dreamweaver CS3 comes complete with its own set of predefined snippets, and you can even create your own. This exercise shows you how to add one of the predefined code snippets to your page and how to add your own snippets to Dreamweaver CS3.

---

1 You should still have the **aboutus.html** file from Exercise 5 open. If not, complete Exercise 5, and then return to this exercise.

---

2 Position your cursor before the **About Us:Our Goal** text at the top of the page.

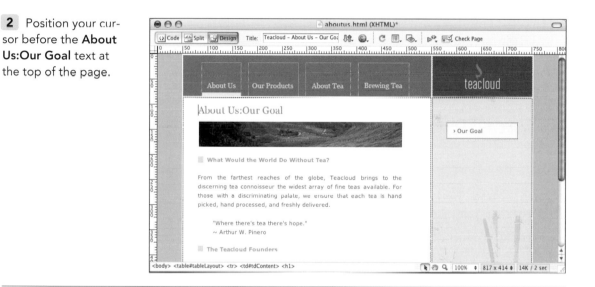

---

3 Choose **Window > Snippets** to open the **Snippets** panel.

---

4 Open the **Navigation** folder, then open the **Breadcrumb** folder, and finally select **Colon as Separator**. Click the **Insert** button to insert the code snippet in the page.

As you select each snippet, you'll see a preview of the code it will insert in the preview window at the top of the Snippets panel.

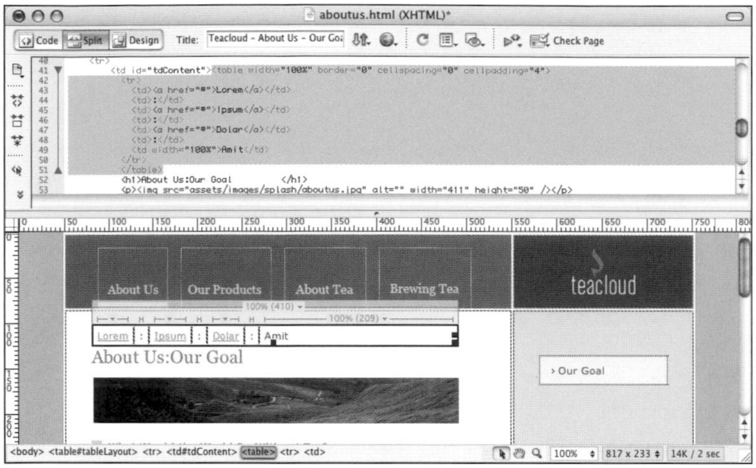

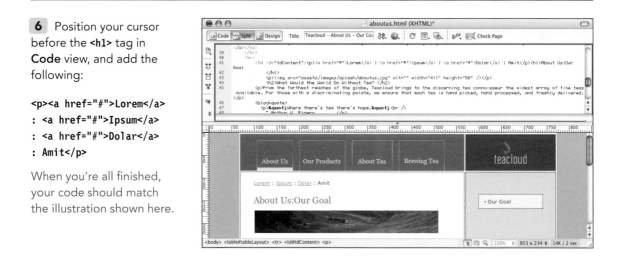

If you switch to Split view, you can see that Dreamweaver CS3 has inserted an entire table, complete with placeholder links for adding your own breadcrumb-style navigation.

---

5 If you're not already in **Split** view, switch to **Split** view. Choose **Edit > Undo** to remove the table you just inserted.

Simple breadcrumb-style navigation doesn't really require an entire table.

---

6 Position your cursor before the **<h1>** tag in **Code** view, and add the following:

```
<p><a href="#">Lorem</a>
: <a href="#">Ipsum</a>
: <a href="#">Dolar</a>
: Amit</p>
```

When you're all finished, your code should match the illustration shown here.

7 Either click and drag to select the entire **<p>** tag and its contents or click in **Design** view, and then select the **<p>** tag in the **Tag Selector**.

Either method will work, as long as you get the content and the opening and closing **<p>** tags. Since you took the time to type that bit of code for the breadcrumb, it's probably a good idea to save it as a snippet so you can quickly use it again on other pages without have to retype everything again.

8 In the **Snippets** panel, click the **New Snippet** button to open the **Snippet** dialog box.

9 In the **Snippet** dialog box, type **Standard Breadcrumb** in the **Name** field. Because this is an entire block of code, select **Insert block**. (If you want to wrap a selection with a snippet, you can select **Wrap selection** and provide **Insert before** and **Insert after** code.) Finally, select **Design** for **Preview type**, and click **OK**.

Your new snippet is now listed in the Snippets panel. You can click the Edit button to change the snippet, or you can click the Delete button to remove it completely.

TIP:

Keyboard Shortcuts for Snippets

If you use a particular snippet frequently, you may want to create a keyboard short-cut to insert the snippet by choosing **Edit > Keyboard Shortcuts** (Windows) or **Dreamweaver > Keyboard Shortcuts** (Mac). In the **Keyboard Shortcuts** dialog box, select **Snippets** in the **Commands** list to define a keyboard shortcut for your favorite snippet.

---

10 Save and close **aboutus.html**.

In this chapter, you learned how to work with the Dreamweaver CS3 Code view. You learned how to use the Code toolbar, how to use code collapse to make your code easier to read, and how to edit your XHTML code directly in Design view. In the next chapter, you'll learn how to work with forms to collect data from your site's users.

13

Working with Forms

Forms are one of the most important elements of a Web site, because they let you ask questions of your audience and receive answers. Forms can be identical to those you're accustomed to in the nonvirtual world (think IRS, car insurance, or loan paperwork), but they can also be used for more exciting things, such as voting, guest books, interactive poetry, or e-commerce. In general, form-based pages are much more interactive than other types of HTML (**H**yper**T**ext **M**arkup **L**anguage) pages, because they can collect and report information to you and give feedback to your users.

Creating forms involves two tasks: creating the form objects (text fields, check boxes, submit buttons, and so on) and making the forms function properly. This chapter focuses on creating form objects, not on the programming required to make forms transmit data to and from your server. Unfortunately, making the forms operational involves programming that goes beyond the capabilities of Adobe Dreamweaver CS3 and the scope of this book. The good news is that almost all reputable Web hosting providers have services to help you get your forms working. You just have to design and create them and then let your hosting provider activate them. At first, forms might not sound like much fun, but they are at the heart of what makes the Web different from the paper and publishing mediums of the past.

Using the Forms Group of the Insert Bar

The objects you use to create a form in Dreamweaver CS3 are referred to as **form objects**. These include text fields, check boxes, buttons, and so on. You'll find all the form objects in the **Forms** group of the **Insert** bar.

The **Forms** group of the **Insert** bar is the easiest way to access many of the objects you will add to your forms. The following chart outlines the objects available in the **Forms** group:

Understanding Form Objects		
Icon	**Name**	**Function**
	Form	This inserts a **<form>** tag into your document. This is required for all forms. If you do not place all your objects in the **<form>** tag, your form will not work properly.
	Text Field	This inserts a **Text Field** object on your form. The text field is the root of all forms. It lets your visitors type information in a field, such as their user name, e-mail address, and street address.
	Hidden Field	This inserts a hidden text field. These fields store information that does not need to be displayed but is necessary for processing the form on the server.
	Textarea	This inserts a multiple-line text field. These are useful for getting large amounts of feedback from users, such as for comments on a site.
	Checkbox	This inserts a **Checkbox** object on your form. You'll use check boxes when you want your visitors to select any combination of a group of responses. For example, "How did you hear about us? Check all that apply."
	Radio Button	This inserts a **Radio Button** object on your form. Use radio buttons when you want users to select one item from a list of available options. For example, "Aisle, middle, or window seat?"
	Radio Group	This inserts a group of **Radio Button** objects on your form, which is just a really fast way to insert multiple radio buttons at once.
	List/Menu	This inserts a **List** or **Menu** object on your form. These two objects allow you to make single (**Menu**) or multiple (**List**) selections in a small area of space. You've probably seen these mostly for choosing the state you live in when shipping something from an online store.

continues on next page

Understanding Form Objects *(continued)*

Icon	Name	Function
	Jump Menu	This inserts a specially formatted **List** object that uses JavaScript to allow the user to select an item from a list and then jump to the URL (**U**niform **R**esource **L**ocator) for that **List** object entry.
	Image Field	This inserts an image on a form that the user can click. You can use image fields to make graphic-based buttons to submit your form.
	File Field	This inserts a text box and button that lets the user browse to a file on the hard drive for uploading. This doesn't mean you can just insert a field and be able to upload, though; you need specialized server-side code to handle file uploads, which isn't covered in this chapter.
	Button	This inserts a **Button** object on your form. A submit button (or an image field) is required in order to actually do anything with a form. You can also make this a reset button, which sets all the form fields to their defaults, or you can set it to not do anything at all, so you can attach your own JavaScript events or behaviors to it.
	Label	This inserts a label on your form. Use labels to attach a text label to a form field to improve accessibility.
	Fieldset	This inserts a container tag for a logical group of form elements. This doesn't affect the functionality of the form, but it does allow you to make larger forms easier to read and work with.
	Spry Validation Text Field	Used when building Spry pages, this is a text field that lets your visitors know whether they've entered valid or invalid information. For example, you can make the field required so that if your visitors try to submit their form data without filling out this field, it will turn red and let them know they must enter information in it before they can continue.
	Spry Validation Textarea	This field is identical to the **Spry Validation Text Field** object in functionality, except it allows your visitors to type a large amount of text, rather than a single line of text.
	Spry Validation Checkbox	This is a check box that can display valid or invalid states. For example, if you're asking your visitors to select three choices, you can use the **Spry Validation Checkbox** objects to confirm that they've made enough selections before submitting the form.
	Spry Validation Select	This is a drop-down menu that can display valid or invalid states, which is useful if you want to require your visitors to select an item from a menu before submitting the form.

Making Forms Function

Dreamweaver CS3 gives you complete control over the layout of your form and the creation of form objects, which is great, but the truth is that there is a bit more to creating forms than just a pretty interface.

Forms are interactive elements that are driven by scripts. Therefore, when users click the submit (or similar) button, the information from the form is processed. This processing isn't something for which XHTML (e**X**tensible **H**yper**T**ext **M**arkup **L**anguage) was designed. So, in order to process forms, you need to use some type of additional scripting beyond XHTML. Although it is possible to process form data through JavaScript or even Java, most Web developers agree the most foolproof way to program forms is through some server-side language, such as CGI (**C**ommon **G**ateway **I**nterface), PHP, ASP (**A**ctive **S**erver **P**ages), .NET, or ColdFusion.

If you have a Web site, chances are good that your Internet service provider or Web administrator has existing server-side code you can use. Because server-side programming involves so many variables, it will be up to you to coordinate obtaining the scripts and implementing the processing of your forms.

The first step is to check with your Web hosting provider to see whether they can assist you. You can also check out these online resources:

HotScripts.com: www.hotscripts.com

The CGI Resource Index: www.cgi-resources.com

Script Search: www.scriptsearch.com

1 | Working with Text Fields and Text Areas

In this exercise, you will get hands-on experience with each of the various form elements. You won't be adding any server-side scripts because doing that would require another book, but you will get everything set up so when you do want to add some server-side functionality, your pages will be ready!

1 If you haven't already done so, copy the **chap_13** folder from the **Dreamweaver HOT CD-ROM** to your desktop. Define your site as **Chapter 13** using the **chap_13** folder as the local root folder. Make sure the **Files** panel is open. If it's not, choose **Window > Files**, or press **F11**.

2 In the **Files** panel, double-click **contactus.html** to open it.

This is the Teacloud contact page for which you're going to create the contact form.

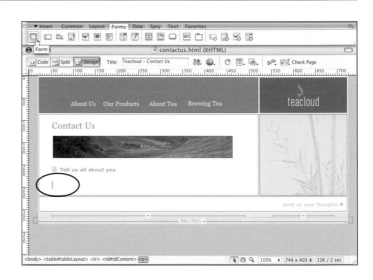

3 If it's not already selected, select the **Forms** group in the **Insert** bar.

4 Position your cursor in the blank space below **Tell us all about you**, and click the **Form** icon in the **Forms** group of the **Insert** bar.

Before you start working with a form, you need a **<form>** tag. All form elements must be contained in a **<form>** tag in order for them to work properly with a server of any sort. The only time you don't need a **<form>** tag is if you're using the form elements for display purposes only and won't actually be collecting information from your users.

5 Your cursor is automatically positioned in the **<form>** tag for you. To organize the form, you'll put all your form elements in a table. Choose **Insert > Table** to open the **Table** dialog box.

6 In the **Table** dialog box, match the settings to the illustration shown here to create a table with 10 rows and 2 columns and no headers. Click **OK**.

Ten rows is a good round number to start. You can always add or delete rows as necessary later.

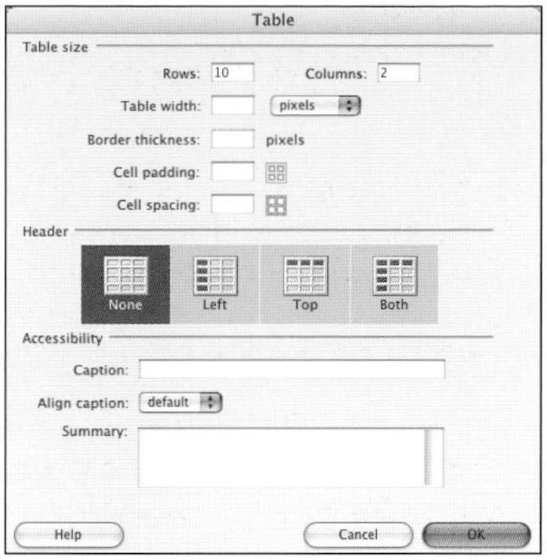

7 Position your cursor in the upper-right table cell, and click the **Text Field** button in the **Forms** group of the **Insert** bar.

8 In the **Input Tag Accessibility Attributes** dialog box, type **Name:** in the **Label** field, and select **Attach label tag using 'for' attribute** in the **Style** section. Leave everything else at its default, and click **OK** to insert the text field.

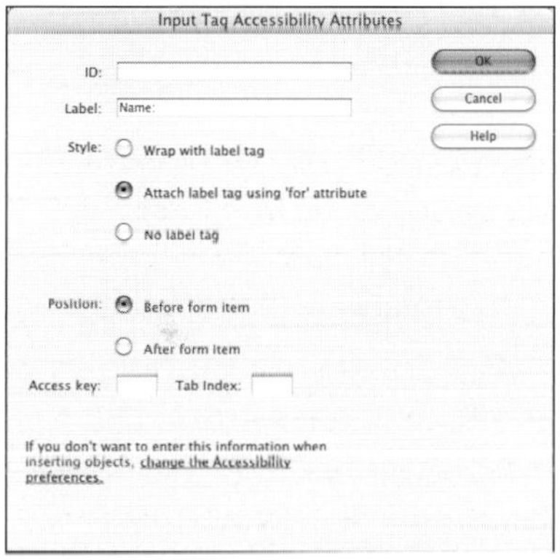

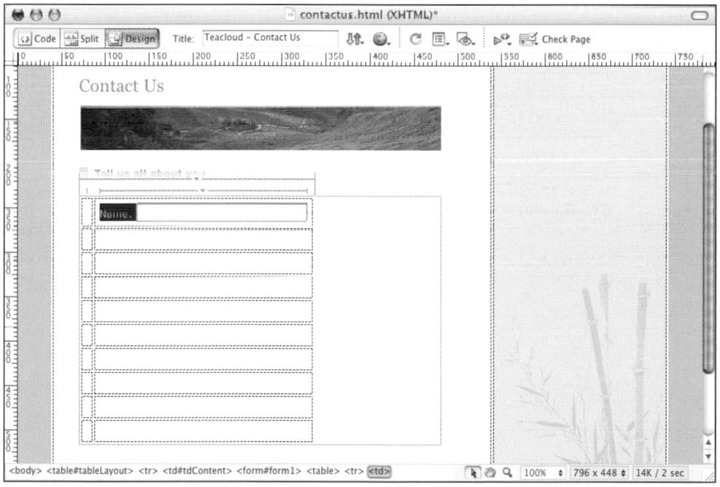

Notice a new text field has been added to the table, along with its associated label.

The Importance of Labels

Labels allow you to attach a text description to a specific form field. This may not seem like a big deal at first, but labels allow browsers to determine what text description goes with what form field. Labels make it possible for screen readers and other assistive devices to tell a user that the text field in the upper-right corner is indeed intended to be the customer's name.

Labels do a little more than actually describe the form fields; they give your visitors a larger target to hit to interact with a form field. In some browsers, clicking the label for a text field positions the user's cursor in the matching text field. Similarly, clicking the label for a check box will actually select and deselect the box.

Attaching a label with a **for** attribute lets you put a label anywhere on the page and associate it with a specific form element. So, the following code associates the label **Name:** with the text field with the same **ID**:

```
<label for="textfield">Name: </label>
<input type="text" name="textfield" id="textfield" />
```

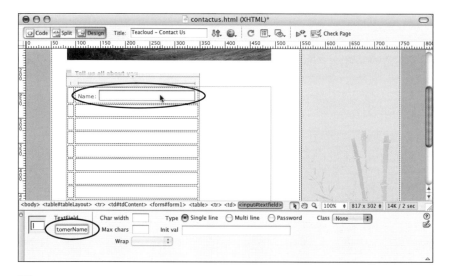

9 Every form field on your page must have a name by which it's going to be referenced. Click the text field in **Design** view, and in the **Property inspector**, set the text field's **Name** field to **CustomerName**.

Form Items Renamed

Generally speaking, Dreamweaver CS3 rewrites code for you when you need it to and leaves it alone when you don't. Unfortunately, when you work with form elements, the default behavior of Dreamweaver CS3 is to rename form elements (and their labels) when you copy, cut, paste, or drag and drop the fields. This can be extremely irritating when you start working with labels and form elements and begin to rearrange your forms. You will oftentimes end up with form elements getting renamed when you didn't want them to, and you won't realize it until your client tells you things aren't working properly.

To get rid of this annoying behavior, choose **Edit > Preferences** (Windows) or **Dreamweaver > Preferences** (Mac), and select **Code Rewriting** in the **Category** list. Deselect **Rename form items when pasting**, and click **OK**. This is always the first option I disable when installing Dreamweaver.

10 If you haven't already, be sure to read the previous warning, and change your preferences so the form items are not renamed. After making the change to the **<label>** tag, the entire tag is selected in **Design** view. Select and drag **Name:** from the right column to the left column.

Your page should now look like the illustration shown here. The label is in the left column, and the text field is on the right. Because you used a **for** attribute for the label instead of wrapping the **<label>** tag around the form element, the *Name:* text is still associated with the text field, even though it's in a separate table cell. You'll be setting up the majority of your form elements this way in order to make the form elements line up nicely with each other.

11 Position your cursor in the second row of the right column, and click the **Text Field** button in the **Forms** group of the **Insert** bar. Type **Email Address:** in the **Label** field, leave everything else at its default, and click **OK**.

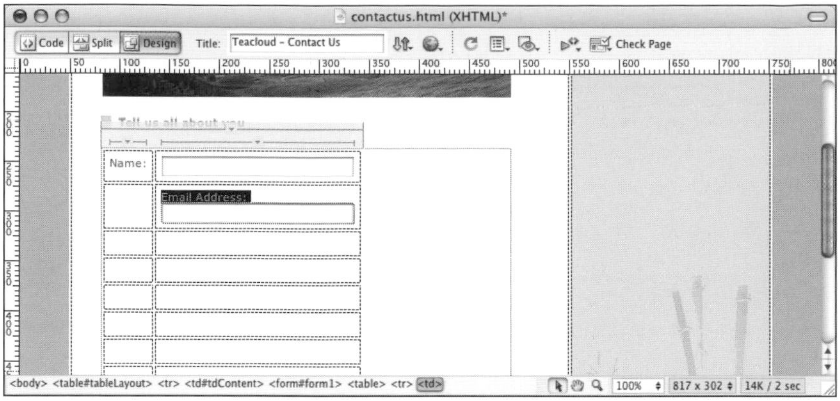

12 In the **Property inspector**, set the field name to **EmailAddress**.

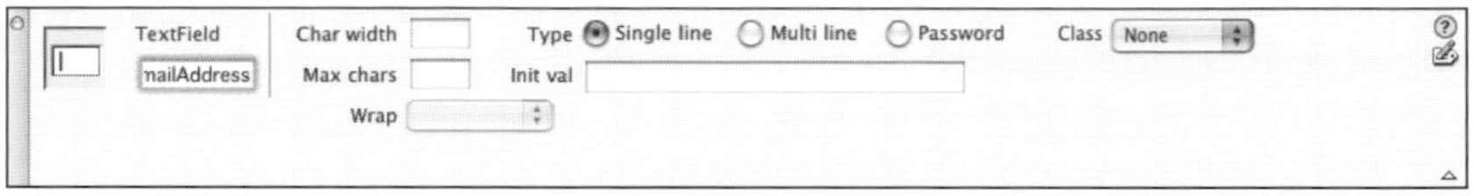

13 Using the **Tag Selector**, select the `<label>` tag around **Email Address:**, and then click and drag the label to the left column of the table.

After the first two form fields are in place, your page will look like the illustration shown here. Next you'll add a Textarea field.

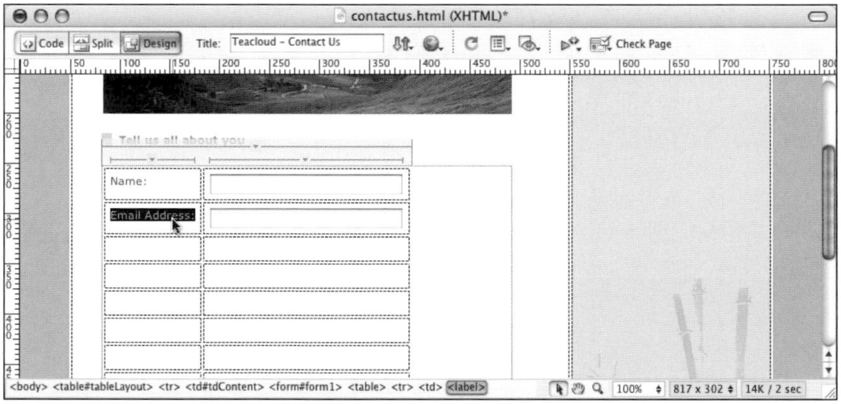

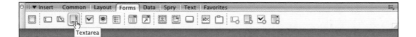

14 Position your cursor in the third row of the right column, and click the **Textarea** button in the **Forms** group of the **Insert** bar.

15 Type **Comments:** in the **Label** field of the **Input Tag Accessibility Attributes** dialog box, and click **OK** to insert the `<textarea>` tag.

16 Select the text area in **Design** view, and in the **Property inspector**, type **Comments** as the text field's name. Then type **5** in the **Num Lines** field.

If you decide you want a standard text field instead of a text area, you can simply change Type to Single line, and Dreamweaver CS3 will convert the text area to a text field for you. Conversely, if you have a text field and you want it to be a text area, select Multi line for Type.

17 Select the **Comments** label, and move it to the left column just as you did with the **Name:** and **Email Address:** labels.

18 Select the left column by dragging through all its cells, and choose **Right** in the **Horz** pop-up menu in the **Property Inspector** to make all the labels line up nicely.

19 Save the page, and press **F12** (Windows) or **Opt+F12** (Mac) to preview your form in your browser.

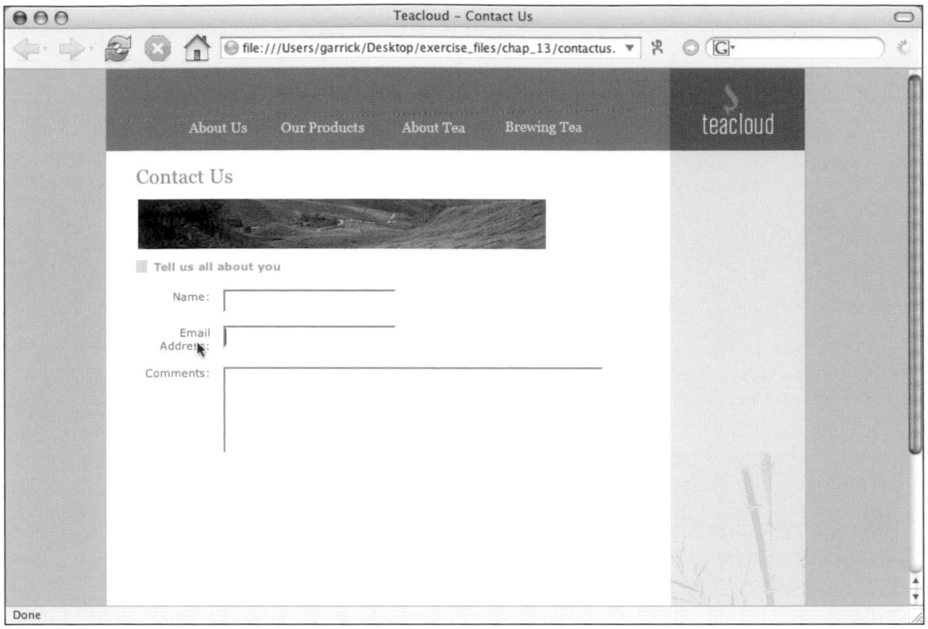

20 Click the labels, and notice that a cursor appears in each corresponding field.

Note: At the time of this book's publication, labels don't work in Apple Safari. Mac users can see labels in action using an alternate browser such as Firefox.

---

21 Return to Dreamweaver. Save **contactus.html**, and leave it open for the next exercise.

In this exercise, you learned how to work with text fields and text areas, as well as how to make sure your form element's labels work correctly. In the next exercise, you'll learn how to work with check boxes and radio buttons.

EXERCISE

2 | Working with Check Boxes and Radio Buttons

Check boxes and radio buttons allow users to make decisions in your form. You can use single check boxes to ask yes or no questions, such as asking users whether they'd like to sign up for a newsletter, or you can use a group of check boxes to allow your visitors to select any combination of choices, as in "Check all available dates." Use radio buttons when you want to limit your visitor's response to just a single choice, as in "Smoking or nonsmoking?" or "Adult, teen, or child?" This exercise shows you how to work with check boxes and radio buttons.

1 You should still have the **contactus.html** file from Exercise 1 open. If not, complete Exercise 1, and then return to this exercise.

2 Position your cursor in the fourth row of the right column (below the text area), and click the **Checkbox** button in the **Forms** group of the **Insert** bar.

3 Type **Add me to the Teacloud newsletter** in the **Label** field of the **Input Tag Accessibility Attributes** dialog box, and select **Wrap with label tag** for the **Style**. Click **OK** to insert the check box.

In this case, you can choose Wrap with label tag because the label is going to be listed after the check box, not in the left column. You might have noticed that the Position was set to After form item in the Input Tag Accessibility Attributes dialog box.

4 Select the check box in **Design** view. In the **Property inspector**, set the name to **Newsletter**, type **Yes** in the **Checked value** field, and leave the **Initial state** set to **Unchecked**.

Check boxes are submitted only if they are selected. If a check box is deselected, it doesn't have a value, so it's completely ignored. For that reason, the Checked value field should almost always be an affirmative response of some sort, such as Yes, True, or YouBetcha.

5 Position your cursor in the fifth row of the right column, and click the **Radio Group** button in the **Forms** group of the **Insert** bar.

6 In the **Radio Group** dialog box, type **Referral** in the **Name** field.

7 Click the first radio button label, and type **Newspaper Ad**. Type **Newspaper Ad** for **Value** as well. Type **Friend** for **Label** and **Value** for the second radio button. Click the **+** button to add a new radio button to the list, and type **Other** for both **Label** and **Value**. Use the **up** or **down** arrows to rearrange the list to match the illustration shown here. Leave the **Lay out using** option set to **Line breaks (
 tags)**, and click **OK**.

The value of a form field is what will actually be sent to the server when you submit a form. The label is what users will actually see in their browsers. In the examples in this chapter, the two are always the same. If you were working with dynamic data or some other form-processing script, this may not always be the case.

8 Select the first radio button in the group, **Newspaper Ad**. In the **Property inspector**, select **Checked** for **Initial state**.

It's always a good idea to select a default value for radio buttons to ensure that at least one of the options is selected. If an initial value is set in a radio group, it's impossible for the user to *not* select something from the group—an option will always be selected.

9 Select each radio button, and notice that they all have the same name, **Referral**, but that each one's **Checked value** is different.

This is the key to making radio buttons work properly—all related items must have the same name. This allows you to have multiple radio button groups in the same form. If you added another radio button group at this point—if, for example, you were asking for the visitor's favorite type of tea—you could name the group FavTea, and the radio buttons in this group would work completely independently of the buttons in the Referral group. If each radio button had a different name, your visitors would be able to select them all, which defeats the purpose of radio buttons and essentially turns them into round check boxes.

10 Save the page, and press **F12** (Windows) or **Opt+F12** (Mac) to preview the page in your browser. Click each of the radio button options to see how they behave in the browser. Notice that you can select only one at time.

11 When you're finished, return to Dreamweaver CS3. Save **contactus.html**, and leave it open for the next exercise.

3 | Working with Lists and Menus

Lists and menus give you a compact way to offer users a large number of choices. These are most often used for letting your visitors select their state or country for mailing addresses. In this exercise, you'll learn how to use lists and menus to allow visitors to select their favorite type of tea and tell you which Teacloud shops they visit the most.

---

1 You should still have the **contactus.html** file from Exercise 2 open. If not, complete Exercise 2, and then return to this exercise.

2 Position your cursor in the table cell below the radio button group you inserted in the previous exercise. In the **Forms** group of the **Insert** bar, click the **List/Menu** button.

3 Type **Your favorite tea:** in the **Label** field of the **Input Tag Accessibility Attributes** dialog box, and select **Attach label tag using 'for' attribute** for **Style**. Click **OK**.

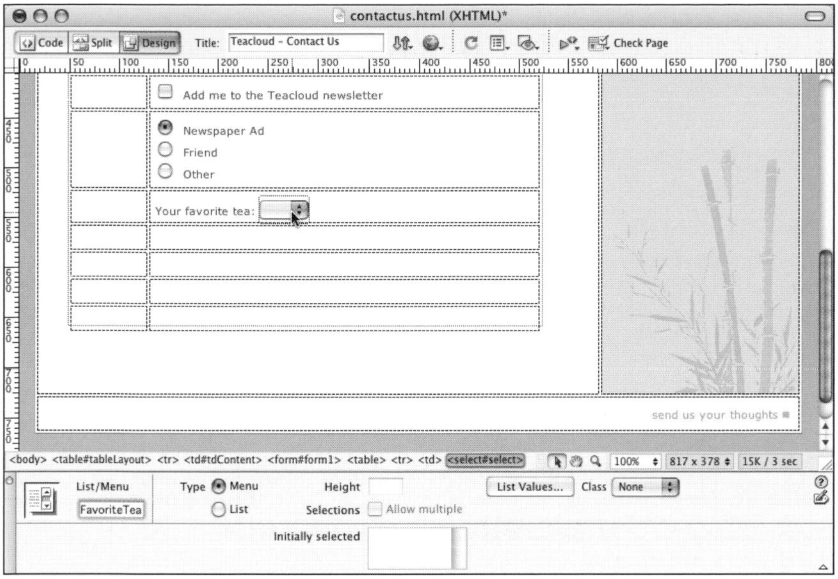

4 Click the menu (or **<select>** tag) in **Design** view. In the **Property inspector**, type **FavoriteTea** for the name.

5 In the **Property inspector**, click the **List Values** button to define the items that will appear in the menu. Click directly below the **Item Label** field, and type **Black Tea**. Press **Tab**, and type **Black Tea** in the **Value** field. Press **Tab** again to go to the next row, and type **Green Tea** for the next **Item Label** and **Value**. Finally, press **Tab** again, and type **Oolong Tea** for the third **Item Label** and **Value**. Click **OK** to add the items to the list.

TIP:

Setting the Initial Value of a List

When a user views your page in a browser, the first item in the menu will be selected by default. You can change the default selection by simply choosing a different item in the **Initially selected** pop-up menu in the **Property inspector**.

6 Select the **FavoriteTea** label, and drag it to the left column.

The text in the left column is starting to look a little cramped. You'll allow that column to get wider by reducing the size of the text area.

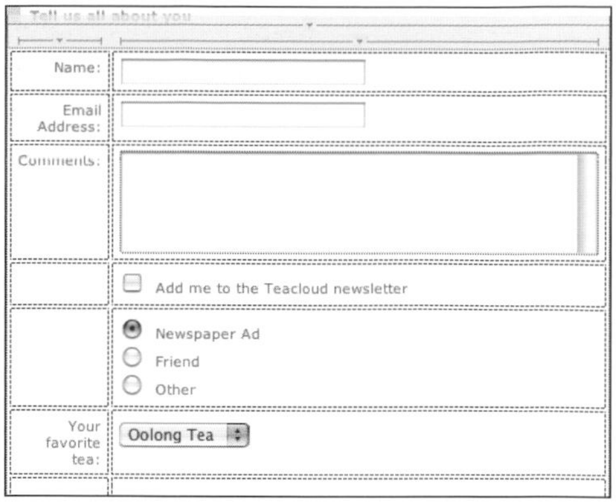

7 Select the text area (the **Comments** field), and change the **Char Width** setting in the **Property inspector** to **30**. Then drag the border between the two columns to the right until all the text labels appear on their own single lines.

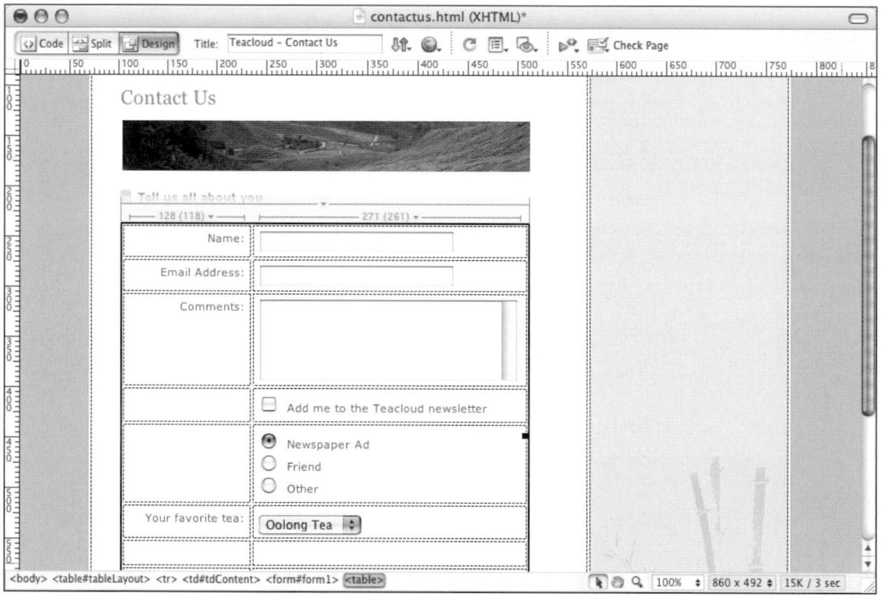

Your page should now look like this illustration after inserting the menu. Next you'll add a **List** object.

8 Position your cursor in the table cell below the menu you inserted, and click the **List/Menu** button in the **Forms** group of the **Insert** bar again.

9 Type **Select your favorite stores:** in the **Label** field, and make sure **Style** is still set to **Attach label tag using 'for' attribute** in the **Input Tag Accessibility Attributes** dialog box. Click **OK**.

Input Tag Accessibility Attributes

ID:

Label: Select your favorite stores:

Style: ◯ Wrap with label tag

● Attach label tag using 'for' attribute

◯ No label tag

Position: ● Before form item

◯ After form item

Access key: ☐ Tab Index: ☐

If you don't want to enter this information when inserting objects, change the Accessibility preferences.

OK

Cancel

Help

List/Menu Type ◯ Menu Height 5 List Values... Class None
roriteStores ● List Selections ☑ Allow multiple
Initially selected

10 Select this new menu, and set the name to **FavoriteStores**. Set **Type** in the **Property inspector** to **List**. Type **5** in the **Height** field, and select the **Allow multiple** check box.

Setting the type of the menu to List lets the menu show more than one item at a time. You can then use the Height field to specify how many items are displayed at once. If you check the Allow multiple check box, visitors can select multiple items by holding down the Ctrl key (Windows) or the Cmd key (Mac) and clicking multiple items in the list. It's usually a good idea to include instructions on how to select multiple items in your form, because users might not know it's even possible.

11 In the **Property inspector**, click the **List Values** button to open the **List Values** dialog box. Add the following store locations to the list:

Anaheim
Beverly Hills
Brea
Ojai
Pasadena
Pomona
Venice

Set **Label** and **Value** to the same values for each store location, and then click **OK**.

List Values

➕ ➖ ▲ ▼ OK

Item Label | Value
Beverly Hills | Beverly Hills
Brea | Brea
Ojai | Ojai
Pasadena | Pasadena
Pomona | Pomona
Venice | Venice

Cancel

Help

12 Select and drag the label to the left column.

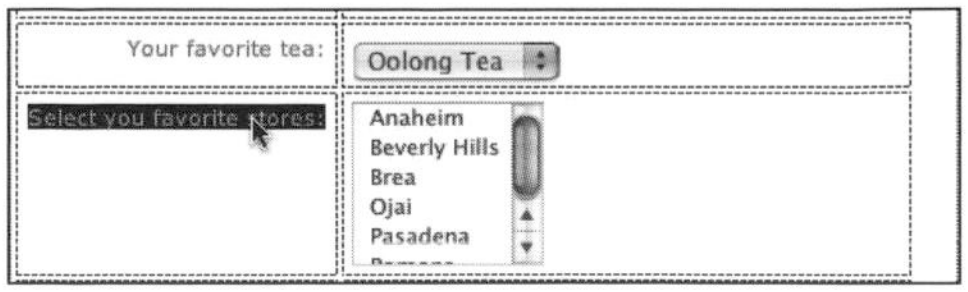

---

13 Position your cursor directly after the list, and press **Shift+Enter** (Windows) or **Ctrl+Return** (Mac) to insert a line break. Type **Hold down Ctrl (Windows) or Cmd (Mac) and click to select multiple stores.**

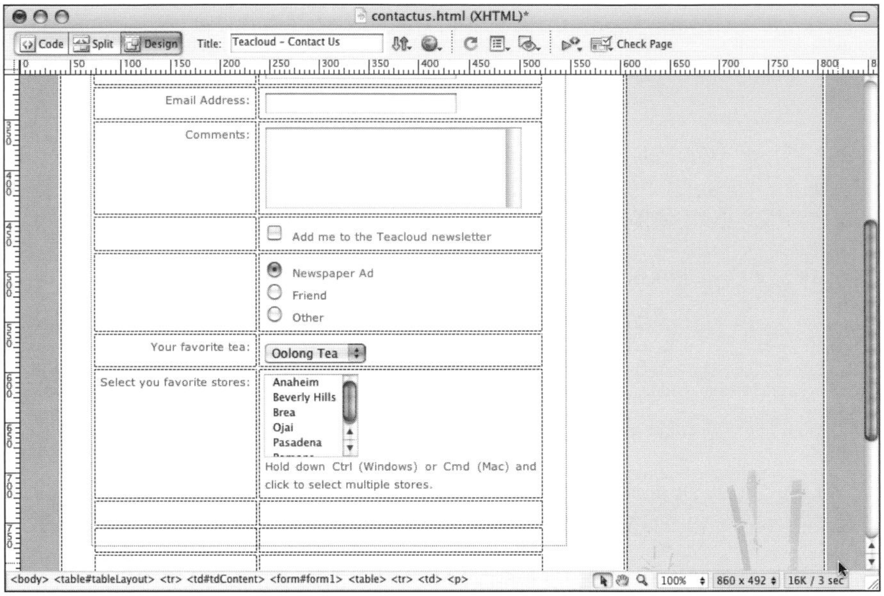

Your page should now match the illustration shown here.

---

14 Save the page, and press **F12** (Windows) or **Opt+F12** (Mac) to preview the page in your browser and experiment with the multiple-select menus.

---

15 When you're finished, return to Dreamweaver CS3. Save **contactus.html**, and leave it open for the next exercise.

VIDEO: | **jump_menu.mov**

Want to learn how to create some fancy navigation using **List** objects? To learn more about how to insert and manipulate a special item called a jump menu, check out **jump_menu.mov** in the **videos** folder on the **Dreamweaver HOT CD-ROM**.

4 | Adding Submit and Reset Buttons

A form is ultimately useless if you don't send the data anywhere. To get your form to actually do anything useful, you'll need to add a submit button and have your visitors actually submit the data to you. This exercise walks you through adding a submit button to your form and explains how you specify which page the form will submit to and how it will send the data.

---

1 You should still have the **contactus.html** file from Exercise 3 open. If not, complete Exercise 3, and then return to this exercise.

2 Position your cursor in the table cell below the favorite stores list, and click the **Button** button in the **Forms** group of the **Insert** bar to open the **Input Tag Accessibility Attributes** dialog box.

As a general rule, you don't need to specify a label for a button, because the button displays its value on the button.

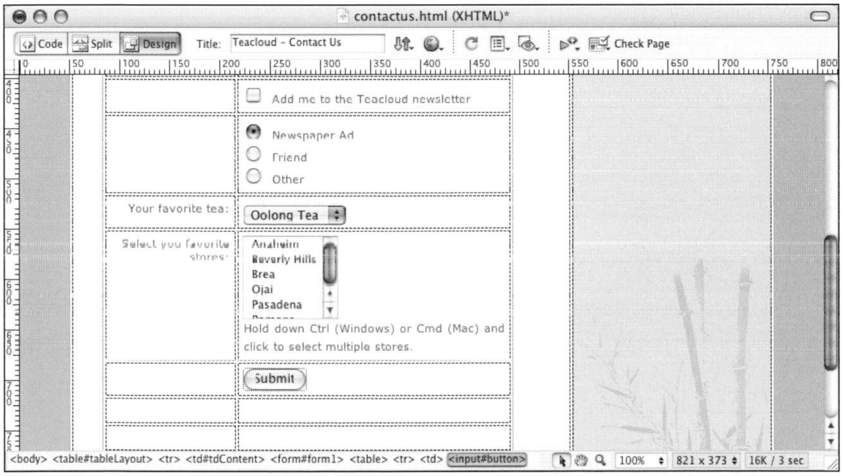

---

3 Click **Cancel** to close the **Input Tag Accessibility Attributes** dialog box.

The button has now been added to the page without a label tag. Notice that by default it's labeled Submit.

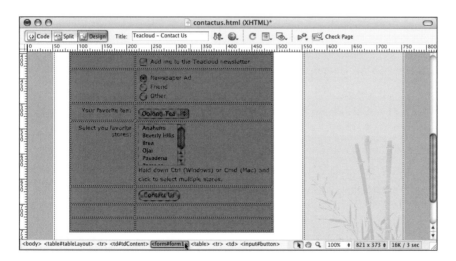

4 With the button selected, type **Contact Us** in the **Value** field in the **Property inspector**.

A button can have one of three actions: Submit, Reset, or None. A submit button actually submits the results of a form to the page specified in the **<form>** tag (more on that next). A reset button sets all the fields in the form to their default values. This is useful for long forms when a user might want to start from scratch. Finally, a button with an action of None doesn't do anything by default. You can click it all day long, and it won't do anything unless you attach a JavaScript event to perform some action.

---

5 Save the page, and press **F12** (Windows) or **Opt+F12** (Mac) to preview the page in your browser. Click the **Contact Us** button.

Because you haven't set an action for the **<form>** tag in the document, nothing happens with the form's information when you submit the form.

---

6 Return to Dreamweaver. Click anywhere in the table. In the **Tag Selector**, select the **<form#form1>** tag, and look at the **Property inspector**. The following chart describes the options available for the **<form>** tag:

You won't change anything in the Property inspector at this time because you aren't actually posting this form to a Web server and also because you have no information about what selections to make in the Property inspector. But just be aware that this is where you set your form submission options when it comes time to build your own forms. For now, you'll just clean up the table a bit.

<table>
<tr><th colspan="2">Form Tag Attributes</th></tr>
<tr><th>Attribute</th><th>Description</th></tr>
<tr>
<td>Action</td>
<td>The <code>action</code> of a form is the name of the page that will receive the form information. This is almost always a dynamic page of some sort (ASP, PHP, ColdFusion, and so on).</td>
</tr>
<tr>
<td>Target</td>
<td>The <code>target</code> of a form is used when working with frames. The target specifies which frame in a frameset will receive the form information.</td>
</tr>
<tr>
<td>Method</td>
<td>The <code>method</code> of a form determines how information is sent to the action page. If you choose <code>POST</code>, the form information is sent as an actual form post to the server, and none of the form information will be visible in the browser. If you choose <code>GET</code>, each form element on the page will be added to the URL in the browser as a name/value pair.</td>
</tr>
<tr>
<td>Enctype</td>
<td>The <code>enctype</code> of a form determines the encoding that will be used to send the information to the browser. Ninety-nine percent of the time you don't need to specify an encoding type, but if you're dealing with file uploads or <code>mailto</code> actions, you'll need to tell the browser how to submit the form information.</td>
</tr>
<tr>
<td>Class</td>
<td>This assigns a CSS class to the <code><form></code> tag.</td>
</tr>
</table>

7 Click and drag to highlight the last two empty rows of the table, and press **Delete** to remove them.

Lastly, you'll add a reset button. This is not absolutely necessary, but it's nice to have one in your form, especially if it's a particularly long form and you want to give your visitors a quick way to clear the form fields in case they mess up and want to start again.

8 Click to the right of the **Contact Us** button, and click the **Button** button in the **Forms** group of the **Insert** bar again. Click **Cancel** in the **Input Tag Accessibility Attributes** dialog box.

9 Select the new button, change its **Value** to **Start Over**, and set its **Action** to **Reset form**.

10 Save the page, and press **F12** (Windows) or **Opt+F12** (Mac) to test your form in your browser. Make some selections, and fill out some text fields. Then click the **Start Over** button to clear all the fields.

11 When you're done, return to Dreamweaver. Save and close **contactus.html**.

VIDEO:

style_forms.mov

You've just finished building a fairly simple contact form. Unfortunately, it's rather bland and could use some styling to make it a bit easier on the eyes. To learn more about form styling, including how to use CSS (**C**ascading **S**tyle **S**heets) to style forms, check out **style_forms.mov** in the **videos** folder on the **Dreamweaver HOT CD-ROM**.

NOTE:

Form Elements in Safari

The Safari browser on Mac computers doesn't allow form elements to be styled. Safari uses the OS X built-in "Aqua" form fields and buttons for all of its form elements, and you can't override their appearance. So if you depend on a certain style for a form element in order to gain users' attention, just remember that if they're using Safari, they'll still be able to fill out your form, but they won't see your styling.

NOTE:

Sending Form Results Through E-mail

Your form information isn't going to do you much good if you can't actually get the information. One way around complex server-side programming is to send the results through e-mail. However, there are too many pitfalls to make e-mail an acceptable solution. You can set the action of the **<form>** tag to **mailto:you@yoursite.com**, which lets the user send the form data through their own e-mail client, but the problems with this method include the following:

- Not everyone has a default e-mail client installed. (Many people use Web-based e-mail accounts, such as Yahoo, Hotmail, or Gmail.)

- Even if your users do have an e-mail client installed, not all have one that supports a **mailto** form.

- If users do have an e-mail client that supports a **mailto** form, it's easy for them to just not send the e-mail at all or for a malicious user to alter the form information before they send. They can also see any hidden form elements that weren't intended for their viewing.

- Many browsers and e-mail clients will prompt the user with a security dialog box before they will allow the e-mail to be created, which can scare away many users.

So, what are you to do? Check with your Web hosting provider to see whether they have any server-side scripts that will send form results for you. Many hosts will already have a form-handling script set up and ready to go. If they don't, several sites will handle sending form information for you. Two of the most popular are **www.response-o-matic.com** and **www.formmail.com**. These sites accept a form post directly from your site and then e-mail you the results. You can find more services of this sort at **http://hotscripts.com/Remotely_Hosted/Form_Processors/index.html**.

In this chapter, you learned how to work with each of the different types of form elements: text fields, text areas, check boxes, radio buttons, lists, and menus. As you begin developing more complicated sites, forms will become increasingly important, and you'll spend a large amount of development time getting those forms just right. Formatting and working with forms is a skill no Web designer can do without. In the next chapter, you'll learn how to use behaviors to add interactivity to your sites (including how to validate forms).

14

Applying Behaviors

Adobe Dreamweaver CS3 uses the term **behaviors** to describe its pre-built scripts, written in JavaScript, that extend XHTML (e**X**tensible **H**yper**T**ext **M**arkup **L**anguage) to perform actions it can't do on its own. Dreamweaver CS3 ships with various behaviors that allow you to do all kinds of cool things, such as open a browser in a smaller window or detect the version of a user's browser.

The Adobe Extension Manager lets you easily install and remove additional behaviors (in the form of extensions) from Dreamweaver CS3. In early versions of Dreamweaver, you had to download and install the Extension Manager application. In Dreamweaver CS3, the Extension Manager comes preinstalled and ready for use.

This chapter shows you how to use some of the behaviors that ship with Dreamweaver CS3. You'll also learn how to download additional behaviors from the free online service Adobe Dreamweaver Exchange, which houses hundreds of additional third-party Dreamweaver extensions.

1 | Using the Open Browser Window Behavior

Times arise when you just can't cram everything on a single Web page. As a result, many Web developers choose to open additional, yet related, information in another window. In this exercise, you'll open a new browser window to display larger images of the Teacloud teapots that simply didn't fit well on the main products page.

---

1 If you haven't already done so, copy the **chap_14** folder from the **Dreamweaver HOT CD-ROM** to your desktop. Define your site as **Chapter 14** using the **chap_14** folder as the local root folder. Make sure the **Files** panel is open. If it's not, choose **Window > Files**.

---

2 In the **Files** panel, double-click **kettlesandteapots.html** in the **ourproducts** folder to open it.

This page has some nice images, but they're simply not big enough. The page doesn't have room for the larger images of the teapots, so you'll open a pop-up window with the larger image of each teapot.

---

3 Select the image of the first teapot on the page, the **Teacloud Azul** teapot. If it's not already open, choose **Window > Behaviors** to open the **Behaviors** panel.

4 In the **Behaviors** panel, click the + button, and choose **Open Browser Window** in the pop-up menu to open the **Open Browser Window** dialog box.

---

5 In the **Open Browser Window** dialog box, click **Browse**, and select **azul.html** in the **ourproducts/kettlesandteapots** folder. Type **530** in the **Window width** field, and type **350** in the **Window height** field. Select the **Status bar** option, and then type **teacloudazul** in the **Window name** field. Click **OK**.

After you click OK, Dreamweaver applies the behavior to the `onclick` attribute of the `<img>` tag, which indicates the pop-up window will open when a user clicks the image.

NOTE:

Open Browser Window Options

The **Open Browser Window** dialog box contains a number of options you need to understand. The window width and height sets the size of the pop-up window you want to open, and you may need to experiment with these settings before finding the right size of window to display the page.

The attribute options affect how the window is created. You can specify whether you want the user to be able to resize the window (resize handles) or whether you want a scroll bar in the pop-up window, if required to view all the content. The other attributes refer to different pieces of the browser elements (the items that actually make up the browser), such as the address bar and the **Forward** and **Back** buttons. The attributes aren't counted as part of the window width and height, so a window with a height of 350 pixels will actually be taller if you choose to display a status bar, navigation toolbar, location toolbar, or menu bar.

The window name provides a JavaScript reference (similar to an ID) in order to manipulate the pop-up window. If you create 10 different pop-up windows and give them all the same name, they would all open using the same window, instead of each opening its own independent window. If you want each pop-up window to open in a separate window, make sure you give each window a unique name.

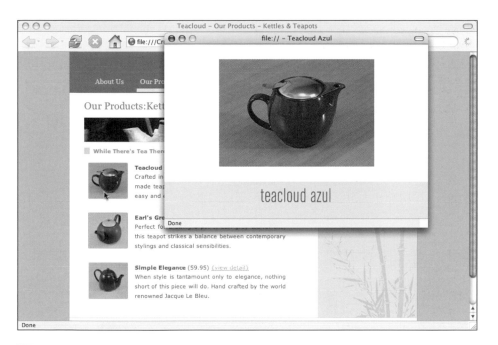

6 Save the page, and press **F12** (Windows) or **Opt+F12** (Mac) to preview the page in a browser. Click the **Teacloud Azul** image to open the pop-up window you just defined.

Notice the pop-up menu has a status bar at the bottom, which reflects the choice you made in the Open Browser Window dialog box, and the dimensions match the ones you specified.

Note: If you're using Apple Safari, you may see a scroll bar and resize handle appear in the window, even though you didn't specify those attributes to appear.

---

7 Return to Dreamweaver CS3. Click to select the **Earl's Grey** image. In the **Behaviors** panel, click the **+** button, and choose **Open Browser Window** in the pop-up menu to open the **Open Browser Window** dialog box.

---

8 In the **Open Browser Window** dialog box, click **Browse**, and select **earlsgrey.html** in the **ourproducts/kettlesandteapots** folder. Match the **Window width**, **Window height**, and **Attributes** options to the ones shown in the illustration here. These settings are the same as you specified in Step 5. Type **earlsgrey** in the **Window name** field. Click **OK**.

When you create multiple pop-up windows from the same page with similar content, you should use the same dimensions and attributes so users have a consistent experience. Having pop-up menus with varying sizes and appearances can be frustrating for users viewing the content. And by specify a unique Window name for each pop-up window, you're making sure each page opens in its own window.

9 Repeat Steps 7 and 8 to create a pop-up window for the **Simple Elegance** image. Set **URL to display** to **kettlesandteapots/simpleelegance.html**, and name the window **simpleelegance**.

---

10 Save the page, and press **F12** (Windows) or **Opt+F12** (Mac) to preview the page in a browser. Click each of the images to open the pop-up windows displaying the larger images.

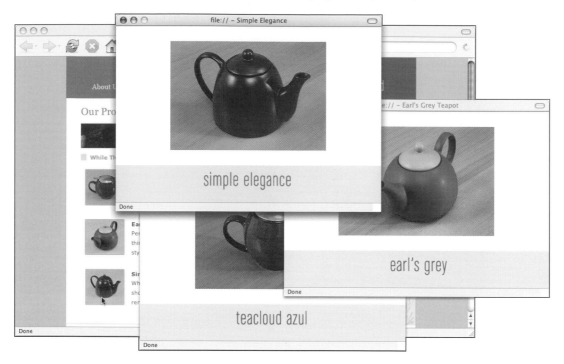

Notice that each image opens in its own pop-up window. As you can see, using a behavior in Dreamweaver CS3 made it really easy to create this functionality.

---

11 Save and close **kettlesandteapots.html**.

---

2 | Using the Popup Message Behavior

In the previous exercise, you learned how to add the Open Browser Window behavior to a Web page, which can be useful when you want to display a second Web page while keeping the original Web page open. In this exercise, you'll learn how to use the Popup Message behavior, which is perfect for times when you want to convey some additional information that might not warrant building an entire Web page to deliver.

1 In the **Files** panel, double-click **index.html** to open it. Scroll down to the bottom of the page where the **Site Design** notice appears. If the **Table Width** display prevents you from seeing this area, choose **View > Visual Aids**, and make sure **Table Widths** is unchecked.

This is a link to lynda.com. Sometimes when linking to an external site, it can be prudent to let your visitors know that by clicking this link they'll be leaving your site and that you are not responsible for the content appearing on the site to which you're linking. You'll add just such a message using the Popup Message behavior.

2 Position your cursor anywhere in the **lynda.com** link. In the **Behaviors** panel, click the **+** button, and choose **Popup Message**.

3 In the **Popup Message** dialog box, type **You are leaving teacloud.com. Teacloud is not responsible for the content of lynda.com.** Click **OK**.

Notice the Popup Message behavior is set to appear when your visitor clicks the link.

4 Save the page, and press **F12** (Windows) or **Opt+F12** (Mac) to view the page in your browser. Click the **lynda.com** link at the bottom of the page.

The pop-up message appears. Notice also that lynda.com does not load in your browser window. The destination page will not load until the visitor clicks OK.

5 Click **OK** to view **lynda.com**. Close your browser, and return to Dreamweaver.

As you can see, adding the Popup Message behavior is incredibly easy. And it provides a great way for you to convey any short message you want to your visitors.

Link Your Text Before Adding Behaviors

In Exercise 1, you attached the Open Browser Window behavior to three images. In this exercise, you attached the Popup Message behavior to the **lynda.com** link. One important fact to keep in mind when you attach behaviors to text is that the text must be a link. You were able to successfully attach the behavior to **lynda.com** in this exercise because it was already set up as a link.

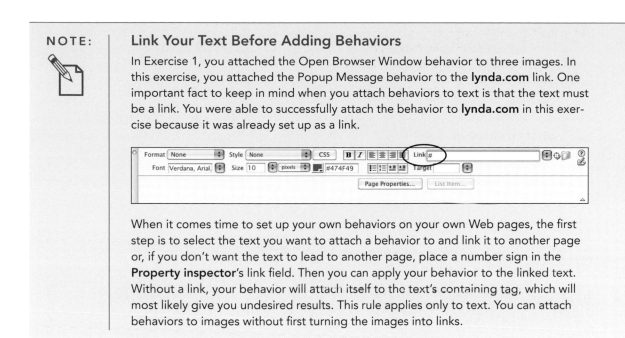

When it comes time to set up your own behaviors on your own Web pages, the first step is to select the text you want to attach a behavior to and link it to another page or, if you don't want the text to lead to another page, place a number sign in the **Property inspector**'s link field. Then you can apply your behavior to the linked text. Without a link, your behavior will attach itself to the text's containing tag, which will most likely give you undesired results. This rule applies only to text. You can attach behaviors to images without first turning the images into links.

6 Save and close **index.html**.

3 | Using the Validate Form Behavior

In the previous chapter, you learned all about creating forms. In this exercise, you'll learn how to validate the information users type into the form. Giving users a place to enter information doesn't guarantee they will enter the information correctly. It also doesn't guarantee they will enter any information at all. Using the behaviors in Dreamweaver CS3, you can **validate**, or verify, the type and format of the information users have provided before it ever gets to your inbox.

---

1 In the **Files** panel, double-click **contactus.html** to open it.

This file contains a version of the form you created in Chapter 13, *"Working with Forms."* You'll be adding validation to the contact form.

2 Click anywhere in the table, and choose the **<form>** tag in the **Tag Selector**. In the **Behaviors** panel, click the **+** button, and choose **Validate Form** in the pop-up menu to open the **Validate Form** dialog box.

The Validate Form dialog box displays all the text fields and text areas in your form. You can select each form element and specify whether the field is required and what type of data the field can accept.

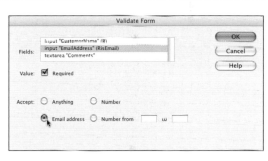

3 Select the **CustomerName** field, and select the **Required** check box to make it mandatory for users to enter their names.

Notice that Dreamweaver CS3 adds *(R)* after the field to indicate that the field is required. The items in parentheses after each field give you a visual cue of what each field requires.

4 Select the **EmailAddress** field, select the **Required** check box, and select **Email address** in the **Accept** section.

The e-mail address validation ensures that the user actually enters a properly formatted e-mail address, including the at (@) sign and the top-level domain name (.com, .net, and so on).

5 Click **OK** to apply the behavior to the **<form>** tag.

The Validate Form behavior is added to the **onSubmit** event of the **<form>** tag. Regardless of how users submit the form (clicking a button, pressing Enter while in a form field, or submitting the form through a JavaScript function), the validation will be automatically processed.

6 Save the page, and press **F12** (Windows) or **Opt+F12** (Mac) to preview the page in a browser. Leave all the fields blank, scroll to the bottom of the page, and click the **Contact Us** button.

Notice an error message appears, indicating the fields that were not filled in correctly. Each of the fields is validated individually, and then the error message lists the errors. As a result, users cannot submit the form until they fill in the information appropriately.

7 Click **OK** to dismiss the error message. Type your name in the **Name** field. In the **Email Address** field, type any text, but don't include an at (**@**) sign. Click **Contact Us** again.

This time you see the warning telling you that you entered your e-mail address incorrectly.

TIP:

Never Trust Strangers

The advice your mother gave you as a child still applies today. Never trust a user filling out a form on your site. Your users aren't necessarily computer-competent individuals, and they may misuse your form, or they could be even worse and be looking for holes in the security of your site. For this reason, you should *always* validate any input that makes it to your server. This includes doing client-side validation (through JavaScript) on any pages containing forms.

Unfortunately, the Validate Form behavior is simply inadequate to get the job done. Happily, Dreamweaver CS3 now offers much better field validation in the form of Spry Form Fields, which you'll learn how to use in Chapter 20, *"Using Spry Tools."*

Spry Form Fields offer far more flexibility and give you control over check boxes, menus, and lists, as well as the standard text fields.

8 Return to Dreamweaver. Save and close **contactus.html**.

Getting More Behaviors

It is possible to create behaviors that are far more complicated than the ones this chapter describes, such as behaviors that script complex interactions between Dreamweaver CS3 and Fireworks CS3. However, creating this type of command requires very strong JavaScript skills.

The good news is that the JavaScript gurus who can create more complicated Dreamweaver extensions often distribute these from their own sites. There is actually a sizable third-party market for Dreamweaver extensions. Read on for information about the Adobe Dreamweaver Exchange and a couple of the third-party sites I've found most useful. Make sure you also check out Appendix B, *"Dreamweaver CS3 Resources,"* for a listing of these sites, and Appendix C, *"Installing Extensions,"* for information about how to install new extensions into Dreamweaver. In addition, you can choose **Help > Dreamweaver Exchange** to access Dreamweaver Exchange, the online community for extensibility developers.

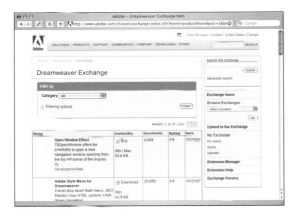

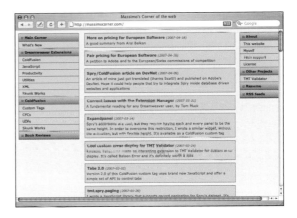

Dreamweaver Exchange

The Dreamweaver exchange contains more than 1,000 extensions for Dreamweaver:

www.adobe.com/exchange

Massimo's Corner

Massimo's is a great Web site for getting some really useful commands and ColdFusion code:

www.massimocorner.com

Hundreds of other Web sites sell commercial extensions, but we'll leave you to find those through the Dreamweaver Exchange.

In this chapter, you learned how to use behaviors to open browser windows, create pop-up messages, and validate forms. There are a number of other built-in Dreamweaver CS3 behaviors, and thousands of third-party behaviors, that allow you to do everything from swapping an image to inserting full-blown mini-calendar applications, and everything in-between. Be sure to take the time to explore more behaviors on your own. In the next chapter, you'll learn how to use Adobe Photoshop and Adobe Fireworks in combination with Dreamweaver CS3 to boost your productivity.

15

Editing Images

Designing and developing Web pages cannot be done with Adobe Dreamweaver CS3 alone. At some point, you'll need a graphics editor to create the various images, buttons, and other visual elements for your pages, and because you're working with the Adobe CS3 suite, your choices are most likely going to be Adobe Photoshop CS3 or Adobe Fireworks CS3 (or both) depending on which version of the suite you purchased. Although you'll see in this chapter that Dreamweaver has some image-editing capabilities, it doesn't even come close to the power of Photoshop or Fireworks, and Dreamweaver's capabilities are limited to working with existing images—it does not offer you the ability to create images from scratch.

Dreamweaver and Fireworks have always had an incredible level of integration with each other, beginning several years ago when they were both Macromedia products. As Adobe CS3 products, they continue to have great interactivity together, but Dreamweaver now boasts great integration with Photoshop as well. In this chapter, you'll first learn about the capabilities and limitations of Dreamweaver's built-in editing tools, and then you'll see how to launch either Fireworks or Photoshop from Dreamweaver, edit your images, and then place the updated images back into your Web page.

1 | Setting External Image Editor Preferences

If you have both Photoshop CS3 and Fireworks CS3 installed on your computer, you'll probably prefer one over the other for editing your Web site's images. Both Photoshop and Fireworks are great tools for creating and editing Web images. Without a doubt, Photoshop CS3 is by far the granddaddy of all image-editing programs in terms of capabilities and features, but you may not need all that power if your primary need in an image editor is to create and optimize Web graphics. From its inception, Fireworks was designed to primarily be a Web graphics program, and although it has become quite a formidable general image-editing program over the past several years, Web graphics are still its specialty.

I won't be covering how to use Photoshop or Fireworks in this book—that would require another book altogether. See the end of this chapter for some recommendations on books and videos to help you learn either or both programs so you can determine for yourself which one best suits your needs. Once you determine that, you'll want to set up either Photoshop or Fireworks as your default external image editor for Dreamweaver, which will allow you to launch either program directly from Dreamweaver and immediately begin editing a selected image on your Web page.

---

1 If you haven't already done so, copy the **chap_15** folder from the **Dreamweaver HOT CD-ROM** to your desktop. Define your site as **Chapter 15** using the **chap_15** folder as the local root folder. Make sure the **Files** panel is open. If it's not, choose **Window > Files**.

Although you just defined a site, be aware that you don't need to define a site to set your image-editing preferences in Dreamweaver. When you set preferences, you're determining your preferences for the entire application, regardless of which site you're working in.

Note: You'll need to have both Fireworks CS3 and Photoshop CS3 installed on your computer to complete this exercise. If you don't have both programs installed, you can still read through the exercise to learn how to set up your preferred image editor in Dreamweaver.

NOTE:

Note for This Chapter

To perform all the exercises in this chapter, you'll need to have Fireworks CS3 and Photoshop CS3 installed. Photoshop CS3 is available as part of the Design Premium, Design Standard, and Web Premium editions of the CS3 suite. Fireworks CS3 is available in the Web Premium and Web Standard editions. You can also download free 30-day trial versions of Photoshop CS3 and Fireworks CS3 from **www.adobe.com/downloads**.

2 Choose **Edit > Preferences** (Windows) or **Dreamweaver > Preferences** (Mac), and select **File Types / Editors** in the **Category** list.

In the Extensions list, you can scroll through all the files types that Dreamweaver CS3 will recognize. The items in the Editors list will change depending on which extension you select.

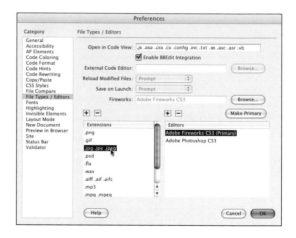

3 Click some of the extensions to see which of the applications installed on your computer are associated with each file type. Selecting **.png**, **.gif**, and **.jpg .jpe .jpeg** should display either Fireworks or Photoshop (or both) in the **Editors** list.

In this exercise, you'll make Fireworks your primary image editor.

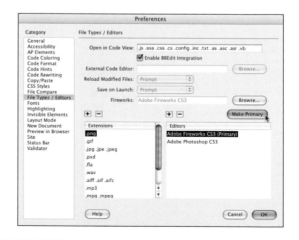

4 Select **.png**. In the **Editors** list, select **Fireworks CS3**, and click the **Make Primary** button. The word **(Primary)** should appear next to Fireworks CS3 (if it wasn't already there). If you have Fireworks CS3 installed on your computer but you don't see it in the **Editors** list, click the **+** button above **Editors**, and locate your copy of Fireworks CS3 to add it to the list.

If you don't have Fireworks CS3 installed on your computer, you won't be able to add it to the list of editors and will have to use Photoshop (or another installed image editor) as your primary image editor.

5 Select **.gif**, and make Fireworks CS3 the primary editor as well. Then do the same with **.jpg .jpe .jpeg**. Click **OK** to close **Preferences**.

You've now made Fireworks CS3 the primary editor for the three most common types of Web graphics.

---

6 In the **Files** panel, open the **ourproducts** folder, and double-click **kettlesandteapots.html** to open it.

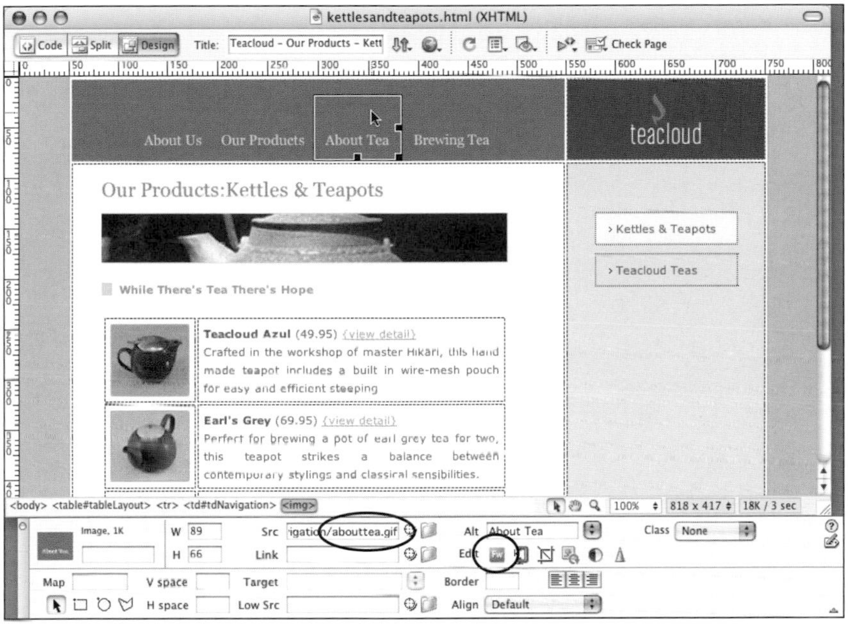

7 Select each of the images in the navigation bar.

These are all .gif files. Notice the Fireworks icon that appears in the Property inspector, indicating that Fireworks is the default editor for this file type.

---

8 Select the **teacloud** logo and each of the teapot images.

The teacloud logo is a .png file, and the teapot images are all .jpg files. Notice their default editor is also Fireworks.

---

9 Choose **Edit > Preferences** (Windows) or **Dreamweaver > Preferences** (Mac), and select **File Types / Editors** in the **Category** list.

Now you'll switch the default editor for one file type.

---

10 Select **.jpg .jpe .jpeg** in the **Extensions** list. Select **Adobe Photoshop CS3** in the **Editors** list, and click the **Make Primary** button. Click **OK** to close **Preferences**.

11 Select each of the teapot images, and notice that the default **Edit** icon is now a **Photoshop** icon.

12 Select **earls-grey.jpg**, and click the **Photoshop** icon in the **Property inspector**.

Photoshop launches and displays the selected teapot image, ready for editing. You won't do any editing in this exercise, however.

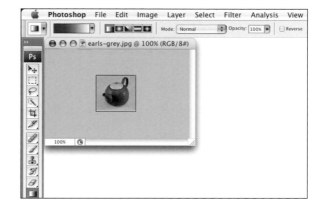

13 Quit Photoshop, and return to Dreamweaver. Close **kettlesandteapots.html**. You didn't make any changes to the file, so you shouldn't be prompted to save it.

In this exercise, you learned how to specify your preferred primary image editor. In the next exercise, you'll learn about Dreamweaver's built-in editing tools before you venture into Fireworks and Photoshop later in this chapter.

2 | Editing Images with Built-in Tools

In this exercise, you will learn to how to edit and manipulate images using Dreamweaver's built-in graphics editing tools, which can be helpful for those small adjustments that don't require the full set of Fireworks CS3 or Photoshop CS3 design tools. Once you get the hang of it, you'll see these tools can help enhance your productivity by letting you crop, resize, and make other minor edits without leaving Dreamweaver CS3.

1 In the **Files** panel, double-click **index.html** to open it. Select the **landing.jpg** image in the center of the page.

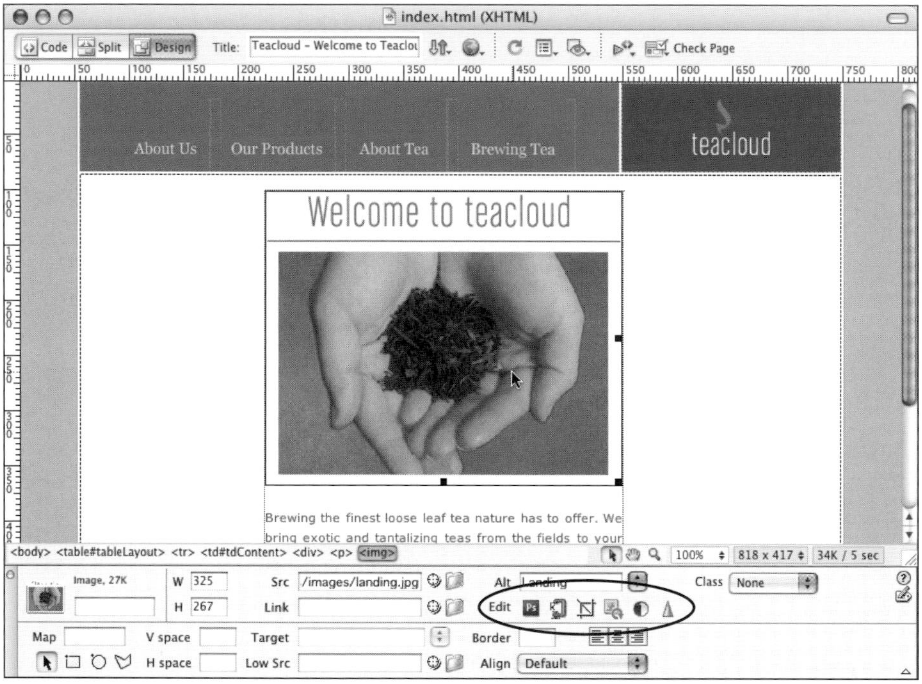

With an image selected, the Property inspector displays the image's properties, as well as Dreamweaver's set of image-editing tools. For this example, you'll adjust the brightness and contrast of this image.

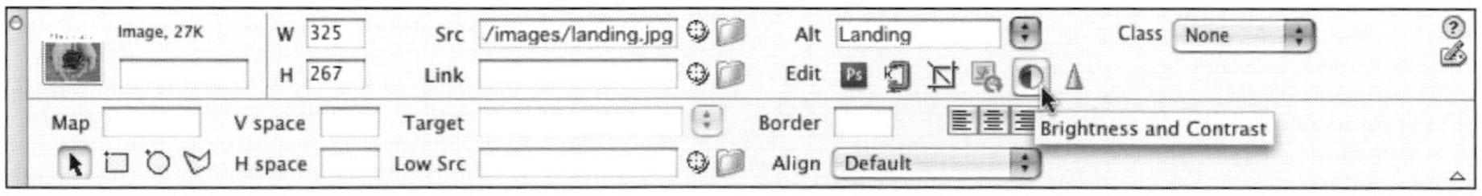

2 In the **Property inspector**, select the **Brightness and Contrast** tool. It's the one that looks like a half moon.

When you click an editing tool, a dialog box will appear warning you that any changes you make will be permanent. If you don't like the way the image looks after you have adjusted it, you can undo the changes, but be aware that if you save and close the page, your change will truly be permanent. So if you're concerned you might accidentally damage an image, make a duplicate of the image and store it somewhere else on your computer before altering your only copy.

3 Click **OK** to close the warning dialog box. The **Brightness/Contrast** dialog box appears automatically, and you can begin editing the image.

4 Experiment by dragging the **Brightness** and **Contrast** sliders to the left and right to decrease or increase the brightness and contrast, respectively. (In the illustration shown here, I used a setting of **12** for **Brightness** and **14** for **Contrast**.) Select the **Preview** check box a few times to compare your settings to the original image. When you are happy with the result, click **OK**.

For a simple edit, such as this one, it was easy to make the changes directly in Dreamweaver CS3 without having to use an external editor.

5 Save **index.html**, and leave it open for the next exercise.

Now that you have an idea of what to expect, you can use the following chart to guide you through your experimentation with the built-in editing tools in Dreamweaver CS3:

Built-in Editing Tools in Dreamweaver CS3

Icon	Name	Function
Ps	**Edit**	Launches either Photoshop or Fireworks, based on your preference settings, for full-featured roundtrip editing of images.
	Optimize	Opens the **Optimize** panel allowing compression changes to images.
	Crop	Activates cropping handle controls allowing for image cropping in Dreamweaver CS3.
	Resample	Allows the scaling of image files to the desired size. Use the image handles around an image to resize it, and then click the **Resample** button to change the actual physical image dimensions to the new size.
	Brightness and Contrast	Activates **Brightness** and **Contrast** controls, which lets you adjust image brightness and contrast directly within Dreamweaver CS3.
	Sharpness	Activates sharpen controls used to increase overall image sharpness directly within Dreamweaver CS3.

<table>
<tr><td>EXERCISE</td></tr>
<tr><td>3</td></tr>
</table>

Roundtrip Editing to and from Photoshop or Fireworks

In the previous exercise, you played around with Dreamweaver's built-in image-editing tools, which can be quite convenient when you need to make a quick change to an image. But many times you'll need more powerful editing tools than what Dreamweaver provides. In this exercise, you'll see how to send an image on a roundtrip from Dreamweaver to either Photoshop or Fireworks, where you can use all the power of those programs to edit the image, and then send the image back to Dreamweaver.

1 You should still have the **index.html** file from Exercise 2 open. If not, complete Exercise 2, and then return to this exercise.

2 Select the **landing.jpg** image in the center of the page. Click the **Photoshop** icon in the **Property inspector** to open **landing.jpg** in Photoshop.

Your preferences should still be set to edit JPEG images with Photoshop. If you see a Fireworks icon in the Property inspector instead of the Photoshop icon and you don't feel like changing your preferences, you can right-click the image and choose Edit With > Adobe Photoshop CS3 to open the image in Photoshop.

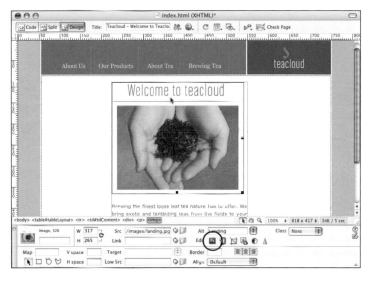

The landing.jpg image is now open in Photoshop. You'll make a quick change to the image and send it back to Dreamweaver.

3 In Photoshop, choose **Image > Adjustments > Hue/Saturation** to open the **Hue/Saturation** dialog box.

4 Select the **Colorize** check box, and drag the **Hue** slider all the way to the left. This tints the image with a reddish tone. Click **OK**.

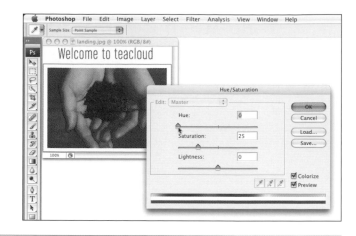

5 Close **landing.jpg**. When Photoshop prompts you to save the image, click **Yes** (Windows) or **Save** (Mac). In the **JPEG Options** dialog box that opens, select **High** for **Image Quality**, and click **OK**.

6 Return to Dreamweaver, and notice that the landing image automatically updates and displays the new version of the image you just created. (If you don't see the updated version immediately upon switching to Dreamweaver, just click the image to nudge Dreamweaver into updating the image.)

You can see how easy it is to take an image from a Web page in Dreamweaver, edit it in Photoshop, and have it reappear in Dreamweaver with your changes. However, working with

images in this way has one slight disadvantage. JPEG images are, by nature, compressed images, and by opening a JPEG in Photoshop, changing it, and resaving it as a JPEG, you're essentially compressing a compressed image. Do that too many times, and your image will start too look degraded and unsharp. One of the advantages of editing an image in Fireworks rather than in Photoshop is that Fireworks prompts you to locate the original uncompressed version of your image (if one exists), allowing you to work from the original to make your changes. This ensures that when you save the image for use in Dreamweaver, it will be the first time that the image is compressed. Next, you'll take a look at how to roundtrip edit an image from Dreamweaver to Fireworks.

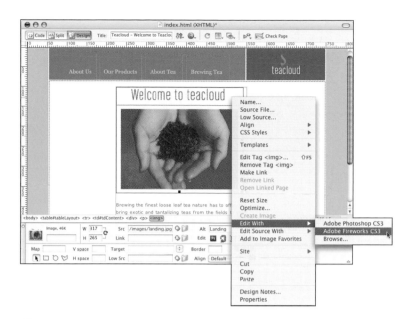

7 Right-click the **landing.jpg** image, and choose **Edit With > Adobe Fireworks CS3** in the contextual menu.

When Fireworks opens, it asks you whether you want to edit the version of the image that currently appears on your Dreamweaver page or whether you want to work with an original PNG source file. If you have access to it, it's almost always better to work with your original, uncompressed image. For this exercise, I've provided the source file for landing.jpg.

8 Click **Use a PNG**. Navigate to the **landing.png** file located in the **FW Files** folder, which is in the **chap_15** folder. Select it, and click **Open**.

9 Press **2** to hide the green slice overlay so you have an unob-structed view of the image. Notice the display at the top of the win-dow, which lets you know that Fireworks knows you're editing this image from Dreamweaver.

The image isn't colorized because you're working with the original version, not the JPEG version you edited in Photoshop. Now you'll apply the same kind of tinting effect you did in Photoshop.

---

10 If it's not selected, click the image to select it. Choose **Filters > Adjust Color > Hue/Saturation**.

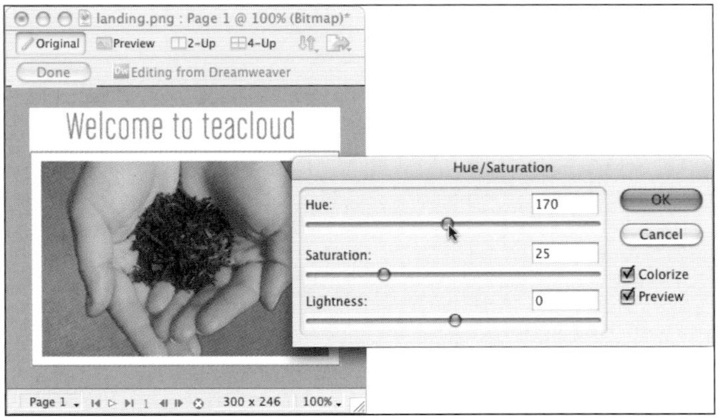

---

11 Check the **Colorize** button, and drag the **Hue** slider to about **170** to give the image a blue-green tint. Click **OK**.

---

12 Click the **Done** button at the top of the window. Notice that Fireworks doesn't prompt you to name or save the file or even compress it as a JPEG. The image just closes.

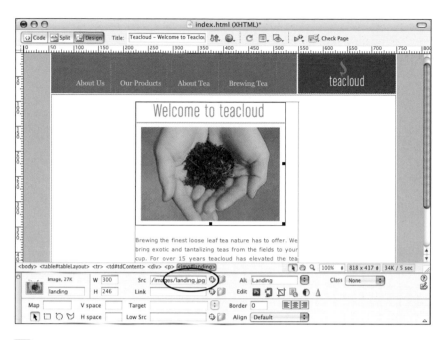

13 Return to Dreamweaver, and observe that the new version of the image now appears here.

Also notice that its name is still landing.jpg—Fireworks automatically saved the PNG image as a JPEG and overwrote the original landing.jpg, and you now have a clean version of the image that wasn't compressed multiple times.

---

14 Save **index.html**, and leave it open for the next exercise.

So, that's the gist of roundtrip image editing from Dreamweaver to Photoshop and Fireworks. As you continue building Web pages, you'll figure out which method works best for you in different editing situations. In the next exercise, you'll learn about a new and incredibly convenient copy-and-paste feature that's now available between Photoshop CS3 and Dreamweaver CS3.

Copying and Pasting from Photoshop into Dreamweaver

Probably one of the most welcome additions to the interaction between the various applications of the CS3 suite is the expanded ability to copy and paste from one application to another. You could always copy and paste text, but in the CS3 suite you now have the ability to copy and paste images from Photoshop and Fireworks into Dreamweaver. In this exercise, you'll copy part of an image from Photoshop and paste it into Dreamweaver.

1 You should still have the **index.html** file from Exercise 3 open. If not, complete Exercise 3, and then return to this exercise.

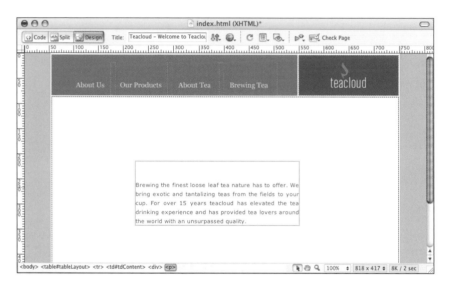

2 Select the **landing.jpg** image in the middle of the page, and delete it.

You'll replace it with a slightly altered version of the image.

3 Switch to **Photoshop CS3**, and open **landing.png** in the **chap_15/FW Files** folder. Click **OK** to dismiss the message about Fireworks data being discarded when you save the file. You won't be saving this file anyway.

> Fireworks Data Found
>
> This PNG contains additional data for Adobe Fireworks, which will be discarded upon save.
>
> OK   Cancel

Let's assume you're interested only in using the Welcome to teacloud portion of this image on your page. In the past you would have had to use Photoshop's Crop tool to crop the image and then save the image in a Web-ready format before you could add it to a Web page. And if you weren't working with a copy of the original image, you were permanently altering the original image. Happily, in the CS3 suite it's much quicker and easier to use just a portion of an image without damaging the original.

4 Press **M** to select Photoshop's **Marquee** tool, and draw a marquee around the **Welcome to teacloud** portion of the image.

---

5 Choose **Edit > Copy** to copy your selection to the **Clipboard**.

---

6 Close the image in Photoshop, and return to Dreamweaver.

Notice you weren't prompted to save the image in Photoshop, because you made absolutely no changes to it. You merely copied a portion of it to your computer's Clipboard.

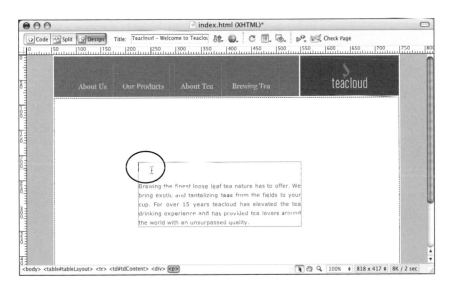

7 Position your cursor in the blank area formerly occupied by the **landing.jpg** image you deleted in Step 2, and then choose **Edit > Paste**.

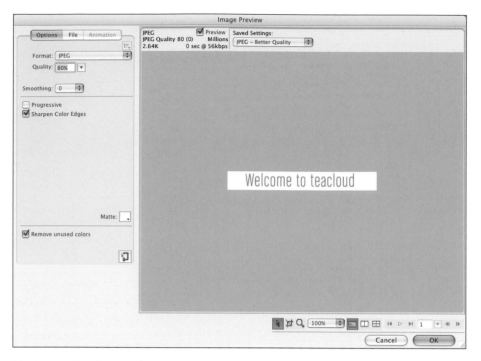

The Image Preview window opens. You can optimize your image for the Web right here in Dreamweaver. Notice it displays just the portion of the image you copied in Photoshop.

---

8 Keep the current settings in the **Image Preview** window where they are, and click **OK**. Save the image as **welcome.jpg** in the **assets/images** folder. If the **Image Description (Alt Text)** dialog box appears, type **Welcome to teacloud** as the description, and click **OK**.

Your new image now appears on the page. If you're new to Dreamweaver, Photoshop, or the Creative Suite in general, you might be thinking, "So, what? That's the way it *should* work." And you'd be right—it should work like that. But this is the first time in the history of these applications that this type of interaction has existed. And if you're a veteran Dreamweaver, Photoshop, or Fireworks user, you should be pretty happy to learn about this new capability. (You can copy and paste from Fireworks just as you did from Photoshop.)

That's all there is for this chapter. You learned how to increase your productivity by moving back and forth between Photoshop CS3, Fireworks CS3, and Dreamweaver CS3. You learned how to edit images directly in Dreamweaver, as well as how to send images to Photoshop or Fireworks and how to copy and paste images into Dreamweaver. In the next chapter, you'll learn how to work with templates and library items.

16

Using Templates and Library Items

Two of the biggest challenges Web designers face are making pages look consistent and updating changes throughout a site. Templates and library items can help you meet both challenges successfully by making it easy to create consistent pages and page elements, and they can automatically update multiple pages when changes are required.

Templates are useful for entire page designs. They can lock in colors, fonts, style sheets, tables, images, and even behaviors while leaving other parts of the document editable. Once you create a template, you can create new pages based on the template.

Library items are useful for page design elements, such as a navigation bar or copyright notice. They are little pieces of HTML (**H**yper**T**ext **M**arkup **L**anguage) or text you can drop anywhere in a page (template-based or not). You'll learn the differences between these two Adobe Dreamweaver CS3 features by following the hands-on exercises in this chapter.

1 | Seeing Templates in Action

The best way to understand templates is to see them in action. In this exercise, you'll modify an existing template and see how Dreamweaver CS3 locks regions of a template so they can't be edited. You'll also see how easy it is to update multiple pages across your site by changing the navigation and updating all the child pages that are based on a template.

---

1 If you haven't already done so, copy the **chap_16** folder from the **Dreamweaver HOT CD-ROM** to your desktop. Define your site as **Chapter 16** using the **chap_16** folder as the local root folder. Make sure the **Files** panel is open. If it's not, choose **Window > Files**.

> **TIP:** ✳
>
> ### Templates and Library Folders
>
> You may have noticed there are two folders in the **chap_16** folder: **Templates** and **Library**. Dreamweaver CS3 automatically creates these folders for you when you create a template or library item. If you do not use templates or library items, Dreamweaver will not put these folders in your directory structure. The **Templates** and **Library** folders do not need to be uploaded to your server when you publish your site to the Web unless you're working with another developer who needs them; they are for use in Dreamweaver CS3 only.

2 In the **Files** panel, double-click **abouttea.html** to open it. This file, as well as several others in the **chap_16** folder, has a template called **AboutTea.dwt** already applied to it. Open **fromthefields.html** and **teatypes.html** in the **abouttea** folder. Notice they all share the same layout and headings. Close all the files except **abouttea.html** before continuing.

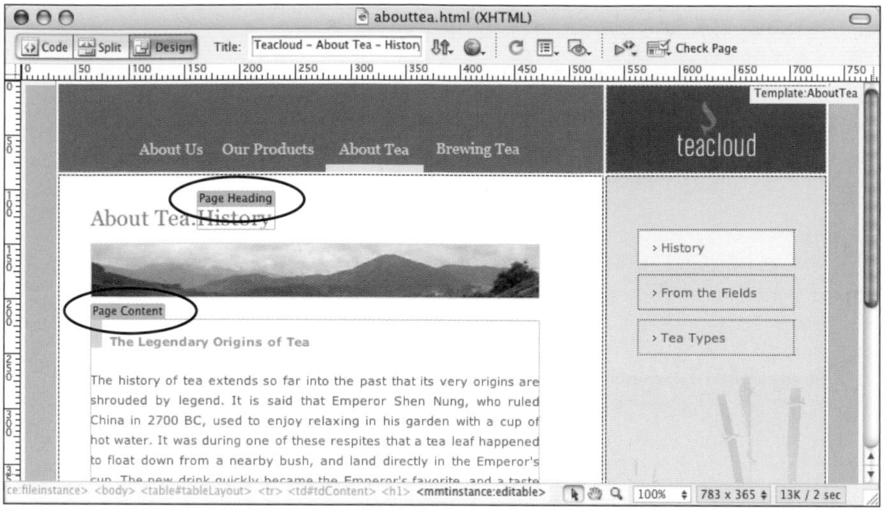

When you open a file with a template attached to it, you will see a tab in the upper-right corner identifying the name of the template file and a tab around each of the template's editable regions. You set the colors of these areas in the Highlighting category of the Preferences dialog box.

---

3 The **Assets** panel can show you all the templates in the current site. If this panel is closed, open it by choosing **Window > Assets**. Then click the **Templates** button to view the templates within your site.

---

4 Select the template called **AboutTea** in the **Assets** panel, and then click the **Edit** button to open the template so you can start editing it.

Tip: As an alternative, you can switch to the Files panel to open AboutTea.dwt in the Templates folder. All templates for a site are stored in the Templates folder at the root of the current site.

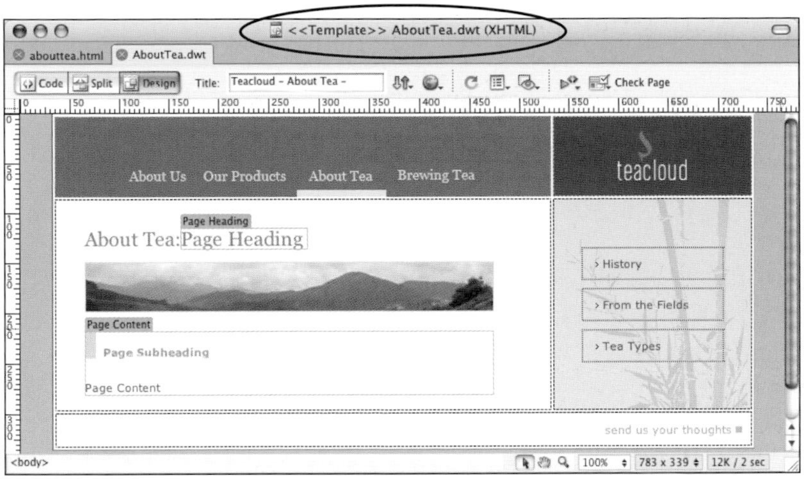

It's easy to tell when you are editing a template because the title bar displays *<<Template>>* and the template file name. All Dreamweaver CS3 templates have a .dwt file extension.

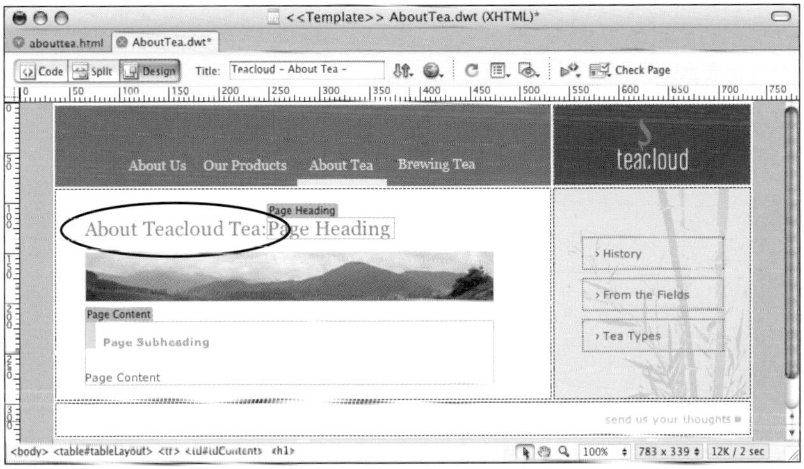

5 Replace the text **About Tea:** with **About Teacloud Tea:**.

Notice the *About Teacloud Tea:* text is not inside any of the bordered regions in the document (editable regions). This area of the page is locked down in any page based on this template, and any changes made to the template will take place in the child pages.

6 Choose **File > Save** to save your changes.

You have just saved a change to the layout of the master template. This change affects the multiple pages you viewed in Step 2, which were created with this template.

7 The **Page Heading** editable region is in a **<p>** tag. Dreamweaver warns you that you have an editable region inside a block-level tag, and it lets you know users won't be able to create new blocks (paragraphs) in this editable region. Click **OK** to acknowledge the warning and continue.

8 After you save the template, the **Update Template Files** dialog box appears. Because you want to apply the layout to all three pages, click **Update** so Dreamweaver will update all the files associated with this template.

Dreamweaver CS3 keeps track of which files are based on which template. Anytime you save a template, Dreamweaver CS3 prompts you to update the files based on that template.

9 As Dreamweaver CS3 updates each template, it will list the status of all the pages in the **Update Pages** dialog box. If you don't see the bottom half of the dialog box, select the **Show log** box to see all the information. In this case, the three files you opened in Step 2 are updated. Once you are finished reviewing this screen, click **Close**.

Note: If you have any files open while performing this operation, the page will be updated, but if you close the file without saving the changes, you'll lose any changes made by the template. Make sure you save your changes to abouttea.html (which is still open) when you close it.

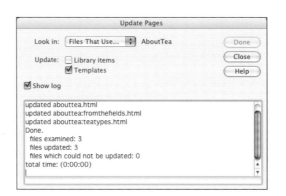

TIP:

Manually Updating Child Pages

If, for whatever reason, a page doesn't get successfully updated, you can always manually update the page. Open the page you want to update, and choose **Modify > Templates > Update Current Page**. The page will immediately update with the latest content from the template. If you want to manually update *all* pages based on a template, choose **Modify >Templates > Update Pages**, select the template you want to update, and click **Start**.

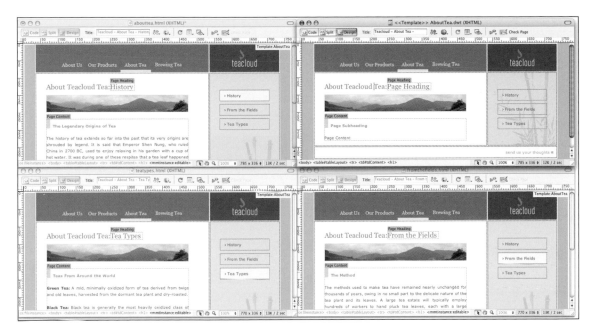

10 Open **fromthefields.html** and **teatypes.html** in the **abouttea** folder. Notice each now has the text change made in **AboutTea.dwt**.

Imagine how much time templates could save you if you had hundreds or thousands of pages that shared the same layout!

---

11 Close all the files. Save any changes to the pages if you're prompted to do so.

Working with templates is an excellent technique to ensure design consistency. The only caveat is that you must create a template file first. How do you do that? Check out the next exercise.

Templates and Teams

Using templates when designing a site on your own can certainly be helpful. It lets you lock down your design and quickly make changes on a large scale. But the real benefit in using templates comes when you're working with other designers or content contributors.

The ability to lock down a design when other team members are working on a site can be invaluable, especially when working with nondesigners. (Would you trust your boss with Dreamweaver?) Giving Dreamweaver CS3 to a novice on a team without using templates can be disastrous. Adobe has done a wonderful job, making it possible to control your design while still giving content editors the ability to do their jobs.

Adobe Contribute (**www.adobe.com/go/contribute**) is part of the CS3 Web Premium and Web Standard editions of the suite, and it allows content editors to work on Dreamweaver sites using templates so they can add content without affecting the design of the site. Contribute lets nontechie editors easily update their sites just like they would update a word processing document. The technical details are hidden from them, but at the same time, all the content is accessible.

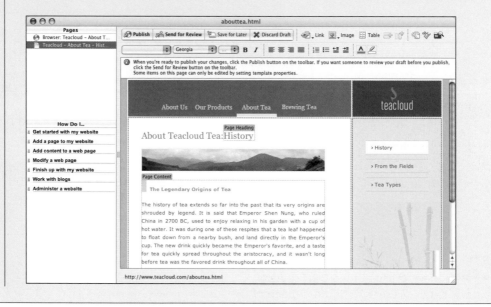

2 | Creating a New Template

Now that you're familiar with the way a template looks and feels, it's time to create your own. In this exercise, you'll take one of the Teacloud pages, convert it to a template, and begin adding editable regions. Editable regions allow you to make specific portions of your pages editable while locking down everything not residing in an editable region.

---

1 In the **Files** panel, double-click **ourproducts-base.html** to open it.

This document was created for you, but the following steps would also work on a document of your own creation. Once you have created the basic layout of your document, the next step is to save it as a template.

(Screenshot of Dreamweaver document window showing ourproducts-base.html (XHTML), with navigation "About Us Our Products About Tea Brewing Tea", teacloud logo, "Our Products:SubSection", "While There's Tea There's Hope", "Content Region", "Kettles & Teapots", "Teacloud Teas", "send us your thoughts", "Site Design by lynda.com (Adam and Dan)")

NOTE:

Everything Is Locked by Default

Templates work by making *everything* locked by default. Unless you specifically say that something is editable by placing it in an editable region, Dreamweaver CS3 will lock it down so that no one can touch it in child pages.

---

2 Choose **File > Save As Template** to open the **Save As Template** dialog box.

---

3 The file name **ourproducts-base** is prefilled in the **Save as** field; change this to **OurProducts**. You can also type a user-friendly description of the template, which is displayed in the **Templates** section of the **New Document** dialog box. Click **Save** to create the new template.

You can see that the other template you worked with in Exercise 1, AboutTea, is already listed in the Existing templates box.

(Screenshot of Save As Template dialog box. Site: Chapter 16. Existing templates: AboutTea. Description: Layout for our products. Save as: OurProducts. Buttons: Save, Cancel, Help)

---

4 A dialog box appears, asking you whether you want to update links. Click **Yes** to close the dialog box and update the links in the document.

When you save a document as a template, Dreamweaver CS3 copies that document to the Templates directory. When the document is copied to the Templates directory, all links (this includes **<img>** tags as well, not just hyperlinks) must be updated so that the template can find all the assets necessary to display the page correctly. Always click Yes to update links when saving a document as a template.

Your new template appears in the Templates category in the Assets panel. If you don't see the template, click the Refresh button in the Assets panel. The top portion of the Assets panel displays a preview of the template.

Now that you have created your template, you need to decide which areas you want to be editable and which areas you want to lock. By default, there are no editable regions in a new template. If you were to save the template as is and create a new child page from this template, you wouldn't be able to make any edits except for the page title. You'll learn how to create editable regions next.

5 Select the word **SubSection** at the top of the page, and choose **Insert > Template Objects > Editable Region** to designate this area as an editable region.

6 In the **New Editable Region** dialog box, type **Sub Section Heading** in the **Name** field, and click **OK**.

Notice the name you typed appears at the cursor location as a label, surrounded by a highlighted box. This indicates this area of the template is editable—you or other members of your team can enter information in this editable region.

TIP:

I Don't See Any Tabs!

If you don't see any tabs or highlighting in Dreamweaver CS3, choose **View > Visual Aids > Invisible Elements**. If you disable this feature, you will not see any tabs or highlighting in your template files. You can choose **View > Visual Aids > Invisible Elements** to turn the tabs on and off whenever you need them.

TIP:

Highlighting Preferences

You can modify your document's highlighting colors in the **Preferences** dialog box. By choosing **Edit > Preferences** (Windows) or **Dreamweaver > Preferences** (Mac) and then selecting **Highlighting** in the **Category** list, you can set the highlighting colors to any color you want.

7 Click and drag to select the **Content Region** text. Choose **Insert > Template Objects > Editable Region**. In the **New Editable Region** dialog box, type **Content**, and click **OK**.

Give your editable regions plain-English names so others working with the templates understand what should go where. You should avoid using special characters, but spaces are just fine.

At this point, your template looks like the illustration shown here.

---

8 Now that you have designated the necessary areas as editable, close this file. When prompted, save your changes. If you see a dialog box warning you about inserting an editable region inside a block tag, click **OK**.

Congratulations—you have just created a custom template. Next, you will create a page based on your newly created template.

---

9 Switch to the **Assets** panel (choose **Window > Assets** if it's not already open), and select the **Templates** category. You will see the new template in the template list. **Right-click** (Windows) or **Ctrl-click** (Mac) the **OurProducts** template, and choose **New from Template** in the contextual menu.

10 After the new page opens, choose **File > Save As**, and save the file as **ordering.html** in the **ourproducts** folder.

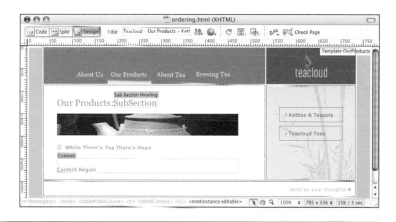

With a template applied to it, the page looks like the illustration shown here. The two areas you designated as editable are labeled and ready to be edited.

11 Click the **Sub Section Heading** tab to select all the text in the editable region. Type **How to Order**.

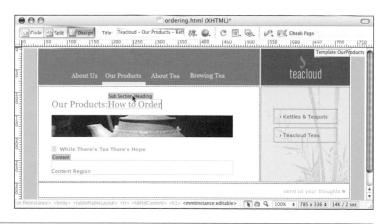

12 Click the **Content** label to select all the text in the editable region.

13 Open **placeholder.txt** in the **chap_16** folder, and copy all the content from the file. Return to **ordering.html**, and paste the text into the **Content** editable region.

With the content inserted into the document, the page looks like the illustration shown here.

14 Save and close **ordering.html** and **placeholder.txt**.

TIP:

![*]

Detaching a Template

You won't detach the template now, but it's good to know how to do so for future reference. You may at some point want to modify sections of a page that has a template applied. Because some areas are locked, you can't modify them with the template still applied. By choosing **Modify > Templates > Detach from Template**, you can detach the template from the page and make the entire document editable again.

---

3 | Applying Templates to Existing Documents

In this exercise, you'll apply a template to an existing document. As you go through the development process, you'll most likely not start by developing a template, and this is completely natural. Templates can be limiting and difficult to work with when you're constantly tweaking a design to get it just right. But once you get it just right and create your first template, you may need to go back and apply that template to documents you've already created.

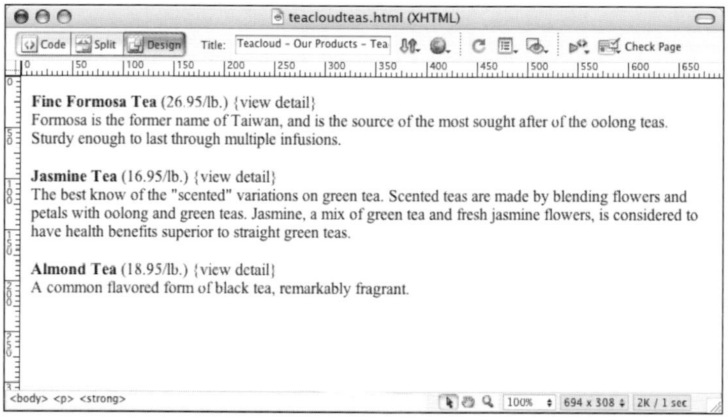

1 In the **Files** panel, double-click **teacloudteas.html** in the **ourproducts** folder to open it. This file doesn't have any design at all, just some product descriptions. You'll apply a design to it using the template you created in the previous exercise.

2 Choose **Modify > Templates > Apply Template to Page** to open the **Select Template** dialog box, which lists all the available templates in the current site. Select the **OurProducts** template, and click **Select**.

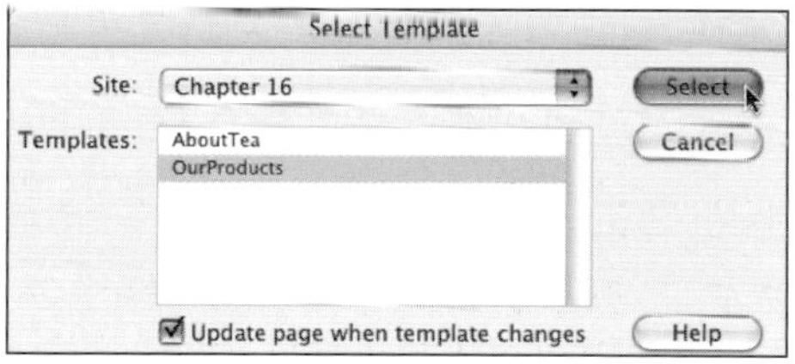

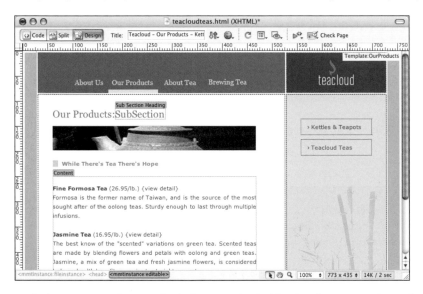

3 When you apply a template to a document, if the editable regions in the document don't match the editable regions in the template you're applying (or there are no editable regions in the current document), the **Inconsistent Region Names** dialog box opens. Select the **Document Body** region (which contains everything between the **\<body\>** tags in your page), and choose **Content** in the **Move content to new region** pop-up menu. Click **OK**.

The Inconsistent Region Names dialog box can look a bit overwhelming at first, but it simply provides a way for you to put your content in the correct editable region when you apply a new template.

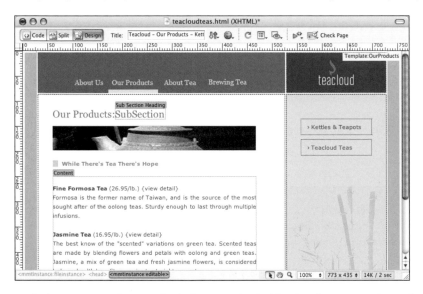

With the new template applied, the page looks like the illustration shown here.

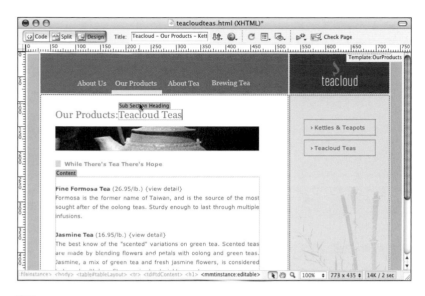

4 Click the **Sub Section Heading** tab, and type **Teacloud Teas**.

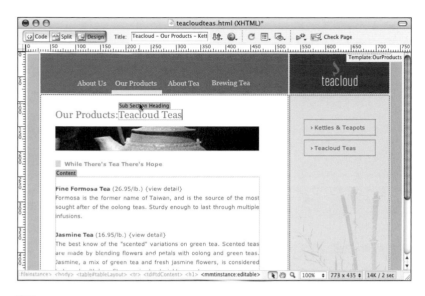

5 One unfortunate side effect of applying a template to an existing document is that you lose the document's title. In the **Document** toolbar, click in the **Title** field, change **Kettles and Teapots** to **Teacloud Teas**, and press **Enter** (Windows) or **Return** (Mac).

6 You now have your new page wrapped up in the **OurProducts** template. Save and close **teacloudteas.html**.

NOTE:

Applying Templates to Fully Designed Pages

At some point you may need to apply a template to a page that already has a full design. When the **Inconsistent Region Names** dialog box opens and you decide to put the **Document** body in the **Content** region of your template, you'll end up with one design inside another, which is probably not what you wanted. The easiest way to make this situation work is to copy the content of your fully designed page, paste it into a new blank document, and then apply the template to the new document. Then just save the new document over the old one. This gets rid of any existing design elements that could break the new template you're applying.

4 | Modifying a Template

Unless you're like me and get everything right on your first try (yeah right), you'll need to modify your existing template to tweak things after you've started working on your child pages. In this exercise, you'll modify the template you created in Exercise 2 to change some text alignment. Once you've made this change, you'll get to watch Dreamweaver CS3 take care of the hard work for you by updating all the child pages based on the template.

1 Before you can modify a template, you must open it in the **Assets** or **Files** panel. In the **Assets** panel, double-click the **OurProducts** template to open it.

2 Position your cursor in the **Our Products:** text, and choose **Edit > Select Parent Tag** to select the entire **<h1>** tag.

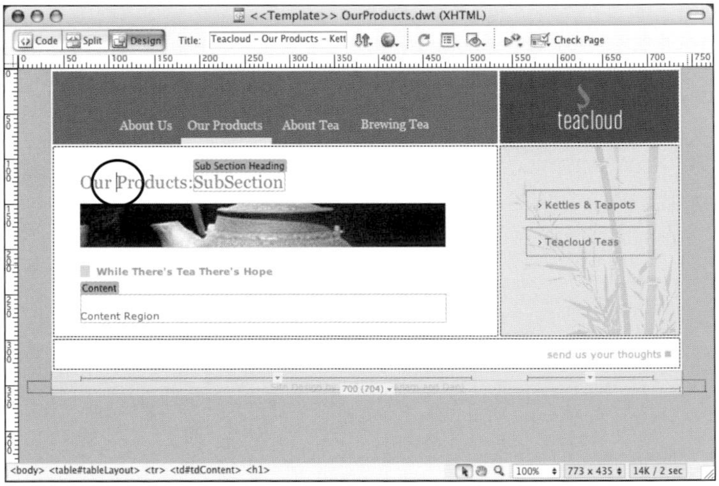

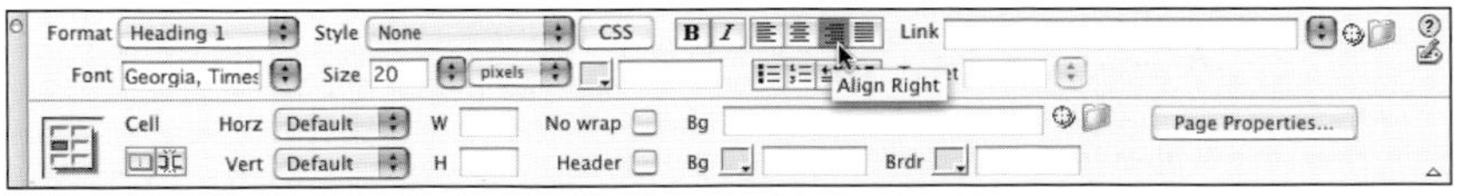

3 In the **Property inspector**, click the **Align Right** button to change the text alignment.

This moves the text to the right of the page.

4 Choose **File > Save** to save the template changes. A dialog box opens, warning you about inserting an editable region in a block tag. Click **OK**.

5 In the **Update Template Files** dialog box, click **Update** to update any files using this template (in this case **ordering.html** and **teacloudteas.html**). The **Update Pages** dialog box will list which files were updated. Click **Close** to close the **Update Pages** dialog box and continue. In the **Files** panel, double-click **teacloudteas.html** to open it.

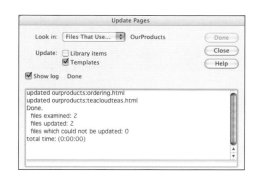

This is what teacloudteas.html looks like with the revised template applied to it. Note that the heading at the top of the page is aligned to the right, just like the template.

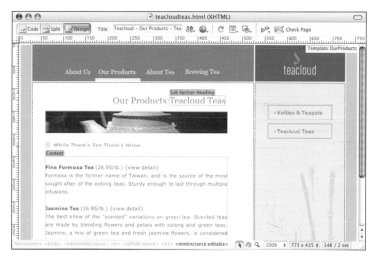

6 Save and close everything but **OurProducts.dwt**; you'll be using it in the next exercise.

NOTE:

Locked Head Content

After you apply a template to a page, you can no longer edit any information in the **<head>** tag that is part of the parent template. You can add JavaScript, styles, or behaviors, but you can't modify or remove any JavaScript, styles, or behaviors that were actually part of the template file. If you do need to edit the code in the locked region of the **<head>** tag, you need to remove the template by choosing **Modify > Templates > Detach from Template**. The downside, of course, is that if you make changes to the template, this unlinked copy will no longer be updated.

5 | Adding Repeating Regions

Repetitive work is the bane of many Web designers' existence. We like to design, not type the same information again and again. Repeating regions (and repeating tables) let you get rid of some of the drudgery and make entering repetitive data quick and precise. One of the problems with data entry is the likelihood for mistakes. Lock repetitive tasks into repeating regions, and you'll cut down on data entry errors significantly. In this exercise, you'll learn how to make the Teacloud catalog pages easier to modify and update by using repeating regions.

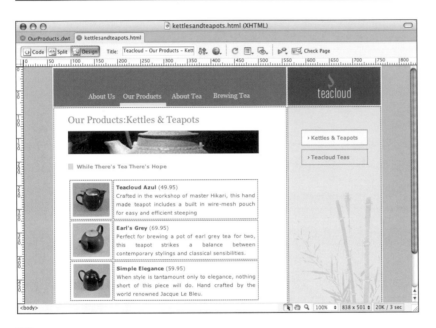

1 To begin, take a look at an existing catalog page that's not based on a template. From the Files panel, open **kettlesandteapots.html** in the **ourproducts** folder.

As you can see, this page is a wonderful candidate for a repeating region. Each teapot is in its own row, and each teapot has the same layout.

---

2 If it isn't already open from the previous exercise, open **OurProducts.dwt** in the **Templates** folder.

You'll add a repeating region to the template you were working with in the previous exercises.

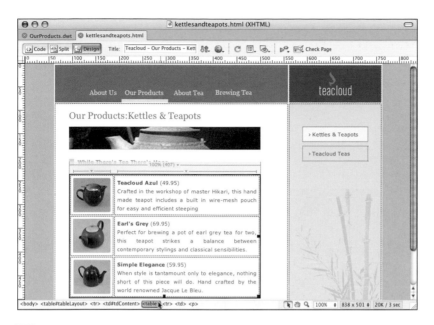

3 Switch to **kettlesandteapots.html** by choosing **Window > kettlesandteapots.html** or by clicking its tab at the top of the **Document** window. Select the entire table containing the teapots, and choose **Edit > Copy** to copy the table.

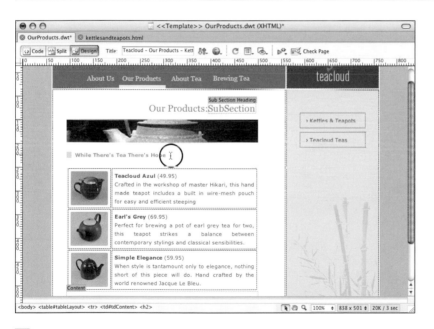

4 Switch back to **OurProducts.dwt**. Position your cursor after **While There's Tea There's Hope**, and choose **Edit > Paste**.

The product table from the existing product page is now part of the template.

5 Click in the second row of the first column, and drag to the bottom right of the table to select the last two rows of the table. Press **Delete** to remove them. You need only one row to create a repeating region.

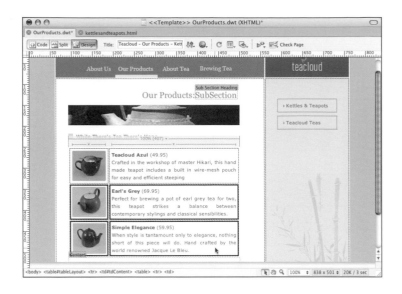

---

6 Click anywhere in the table cells in the table, and click the **<tr>** tag in the **Tag Selector** to select the entire row.

---

7 Choose **Insert > Template Objects > Repeating Region** to open the **New Repeating Region** dialog box.

---

8 Type **Catalog Row** as the **Name** of the repeating region, and click **OK**.

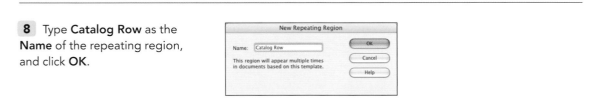

After you add the repeating region to the page, the file looks like the illustration shown here. You can see a new tab wrapped around the table row, with the label *Repeat: Catalog Row*. This easily identifies this row as a repeating region.

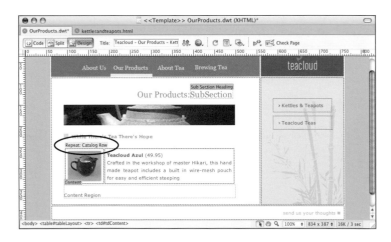

9 Select the teapot photo in the first table column, and choose **Insert > Template Objects > Editable Region**. In the **New Editable Region** dialog box, name the region **Product Image**, and click **OK**.

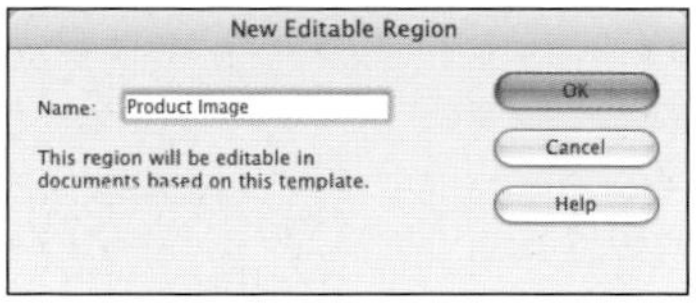

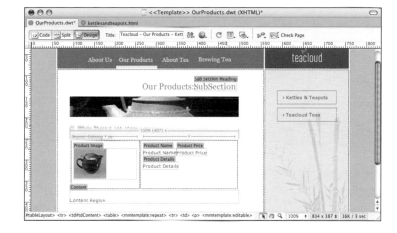

You added a repeating region, but you needed some editable regions as well. If you don't specify any editable regions in the repeating region, you won't be able to add any content to the rows in the child pages.

---

10 Click and drag to select the teapot name, **Teacloud Azul**, and press **Delete**. With the cursor still in the same location, choose **Insert > Template Objects > Editable Region**. In the **New Editable Region** dialog box, name the region **Product Name**, and click **OK**.

---

11 Do the same for the product price and the details, naming the regions **Product Price** and **Product Details**.

After all the editable regions are in place, the template looks like the illustration shown here. The product image, name, price, and details are all in editable regions, and the rest of the page is still locked.

---

12 Save the template, and update all the pages based on the template. If a warning message appears about placing an editable region in a block tag, click **OK** to dismiss it. Close any open documents before continuing to the next exercise.

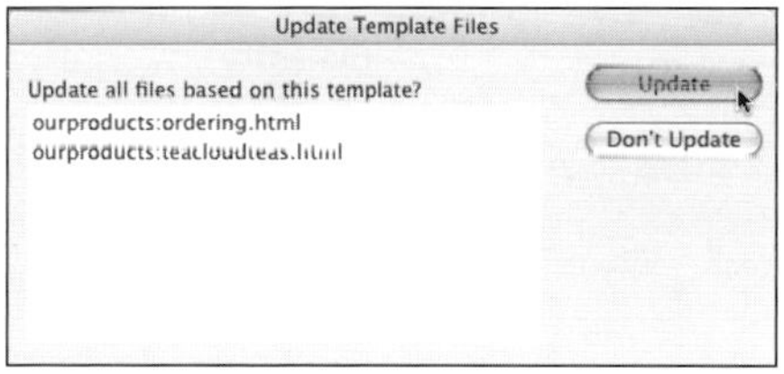

You're probably thinking this is all very unexciting at this point. But now it's time to create a new page and start working with the repeating region. Continue to the next exercise to learn how to *use* those repeating regions.

In the previous exercise, you added a new repeating region to a template. Looking at it inside the template wasn't all that awe inspiring, but now you get to play with the repeating regions. In this exercise, you'll create a new page based on the template you saved in the previous exercise, and you'll add some new catalog entries.

1 In the **Assets** panel, select the **Template** category. **Right-click** the **OurProducts** template, and choose **New from Template** in the contextual menu. Save the new document as **kettlesandteapots-new.html** in the **ourproducts** folder.

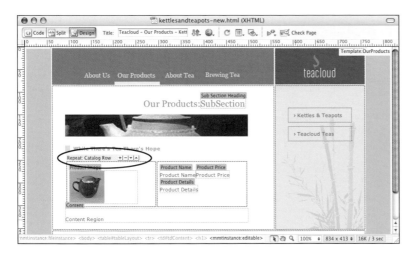

2 The first thing you should notice is the **Repeating Region** controls above the repeating region you added in the previous exercise.

The Repeating Region controls let you add a new row after the currently selected row (+), delete the selected row (–), and move the selected row up (up arrow) or down (down arrow). The selected row in this case is whichever row the cursor is currently in.

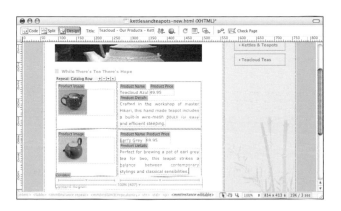

3 For the first product, click the tab for each editable region, and specify the following:

Product Image: Leave the default image, since it's already the image of the Teacloud Azul teapot.

Product Name: Type **Teacloud Azul**.

Price: Type **49.95**.

Product Details: Type **Crafted in the workshop of master Hikari, this handmade teapot includes a built-in wire-mesh pouch for easy and efficient steeping.**

4 In the **Repeating Region** controls, click the **+** button to add a new row directly below the **Teacloud Azul** row. Specify the following for each editable region in the new row:

Product Image: Set the image source to **../assets/images/products/kettles/earls-grey.jpg** in the **Property inspector**.

Product Name: Type **Earl's Grey**.

Price: Type **69.95**.

Product Details: Type **Perfect for brewing a pot of earl grey tea for two, this teapot strikes a balance between contemporary stylings and classical sensibilities.**

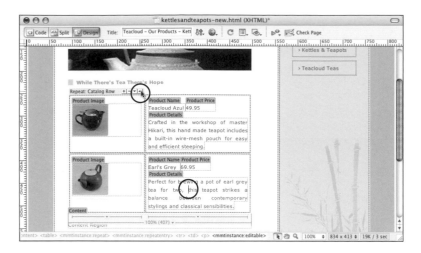

5 Now that you have two products set up, you can play with changing the order. Position your cursor in any of the editable regions in the second row. In the **Repeating Region** controls, click the **up arrow** button to move the second row above the first.

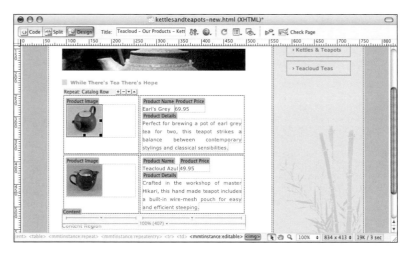

After moving the rows around, your page looks like the illustration shown here.

6 Save and close **kettlesandteapots-new.html**.

In this exercise, you learned how to work with the Repeating Region controls to manipulate the repeating region you added in the previous exercise. You can now take your templates to the next level and make sure others on your team (or your boss who wants to be a Web designer) don't make a mess of the design you spent so much time putting together.

7 | Adding Optional Regions

Sometimes you'll want to hide or display elements on a per-page basis. With optional regions, you can turn sections of a template on and off using template parameters (which you'll learn to modify in the next exercise). In this exercise, you'll create an optional region that will allow you to easily turn off the product repeating region you added in Exercise 5, because the **Teacloud Teas** page doesn't need the product display, even though it's based on the **OurProducts** template.

1 In the **Files** panel, double-click **teacloudteas.html** in the **ourproducts** folder to open it.

As you can see, when you added the repeating region to the OurProducts template, it added that repeating region to the Teacloud Teas page as well, an unintended side effect of making the kettles and teapots easier to add.

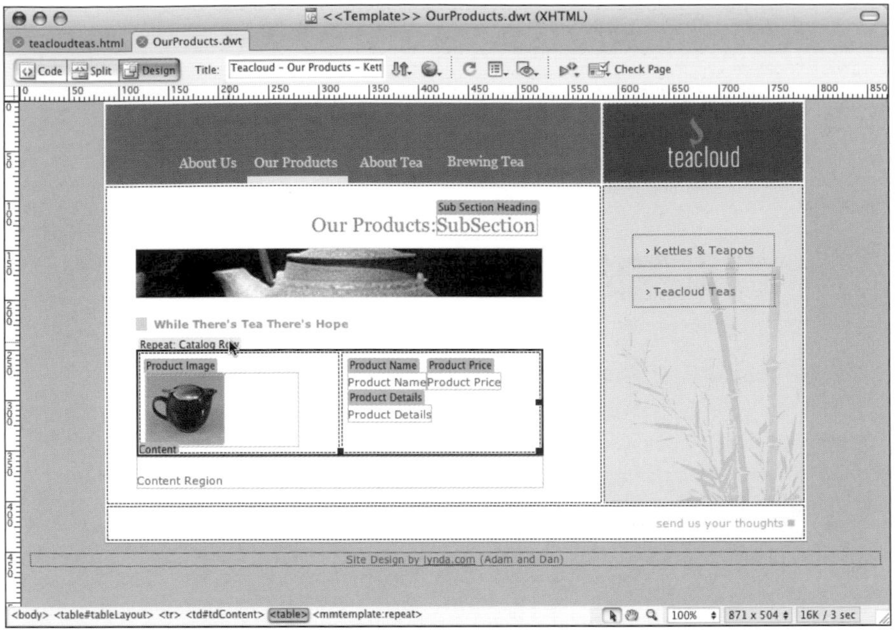

2 Open **OurProducts.dwt** in the **Templates** folder. Click the **Repeat: Catalog Row** tab, and choose **Edit > Select Parent Tag** to select the entire product table. (If the table widths get in the way, choose **View > Visual Aids > Table Widths** to turn them off.)

---

3 Choose **Insert > Template Objects > Optional Region** to open the **New Optional Region** dialog box.

The New Optional Region dialog box lets you give the optional region a friendly name for references in the Template Properties dialog box (which you'll learn more about in the next exercise).

---

4 Type **Show Product Table** as the **Name** of the optional region, and leave the **Show by default** box selected. Click **OK** to add the new region to the page.

The Basic tab of the New Optional Region dialog box will do everything you need to do for 99 percent of the templates you'll build. You may eventually have need for the Advanced tab, which lets you pick from existing template parameters already on the page and lets you specify custom template parameter expressions to decide whether to show a region.

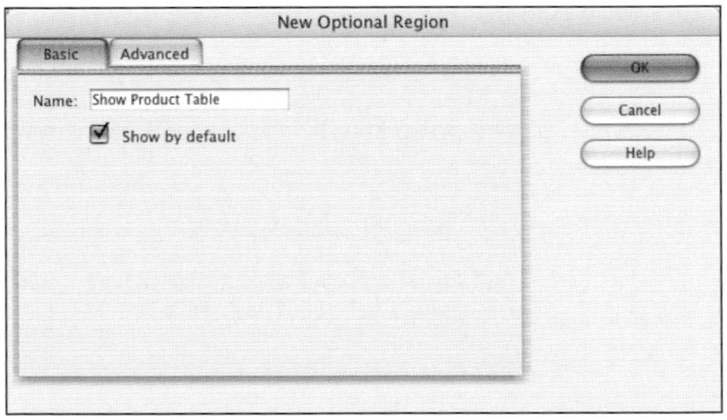

404   **Adobe Dreamweaver CS3** : H·O·T

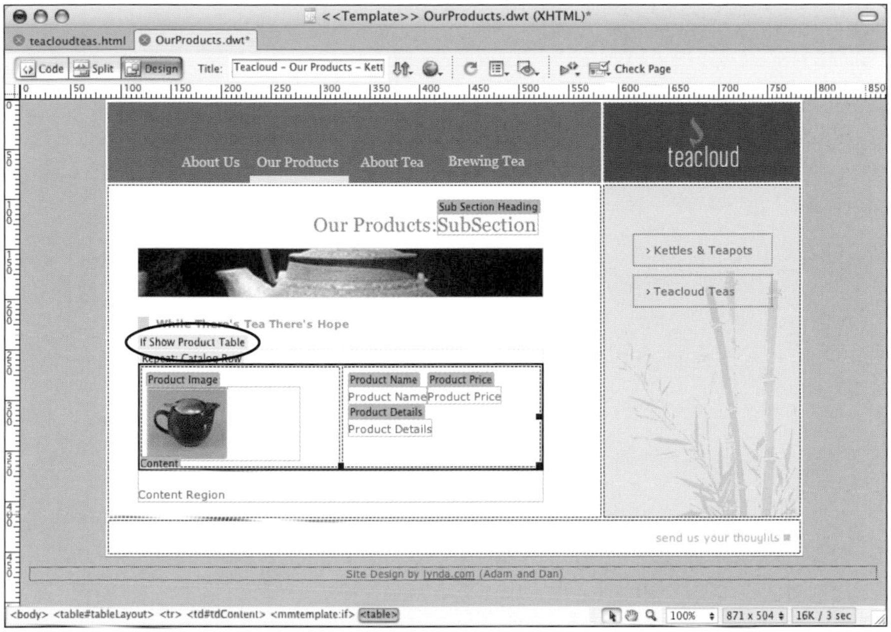

With the new optional region added to the page, the OurProducts template looks like the illustration shown here. Notice the new tab wrapped around the product table, labeled *If Show Product Table*. This tab gives you a quick reference to let you know that an optional region is wrapped around the content.

5 Save the **OurProducts** template. When the **Update Template Files** dialog box appears, click **Update**. Click **Close** in the **Update Pages** dialog box after everything has been updated.

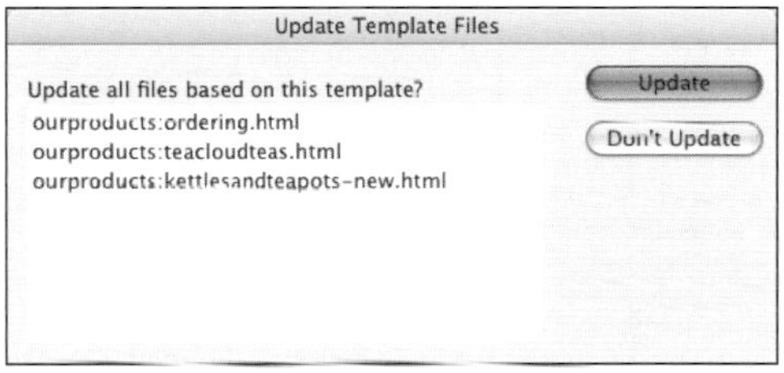

6 Switch to **teacloudteas.html** to see what has changed. Leave this file open—you'll be using it in the next exercise.

Surprised? There's absolutely no change to the way the document looked before you added the optional region. That's because when you defined the optional region, you left the Show by default box selected, so the optional region is being shown. Check out the next exercise to see how to hide the optional region in your page.

Modifying Template Properties

When you created the optional region in the previous exercise, Dreamweaver CS3 created a template parameter for you to control the display of that optional region. In this exercise, you'll learn how to modify template properties on your child pages.

---

1 You should still have the **teacloudteas.html** file from Exercise 7 open. If not, complete Exercise 7, and then return to this exercise. Switch to **Code** view, and scroll up to line **35**. (This may be slightly different on your machine.)

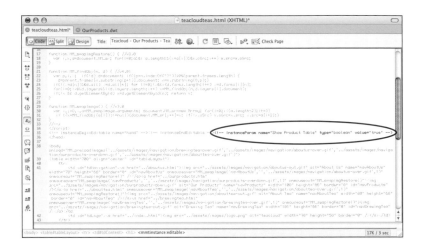

The HTML comment is how Dreamweaver CS3 defines template parameters in your documents. Template parameters control any optional regions on your page. As you can see, the name of the template parameter is Show Product Table (just like you defined in the previous exercise), the type of parameter is **Boolean** (meaning true or false), and the default value is **true**.

---

2 Switch back to **Design** view, and choose **Modify > Template Properties** to open the **Template Properties** dialog box.

---

3 With the **Show Product Table** template parameter selected in the top half of the dialog box, deselect the **Show Show Product Table** box. Notice **Value** changes to **false**. Click **OK** to close the dialog box and update the page.

It may seem odd that the dialog box says *Show Show Product Table*, but the default behavior for the Template Properties dialog box is to put the word *Show* before the optional region name. Regardless of the goofy wording, we prefer to give optional regions names that read well with the word *If* in front of them so they make sense when looking at the labels for the optional regions in the template.

Adobe Dreamweaver CS3 : H·O·T

4 You should now see that the product table is no longer displayed on the page. Save and close all open files.

Knowing When to Use Library Items

One of the biggest issues with using templates and library items is trying to figure out when to use which. Templates are good for locking down entire layouts, whereas library items let you lock down small pieces of code that you want to use on multiple pages, whether you're using a template or not.

One of the best examples of when to use library items is with copyright statements (which we'll show you in the next few exercises). In most sites,

you'll have two or three different page layouts, perhaps with three or four different templates. You might have pop-up windows that contain copyright statements, along with all your standard pages. It's far easier to make that copyright statement a library item and include it in each of your templates and pop-up windows than it is to change the copyright every year in each template and each pop-up window.

9 | Creating a Library Item

Library items and templates are somewhat similar in function. Both let you apply changes to multiple pages with ease. The difference is that templates affect the entire page design, whereas you use library items for individual page elements, both inside and outside templates. In this exercise, you will create a library item for a copyright statement and then apply it to a page by simply dragging it to **Design** view in Dreamweaver CS3.

---

1 In the **Files** panel, double-click **index.html** to open it. Scroll to the bottom, and you'll see the copyright statement that needs to be on every page of the site. Click and drag to select all the copyright text.

2 In the **Assets** panel, select the **Library** category. Click the **New Library Item** button. Your new library item instantly appears in the category. If you get a warning stating that the library item may not look the same in other documents, just click **OK**. It needs a name, so type **Copyright** in the bounding box.

When you click the New Library Item button, Dreamweaver takes any highlighted text in the current document and adds it as a new library item. It will then convert the selection in your document to the new library item.

Dreamweaver CS3 took the liberty of converting the selection in index.html to a library item for you. You can tell that a block of text is part of a library item because of the yellow highlighting.

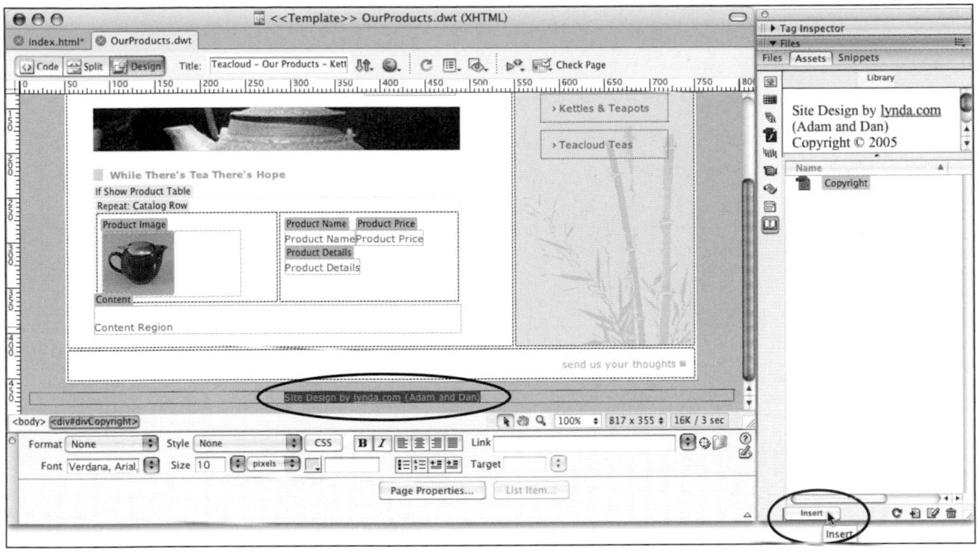

3 Now that you have created your library item, you can apply it to any page in the site. Open the file **OurProducts** template. Scroll to the bottom, and click and drag to select the text in the footer. In the **Assets** panel, select the **Copyright** library item, and click **Insert**.

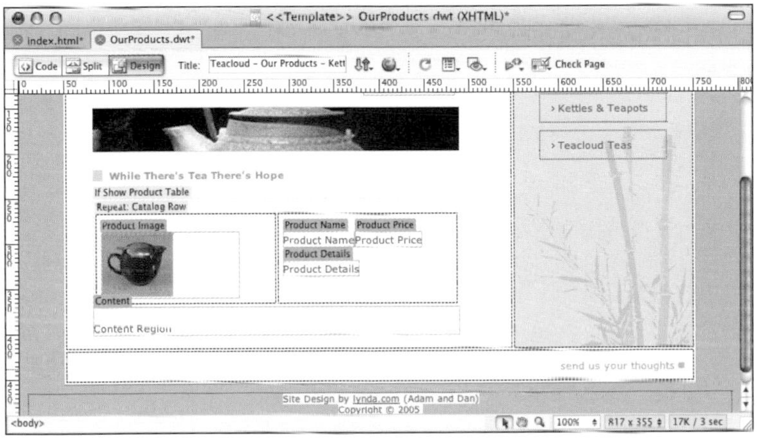

The template is now using the library item for the copyright statement in the footer.

---

4 Save the **OurProducts** template, and update all the pages based on the template. All the template-based pages are now using the same library item.

---

5 Save and close any open documents.

In the next exercise, you'll modify the Copyright library item and see that it's just as easy to update a library item as it is to update a template.

---

10 | Modifying a Library Item

Now that you know how to create library items, you'll modify the one you just created and then watch Dreamweaver CS3 quickly update your pages.

---

1 In the **Library** category of the **Assets** panel, select the **Copyright** library item, and click the **Edit** button.

TIP: | ### Edit Right from the Page

You can also edit library items by **right-clicking** the library item on any page in which it's applied. Then just choose **Open Library Item** in the contextual menu.

```
<<Library Item>> Copyright.lbi*

Code   Split   Design   Title:                         Check Page

Site Design by lynda.com (Adam and Dan)
Copyright © 2005-2007|

                                    100%   817 x 381   1K / 1 sec
```

2 Change the copyright statement to read **Copyright © 2005-2007**.

---

3 Close the library item file, and when you are prompted, make sure you save your changes. In the **Update Library Items** dialog box, click **Update**.

Notice that not only is index.html listed but the OurProducts template and all the pages based on that template will also be updated.

4 Click **Close** to close the **Update Pages** dialog box when you are done reviewing it.

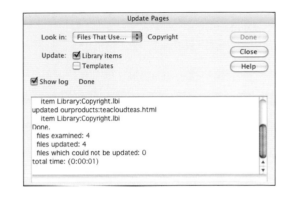

5 Open **index.html** again, and you'll see that the new copyright dates are now listed on the page. Close all open documents.

In this chapter, you learned how to work with templates and library items. You learned how to add editable regions, repeating regions, and optional regions to a template to make it easy to manage all the product documents for your site. You also learned how to lock down smaller areas of a page by using library items. These solutions make it possible to make changes in large numbers of documents all at once. In the next chapter, you'll learn how to use a different type of automation in Dreamweaver CS3.

17

Automating Repetitive Tasks

As you design Web pages, you'll quickly notice that an abundance of incredibly repetitive and boring tasks are required to do your work. Fortunately, Adobe Dreamweaver CS3 has several features to help you automate many of these boring tasks, such as the **History** panel and custom objects and commands. In this chapter, you'll learn about the **History** panel, which memorizes and replays steps you've performed while creating a Dreamweaver CS3 document. You can script this panel to replay these steps, which is one great way to automate repetitive tasks. This chapter also introduces you to the powerful **Find and Replace** feature, which can efficiently make changes to your current page, a range of pages, or your entire site. You will also work with one of the preexisting commands that comes with Dreamweaver CS3: **Create Web Photo Album**.

What Is the History Panel?

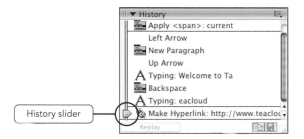

History slider

By default, the **History** panel displays the last 50 steps you performed since creating or opening a file. This offers a nice visual overview of the different steps you've completed. You can use the slider to quickly undo and redo these steps. This visual approach to stepping backward and forward through your document gives you more feedback than pressing **Ctrl+Z** and **Ctrl+Y**

(Windows) or **Cmd+Z** and **Cmd+Y** (Mac). In addition, you can copy the steps in the **History** panel from one document to another, which is helpful when you want to perform identical actions on multiple documents. You can also copy steps from the **History** panel and save them as commands, which lets you replay them later, in any document, with a just single click.

1 | Using the History Panel for Undo/Redo

This exercise gets you comfortable working with the **History** panel. You'll learn how to use this panel to repeat or delete operations you've performed. Working with the **History** panel can be much easier than choosing **Undo** or **Redo** multiple times.

---

1 If you haven't already done so, copy the **chap_17** folder from the **Dreamweaver HOT CD-ROM** to your desktop. Define your site as **Chapter 17** using the **chap_17** folder as the local root folder. Make sure the **Files** panel is open. If it's not, choose **Window > Files**.

---

2 In the **Files** panel, double-click **contactus.html** to open it. Position your cursor in the table cell containing the **Name:** label.

To make the labels for the form fields easier to see on this page, you'll change the formatting for the table cells containing the labels.

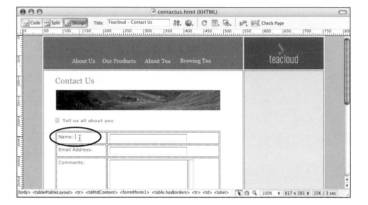

---

3 In the **Property inspector**, choose **Right** in the **Horz** pop-up menu, and type **#E3E5DC** in the **Bg** field.

---

4 If the **History** panel isn't already open, choose **Window > History** to open it.

The History panel displays the change you made to the table cell in Step 3. As you continue to make additions and changes to your document, your steps appear here automatically.

5 With the table cell still selected, select the **Header** check box in the **Property inspector** to change the **<td>** tag to a **<th>** tag.

Notice the History panel records this step as well.

6 In the **History** panel, click and drag the **History** slider to the top so the first step is highlighted. This undoes the last formatting you applied to the page, just as though you had used the **Undo** command. Click and drag the **History** slider back down to the bottom of the list to reapply the text formatting.

This is a nice way to step through the changes you have made to a document. It beats having to press Ctrl+Z (Windows) or Cmd+Z (Mac) because you can see a description for every step you're undoing.

7 Position your cursor in the table cell containing the **Email Address** label, and click the **<td>** tag in the **Tag Selector** to select the table cell.

To make sure the History panel actually applies the changes to the proper element, you need to make sure the actual table cell is selected.

8 Select the last item in the **History** panel, hold down the **Shift** key, and select the first item to select all the steps. Click the **Replay** button.

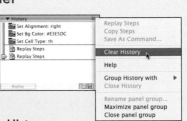

The table cell containing the Email Address label now has the same formatting as the Name label's table cell. As you can see, you can apply or replay the steps in the History panel. In this case, you manually formatted the Name field and used the recorded steps in the History panel to replay the actions to apply the same formatting to the Email Address field. As you can see, replaying actions is a huge timesaver and saves you from repeating multiple steps over and over, which can be tedious and rather boring.

9 Save **contactus.html**, and leave it open for the next exercise.

NOTE:

Saving Files and Clearing the History Panel

The **History** panel does not clear automatically when you save a file. This is great if you want to use it to make changes even after you save the document. If you close the file and reopen it, however, the history is cleared.

You can clear the **History** panel at any time. Why would you want to clear the **History** panel? The **History** panel uses a lot of RAM (**R**andom **A**ccess **M**emory) if you have made a lot of changes to your document. Clear the history by clicking the **Panel Options** menu button in the upper right of the **History** panel and choosing **Clear History** in the pop-up menu. You can't undo this action, so be careful when you use it.

Note: Don't clear the history if you just completed Exercise 1, because you'll need the history steps for Exercise 2.

---

2 | Saving History Steps as Commands

In the previous exercise, you learned how to use the **History** panel to undo and redo changes. You also learned how to replay the history steps to perform repetitive operations. What would you do if you needed to perform those same steps in multiple documents, perhaps hundreds of times over the course of a site's design? Dreamweaver CS3 makes it easy to replay steps as many times as you like by saving the steps in the **History** panel as a command.

---

1 You should still have the **contactus.html** file from Exercise 1 open. If not, complete Exercise 1, and then return to this exercise. The **History** panel should match the illustration shown here.

In this exercise, you'll use the existing steps in the History panel to create a command you can use over and over to format multiple pages.

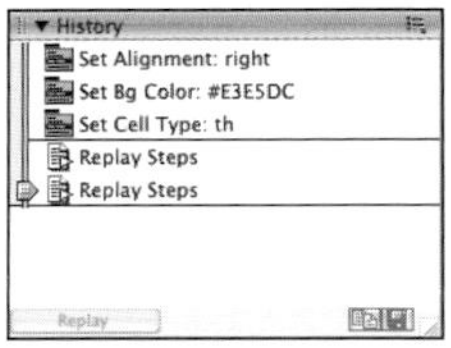

NOTE:

What Is a Command?

A **command** is a small JavaScript file that performs specific functions in Dreamweaver CS3. These files are stored in the **Configuration\Commands** folder. Some commands ship with Dreamweaver CS3, such as the **Create Web Photo Album** command. You can even create your own custom commands using the **History** panel or write them from scratch using JavaScript. For example, you can copy steps from the **History** panel and save them as a command. Dreamweaver CS3 converts the selected steps into JavaScript so you can replay them from any document. As you'll see in a moment, commands can be powerful and can save you a lot of time.

---

2 Click the first step in the **History** panel. Hold down the **Shift** key, and click **Set Cell Type: th** step to select all three steps in the **History** panel.

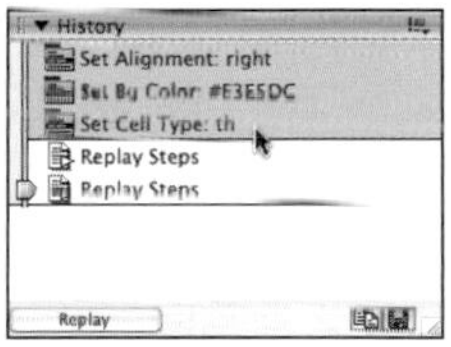

3 Click the **Save** button to open the **Save As Command** dialog box.

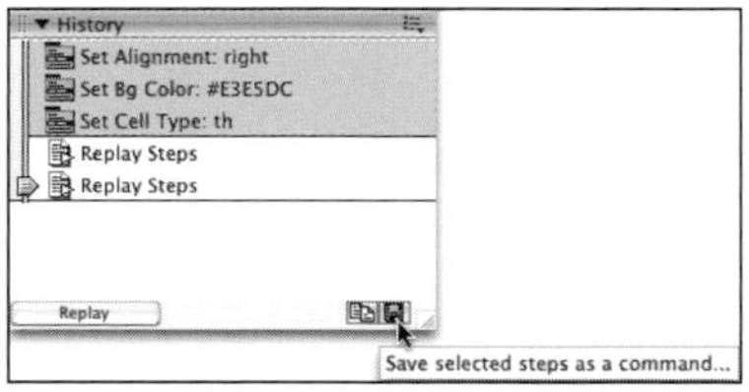

4 In the **Save As Command** dialog box, type **Format Table Label** for **Command Name**, and click **OK**.

When you name commands, try to be specific about what steps the command performs. As you create more and more commands, it can be hard to remember which command does what. By using a descriptive name, you'll be able to easily know what steps the command performs.

5 Position your cursor in the table cell containing the **Comments** label, and click the **<td>** tag in the **Tag Selector** area to select the table cell. Choose **Commands > Format Table Label**.

The Comments table cell is now formatted the same as the other two table cells. Saving a set of history steps as a command makes it easy to perform the same steps as many times as you need and on any page you want (not just on documents in the current site).

6 Close **contactus.html**. You don't need to save your changes.

NOTE: | **Not All Steps Can Be Saved**

Before you get too excited about saving history steps as commands, be aware that you can't save all history steps. When you look through the steps of the **History** panel, if you see a little red X next to a step or you see a line dividing some of the steps, that's Dreamweaver's way of letting you know you can't save those particular steps.

VIDEO: | **webphotoalbum.mov**

Saving your own history steps as a command is great, but commands can do so much more. Commands can do as little as setting some table formatting to as much as creating entire Web sites and pages. Dreamweaver CS3 ships with a number of commands that you'll find useful. One of the commands is the **Create Web Photo Album** command, which will automatically convert an entire folder of images to a **Web Photo Gallery**. To learn how to use the **Create Web Photo Album** command to build your own online photo albums, check out **webphotoalbum.mov** in the **videos** folder on the **Dreamweaver HOT CD-ROM**.

---

3 | Using Find and Replace

One of the most powerful (and least acclaimed) features in Dreamweaver CS3 is the **Find and Replace** feature. With it you can perform what would normally be very time-intensive tasks in an incredibly short amount of time. The **Find and Replace** feature is similar to the find-and-replace features in other programs, such as Microsoft Word, but it's geared specifically toward Web development. In this exercise, you'll learn how to use this feature to replace text on a page and how to replace text in the source code of your documents.

1 In the **Files** panel, double-click **aboutus.html** to open it.

Notice this page incorrectly uses *tea cloud* in the page title and in the body text. The proper name for this company is *Teacloud*. Unfortunately, every page in the site uses the wrong company name. You could open each page in your site and make the corrections manually, but that would be an inefficient way to work. This site has fewer than 10 pages with the wrong company name, but what if you had a site that had a similar problem on hundreds of pages? By using the Find and Replace feature, you can make these changes quickly and accurately.

2 Click to select the **tea cloud** text in the either the first or second paragraph of the document. Choose **Edit > Find and Replace** to open the **Find and Replace** dialog box with your selection already in the **Find** field.

3 In the **Find in** pop-up menu, choose **Entire Current Local Site** to ensure Dreamweaver CS3 searches all the pages within the current local site.

Take a moment to examine the other available options. As you can see, Dreamweaver CS3 lets you modify as little or as much of your site as you want. You can search in as little as a few selected words, in a specific folder, or across the entire site.

4 Choose **Text** in the **Search** pop-up menu to ensure Dreamweaver CS3 searches only the text on each affected page. You can also search through the source code or even specific tags.

---

5 The **Find** field should automatically contain the text you select in Step 2. If it doesn't, type **tea cloud** in the **Find** field.

---

6 In the **Replace** field, type **Teacloud** to define the text that will replace the text in the **Find** field. Click **Replace All** to have Dreamweaver search the text on all the pages in your site and make the necessary replacements.

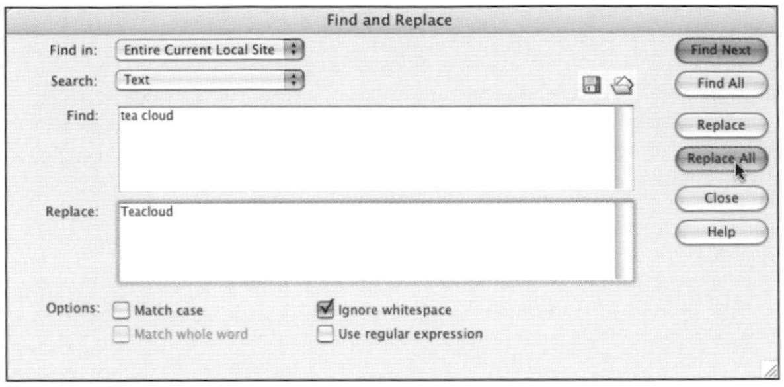

There are plenty of other options, such as making sure the Find and Replace operation matches the case exactly. Click the Help button to learn more about these options.

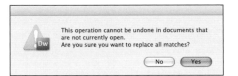

---

7 Because you don't have every page in your site open, Dreamweaver CS3 displays a warning telling you that this operation cannot be undone in pages that aren't open. Click **Yes** to continue.

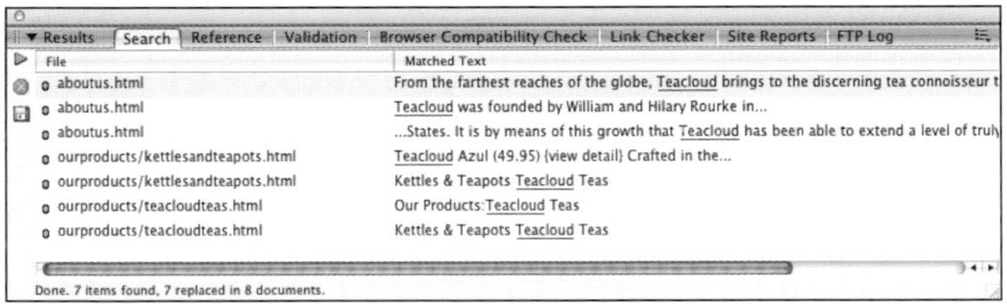

Dreamweaver CS3 opens the Results panel, which shows you every replace that Dreamweaver CS3 performed. This lets you make sure everything was replaced correctly.

---

8 Double-click any entry in the **Results** panel to open the page. Dreamweaver highlights the first instance of the replaced text, just in case you replaced something you shouldn't have.

Notice only the text on the page was replaced; the text in the **<title>** tag was left alone. When you set the Search option to Text in the Find and Replace dialog box, Dreamweaver CS3 limited the search to the text within the **<body>** tag of the page. Because the **<title>** is outside the **<body>** tag, that text was not replaced.

---

9 Choose **Edit > Find and Replace** again.

---

10 If the fields aren't already filled, type **tea cloud** in the **Find** field and **Teacloud** in the **Replace** field. In the **Search** pop-up menu, choose **Source Code**. This causes Dreamweaver CS3 to search through all the source code on the page, including the **<title>** tag, instead of just the text contained in the **<body>** tag. It will also find any problems with tag attributes, such as a misspelling in an **alt** attribute for an image. Click **Replace All**.

---

11 When the warning dialog box appears, click **Yes**.

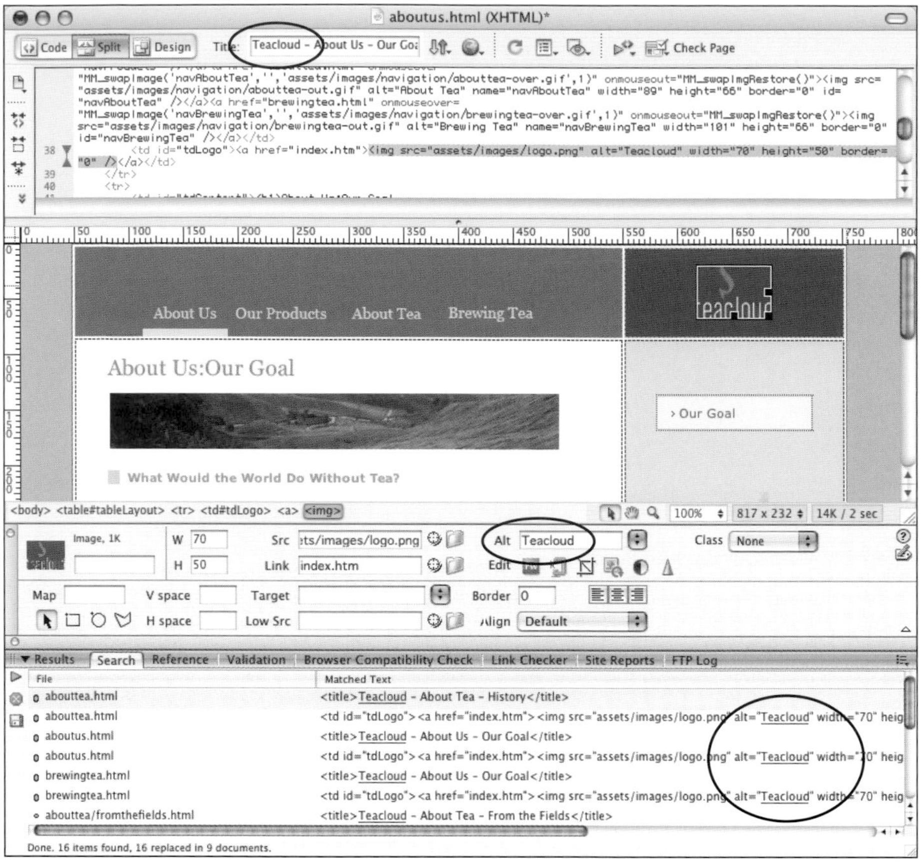

Because you are replacing text in the source code of the page, Dreamweaver opens the current page in Split view and highlights one instance of the text that has been changed. As you can see in this image, the page title has been fixed, as have several problems with alt attributes.

---

12 Save and close **aboutus.html**.

In this chapter, you learned how to speed up your development processes using some of the automation tools in Dreamweaver CS3. You learned how to use the History panel to quickly undo and redo steps, how to save those steps as a command that you can run anytime you want, and how to use the Find and Replace feature to make changes to large numbers of documents at once. In the next chapter, you'll learn how to make your pages more accessible to people with disabilities.

18

Understanding Accessibility

Accessibility is one of the hottest buzzwords in the Web design industry today because it remains one of the most significant issues Web design-ers have faced in the past few years. **Accessibility** means making your Web pages accessible to everyone, including people with disabilities. With the passing and enforcement of Section 508 of the Rehabilitation Act, Web designers are now charged with not only making their sites visually appealing but with also making them "accessible." This law applies mostly to federal and state agencies, schools, and government vendors. Its direct impact on most other sites is expected to be less seri-ous. Regardless, Web designers should make their pages as accessible as possible for everyone.

Dreamweaver CS3 has a suite of features that help you create accessible Web pages. It even has a great reporting feature that can help you iden-tify accessibility problems in existing Web pages. In this chapter, you'll learn how to use the accessibility features in Dreamweaver CS3 to ease the process of creating accessible Web pages. Whether you know it or not, you've already been using several accessibility features as you worked through the previous chapters.

Understanding the W3C Accessibility Guidelines

Before you learn the nuances of accessibility in Dreamweaver CS3, it's important to first establish what the term **accessibility** does and doesn't mean, specifically in the context of Web design. In a Web design arena, accessibility simply means "online content that can be used by someone with a disability." Although this definition is accurate, consider this as one part of the accessibility equation.

Making your Web sites accessible does not mean you make them accessible only to persons with disabilities but that you make them more accessible to *all* people who visit your site, including those with and without disabilities. For example, if you implement a technique that makes your site more accessible to a person with impaired vision and it then becomes less accessible to someone who has good vision, you have failed in making your site accessible.

The W3C (**W**orld **W**ide **W**eb **C**onsortium) has developed a collection of documents to help you understand accessibility and how to create accessible documents. You don't have to memorize these documents, but familiarizing yourself with what's contained within each will be of great help when you have an accessibility question and no one is around to ask.

The following four documents are the de facto standards for understanding, creating, and developing accessible Web pages.

Web Content Accessibility Guidelines 1.0
www.w3.org/TR/WCAG10/

This is one of the most important documents on Web accessibility. It identifies and explains the 14 guidelines and their checkpoints, and it prioritizes each. This is the place to start learning more about Web accessibility.

Techniques for Web Content Accessibility Guidelines 1.0
www.w3.org/TR/WCAG10-TECHS/

This document gives you techniques and examples for making your Web sites accessible. Once you understand the 14 guidelines of Web accessibility, this document helps you create accessible pages by giving you sample code and different scenarios you might encounter. You might want to print this document and keep a copy nearby.

CSS Techniques for Web Content Accessibility Guidelines 1.0
www.w3.org/TR/WCAG10-CSS-TECHS/

This document focuses on (and gives examples for) creating accessible Web pages using CSS (**C**ascading **S**tyle **S**heets). (You can also find examples using deprecated code to illustrate things developers should not do.)

HTML Techniques for Web Content Accessibility Guidelines 1.0
www.w3.org/TR/WCAG10-HTML-TECHS/

This document focuses on creating accessible Web pages using HTML (**H**yper**T**ext **M**arkup **L**anguage). You can probably imagine why this document is so important. Similar to the CSS techniques document, this one also provides readers with good and bad code examples that illustrate what developers should and should not do.

1 | Setting Accessibility Preferences

One of the most important steps in creating an accessible site is learning how to turn the **Accessibility** preferences on and off in Dreamweaver CS3. These options let you create accessible pages as you add content, instead of adding them when the page is finished. This proactive approach saves you time and ensures you don't forget to add accessibility features later. If you learn to work with these options turned on, creating accessible Web pages is no more difficult than creating nonaccessible Web pages. Dreamweaver CS3 turns all these options on by default, but you should still know where to find them.

1 In Dreamweaver CS3, choose **Edit > Preferences** (Windows) or **Dreamweaver > Preferences** (Mac) to open the **Preferences** dialog box.

Mac Accessibility Preferences

Windows Accessibility Preferences

2 Select **Accessibility** in the **Category** list to see what accessibility options are available in Dreamweaver CS3. By default, each of the **Show attributes when inserting** check boxes is selected. Windows users have two additional check boxes: **Offscreen rendering (need to disable when using screen readers)**, which is selected by default, and **Keep focus in the panel when opening**, which you can select if you want access to a panel after you open it; by default, Dreamweaver CS3 keeps the focus in the **Document** window.

If, for whatever reason, you don't want or need the accessibility options for a particular object to display, deselect the appropriate box. You don't have to turn on all the accessibility options; you can turn on only the options you want. At any time, you can return to this dialog box and deselect any of these options to turn them off.

3 Leave all the accessibility boxes selected, and click **OK** to close the **Preferences** dialog box.

2 | Inserting Accessible Images

Millions of people throughout the world have some type of visual impairment, such as color blindness and partial or total blindness. Because the Web is a visual-centric environment, making the images on your pages accessible should be a priority. In this exercise, you'll learn how to add alternate text (**alt** attribute) and a long description for images on a Web page. The **alt** attribute is important because screen readers read its information aloud.

---

1 If you haven't already done so, copy the **chap_18** folder from the **Dreamweaver HOT CD-ROM** to your desktop. Define your site as **Chapter 18** using the **chap_18** folder as the local root folder. Make sure the **Files** panel is open. If it's not, choose **Window > Files**.

---

2 In the **Files** panel, double-click **accessibility.html** to open it.

This is just a blank page you'll use to learn more about the accessibility attributes.

---

3 Choose **Insert > Image**, and navigate to the **products/kettles** folder. Select **teacloud-azul.jpg**, and click **OK** (Windows) or **Choose** (Mac).

Because the accessibility attributes for images are turned on, the Image Tag Accessibility Attributes dialog box appears automatically. If the accessibility attribute for images is disabled (in the Preferences window), this dialog box will not appear automatically, which means you won't be prompted to add **alt** text. Leave this option turned on so you never forget to add **alt** text to the graphics on your pages.

---

4 In the **Alternate text** field, type **Teacloud Azul Teapot** to add the **alt** attribute to the image tag.

When you're creating the **alt** attribute, keep it short but descriptive. The **alt** attribute helps visually impaired people because that text is read aloud by screen reader programs. Additionally, in some browsers, the text appears in a small help tag (tool tip) when the cursor moves over the image.

---

5 Click the **Browse** folder icon next to the **Long description** field, and select the **teacloud-azul.html** file in the **products** folder. Click **OK**.

NOTE:

The longdesc Attribute

Adding the **alt** attribute to all the images on your pages is a big part of making accessible Web pages. However, sometimes you may want to offer a more verbose explanation of an image. In these cases, you should use the **longdesc** attribute as well, which lets you link to a text file that contains a longer description of the image. The link is no different from any other link, except it won't appear to people who aren't using a screen reader. If an image has a **longdesc** attribute applied and a screen reader program encounters the image on the page, it is read as a link so a person with a visual impairment knows that particular image contains a longer description. Open **products/teacloud-azul.html** to see an example of a long description file.

---

6 Switch to **Code** view.

Notice Dreamweaver CS3 added **alt** and **longdesc** attributes to the **<img>** tag; Dreamweaver added this code when you entered information in the Image Tag Accessibility Attributes dialog box.

Adding the **alt** and **longdesc** attributes to all the images on your page is one of the easiest and most significant ways you can help make your Web pages accessible to everyone.

7 Switch back to **Design** view. Save the page, and press **F12** (Windows) or **Opt+F12** (Mac) to view the page in your browser.

If you're using Internet Explorer, you can move your cursor over the image to see the `alt` text appear. (Safari and Firefox don't display `alt` text.) Notice that clicking the image does nothing either. Only screen-reading software is able to detect the long description associated with this image.

---

8 Return to Dreamweaver. Select the image on the page, and press **Delete** on your keyboard to revert to a blank page for the next exercise.

3 | Inserting Accessible Tables

Tables can be particularly frustrating if you can't see how they're laid out, because screen-reading software can have difficulty figuring out which columns or rows to read in which order. When you're using tables for data in your sites, do your best to make them usable for those with disabilities. This exercise shows you how to add accessibility attributes to your tables and show you what they're used for.

1 You should still have the **accessibility** file from Exercise 2 open. If it's not, double-click **accessibility.html** in the **Files** panel to open it.

2 Choose **Insert > Table** to open the **Table** dialog box. Match all the settings to the ones shown in the illustration here (paying particular attention to the **Accessibility** section), and click **OK** to insert the table.

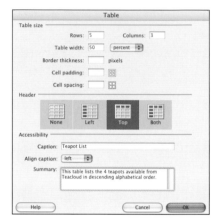

At this point, the table should look like the illustration shown here. Dreamweaver has added the caption for the table above the table, but the summary isn't visible.

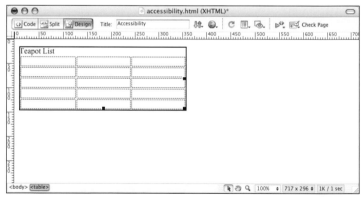

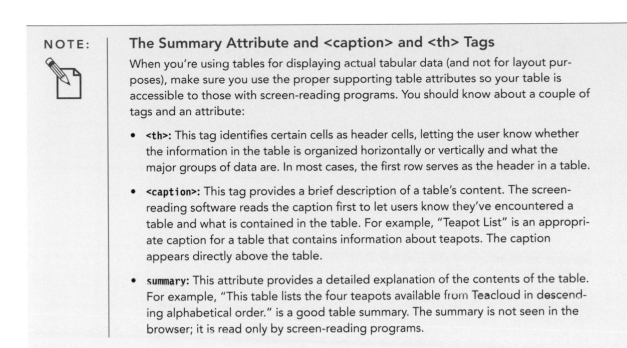
The Summary Attribute and <caption> and <th> Tags

When you're using tables for displaying actual tabular data (and not for layout purposes), make sure you use the proper supporting table attributes so your table is accessible to those with screen-reading programs. You should know about a couple of tags and an attribute:

- **<th>:** This tag identifies certain cells as header cells, letting the user know whether the information in the table is organized horizontally or vertically and what the major groups of data are. In most cases, the first row serves as the header in a table.

- **<caption>:** This tag provides a brief description of a table's content. The screen-reading software reads the caption first to let users know they've encountered a table and what is contained in the table. For example, "Teapot List" is an appropriate caption for a table that contains information about teapots. The caption appears directly above the table.

- **summary:** This attribute provides a detailed explanation of the contents of the table. For example, "This table lists the four teapots available from Teacloud in descending alphabetical order." is a good table summary. The summary is not seen in the browser; it is read only by screen-reading programs.

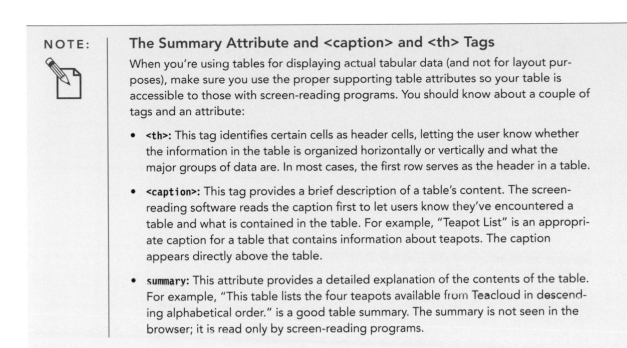

3 Switch to **Code** view to view the XHTML (e**X**tensible **H**yper**T**ext **M**arkup **L**anguage) code for this page. Here, you can see the various tags that were added to make this table accessible.

---

4 Switch back to **Design** view, and choose **Edit > Undo** to return to a blank page for the next exercise.

4 | Inserting Accessible Form Objects

Form objects tend to be one of the most overlooked elements on an accessible Web page. For some reason, many people don't know that forms can cause accessibility problems or that there are good ways to make form objects accessible. Fortunately, Dreamweaver CS3 has a feature to help you make your form objects accessible, which is exactly what you'll learn to do in this exercise.

1 You should still have the **accessibility.html** file from Exercise 3 open. If it's not, double-click **accessibility.html** in the **Files** panel to open it.

2 Choose the **Forms** group of the **Insert** bar to display a collection of buttons that let you add various form objects to your page.

3 Click the **Text Field** button to insert a text field on the page and to open the **Input Tag Accessibility Attributes** dialog box.

4 Type **First Name:** in the **Label** field. This text appears on the Web page as normal text and lets the user know what information should be entered in this text field.

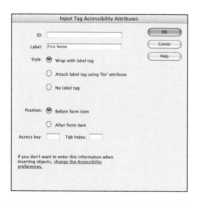

5 Select **Wrap with label tag** for **Style**.

6 Make sure the **Before form item** radio button is selected for **Position**. This places the label text before the form object. Click **OK**.

Understanding the Input Tag Accessibility Attributes

The **Input Tag Accessibility Attributes** dialog box has a number of options. Here's an overview of each:

Input Tag Accessibility Attributes	
Option	Description
Label	This text appears next to the form object. Depending on which **Position** option you choose, the text appears before or after the form object.
Style: Wrap with label tag	This wraps both the label text and form object with a `<label>` tag.
Style: Attach label tag using 'for' attribute	This option uses the **for** attribute to associate the `<label>` tag with the form element to which it's related.
Style: No label tag	This option does not add a `<label>` tag around the form object.
Position: Before form item	This radio button places the label text before the form object.
Position: After form item	This radio button places the label text after the form object.
Access key	You can use the key you enter here plus the **Ctrl** key to select this object in the browser window.
Tab Index	This option sets the tab order of the form objects. This helps you specify someone using the **Tab** key can move from one form object to the next.

7 Click **Yes** when you are prompted with **Add form tag?**.

The form object won't work properly unless it's enclosed in the `<form>` tag. For more information about forms, check out Chapter 13, *"Working with Forms."*

8 Switch to **Split** view.

Dreamweaver adds the label to the left of the input field and wraps the entire block in a **<label>** tag. Now, instead of just normal text in front of an element, the **<label>** tag allows that text to identify with a specific form element within screen readers. It won't appear any different to other users, but it will be more accessible to those with a disability.

---

9 Save the page, and press **F12** (Windows) or **Opt+F12** (Mac) to preview the page in your browser. Click the **First Name** text, and your cursor will be positioned in the text field. This lets you know you should enter your first name into that particular text field.

Users can click labels to select and deselect check boxes, select radio buttons, and set lists and menus to their default selections. Labels are far more useful than simply making it easier for screen readers.

Note: This label functionality doesn't work in Apple Safari.

If you want, try adding other form objects to your page. There's no harm in experimenting with these settings, and practice will definitely make you feel more comfortable. I especially encourage you to work with the check boxes and radio buttons to see how the labels affect them.

---

10 Return to Dreamweaver, and save and close **accessibility.html**.

Accessibility Testing

This chapter showed you how to create accessible Web pages as you created the pages. What can you do if you already have a completed Web site and you want to make sure it's accessible? Dreamweaver CS3 allows you to analyze your Web pages and report any accessibility errors. Simply choose **File > Check Page > Accessibility**, and Dreamweaver CS3 analyzes the page you have open and provides you with a list of errors.

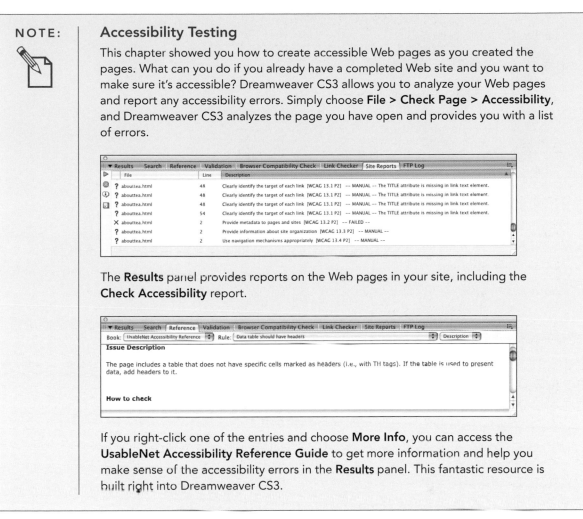

The **Results** panel provides reports on the Web pages in your site, including the **Check Accessibility** report.

If you right-click one of the entries and choose **More Info**, you can access the **UsableNet Accessibility Reference Guide** to get more information and help you make sense of the accessibility errors in the **Results** panel. This fantastic resource is built right into Dreamweaver CS3.

This chapter showed you how to make your Web pages more accessible by using the Dreamweaver accessibility attributes as you work with images, tables, and form objects. In the next chapter, you'll learn how to insert media objects, such as Adobe Flash files and MP3 files.

19

Inserting Media Objects

You've learned a lot working through this book, but there's still another important Adobe Dreamweaver CS3 feature to learn about—how to work with media objects. **Media objects** are items you add to your pages that typically require a plug-in to play back properly in a browser, such as Adobe Flash movies or objects, Apple QuickTime or Adobe Shockwave movies, Java applets, ActiveX controls, or other audio or video objects. **Plug-ins** are special program extensions installed in your visitors' browsers that let them view multimedia content.

In this chapter, you'll learn how to add media objects to your sites and how to use their associated plug-ins. You'll also learn how to set parameters in the **Property inspector** to control how and when your media objects play.

As exciting as this may seem, it's also the area of Web development where compatibility issues between browsers really get intense. Not everyone has the same plug-ins loaded to support the playback of media objects, and some plug-ins work differently on Macs than they do in Windows. Dreamweaver CS3 does a great job of letting you put this content on your site. It's the rest of the Web's limitations that you'll likely have to struggle with.

What Is a Plug-In?

In the early days of the Web, any file that wasn't an HTML (**H**yper**T**ext **M**arkup **L**anguage) file had to be downloaded and required a separate "player" for the content to be seen. This process was a hassle for most Web users because it meant breaking the flow of the browsing experience to view material in an external application. In response to this problem, Netscape introduced the idea of plug-ins, which extended the capability of HTML pages to display non-HTML-based content. Today, browsers ship with a variety of preinstalled plug-ins, including QuickTime Player, Flash Player, and RealPlayer. This chapter focuses on techniques to insert plug-in–based content into your pages so it can be viewed directly in the browser, without requiring an outside player application.

Downloading Plug-Ins

As you work through these exercises, you might find yourself being directed to download plug-ins from the Internet or to reassign them in your browser preferences. If this seems like a hassle, remember that you ask your audience to do the same thing when you present plug-in-based content to them. Here's where you can download plug-ins:

URLs for Downloading Plug-Ins	
Plug-In	URL
QuickTime	www.apple.com/quicktime/download/
Flash	www.adobe.com/products/flashplayer/
Shockwave	www.adobe.com/products/shockwaveplayer/
RealPlayer	www.real.com/player/

1 | Linking to Sounds

You can add sound to your page in multiple ways. In this exercise, you'll learn to add sound to your page simply by creating a link to a sound file. As you will see, you must consider some nuances when you work with sound files. For example, no standard format for sounds exists on the Web. Sounds are handled differently between browsers and operating systems (as if designing Web pages wasn't difficult enough). Fortunately, by the time you finish the hands-on exercises in this chapter, you'll have a better understanding of how to add sound to your site.

1 If you haven't already done so, copy the **chap_19** folder from the **Dreamweaver HOT CD-ROM** to your desktop. Define your site as **Chapter 19** using the **chap_19** folder as the local root folder. Make sure the **Files** panel is open. If it's not, choose **Window > Files**.

2 In the **Files** panel, double-click **audio.html** to open it.

You will see two links at the top of the page. These two links point directly to two different sound files. The first link points to a WAV file, and the second link points to an MP3 file.

3 Position your cursor in the **.wav** link at the top of the page. In the **Property inspector**, notice this links to the **timefortea.wav** file in the **assets/sound** folder.

That's all there is to it. When a user clicks this link in a browser, the file will open in the user's default application for Windows Audio files.

4 Place your cursor in the **.mp3** link.

This link points to the timefortea.mp3 file in the assets/sound folder.

Nothing is too complicated about this so far. The process of linking to a sound file is no different from linking to a Web page.

---

5 Press **F12** (Windows) or **Opt+F12** (Mac) to preview this page in a browser. Click each of the links. Clicking either link will play a 30-second sample of music.

Depending on how your browser preferences are set up and what operating system you use, clicking the links might launch different audio players—on Windows, the .wav file might launch Windows Media Player, while the .mp3 file might launch the QuickTime plug-in. On a Mac, the QuickTime plug-in might handle both file types. Which plug-in handles which type of audio file depends on how your visitors has their browsers configured and is out of your hands.

---

6 Return to Dreamweaver CS3, and keep **audio.html** open for the next exercise.

In this exercise, you saw that it's pretty easy to link to any audio file. But there may be times when you want an audio file to be part of a page layout rather than just opening in its own window. In the next exercise, you'll learn how to embed the sound directly in the page.

TIP: | **Different Sound Players**

Just about every browser will let you choose which application or plug-in plays the audio files you find on Web pages. In fact, you can set a different one for each type of audio format. For example, you might choose to have the QuickTime plug-in play AIF and WAV files and have the Flash plug-in play SWF files. You can control this by modifying your browser preferences. Check these settings if you experience any problems while trying to play sound files. For instructions on how to change these settings, see your browser's **Help** feature.

Understanding Different Sound Formats

One of the problems with adding sound to your Web page is deciding which format to use. Most Web publishers use MP3, RealPlayer (RAM), or WAV files—the most commonly supported audio formats. It is a good idea, however, to be familiar with the other formats you might run into on the Web. The following chart gives you an idea of what's available:

Sound Formats	
Extension	**Description**
.au	This format was one of the first introduced on the Internet. It was designed for NeXT and Sun Unix systems.
.aiff/.aif	The AIF (**A**udio **I**nterchange **F**ormat) format was developed by Apple and is used on SGI machines. It is the main audio format on Mac computers.
.midi/.mid	The MIDI (**M**usical **I**nstrument **D**igital **I**nterface) format was designed to translate how music is produced. MIDI files store just the sequencing information (notes, timing, and voicing) required to play back a musical composition, rather than recording the composition itself, so these files are usually small, but playback quality is unpredictable.
.MP3	The MP3 (**MP**EG-1 Audio Layer-**3**) format is the hottest audio file format on the Web. It offers superior compression and great quality. This file format is widely used in Adobe Flash content.
.ra/.ram	The RA (**R**eal **A**udio) format was designed to offer streaming audio on the Internet.
.rmf	The RMF (**R**ich **M**usic **F**ormat) was designed by Headspace and is used in the Beatnik plug-in. This format offers good compression and quality.
.swa	The SWA (**S**hock **w**ave **A**udio) format was developed by Macromedia and is used in Flash.
.wav	This format was developed by IBM and Microsoft. This is the main audio format for the Windows operating system, but WAV files play on Macs and other systems.

2 | Embedding Multimedia Files

In addition to linking to a sound file, there is another approach to adding multimedia files to your Web pages. You can embed multimedia files so they play directly in your Web page instead of linking to the physical file (as shown in the previous exercise). This approach is good if you just want to play—not download—files in the browser. Embedding multimedia files gives you more control over them because they actually appear in your HTML files, along with the other content. By modifying specific parameters, you can control when the player starts, how it appears on the page, and whether it loops (continuously plays), as well as several other settings. In this exercise, you'll be inserting one of the sounds from the previous exercise.

1 You should still have the **audio.html** file from Exercise 1 open. If not, complete Exercise 1, and then return to this exercise.

In this exercise, you'll embed the WAV file from the previous exercise directly into the page.

2 Position your cursor at the end of the first line of text, and press **Enter** (Windows) or **Return** (Mac) to create a new paragraph.

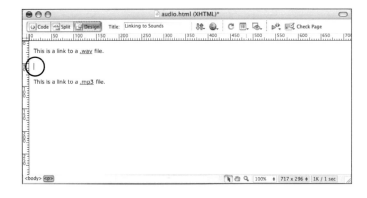

3 Choose **Insert > Media > Plugin** to open the **Select File** dialog box. Browse to the **assets/sound** folder, and select the **timefortea.wav** file. Click **OK** (Windows) or **Choose** (Mac).

Dreamweaver CS3 displays a plug-in icon on the page to indicate where the plug-in will appear.

4 Select the plug-in icon, and click the **Parameters** button in the **Property inspector** to open the **Parameters** dialog box.

The Parameters dialog box is where you will insert any parameters and values you need. See the note at the end of this exercise to learn a bit more about parameters.

5 In the **Parameter** column, type **autoplay**, and then press **Tab**. Type **false** in the **Value** column, and click **OK**.

This prevents the sound file from playing automatically; to play the sound file, the user will have to click the Play button.

6 In the **Property inspector**, type **150** in the **W** field to change the width of the plug-in.

You need to widen the plug-in so your visitors will be able to see all the playback controls (Play, Pause, Stop, and so on).

7 Save the file, and press **F12** (Windows) or **Opt+F12** (Mac) to preview your page in a browser. Click the **Play** button to hear the sound. Here, you can see that QuickTime is being used to play WAV files in Firefox for Mac OS X.

8 Return to Dreamweaver CS3, and close **audio.html**.

NOTE:

What Is a Parameter?

Most plug-in content is controlled by various parameters (sometimes referred to as **attributes**), which are different for each kind of plug-in. A **parameter** is an option passed to the plug-in that tells it how to behave. In Exercise 2, you learned how to set the `autoplay` parameter to `false`. That parameter is part of the QuickTime specification.

This chapter covers sound, Flash, Flash Video, and QuickTime, but many other types of plug-ins are available on the Web. To learn what all the parameters are for a plug-in, it's best to visit the site from which you downloaded the plug-in.

VIDEO:

parameters.mov

To learn more about working with parameters, check out **parameters.mov** in the **videos** folder on the **Dreamweaver HOT CD-ROM**.

In this exercise, you inserted a sound file directly into an XHTML document. You can insert just about any type of media file that has a valid player associated with it, including QuickTime movies, Windows Media files, RealPlayer movies, and so on. You'll find a MOV file (photos.mov) in the assets/video folder if you want to practice inserting additional multimedia files.

3 | Inserting Flash Content

Because both Dreamweaver CS3 and Flash CS3 are Adobe products, it is not surprising that Dreamweaver CS3 supports Flash content. Instead of the generic plug-in object that you used in the previous exercise, Dreamweaver CS3 has several specific Flash objects you can add to your pages. In previous chapters, you already saw how to create Flash Buttons and Flash Text directly from Dreamweaver. In this exercise, you'll see how to add content that was created in Flash.

---

1 In the **Files** panel, double-click **index.html** to open it.

This is the same index.html file you've been using throughout the book, but we've removed the image that has been there all along. In this exercise, you'll replace it with a Flash movie.

---

2 Position your cursor above the opening paragraph of text, and choose **Insert > Media > Flash**.

3 In the **Select File** dialog box, browse to the **assets/flash** folder, and select **teacloud_home.swf**. Click **OK** (Windows) or **Choose** (Mac) to insert the Flash file. If the **Object Tag Accessibility Attributes** dialog box appears, type **Welcome to Teacloud** in the **Title** field, and click **OK**.

---

4 Select the Flash movie, and look at the **Property inspector**.

Dreamweaver CS3 inserts the Flash movie, automatically determines the height and width of the movie, and sets a number of other defaults, such as whether to loop the movie and whether it should play as soon as it loads.

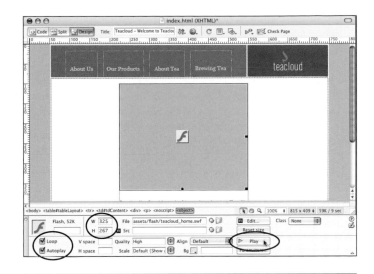

5 Save the page, and press **F12** (Windows) or **Opt+F12** (Mac) to view the content in your browser. If you see a message about copying dependent files, click **OK**.

As you can see, Flash content can be much more dynamic and attention grabbing than static images.

6 Return to Dreamweaver CS3. Close **index.html**.

4 | Inserting Flash Video Content

The Flash Video format has become an incredibly popular way to provide high-quality video on your Web site because of the ubiquitousness of the Flash plug-in. So if you're considering adding video content to your Web site, consider using Flash Video because nearly everyone in the entire world has the Flash Player. The Adobe Flash CS3 Video Encoder comes included in the Design Premium, Web Premium, and Web Standard editions of the CS3 suite. We won't be covering how to create Flash Video in this book, but in this exercise you'll learn how to insert videos into a Web page. Dreamweaver CS3 makes it easy to insert Flash Video content, and you can even choose from a nice selection of prebuilt playback controls.

1 In the **Files** panel, double-click **brewingtea.html** to open it.

2 Position your cursor before **1. The Infuser**, and choose **Insert > Media > Flash Video** to open the **Insert Flash Video** dialog box.

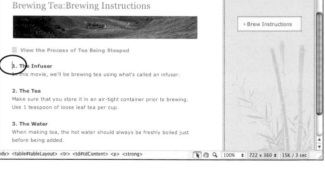

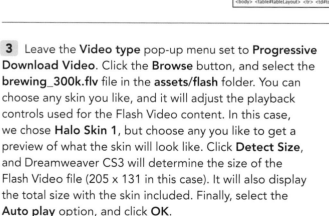

3 Leave the **Video type** pop-up menu set to **Progressive Download Video**. Click the **Browse** button, and select the **brewing_300k.flv** file in the **assets/flash** folder. You can choose any skin you like, and it will adjust the playback controls used for the Flash Video content. In this case, we chose **Halo Skin 1**, but choose any you like to get a preview of what the skin will look like. Click **Detect Size**, and Dreamweaver CS3 will determine the size of the Flash Video file (205 x 131 in this case). It will also display the total size with the skin included. Finally, select the **Auto play** option, and click **OK**.

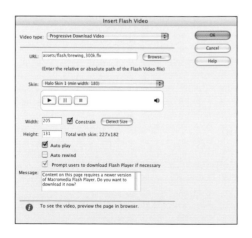

There's a lot going on in this dialog box. You can click the Help button to learn more about the Insert Flash Video options.

4 Position your cursor directly after the Flash Video placeholder, and press **Enter** (Windows) or **Return** (Mac) to put the Flash Video in its own paragraph.

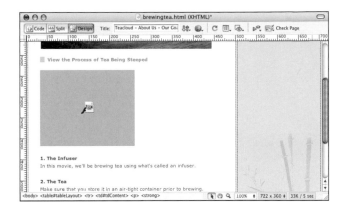

5 In the **Files** panel, notice Dreamweaver CS3 has added two files to your site: **FLVPlayer_Progressive.swf** and **Halo_Skin_1.swf**. If you don't see the files, click the **Refresh** icon in the **Files** panel. Both of these files are necessary for the Flash Video to play correctly, and they should always be located at the root of your site.

6 Save the page, and press **F12** (Windows) or **Opt+F12** (Mac) to preview the page in your browser.

The Flash Video file should start playing immediately, showing you how to brew a perfect cup of tea. Click the playback controls to play, pause, and stop the movie playback.

7 Return to Dreamweaver CS3. Close **brewingtea.html**.

In this chapter, you learned how to insert multimedia files, Flash movies, and Flash Video. Learning how to work with media objects can greatly improve the visual interest of your site.

20

Using Spry Tools

So far, all the Web pages you've built in this book have been traditional, static Web pages. As varied as you can make your pages, they all essentially behave the same way when loaded into a browser: a visitor types your site's Web address or clicks a link in their browser, the browser downloads and renders the entire Web page, the visitor clicks a link on this page, the browser downloads and displays that page, and so on. This is the way Web pages have worked since their inception.

But in recent years, there has been a growing movement in the Web development community to transition to more dynamic and data-driven Web pages. Some have referred this movement as **Web 2.0**. Not everyone has agreed on what exactly Web 2.0 entails, but a major part of the movement deals with creating pages that can automatically update certain areas of themselves rather than loading an entirely different page. In the past, if you wanted to display additional information about an item on a Web page, you had to create and link to an entirely new page containing the relevant information. But in the Web 2.0 era, you can create pages containing all the necessary data but display only certain aspects of that data based on how your visitors interact with the page.

In this chapter, you'll learn all about Ajax as well as the tools that Adobe Dreamweaver CS3 uses to implement this kind of functionality: Spry.

What Is Ajax?

The major driving technology behind this kind of interactivity is known as Ajax (which was originally an acronym for **A**synchronous **JA**vaScript and **X**ML). Normally, using Ajax on your Web pages requires an advanced understanding of JavaScript, but fortunately, Dreamweaver CS3 contains a framework known as Spry, which allows you to visually create Ajax implementations without having to know or type a lot of code. In this chapter, you'll explore Dreamweaver CS3's new Spry tools.

Although Dreamweaver's Spry tools make it relatively easy to implement Ajax in your Web site, this is still a fairly advanced topic, requiring a working knowledge of XML (e**X**tensible **M**arkup **L**anguage), which won't be covered in this chapter. But don't worry, I've included a complete example XML file with the exercise files so you can concentrate on learning how to use the Spry tools.

What Is Spry?

In a nutshell, **Spry** is the framework Dreamweaver CS3 uses to allow you to integrate complex Ajax implementations into your Web pages and provide a much richer Web experience for your visitors. Instead of creating a site of completely

static pages, you can use the Spry framework to generate interactive, dynamic, and compelling pages. You can find Dreamweaver's Spry tools in the **Spry** group of the **Insert** bar; they come in three categories:

Spry Tools	
Name	Description
Spry data widgets	These are used to incorporate XML data into a Web page. Dreamweaver can display this data interactively.
Spry form widgets	Similar to Dreamweaver's regular form tools, Spry Form widgets allow you to perform JavaScript validation functions and supply your visitors with user-friendly error messages when they complete your form incorrectly. You'll learn how to use Spry Form widgets later in this chapter.
Spry layout widgets	These allow you to insert complex and sophisticated layout controls such as tabbed and accordion panels. You'll learn how to add accordion panels later in this chapter.

1 | Adding an XML Data Source

Before you can use Spry to display data on a Web page, you need to first establish an XML data source. As mentioned in Chapter 1, *"Getting Started,"* XML is a strict set of guidelines for tagging data in a text file in such a way that it can be read and processed by any system or device capable of reading text files. Using Dreamweaver CS3's Spry data tools, you can establish a link to an XML file containing all the information you want to display on your page and then customize when and how that data is displayed. In this exercise, you'll examine an XML file and then establish it as the data source for a Web page.

1 If you haven't already done so, copy the **chap_20** folder from the **Dreamweaver HOT CD-ROM** to your desktop. Define your site as **Chapter 20** using the **chap_20** folder as the local root folder. Make sure the **Files** panel is open. If it's not, choose **Window > Files**.

First you'll take a look at the XML file I've created for this exercise.

2 In the **Files** panel, double-click **teapots.xml** to open it.

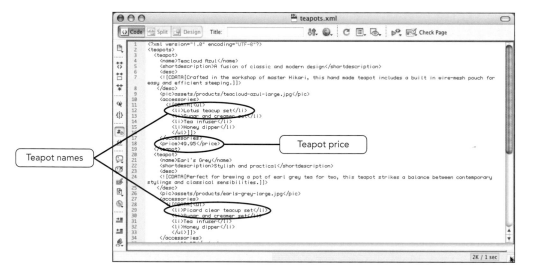

Even if you've never seen an XML document before, you can probably figure out how they work just by taking a closer look at this one. Similar to XHTML (e**X**tensible **H**yper**T**ext **M**arkup **L**anguage), all the data in this file is surrounded by tags. But unlike in XHTML, in XML you can create all the tag names yourself. Notice the tags that specify items such as a teapot's name, its description, its price, and so on. XML is simply a way of marking up a text document so you can call up certain parts of the data later.

Here is what each of the teapot records looks like without the data:

```
<teapot>
  <name> </name>
  <shortdescription> </shortdescription>
  <desc> </desc>
  <pic> </pic>
  <accessories> </accessories>
  <price> </price>
</teapot>
```

Each teapot's information has been added to three repetitions of these tags.

NOTE:

Learning XML

If you're interested in learning how to create your own XML documents, check out **XML Essential Training with Joe Marini** at **www.lynda.com**.

You can find another excellent learning resource at **http://w3schools.com/xml**.

3 After you're done examining **teapots.xml**, close the file, and open **teapots.html** in the **Files** panel.

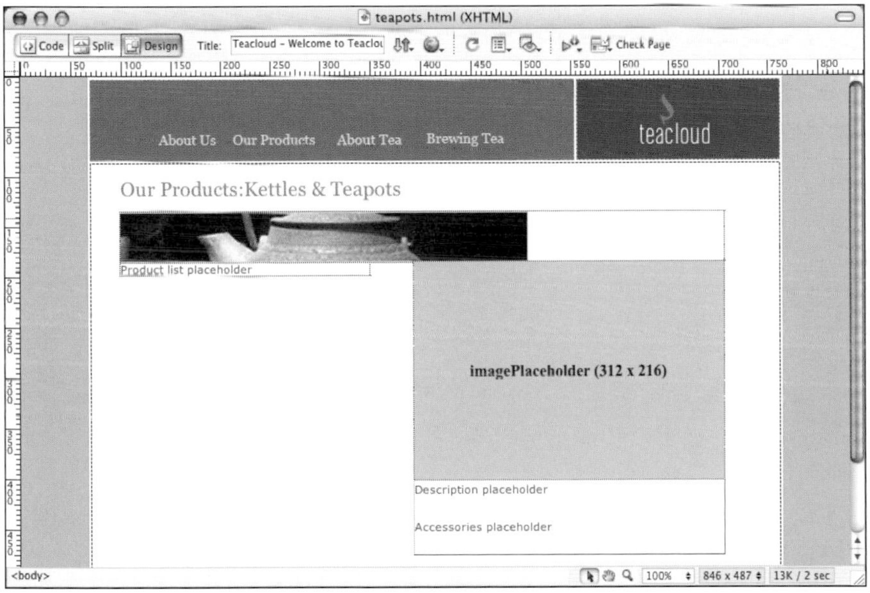

This is a partially built page containing several placeholders for elements you'll be adding in this chapter. Next you'll establish the teapots.xml file as the data source for this page.

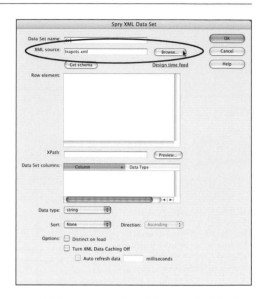

4 In the **Insert bar**, switch to the **Spry** group. Click the **Spry XML Data Set** icon on the left of the **Insert** bar. The **Spry XML Data Set** dialog box opens.

5 In the **Spry XML Data Set** dialog box, leave the default **Data Set name** as **ds1** (for **D**ata **S**et **1**), and click **Browse** to select an XML source. Select **teapots.xml** in the **chap_20** folder on your desktop. Leave the **Spry XML Data Set** dialog box open for the next step.

Next you'll specify which set up data you'll want to load and use on this page. Three teapot models are listed in the XML file you want to display. The **<teapot>** entry appears three times and is known as a **repeating entry**.

6 Click the **Get schema** button to display all the XML entries in the **Row element** area. In the **Row element** area, select the **teapot** repeating entry.

Note: Repeating entries are designated with the **<>+** symbol.

452 | **Adobe Dreamweaver CS3** : H•O•T

7 Click **Preview** to see a preview of the data contained within the first 20 rows of the XML document. Since only three teapots are listed in the entire file, you can see all of them.

This preview window is a good tool for checking your data to make sure you know what kind of information each tag is designating.

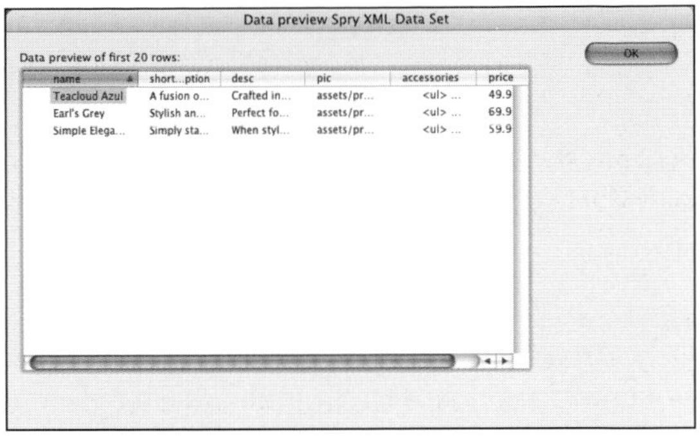

8 Click OK to close the preview window and return to the **Spry XML Data Set** dialog box. In the **Data Set columns** area, select **pic**, and then select **image link** in the **Data type** pop-up menu. Then select **price** in the **Data Set columns** area, and set **Data type** to **number**.

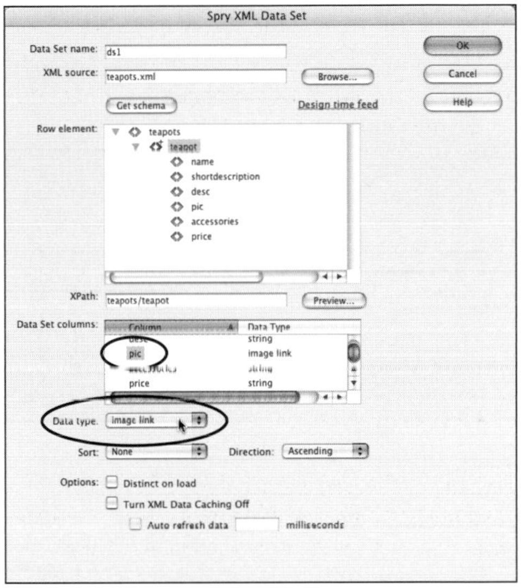

NOTE:

The Importance of Data Types

In Step 8 of this exercise, you change the data types for the **pic** and **price** entries. Using the proper data type is necessary if you want to be able to sort your data properly. For example, by designating the price entry as a number, you ensure that when you or a visitor choose to sort the data by price (which you'll do in an upcoming exercise), the Ajax engine will sort the data numerically.

These are the available data types:

- **string:** Any data that doesn't fall in the other three categories

- **number:** Any numeric data

- **date:** Any complete date such as 11/17/2007 or November 17, 2007

- **image link:** Any file name or path to an image

9 In the **Sort** menu, choose **name**. This sets up your data to initially be sorted by the teapot name. Keep all the other settings in this dialog box at their defaults, and click **OK** to close the **Spry XML Data Set** dialog box.

---

10 Save the page. The **Copy Dependent Files** dialog box opens, indicating that Dreamweaver needs to save some JavaScript files in order for your Spry data to properly function. Click **OK**. If you look in the **Files** panel, you'll see that Dreamweaver has created a folder called **SpryAssets**, containing the JavaScript you just saved.

Even though the Web page doesn't appear to have changed at all, Dreamweaver has inserted some key lines of code, establishing teapots.xml as the XML data source for this page.

Copy Dependent Files

This page uses an object or behavior that requires supporting files. The following files have been copied to your local site. You must upload them to your server in order for the object or behavior to function correctly.

SpryAssets/SpryData.js
SpryAssets/xpath.js

OK

---

teapots.html (XHTML)

Code   Split   Design   Title: Teacloud – Welcome to Teaclou   Check Page

```
23    if(!x && d.getElementById) x=d.getElementById(n); return x;
24  }
25
26  function MM_swapImage() { //v3.0
27    var i,j=0,x,a=MM_swapImage.arguments; document.MM_sr=new Array; for(i=0;i<(a.length-2);i+=3)
28     if ((x=MM_findObj(a[i]))!=null){document.MM_sr[j++]=x; if(!x.oSrc) x.oSrc=x.src; x.src=a[i+2];}
29  //-->
30  </script>
31  </script>
32  <script src="SpryAssets/xpath.js" type="text/javascript"></script>
33  <script src="SpryAssets/SpryData.js" type="text/javascript"></script>
34  <script type="text/javascript">
35  <!--
36  var ds1 = new Spry.Data.XMLDataSet("teapots.xml", "teapots/teapot",{sortOnLoad:"name",sortOrderOnLoad:
      "ascending"});
37  ds1.setColumnType("pic", "image");
38  ds1.setColumnType("price", "number");
39  //-->
40  </script>
41  </head>
42
43  <body onload=
      "MM_preloadImages('assets/images/navigation/abouttea-over.gif','assets/images/navigation/ourproducts-over.gif
      ','assets/images/navigation/brewingtea-over.gif','assets/images/navigation/aboutus-over.gif')">
44  <table width="700" align="center" id="tableLayout">
45    <tr>
46      <td id="tdNavigation"><a href="aboutus.html"><img src="assets/images/navigation/aboutus-out.gif" alt=
      "About Us" name="navAboutUs" width="78" height="66" border="0" id="navAboutUs" onmouseover=
      "MM_swapImage('navAboutUs','','assets/images/navigation/aboutus-over.gif',1)" onmouseout=
```

<head>   179K / 26 sec

---

11 Switch to **Code** view. At about line 32, you can see the links to the JavaScript code Dreamweaver saved for you. And at about line 36, you can see the JavaScript function that establishes **teapots.xml** as the XML data source. Switch back to **Design** view, and keep **teapots.html** open for the next exercise.

Now that you've connected teapots.xml to this page, in the next exercise you'll put the XML file to use by displaying some of its data in a Spry table object.

Adobe Dreamweaver CS3 : H·O·T

2 | Adding a Spry Table

In the previous exercise, you established **teapots.xml** as the XML data source for **teapots.html**. In this exercise, you'll use a Spry table to display some of the data from the XML file, and you'll see how easy it is to use just the data you want.

---

1 You should still have the **teapots.html** file from Exercise 1 open. If not, complete Exercise 1, and then return to this exercise.

---

2 Select the text **Product list placeholder**, and delete it.

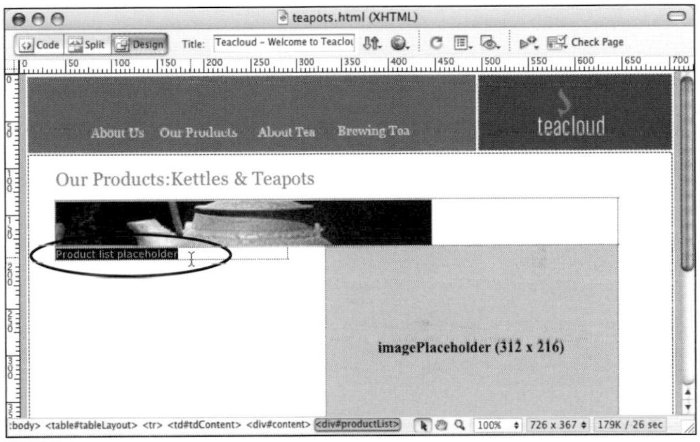

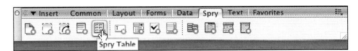

---

3 In the **Spry** group of the **Insert bar**, click the **Spry Table** object. The **Insert Spry Table** dialog box opens.

In Spry Data Set menu, ds1 is already selected because it's the only data set associated with this page. Now you need to specify which data you want to display in this table. For this exercise, you'll display each teapot's name and price.

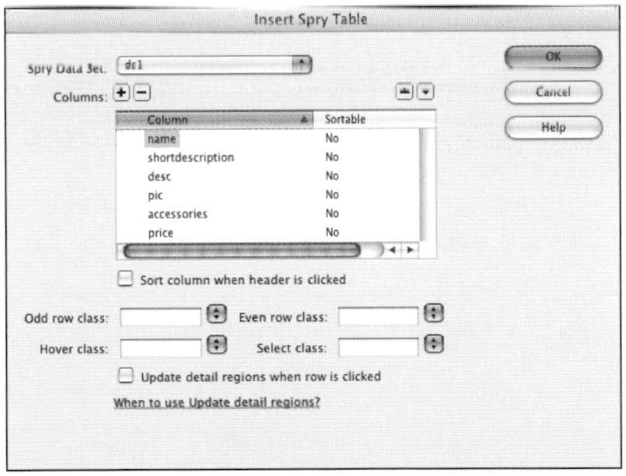

4 In the **Columns** area, select **shortdescription**, and click the – button to remove it from the list. Click the – button three more times to delete **desc**, **pic**, and **accessories**, leaving only **name** and **price**.

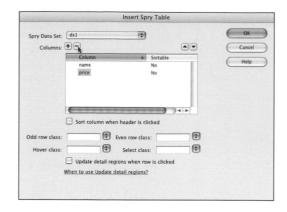

5 Select **name**, and select the **Sort column when header is clicked** check box. Do the same with **price**.

This allows your visitors to sort your table by name or by price simply by clicking the table headers—something you can't do with regular tables. Next, you'll apply some CSS class styles to format the table. These styles have been created for you and are saved in the assets folder. They automatically appear in the menus next to Odd row class, Hover class, Even row class, and Select class.

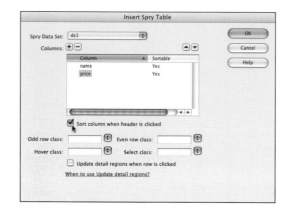

6 In the **Odd row class** menu, select **oddRow**. This style will be applied to odd-numbered rows in the table.

7 In the **Hover class** menu, select **hoverRow**. This style determines the appearance of each row when your visitor's cursor moves over them.

8 Leave the **Even row class** menu untouched, and select **selectRow** in the **Select class** menu. This style specifies the appearance for rows that have been clicked.

9 Check **Update detail regions when row is clicked**. This sets the stage for the next exercise, where you'll have the details of each teapot appear elsewhere on the page when the teapots are selected.

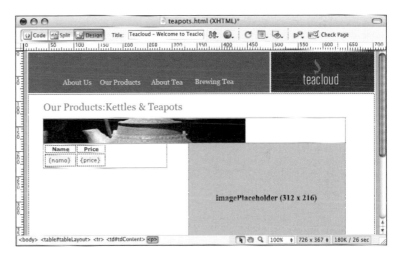

10 Click **OK**. When Dreamweaver asks whether you want to add a Spry region, click **Yes**.

Your new Spry table has been inserted on the page. For the most part, this is a regular table, meaning you can format and customize it just like a regular table.

11 Click anywhere in the table, and then select the **<table>** tag in the **Tag Selector** to select the entire table. In the **Property inspector**, set **CellSpace** to **0** to remove any spacing from between the cells.

12 Drag from the top-left cell to the bottom-left cell to select the entire column. In the **Property Inspector**, choose **Left** in the **Horz** pop-up menu.

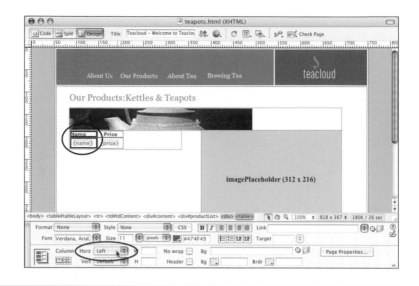

13 Save the page, and press **F12** (Windows) or **Opt+F12** (Mac) to preview the page in your browser.

Notice that the table displays the name and price of each teapot and that rows 1 and 3 (the odd rows you specified) have both been styled with color. You can move your cursor over the rows to see the hover style applied and click the rows to see the select style applied.

14 Click the **Name** and **Price** headers, and notice how the table sorts itself in ascending and descending alphabetical or numeric order.

15 Return to Dreamweaver, and leave **teapots.html** open for the next exercise.

Now that you've successfully added the listing of teapots and their prices, you can add the functionality to display the details of each item, which you'll do in the next exercise.

3 | Adding Spry Detail Regions

In this exercise, you'll define a Spry detail region that's tied into the data set and Spry table you established in the previous two exercises. The goal of this exercise is to have details and an image of each teapot appear when that particular teapot is selected in the Spry table.

1 You should still have the **teapots.html** file from Exercise 2 open. If not, complete Exercise 2, and then return to this exercise.

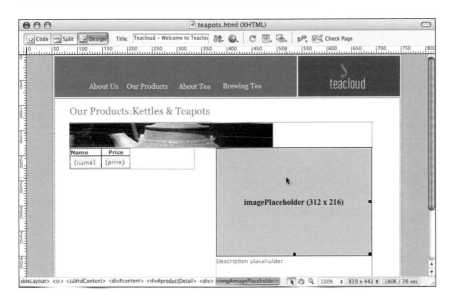

2 Double-click **imagePlaceholder**. In the **Select Image Source** dialog box, instead of selecting a single image, click the **Data Sources** button. This allows you to associate the image placeholder with a data source so the image that appears in its place will dynamically change based on what your visitors click.

3 In the **Field** list, select **pic** to indicate you want to use the **pic** image entry from the data source. Click **OK**.

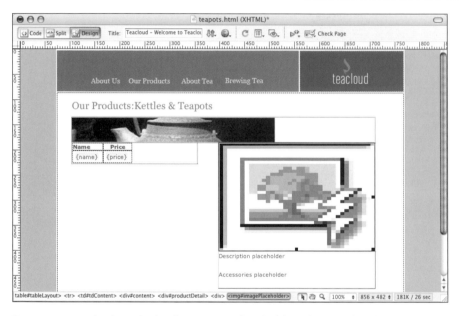

Dreamweaver displays the broken image placeholder. This may be disconcerting at first, but you'll be able to view the proper images in your browser. First, though, you'll make some additional changes to the detail area of this page.

4 Select the **Description placeholder** text, and delete it. Open the **Bindings** panel by clicking its tab or by choosing **Window > Bindings**. In the **Bindings** panel, select **desc**, and click the **Insert** button at the bottom of the panel.

Dreamweaver inserts the code for Spry dynamic text, **{ds1::desc}**. This will display the description text from the XML file for whichever teapot is selected in the Spry table. Now you'll add the second data text element.

5 Select the text **Accessories placeholder**, and delete it. In the **Bindings** panel, select **accessories**, and click the **Insert** button.

To complete the connection between the Spry table and the detail regions, you need to add a little bit of code to specify that the image and the two data text elements are connected to the table. This requires typing some code by hand.

6 In the **Tag Selector**, click **<div#productDetail>** to select the **<div>** tag surrounding the image and data text elements. Press **Ctrl+T** (Windows) or **Cmd+T** (Mac) to open the **Quick Tag Editor**. In the **Quick Tag Editor**, position your cursor between the closing quotation mark and the closing angle bracket, and press the **spacebar**. Type **spry:detailregion= "ds1"**, and press **Enter** (Windows) or **Return** (Mac).

Notice that the **<div#productDetail>** tag in the Tag Selector has been highlighted in orange, indicating that this tag has Spry attributes. Also observe that the dynamic text areas have been changed to **{desc}** and **{accessories}**.

---

7 Save the page, and press **F12** (Windows) or **Opt+F12** (Mac) to preview the page in your browser.

Click each one of the teapot names in the table to see the image, description, and accessory list appear on the right.

---

8 Return to Dreamweaver, and leave **teapots.html** open for the next exercise.

---

4 | Using Spry Widgets

In the previous exercise, you created a Spry detail region to display the details of the teapots listed in the Spry table. In this exercise, you'll increase the functionality of interactivity of the detail region by adding a Spry layout widget.

---

1 You should still have the **teapots.html** file from Exercise 3 open. If not, complete Exercise 3, and then return to this exercise.

In this exercise, you'll remove the dynamic data text you inserted in the previous exercise and replace it with a Spry widget. This is an alternative way to display the same information, so you'll need to undo some of the work you did in the previous exercise.

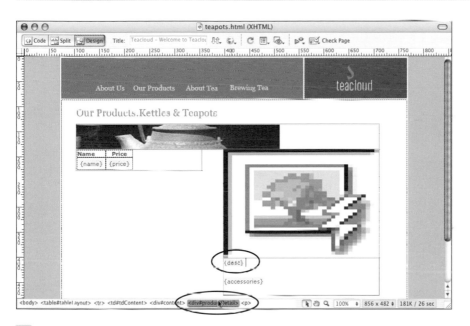

---

2 Position your cursor next to **{desc}** in the detail region. In the **Tag Selector**, select **<div#productDetail>**.

---

3 Press **Ctrl+T** (Windows) or **Cmd+T** (Mac) to open the **Quick Tag Editor**. Select the code you typed in the previous exercise, **spry:detailregion="ds1"** (including a single space before it), and delete it. Press **Enter** (Windows) or **Return** (Mac) to close the **Quick Tag Editor**.

---

4 On the Web page, select both **{ds1::desc}** and **{ds1::accessories}**, and delete them. Finally, select the **<p>** tag in the **Tag Selector**, and delete that as well.

At this point, your page should look like the illustration shown here. You're now ready to add a Spry widget.

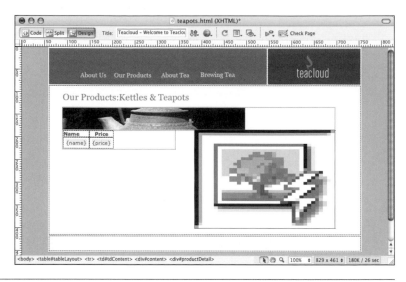

5 In the **Spry** group of the **Insert bar**, click the **Spry Accordion** object.

Dreamweaver places the default Spry Accordion on the page, which includes two accordion panels with the top panel open.

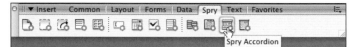

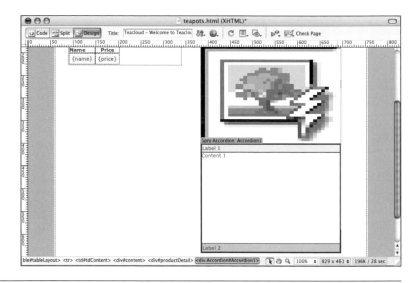

Spry Widgets

Spry Tabbed Panels   Spry Collapsible Panel

▼ Insert   Common   Layout   Forms   Data   Spry   Text   Favorites

Spry Menu Bar   Spry Accordion

You can choose from four built-in Spry widgets in Dreamweaver. Each one provides a way for you to dynamically display or hide data.

- **Spry Menu Bar:** Inserts a navigation bar with pop-up menus on your page

- **Spry Tabbed Panels:** Inserts a series of containers on your page, each revealed with the click of its tab

- **Spry Accordion:** Inserts two or more collapsible panels that independently slide open when selected

- **Spry Collapsible Panel:** Similar to the **Accordion** panel but adds only a single collapsible panel to the page.

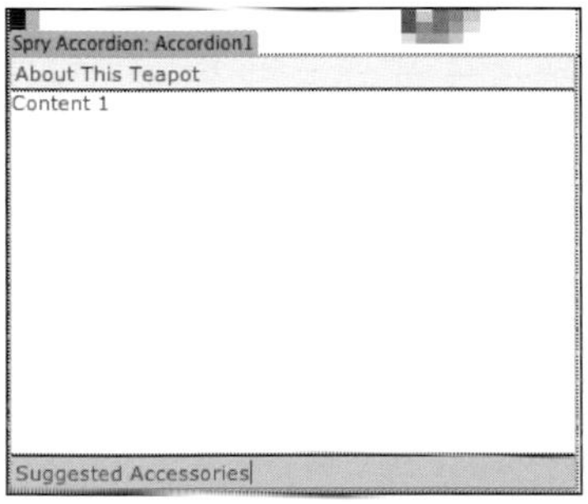

Spry Accordion: Accordion1
About This Teapot
Content 1

Suggested Accessories

6 In the **Spry Accordion** panel, select the placeholder text **Label 1**, and delete it. In its place, type **About This Teapot**. Select and delete the **Label 2** placeholder, and in its place type **Suggested Accessories**.

Next, you'll add the dynamic data content in much the same way as you did in the previous exercise.

7 Select the placeholder text **Content 1**, and delete it. In the **Bindings** panel, select **shortdescription**, and click the **Insert** button. Click to the right of the **{ds1::shortdescription}** text that was just added, and press **Enter** (Windows) or **Return** (Mac) to enter a paragraph break. In the **Bindings** panel, select **desc**, and click the **Insert** button.

Your Spry Accordion widget should match the illustration shown here. Next, you need to add the dynamic data text to the Suggested Accessories panel of the accordion.

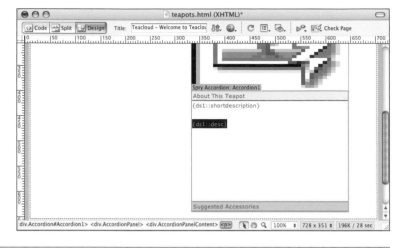

8 Position your cursor over the currently collapsed **Suggested Accessories** panel. Notice that an **eye** icon appears. Click the **eye** icon to expand the panel.

9 Select the placeholder text **Content 2**, and delete it. In the **Bindings** panel, select **accessories**, and click the **Insert** button.

All the dynamic data sources are now in place. Now you need to reapply the Spry detail region attributes to each item you want associated with the Spry table.

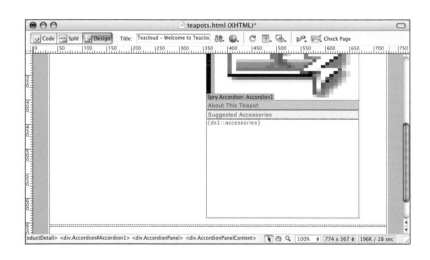

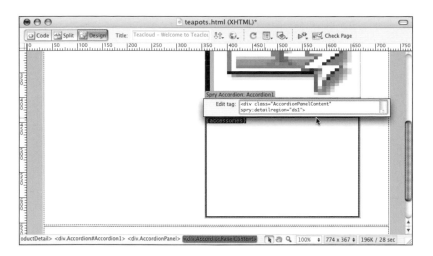

10 With the cursor in the bottom accordion panel, select **<div.AccordionPanelContent>** in the **Tag Selector**. Press **Ctrl+T** (Windows) or **Cmd+T** (Mac) to open the **Quick Tag Editor**. In the **Quick Tag Editor**, place your cursor between the closing quotation mark and the closing angle bracket, and press the **spacebar**. Type **spry:detailregion="ds1"**, and press **Enter** (Windows) or **Return** (Mac).

Now you'll add the same attribute to the other dynamic content.

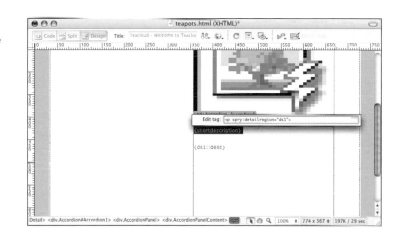

11 Position your cursor on the top accordion panel, and click the **eye** icon to expand the panel. Position your cursor somewhere in the **{ds1::shortdescription}** text, and click the **<p>** tag in the **Tag Selector**. Press **Ctrl+T** (Windows) or **Cmd+T** (Mac) to open the **Quick Tag Editor**. In the **Quick Tag Editor**, position your cursor between the **p** and the closing angle bracket, and press the **spacebar**. Next type **spry:detailregion="ds1"**, and press **Enter** (Windows) or **Return** (Mac).

12 Position your cursor in **{ds1::desc}**, and add the Spry detail region attributes as you did in the previous step for **shortdescription**.

Lastly, you need to add the Spry detail region attribute to the image placeholder.

13 Select the image placeholder, and select the **<div>** tag in the **Tag Selector**. Press **Ctrl+T** (Windows) or **Cmd+T** (Mac) to open the **Quick Tag Editor**. In the **Quick Tag Editor**, position your cursor before the closing bracket press **Space**. Type **spry:detailregion="ds1"**, and press **Enter** (Windows) or **Return** (Mac).

All of your Spry functionality is now in place.

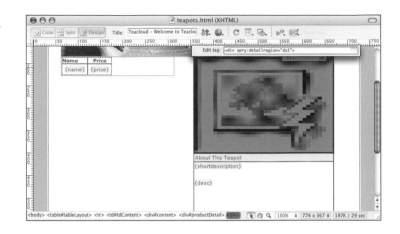

---

14 Save the page, and press **F12** (Windows) or **Opt+F12** (Mac) to preview the page in your browser. When Dreamweaver prompts you with the **Copy Dependent Files** dialog box, click **OK**.

---

15 Click the bottom and top accordion panels to see them in action. Click the other teapots in the table to see their data in the Spry Accordion widget as well.

As you can see, Spry widgets give you the kind of interactivity that simply isn't possible with plain XHTML pages.

---

16 Return to Dreamweaver, and close **teapots.html**.

VIDEO: | **spry_effects.mov**

Dreamweaver CS3 includes additional Spry-based functionality in the form of Spry Effects. To see a demonstration, check out **spry_effects.mov** in the **videos** folder of the **HOT CD-ROM**.

5 | Adding Spry Form Fields

In this exercise, you'll learn to add and customize Spry form fields. Spry form fields and nearly identical to the regular form fields you learned about in Chapter 13, *"Working with Forms,"* but Spry form fields offer the additional advantage of built-in validation to help ensure that your visitors fill out your forms correctly.

1 In the Files panel, double-click **contactus.html** to open it.

This page contains a single-column table into which you'll add some Spry form fields.

2 Position your cursor in the top row of the table. In the **Spry** group of the **Insert** bar, click the **Spry Validation Text Field** object.

3 In the **Input Tag Accessibility Attributes** dialog box, type **name** for **ID** and **Name** for **Label**. For **Style**, select **Attach label using 'for' attribute**, and for **Position** select **Before form item**.

This is the same dialog box you see when you add a regular text field, but you'll see the difference found in a Spry text field in a moment.

4 Click **OK**. The Spry text field appears in the table row. (The table has been preformatted to align all content to the right.) Click **Spry TextField tab** to open its attributes in the **Property inspector**.

The Spry TextField has many more customizable attributes than a regular text field. Next, you'll make this a required field.

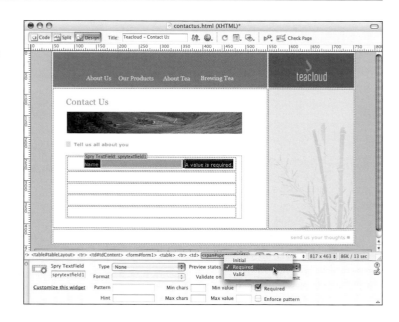

5 Leave the **Type** menu set to **None**, since this is a **Name** field and you want to allow any kind of characters to be typed in this field. Set the **Preview states** menu to **Required**. This shows you the text that will be displayed if the user leaves the field blank: **A value is required**. It's a little verbose, however. Change the text to simply read **Required**.

By default, all validations are triggered when a form is submitted, which is fine in many cases, but it can make for a better user experience if your visitors are prompted to correct errors as soon as they complete a field, rather than having to potentially correct multiple errors once all the fields have been filled out.

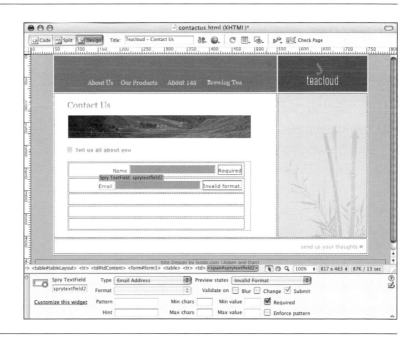

6 Select **Blur** next to **Validate on**.

The term *blur* refers to the moment when visitors leave this field and position the cursor in another one. The selected field is said to be in *focus*, and the other fields are *blurred*. By selecting Blur here, you're telling the TextField to validate itself the moment the visitor's cursor leaves the field. Next, you'll add a field for your visitors' e-mail addresses.

7 Position your cursor in the second row of the table, and click the **Spry Validation Text Field** object in the **Insert** bar. In the **Input Tag Accessibility Attributes** dialog box, type **email** for **ID**, and type **Email** for **Label**. Leave the rest of the settings as they are, and click **OK**.

You'll set up this field to accept only e-mail addresses.

8 Click the tab for the **Spry TextField** you just added. In the **Property inspector**, choose **Email Address** in the **Type** menu. Notice when you do that, the **Preview states** menu is automatically set to **Invalid Format**, showing you the text that will appear if your visitor types an improperly formatted e-mail address. Leave the text as it is for now.

9 Next to **Validate on**, select **Blur**.

Next, you'll add a text area field.

10 Position your cursor in the third row of the table, and click the **Spry Validation Textarea** object.

---

11 In the **Input Tag Accessibility Attributes** dialog box, type **comments** for **ID**, and type **Comments** for **Label**. Leave the rest of the settings as they are, and click **OK**.

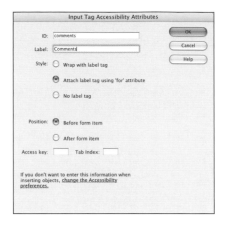

---

12 With the **Spry Textarea** object selected, make sure **Required** is selected in the **Property inspector** to make sure visitors submitting their names and e-mail addresses also ask you a question or make a comment. Choose **Required** in the **Preview states** menu to display the text that will appear if a visitor leaves this field blank. Change the text from **A value is required** to **Please enter a question or comment**.

You'll complete this form by adding a submit button.

13 Position your cursor in the bottom row of the table (leaving the fourth row empty). Switch to the **Forms** group of the **Insert bar**, and click the **Button** object. You don't need to label the button, so just click **OK** when the **Input Tag Accessibility Attributes** dialog box opens.

---

14 Save the page. The **Copy Dependent Files** dialog box opens, letting you know that Dreamweaver needs to save several JavaScript and CSS (**C**ascading **S**tyle **S**heets) files for your Spry form fields to function correctly. Click **OK**.

15 Press **F12** (Windows) or **Opt+F12** (Mac) to preview this page in your browser. Without typing anything in any of the fields, click the **Submit** button. Notice the validation messages that appear, indicating that all the fields are required.

16 Type your name in the **Name** field, and type **I like your site.** in the **Comments** field. In the **Email** field, type **me at lynda.com**. Click **Submit**. Notice the **Name** and **Comments** fields are displayed in green, indicating that the entries are valid but that the **Email** field's alert has changed to **Invalid format**.

As you can see, being able to validate your Spry form fields can make for a much more user-friendly experience and can also save you from having to spend a lot of time searching through the incorrectly completed form data you receive.

17 Return to Dreamweaver, and close **contactus.html**.

In this chapter, you learned about Dreamweaver CS3's powerful new Spry tools for adding data-driven content and self-validating form fields. If you know how to write XML, you should be ready to tackle creating your own data-driven pages using Spry. If you're not comfortable writing XML yet, at least you're now aware of some of the features you can create with XML data in Dreamweaver. In the next and final chapter, you'll learn how to publish your Web site to the World Wide Web.

21

Getting Your Site Online

It's one thing to design a Web page and an entirely different thing to get what you've designed online for everyone else to see. One of the features I have always thought was missing from other books was concrete instructions covering how to access, upload, and update files to a Web server. Until now, you were forced to struggle through this process on your own, which could prove frustrating. Fortunately, this chapter walks you through the process of uploading your pages to a real live Web server. This means anyone with an Internet connection and your Web address will be able to see the results of whatever you publish on the Web.

This chapter shows you how to create a free Web hosting account with Tripod and then use Adobe Dreamweaver CS3 to upload a Web site so others can view it live on the Internet. You do not have to sign up for the Tripod account unless you want to follow along with the exercises. If you already have a Web hosting account, you can learn to use it by reading this chapter as well. Either way, this chapter shows you how to set up your FTP (**F**ile **T**ransfer **P**rotocol) preferences and upload your site to a Web server using Dreamweaver CS3.

Hosting Your Pages with Tripod for Free

Tripod is one of many Web services offering free Web hosting to anyone who wants to sign up. Within just a few minutes, you can have a place to upload your files to the Web, if you don't already have another spot reserved.

And you'll be pleasantly surprised by how much you get for free. The Tripod free Web hosting package includes a lot of extras. All you need to complete the exercises in this chapter are the 20 megabytes of free disk space and FTP access that are provided with the free Web hosting account. The only disadvantage to the free service is that it does include advertising. It's the perfect place to get started, though, and when you're ready to go "pro" and get rid of the ads, you can upgrade to a low-cost service with Tripod or seek out other service providers that will meet your needs.

If you already have a hosting service of your own, feel free to work with your own settings in the exercises, rather than those described for Tripod. For the FTP settings, just substitute your own settings instead of Tripod's. You can acquire your FTP settings from your own hosting service or the Web administrator for your company.

1 | Signing Up with Tripod

The first step in getting your free Tripod Web site online involves filling out a form on Tripod's site. This exercise shows you what parts of the form to complete. If you plan to use your own Web server instead of Tripod's, you can skip this exercise.

---

1 Launch your preferred browser, and browse to the Tripod home page at **www.tripod.lycos.com**. Click the **Start Now** button to go to the **Plan Selection** page.

Note: Since this is the ever-changing Web, the Tripod site may look different than it does in the illustrations shown in this chapter. The basic steps of signing up for an account should remain the same, however.

---

2 Choose to sign up for the **Tripod Free** plan. This takes you to another Web page where you can create your own Tripod account.

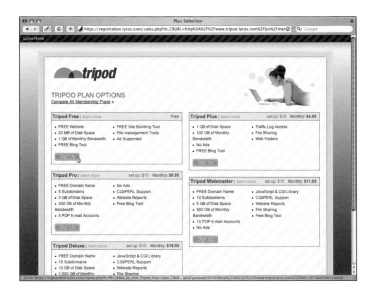

---

3 Fill in all the information requested on the form. Your **Member Name** will appear as part of your Tripod URL (**U**niform **R**esource **L**ocator). For my ID, I used **dwcs3hot**; therefore, when the account is set up, my address for the site will be **http://dwcs3hot.tripod.com**.

Note: Do not use dwcs3hot as your ID; be sure to use your own unique ID, and make sure to write it down because you'll be using your user ID and password in the next exercise.

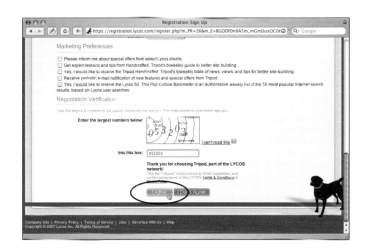

4 When you are finished typing your information, click **I Agree** at the bottom of the page to submit your information.

NOTE:

Privacy Policies

Anytime you provide personal information about yourself on a Web site, you should be familiar with the recipient's privacy policy. Some sites gather personal information that they then sell to marketing companies, which oftentimes results in some extra and unsolicited e-mails in your inbox. If this is of serious concern to you, be sure to deselect everything in the **Marketing Preferences** area of the sign-up form, and be sure you review Tripod's privacy policy (**www.lycos.com/privacy/**) before you provide them with information.

---

5 Skip any special offers that are made on the next page. Tripod will take a few moments to process your new account.

6 You have successfully set up this account and should receive a welcome e-mail from Tripod with your user-name information shortly. Although Tripod offers several tools to help you build and publish a Web site, you won't need any of them since you're using Dreamweaver. Quit the browser; you will return to it later after you have published your site from Dreamweaver CS3.

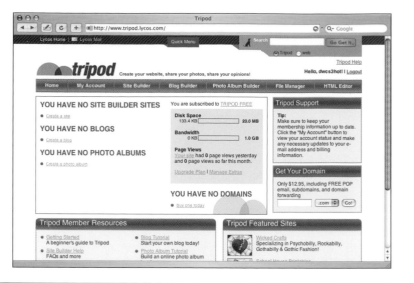

Adobe Dreamweaver CS3 : H•O•T

2 | Setting FTP Connection Information

For your site to be seen on the World Wide Web, you need to upload, or **publish**, your files to a publicly available Web server. Most Web developers and designers build pages on their hard drives (as you have done in this book) before transferring their files to a live Web server. In Dreamweaver CS3 terminology, the files on your hard drive are referred to as **local files**, and the files on a live Web server are referred to as **remote files**. When you publish your Web site, you're simply copying the files on your computer to another computer, called a **Web server**, that's connected to the Internet 24/7. You can publish your files directly from Dreamweaver CS3 without needing any additional software. But first, you need to enter your FTP settings, which you'll do in this exercise.

Note: To complete this exercise, you need to know the member name and password you selected when you created your Tripod account or have the information handy from your own account. If you forgot that information or have not signed up for a Tripod account yet, complete Exercise 1 before beginning this exercise.

---

1 If you haven't already done so, copy the **chap_21** folder from the **Dreamweaver HOT CD-ROM** to your desktop. Define your site as **Chapter 21** using the **chap_21** folder as the local root folder. Make sure the **Files** panel is open. If it's not, choose **Window > Files**.

---

2 Choose **Site > Manage Sites**. In the **Manage Sites** dialog box, select **Chapter 21**, and click **Edit**.

---

3 Make sure the **Advanced** tab is selected. Select **Remote Info** in the **Category** list, and then choose **FTP** in the **Access** pop-up menu.

Next, you'll modify your FTP settings before you upload files to your site.

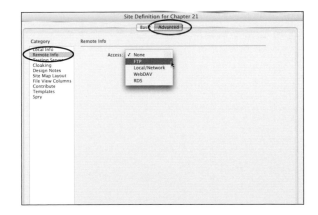

4 Match the settings to the ones shown here, making sure you specify the **Login** and **Password** settings for the Tripod account you created in Exercise 1. Click **Test**.

If you signed up for the free Tripod account, your FTP information should be similar to the information shown here, except for Login. If you are using your own Web hosting service, your Web hosting provider will provide the proper FTP login information to you.

Be sure to use your own Tripod ID and password here.

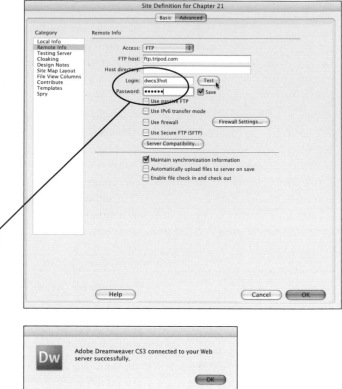

If you set up your connection correctly, Dreamweaver CS3 displays a message saying that it has successfully connected to the server. If you receive an error message, you'll need to verify your FTP settings and potentially check with your ISP (Internet Service Provider) or network administrator for possible firewall settings you may need to adjust.

5 After you've successfully tested your connection, click **OK**. If you see a message telling you Dreamweaver needs to rebuild your site cache, click **OK**. When you return to the **Manage Sites** dialog box, click **Done**.

What Is FTP?

FTP stands for **F**ile **T**ransfer **P**rotocol. This term is usually associated with the process of uploading files to a server. You will hear this term used as a verb, as in, "I am going to FTP all of my files now."

FTP is the most common method used for transferring files from a local computer to a Web hosting server. Dreamweaver is also capable of using the WebDAV (**Web**-based **D**istributed **A**uthoring and **V**ersioning) and RDS (**R**emote **D**evelopment **S**ervices) protocols, and if you need to use either of those, your Web hosting provider will instruct you how to set up your Dreamweaver settings.

But chances are good that you'll be using FTP to publish your site.

It is important to note that you do not have to use Dreamweaver CS3 to exchange files with the remote server. You can use other FTP applications as well, such as WS_FTP (Windows) or Fetch (Mac). There are advantages to using Dreamweaver CS3 over these applications, however, such as file synchronization and site management. You'll learn about these advantages shortly.

Here is a handy chart that describes the FTP settings in Dreamweaver CS3:

FTP Settings in Dreamweaver CS3

Setting	Description
FTP host	This will typically be an address similar to the URL of your Web site. In some cases, it may begin with the prefix *FTP* but may also be an IP (Internet Protocol) address such as 72.14.207.99.
Host directory	If you have a specific folder on the server where you are supposed to place your files, you would type it here. This option is not always used. Your Web hosting provider will let you know whether you need to enter any host directory information.
Login	You will be given a user name or ID to use to access the remote server. It is important you type this information exactly as it is given to you; otherwise, you will have problems connecting.
Password	In addition to a user name or ID, you will also be given a password to use when accessing the remote server. If you don't want to enter the password every time you connect to the remote server, select the **Save** check box, and Dreamweaver CS3 will remember your password. **Note:** The password you type here is just stored in a text file on your hard drive, so anyone can read it. Don't select the **Save** check box if security is a concern at your location.
Use passive FTP	The **Passive FTP** option lets your local software set up the FTP connection rather than the remote server. Leave this option deselected unless directed by your Web hosting provider.
Use firewall	Select this box if you are connecting to the FTP server from behind a firewall.

3 | Putting Files onto the Web Server

Now that you have set up your FTP preferences, you're ready to use Dreamweaver CS3 to connect to a Web server and upload your files. Once you have completed this exercise, you'll be able to see your Web site live on the Internet.

1 Before you try to upload your files to the Web server, make sure you have a live Internet connection. You should be able to browse the Web and look at other sites as a test to see that your Web connection is working.

2 Make sure the **Files** panel is open; if it is not, choose **Window > Files**.

Notice the Connect button, at the top of the panel, is no longer dimmed. Once you specify your FTP preferences, you will have access to the Connect feature.

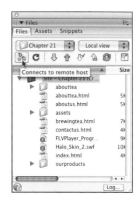

3 Click the **Connect** button. Dreamweaver CS3 will connect to your Web server. If you don't have an active Internet connection or if the FTP details are incorrect, you will receive an error message.

4 With your local root folder selected, you are ready to upload the files for your site. Click **Put Files**.

Note: If you wanted to upload a single file, you wouldn't select the local root folder; instead, you'd select just the particular file and then click Put Files.

5 You are asked whether you want to upload your entire Web site. Because this is the first time you are uploading your site, click **OK**.

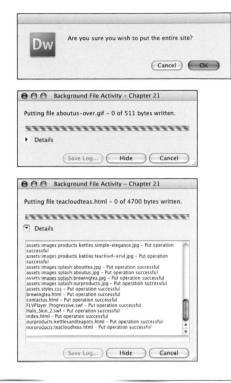

After Dreamweaver CS3 starts to upload, you will see the Background File Activity dialog box, which shows you the FTP progress—whether you're uploading or downloading files.

If you click the triangle next to Details, you can see a detailed list of what's happening on the server. You can also just click Hide and continue working in Dreamweaver CS3. The only things you can't do while Dreamweaver CS3 is interacting with the server is switch to a different site or perform any action that would cause Dreamweaver CS3 to interact with the server. Dreamweaver can do only one thing with the server at a time.

6 After all the files have finished uploading, click the **Expand** icon in the **Files** panel.

You can now see the remote files (on the left side) are nearly identical to the local files (on the right side). Tripod automatically adds the folders _private and cgi-bin. Those folders are needed on the server, so don't change or delete them. You'll also notice that a file called index.htm is on the remote side. This is the place-holder page that Tripod inserts on your site before you publish your site. But since the teacloud site uses index.html, both index files are now on the server, and Tripod will display the .htm page as your site's default.

7 On the **Remote Site** side of the **Files** panel, select **index.htm**, and press **Delete** on your keyboard. Dreamweaver will ask you to confirm that you really want to delete this file. Click **Yes**.

Now, when you browse to your site, index.html will be the default page that displays.

NOTE: | **The Difference Between Getting and Putting**

You can transfer files between the local site and the remote site (the Web server) in two ways. The **Get** command copies the selected files from the remote site to your local site. This process is referred to as **downloading**. The **Put** command copies the selected files from the local site to the remote site. This process is referred to as **uploading** or **publishing**.

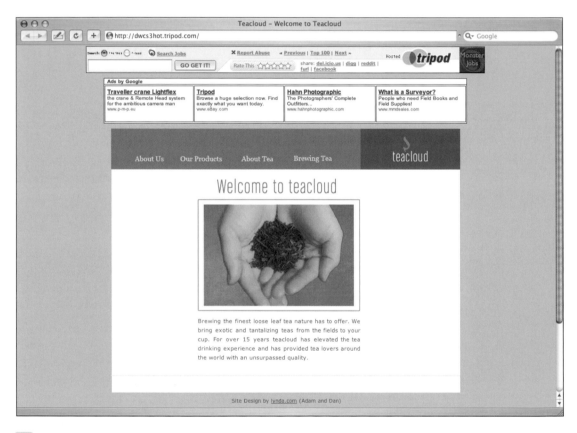

8 Open a browser, and type the URL for the tripod account you created in Exercise 1.

Because my Tripod ID was dwcs3hot, the URL will be http://dwcs3hot.tripod.com. Of course, your URL will be different. Just replace *dwcs3hot* with your own Tripod ID, and voilà—your Web site is live on the Web (albeit with annoying advertisements). Congratulations!

4 | Running Site Reports

As your sites get larger, you will find it increasingly difficult to manage all the files that continue to add up. Trying to locate untitled documents, files with missing **alt** text descriptions, redundant nested tags, and so on, can prove to be a very time-consuming task. Dreamweaver CS3 lets you identify and locate files that meet specific criteria. This feature can save you time hunting for the files manually and will make sure your files are in good shape. In this exercise, you will run a report on a finished site and fix some of the problems identified in the report.

1 In Dreamweaver, choose **Site > Reports** to open the **Reports** dialog box, where you can specify the type of report you want to generate.

2 In the **Report on** pop-up menu, choose **Entire Current Local Site**.

This option ensures that all the files within the current site are processed. Take a moment to read through the Select reports section to see what kind of searches you can perform here.

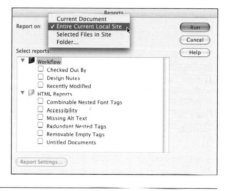

3 Select the **Untitled Documents** check box.

This option examines all the documents in your site to make sure each one has a valid name instead of the default *Untitled Document* Dreamweaver CS3 uses for each new file. As you've already learned, some search engines use the page title as part of their listings, so you don't want any of your site's pages to be untitled.

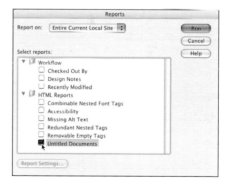

4 Click **Run** to begin scanning all the files in your site, looking for ones that have **Untitled Document** as the page title.

When Dreamweaver CS3 is finished scanning your site, the Site Reports tab of the Results panel will open and display the files that meet the criteria you specified. In this case, you are looking for files that have *Untitled Document* as the page title.

5 Double-click **brewingtea.html** to open the file so you can correct the problem.

The page opens in Split view, and Dreamweaver highlights the code matching the criteria you want to find. Notice the title of the document is set to *Untitled Document*.

---

6 Type **Teacloud – Brewing Tea** in the **Title** field of the **Document** toolbar, and press **Enter** (Windows) or **Return** (Mac).

---

7 Save your changes, and close **brewingtea.html**.

VIDEO: | **check_links.mov**

Another useful report you can run from Dreamweaver is called **Check Links Sitewide**, which allows you to examine your site for broken links and orphaned files, and also get a list of external links you've created. To see a demonstration, watch **check_links.mov** in the **videos** folder of the **HOT CD-ROM**.

Using the Reports Dialog Box

The **Reports** dialog box offers a wide range of options and flexibility. The following chart outlines these options and provides a brief description of each:

Reports Dialog Box Options		
Option	Selection	Description
Report On		
	Current Document	Checks only the active document.
	Entire Local Site	Checks every file within the local root folder.
	Selected Files in Site	Checks only the files that are selected within the **Site** window. You must have the files selected before choosing this option.
	Folder	Checks a specific folder. When you choose this option, you can browse to the specific folder you want to process.
Workflow		
	Checked Out By	Identifies files that have been checked out by a specific user (when using the Dreamweaver CS3 **Check In/Check Out** feature). When this option is selected, you can specify the name by clicking the **Report Settings** button.
	Design Notes	Searches all the **Design Notes** in your documents. The **Report Settings** button will give you access to specific search criteria.
	Recently Modified	Reports files that have been modified within a specified date range. You can click the **Report Settings** button and check for files that have been edited within a certain number of dates or any other arbitrary date range you want to review.
HTML Reports		
	Combinable Nested Font Tags	Reports all nested font tags that could be combined into a single `<font>` tag. For example, `<font color= "#CC3366"><font size="1">Hello</font></font>` would be reported.

continues on next page

continues on next page

Reports Dialog Box Options *(continued)*		
Option	Selection	Description
HTML Reports *(continued)*	**Accessibility**	Analyzes the Web pages against the Section 508 Guidelines to determine whether your pages meet these accessibility requirements. This is a useful feature and can even help you make existing Web pages accessible. See Chapter 18, *"Understanding Accessibility,"* for more information.
	Missing Alt Text	Identifies all images that do not have an `alt` attribute applied to them.
	Redundant Nested Tags	Reports nested tags that can be combined.
	Removable Empty Tags	Reports any tags that don't contain any content, such as empty `<div>` or `<p>` tags.
	Untitled Documents	Searches documents to see whether any have a page title of *Untitled Document*.

After learning how to put Dreamweaver CS3 to use, you've finally learned how to get that site online. Congratulations! I hope this book helped you get up to speed with Dreamweaver CS3 quickly and you now feel ready to tackle your next Web project. I wish you the best of luck with all your future projects.

A

Troubleshooting FAQ and Technical Support

If you run into problems while following the exercises in this book, you might find the answer in the "Frequently Asked Questions" section of this appendix. If you don't find the information you're looking for there, use the contact information provided in the "Technical Support Information" section.

Frequently Asked Questions

Q When I preview my files locally, I get an error that the file or image cannot be found. What's wrong?

A This is one of the most common problems beginners encounter when creating links in Adobe Dreamweaver CS3. This almost always occurs when you create a link that is site root relative instead of document relative. Creating a site root relative link will cause a slash (/) to appear at the beginning of the path to the file, which will cause images to disappear, frames to not function properly, and file links to break when previewed locally. You can correct this problem by relinking the file/image and making sure you are using the **Document** option for **Relative to**.

Q I can't find a feature that existed in previous versions of Dreamweaver. What happened?

A Some features found in previous versions of Dreamweaver have been removed in Dreamweaver CS3. Adobe did this because these features were obsolete or recommended a workflow that is no longer current with modern Web practices.

Q How do I open the **Property inspector** (or any other panel)?

A If you can't see the **Property inspector**—or, for that matter, any of the Dreamweaver panels—choose the **Window** menu, and choose the panel you want to open. The menu also lists shortcut keys that will help you quickly access all of the Dreamweaver panels.

Q The **Document** toolbar has gone missing from the top of my **Document** window. How do I get it back?

A **Right-click** the **Insert** bar, and choose **Document**. Alternatively, choose **View > Toolbars > Document**.

Q I defined my site for a chapter, but files that are listed in the exercises aren't there. What happened?

A When you were defining the site, you may have specified a subfolder of the chapter folder instead of the chapter folder itself. Go ahead and redefine the site. (If you need to revisit these steps, visit Exercise 1 in Chapter 3, "Managing Your Sites.")

You select the correct folder differently on a Mac and in Windows, as shown here:

- **Windows:** When you're browsing to define the chapter folder and the **Choose Local Folder** dialog box opens, select the chapter folder, and then click **Open**. After the folder opens, click **Select**.

- **Mac:** When you're browsing to define the chapter folder and the **Choose Local Folder** dialog box opens, select the chapter folder, and click **Choose**.

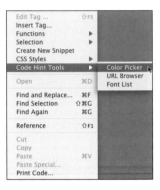

Q Where's the **color picker**?

A Because it's context-sensitive, the **color picker** appears when you click one of the Dreamweaver CS3 color wells. Color wells appear in the **Property inspector** and the **Page Properties** dialog box. You can also find the **color picker** in Dreamweaver's **Code** view by **right-clicking** and choosing **Code Hint Tools > Color Picker** in the contextual menu.

Q I put one AP Div on top of another! How do I delete it?

A To delete an AP Div, select it by the handle at its top, and press **Delete**. You can also use the **AP Elements** panel to select the AP Div, which might be easier in some cases where they overlap. Of course, you can always use the universal undo command, **Ctrl+Z** (Windows) or **Cmd+Z** (Mac).

Q I just specified a tracing image in my **Page Properties** dialog box, but I can't see it when I preview the page in my browser.

A The tracing image is a template to be used for layout in Dreamweaver. It is invisible in the browser window. It's there for your reference only, and your visitors will never see it.

Q Why do I get the "To make a document-relative path, your document should be saved first" message?

A It would be nice if the dialog box simply stated, "Save your file now, or Dreamweaver can't keep track of your files," because that's all it's asking you to do. All you need to do is click **OK** and save your file (inside the defined site), and Dreamweaver CS3 will write the path correctly.

Q Why do I get the message that my file is located outside the root folder?

A Dreamweaver CS3 is asking you to move the file into the root folder you defined as your site. If you work with files outside your defined root folder, Dreamweaver CS3 cannot keep track of your links or manage your site, which is counterproductive to the way the program is structured and to your workflow. This message is there to help you maintain a healthy site without experiencing broken links and problems uploading your files when you publish it. You can handle this message in different ways, depending on the system you are running:

- **Windows:** Click **Yes**, and Dreamweaver CS3 will automatically put you in the correct folder. Click **Save**, and the file will be moved.

- **Mac:** Click **Yes**, and then browse to the correct folder. At that point you will be prompted to save, which you should do.

Q When I try to locate files, why can't I see the file extensions at the end of file names, such as **.gif**, **.jpg**, and **.html**?

A On Windows, you will need to change your preferences to view file name extensions. See the introduction at the beginning of this book for instructions on how to do this.

Technical Support Information

The following is a list of technical support resources you can use if you need help.

lynda.com

If you run into any problems as you work through this book, check the companion Web site for updates:

www.lynda.com/info/books/dwcs

If you don't find what you're looking for on the companion Web site, send the authors an e-mail:

dwcs3hot@lynda.com

We encourage and welcome your feedback, comments, or error reports.

Peachpit Press

If your book has a defective CD-ROM, please contact the customer service department at Peachpit Press:

customer_service@peachpit.com

Adobe Technical Support

If you're having problems with Dreamweaver CS3, please visit the Adobe Technical Support Center:

www.adobe.com/support

B

Dreamweaver CS3 Resources

There are many great resources for Adobe Dreamweaver CS3 users. You have ample choices among a variety of newsgroups, conferences, and third-party Web sites that can really help you get the most out of the new skills you've developed by reading this book. In this appendix, you'll find a list of the best resources for further developing your skills with Dreamweaver CS3.

lynda.com Training Resources

lynda.com is a leader in software books and video training for Web and graphics professionals. To help further develop your skills in Dreamweaver CS3, check out the following training resources from lynda.com.

lynda.com Books

The Hands-On Training series was originally developed by Lynda Weinman, author of the revolutionary book, *Designing Web Graphics*, first released in 1996. Lynda believes people learn best from doing and has developed the Hands-On Training series to teach users software programs and technologies through a progressive learning process.

Check out the following books from lynda.com:

Designing Web Graphics 4 by Lynda Weinman. New Riders, ISBN: 0735710791.

CSS Web Site Design Hands-On Training by Eric Meyer. lynda.com/books and Peachpit Press, ISBN: 0321293916.

Adobe Flash CS3 Professional Hands-On Training by Todd Perkins. lynda.com/books and Peachpit Press, ISBN: 0321509838.

ActionScript 3.0 for Adobe Flash CS3 Professional Hands-On Training by Todd Perkins. lynda.com/books and Peachpit Press, ISBN: 0321293908.

lynda.com Video-Based Training

lynda.com offers video training as stand-alone CD-ROM and DVD-ROM products and through a monthly or annual subscription to the **lynda.com Online Training Library**.

For a free, 24-hour trial pass to the lynda.com Online Training Library, register your copy of *Adobe Dreamweaver CS3 Hands-On Training* at the following link:

www.lynda.com/register/HOT/dwcs3

Note: This offer is available for new subscribers only and does not apply to current or past subscribers of the lynda.com Online Training Library.

To help you build your skills with Dreamweaver CS3, check out the following video-based training titles from lynda.com.

Dreamweaver Video-Based Training
Dreamweaver CS3 Essential Training with Garrick Chow

Web Design Video-Based Training
Flash CS3 Professional Essential Training with Rich Shupe

Photoshop CS3 for the Web Essential Training with Jan Kabili

Fireworks CS3 Essential Training with Tom Green

CSS for Designers with Andy Clarke and Molly E. Holzschlag

CSS Web Site Design with Eric Meyer

Web Development Video-Based Training

CSS 2 Essential Training with Christopher Deutsch

XML Essential Training with Joe Marini

XHTML Essential Training with William E. Weinman

HTML Essential Training with William E. Weinman

JavaScript Essential Training with Charles G. Hollins

Flashforward Conference

Flashforward is an international educational conference dedicated to Adobe Flash, a multimedia authoring program which can be used on its own or in conjunction with Adobe Dreamweaver to build Web sites. Flashforward was first hosted by Lynda Weinman, founder of lynda.com, and Stewart McBride, founder of United Digital Artists. Flashforward is now owned exclusively by lynda.com and strives to provide the best conferences for designers and developers to present their technical and artistic work in an educational setting.

For more information about the Flashforward conference, visit **www.flashforwardconference.com**.

Online Resources

Dreamweaver Support Forum
www.adobe.com/cfusion/webforums/forum/index.cfm?forumid=12

Other Books

Eric Meyer on CSS by Eric Meyer. New Riders, ISBN: 073571245X.

More Eric Meyer on CSS by Eric Meyer. New Riders, ISBN: 0735714258.

Installing Extensions

Although Adobe Dreamweaver CS3 is a massive and highly capable application, it simply can't do everything for everyone. If Dreamweaver tried to do all things for all people, it would probably fail miserably at most of them. But one of the great features of Dreamweaver is that it has always been incredibly extensible, which means it's possible for a third party to extend the functionality of Dreamweaver through plug-ins called **extensions**.

Extensions can add behaviors, commands, toolbars, and server behaviors, and they can even change the way the core functionality of Dreamweaver behaves. Each extension is a collection of HTML (**H**yper**T**ext **M**arkup **L**anguage), JavaScript, CSS (**C**ascading **S**tyle **S**heets), or even DLLs that create all this new and wonderful functionality. If there's a feature you think is missing from Dreamweaver, chances are good someone else thought that too and wrote an extension to solve the problem. You can find thousands of third-party extensions at **http://adobe.com/exchange**. Some extensions cost money, but many are free. In either case, once you've browsed around and downloaded an extension, you'll need to run the Adobe Extension Manager application that was installed with your copy of Dreamweaver.

Using the Adobe Extension Manager

The Adobe Extension Manager is the brains of the Dreamweaver CS3 extensibility engine. It manages all the information relating to extensions in each of the Adobe products. The Extension Manager handles all the installation tasks for

Dreamweaver CS3 (and other Adobe products) automatically. You simply double-click an extension file (which has an **.mxp** file extension), and the Extension Manager takes care of the rest.

Installing an Extension

Here's how to install an extension:

1 In Dreamweaver, choose **Help > Manage Extensions** to open the **Extension Manager**.

2 Click the **Install** button to open the **Install Extension** dialog box.

3 In the **Install Extension** dialog box, browse to the extension file you downloaded. (It has an **.mxp** extension.) Double-click it to install.

4 You need to click either **Accept** or **Decline** after reading the end user license agreement for the extension. Click **Accept** to continue the installation. (Click **Decline** if you don't want to continue with the installation.)

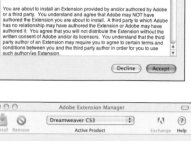

A progress bar shows how much time remains to complete the extension installation.

5 After the installation is complete, Dreamweaver CS3 lets you know the installation was successful. If you have Dreamweaver CS3 open, you may need to restart it before you can use the extension. Click **OK**.

The extension is now displayed in the Extension Manager. Be sure to read the information at the bottom to see where in Dreamweaver you can find the new extension. Depending on the extension you downloaded, it could be in the Insert bar, the Commands menu, or the Behaviors panel.

Adobe Dreamweaver CS3 : H·O·T

Disabling an Extension

Disabling an extension allows you to easily remove an extension from Dreamweaver CS3 and add it back at a later date. To disable an extension, simply deselect the box next to the extension in the Extension Manager, which will leave a copy of the extension files on your local system for the Extension Manager but will remove them from Dreamweaver CS3.

Uninstalling an Extension

Uninstalling an extension removes the extension from Dreamweaver and your computer.

1 To completely remove an extension from Dreamweaver CS3 and your local machine, select the extension in the Extension Manager, and click the **Remove** button.

2 The Extension Manager will prompt you to confirm the removal of the extension. Click **Yes** to permanently remove the extension, or click **No** to cancel the operation.

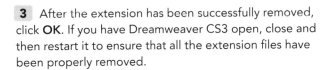

3 After the extension has been successfully removed, click **OK**. If you have Dreamweaver CS3 open, close and then restart it to ensure that all the extension files have been properly removed.

Index

Symbols

  element (nonbreaking space), 197–199
(number sign), 92, 132
% (percent) measurement unit, 163
(|) pipe symbol, 67
; (semicolon), 102
+ (plus) sign, 309
< > (angle brackets), 452

A

<a> tag, 88, 145
absolute links
  creating, 72–74
  identifying, 38–39
  path structures and, 42
  relative vs., 37
Absolutely Positioned tags. *see* AP Divs (Absolutely Positioned) <div> tags
accessibility, 424–435. *see also* Image Tag Accessibility Attributes dialog; Input Tag Accessibility Attributes dialog
  inserting form objects for, 432–434
  inserting images for, 427–429
  inserting tables for, 430–431
  overview of, 424
  setting preferences, 426
  testing, 435
  W3C guidelines for, 425
action attribute, <form> tag, 345
:active pseudo-class, 145

Add Property link, CSS Styles panel, 203, 240
Adobe Contribute, 384
Adobe CS3 suite, 3
Adobe Device Central, 268–271
Adobe Extension Manager, 348, 499–501
Adobe Fireworks
  copying/pasting images into Dreamweaver from, 374–377
  image editing to/from, 369–373
  round corner construction and, 229
  setting preferences, 361–365
Adobe Photoshop
  copying/pasting images into Dreamweaver from, 374–377
  image editing to/from, 369–373
  setting preferences, 361–365
Adobe Reader plug-in, 97
Adobe Technical Support, 493
Advanced tab, Site Definition dialog, 49
.aiff/.aif extension, 440
Ajax (Asynchronous JAvaScript and XML), 449
alignment
  images, 65–68
  table content, 211–216
  templates, 394
  text, 65–68, 175–177
all media type, 257
All mode, CSS Styles panel
  applying AP Divs, 239–242
  creating class selectors, 142
  formatting headings, 158–160
  using, 119–120
Alt (Windows), 310
alt attribute, for accessible images, 427–428

animation
  Flash Button, 292
  rollover, 279
AP Divs (Absolutely Positioned) <div> tags
  absolute positioning of, 242
  applying, 235–241
  converting to tables, 241
  defined, 231
  deleting, 492
  function of, 235
  Layout mode vs., 242
appearance
  page properties settings for, 109
  table borders improving, 197
Assets panel
  creating templates in, 388–390
  drag and drop images and, 64
  library items in, 408–411
  overview of, 60–61
  viewing/editing templates in, 380
Asynchronous JavaScript and XML (Ajax), 449
Attach Style Sheet button, 117, 259–260
Attributes tab, Tag inspector, 137
.au extension, 440
Auto indent option, 301
automating repetitive tasks, 412–423
  Find and Replace feature, 419–423
  History Panel, overview of, 413
  History Panel, Undo/Redo using, 414–416
  History steps, saving as commands, 417–418
Autostretch layout cells, 250–254
Available fonts list, 172–174

Document Type Definition. *see* DTD (Document Type Definition)

Document window
  defined, 296
  docking panels, 25
  features, 22
  Mac interface, 14
  multiple, 24
  overview of, 21
  splitting, 298
  views, 23, 297–301
  Windows interface, 13

documents, 53–57

DOM (Document Object Model), DHTML, 10

down state, rollover graphics, 284

drag and drop insert method, images, 64

Draw Layout Cell, 245–249

Draw Layout Table, 244–245

Dreamweaver CS3
  defined, 3
  extensions, 11
  XHTML and, 3–4

Dreamweaver HOT CD-ROM
  Check Links Sitewide report, 486
  Code toolbar, 304
  Create Web Photo Album command, 418
  CSS Styles panel, 122
  form styling, 346
  ID selectors, 138–139
  image maps, 99
  jump menus, 342
  named anchors, 94
  parameters, 443
  site maps, 48
  Swap Image behaviors, 283
  technical support, 493
  understanding paths, 45
  Welcome Screen, 15

Dreamweaver Support Forum, 496

<dt> tag, 153

DTD (Document Type Definition)
  choosing DOCTYPES, 55
  creating new documents, 54
  Page Properties dialog box settings, 110
  XHTML DOCTYPES, 6

.dwt file extension (templates), 381

E

Edit tool, 368

editable regions
  applying templates to documents, 392
  creating templates, 386–388
  modifying templates, 394
  Page Heading, 382
  repeating regions, 399, 401–402

editing
  in Code view, 302–305
  font lists, 172–174
  images. *see* images, editing
  library items, 410–411
  with Quick Tag Editor, 312–313
  with Tag Chooser, 314–316
  with Tag Editor, 316–317
  templates, 380–383

Editor list, 362–365

elements, block level vs. inline, 147

elements, HTML vs. XHTML, 5

<em> tag, 154, 304

e-mail
  creating links, 87–89
  sending form results through, 345

Email Address field, forms, 332, 357–358, 471–473

Email Link dialog box, 87–88

embedded multimedia files, 441–443

embedded style sheets
  converting to external CSS file, 112–118
  defined, 107
  overview of, 111
  Page Properties creating, 108

embossed media types, 257

empty tags, HTML vs. XHTML, 5

ems, CSS screen measurement unit, 163–164

encoding, Page Properties dialog, 110

enctype attribute, **<form>** tag, 345

Enter (Windows OS), 65

Eric Meyer on CSS (Meyer), 101, 496

error messages, 358, 480

Expand All button, Code toolbar, 311

Expanded Tables Mode, 190–191

exporting, external CSS files, 112–118

exs, CSS screen measurement unit, 163

eXtensible HyperText Markup Language. *see* XHTML (eXtensible HyperText Markup Language)

eXtensible Markup Language (XML), 5, 9, 450–454

Extension Manager, 348, 499–501

extensions. *see also* behaviors
  disabling, 501
  installing, 499–500
  overview of, 498
  specifying preferred image editor, 362–365
  uninstalling, 501

external (linked) style sheets
  exporting and linking, 112–118
  formatting headings, 158–160
  overview of, 111

F

F11 (Windows), 60

F12 (Windows), 58

F5 (Windows), 192

FAQs, troubleshooting, 490–493

favorites, 18, 60

features, removed from Dreamweaver, 491

Fieldset object, 326

file extensions, XHTML, 7–8

file fields, 326

file naming conventions
  creating templates, 388
  file names vs. titles, 59
  form items, 331
  ID selectors, 133
  for named anchors, 91
  saving templates, 385–386
  XHTML, 7

File Transfer Protocol (FTP), 36, 479–481